2016 Growth Slowdown Analysis, Ease of Doing Business Index, and Annual Competitiveness Studies of Indonesia's Sub-National Economies

NUS National University of Singapore

LKY Lee Kuan Yew School of Public Policy

ASIA COMPETITIVENESS INSTITUTE

In 2016 and 2017, ACI was ranked 13th globally, 2nd in Asia and 1st in Singapore amongst 90 think tanks worldwide under the "Best University Affiliated Think Tank" category by the Think Tanks and Civil Societies Program at the University of Pennsylvania, USA.

About ACI

The Asia Competitiveness Institute (ACI) was established in August 2006 as a research centre at the Lee Kuan Yew School of Public Policy (LKYSPP), National University of Singapore (NUS). It aims to build the intellectual leadership and network for understanding and developing competitiveness in the Asia region. ACI seeks to contribute to the enhancement of inclusive growth, living standards and institutional governance through competitiveness research on sub-national economies in Asia. It identifies mitigating issues and challenges for potential public policy interventions through close collaboration with regional governments, business corporations, policy think-tanks and academics. ACI's three key research pillars include (i) sub-national economies level competitiveness analysis and city-level liveability analysis, (ii) firm-level competitiveness analysis in 16 Asia economies, and (iii) Singapore's long-term growth strategies and public policy analysis.

ACI's value propositions may be encapsulated in its acronym:
Analytical inputs to initiate policies for policy-makers and business leaders in Asia
Capacity building to enable others through improvement in productivity and efficiency
Intellectual leadership to create pragmatic models of competitiveness and inclusive growth

The institute's core research competencies can also be encapsulated in this acronym describing our evidence-based assessments conducted on public policies for ASEAN in the context of the rise of China and India.

Vision and Mission

- ACI's over-arching vision is to build up its research credibility with policy impact, contributing as a professional, world-class think-tank.
- ACI's mission is to establish our niche as a leading policy think-tank by identifying competitiveness trends, opportunities and challenges, as well as promoting competition and synergising complementarities amongst Asian economies and business corporations.
- ACI endeavours to articulate sound recommendations, entice discourse, and shape agenda in the arena of public policy amongst Asian governments.
- ACI undertakes evidence-based analysis of public policy issues and decisions, in order to provide assessment of their effectiveness as well as economic and societal impact.

Research Initiatives and Collaborations

I. Identify trends of competitiveness and policy analysis on trade and investment of ASEAN, within the regional context of competition and complementarities with China and India.

II. Identify competitive strengths and conduct policy analysis on Singapore within the context of regional economies with international benchmarking.

III. We are regularly releasing three indices on liveability ranking including 64 Global Cities, 100 Greater China Cities and 17 Shandong Cities.

IV. We have established an Ease of Doing Business Index on Attractiveness to Investors, Business Friendliness and Competitive Policies for 21 sub-national economies of India and 33 sub-national economies of Indonesia.

V. We have signed Memoranda of Understanding with The World Bank (2015), SPRING Singapore (2014) and European Central Bank (2014). The Memorandum of Understanding between The World Bank and National University of Singapore, coordinated through ACI, was signed in 2016.

VI. We have signed Memoranda of Understanding with various institutions in Greater China economies, including Shanghai Academy of Social Sciences (2016), Shandong Academy of Social Sciences (2015), Chongqing Municipal People's Government (2015), China Institute for Reform and Development, Haikou (2015), Counsellors' Office of the People's Government of Guangdong Province (LOI, 2014) and Chung-Hua Institution for Economic Research, Taiwan (2015).

VII. We have signed Memoranda of Understanding with six Chief Ministers' Offices in Andhra Pradesh (2015), Bihar (2015), Chhattisgarh (2015), Madhya Pradesh (2015), Odisha (2015) and Punjab (2015).

VIII. We have signed Memoranda of Understanding with Committee for Acceleration of Priority Infrastructure Delivery at Coordinating Ministry for Economic Affairs, Indonesia (2016), Indonesia Investment Coordinating Board (2014), Indonesian Agency for Agricultural Research and Development at Ministry of Agriculture (2014), Indonesian President's Delivery Unit for Developing Monitoring and Oversight (2013) and Employer's Association of Indonesia (2013).

IX. We have signed Memoranda of Understanding with ASEAN think-tanks and institutions, including Vietnam Chamber of Commerce and Industry (2016), Centre for Strategic and International Studies, Indonesia (2015), Institute of Strategic & International Studies, Malaysia (2015), Philippine Institute for Development Studies (2015), Thailand Development Research Institute (2015) and Central Institute for Economic Management, Vietnam (2015).

About ACI's Research Pillars

ACI has consciously engaged in economic research that has significant relevance to Singapore and the Asian region. Over the years, ACI has focused on our expertise in quantitative competitiveness analysis and simulation, spinning off volumes of research output in the applications of our methodology and regional insight. At this stage, ACI has identified three core research pillars that will guide and define its research efforts moving forward. The three research pillars are as follows:

Pillar I. Sub-national Economies Competitiveness Analysis

ACI engages in systematic and methodical competitiveness analyses of the *sub-national economies* by using an evidence-based, empirical approach involving a comprehensive list of relevant indicators, which are categorised under multiple layers called the 'environments'. A number of our projects, including competitiveness analyses of Greater China, ASEAN-10, India, and Indonesia, as well as other thematic research projects, were conducted by adopting this common methodology, with potential variations in the specific environments and indicators. ACI's competitiveness analysis of Asian economies goes beyond the usual ranking to offer constructive policy recommendations on how individual member states can improve their rankings vis-à-vis their sub-national or regional peers through the application of the 'what-if' simulation, which provides the projected improvements of each state's ranking whereby the bottom one-fifth of its indicators are enhanced.

Pillar II. Micro-based Firm Level Competitiveness Analysis

Micro-based firm level competitiveness analysis is ACI's second research pillar that has been developed in view of the intrinsic importance of firm-level competitiveness in terms of productivity, efficiency, and governance. In the context of globalisation, mobility of economic activities, and blurring of borders, an understanding of the determinants and dynamics of firm-level competitiveness is paramount, in order for policy makers to make adjustments and prepare their industries for an increasingly competitive economic landscape. To this end, ACI has partnered with the European Central Bank to carry out research in this area, possessing a solid foundation in firm-level productivity research in the form of European Competitiveness Network database and methodology. ACI envisaged the expansion of CompNet into Asia, thereby pioneering the Asia CompNet research network encompassing 16 economies in Asia.

Pillar III. Singapore's Long-term Economic Growth Strategies and Public Policies Analysis

The third and imminent research pillar focuses on Singapore's long-term economic growth strategies in the context of changing circumstances, future trends, and emerging opportunities for Singapore in the decades ahead. In particular, ACI will take on the task of critically examining Singapore's public policy strengths and areas of improvement by assessing policy successes of the past, identifying new issues to address and the current policy gaps, through a systematic and evidence-based research inquiry using quantitative methodology and empirical data, leveraging on our network of policy experts.

Founding Patron and International Advisory Panel

Founding Patron

Mr George Yeo
Visiting Scholar, Lee Kuan Yew School of Public Policy, National University of Singapore & Former Minister of Foreign Affairs, Singapore

International Advisory Panel

Co-Chairs:

Professor Michael Porter (2006–2010)
Bishop William Lawrence University Professor

Ms Marjorie Yang (2006–2012)
Chairman, Esquel Group

Members:

Professor Kishore Mahbubani
Dean, Lee Kuan Yew School of Public Policy, National University of Singapore

Dr Kuntoro Mangkusubroto
Head, President's Delivery Unit for Developing Monitoring and Oversight (UKP4), Indonesia

Mr Narayana Murthy
Chairman, Infosys Technologies Limited

Mr Philip Yeo
Chairman, SPRING Singapore

Mr Loh Khum Yean
Permanent Secretary, Ministry of Trade and Industry

Ms Yong Ying-I
Permanent Secretary, Public Service Division

Professor Chan Kam Leung Alan
Dean, College of Humanities, Arts and Social Sciences, Nanyang Technological University

Asia Competitiveness Institute

Co-Directors:

Associate Professor Tan Khee Giap (2011 till now)
Professor Tan Kong Yam (2011 till now)

Asia Competitiveness Institute - World Scientific Series

(ISSN: 2424-9912)

Series Editor: Tan Khee Giap (*Lee Kuan Yew School of Public Policy, NUS, Singapore*)

In the tradition of the Asia Competitiveness Institute (ACI) at the Lee Kuan Yew School of Public Policy, National University of Singapore (NUS), our research publications make a distinctive contribution to the understanding of economic development in Asia. These books, first published in 2013, in the Asia Competitiveness Institute - World Scientific Series evaluate and track competitiveness for the sub-national economies of China, India, Indonesia and ASEAN annually through combining leading-edge methodologies with an extensive dataset. The study covers four environments of competitiveness: (1) Macroeconomic Stability, (2) Government and Institutional Setting, (3) Financial, Businesses and Manpower Conditions, and (4) Quality of Life and Infrastructure Development. It also conducts "what-if" policy simulations to propose policy suggestions.

2016

2016 Annual Competitiveness Analysis and Growth Slowdown Analysis for ASEAN-10
by Tan Khee Giap, Nguyen Le Phuong Anh & Luu Nguyen Trieu Duong (Lee Kuan Yew School of Public Policy, NUS, Singapore)

2016 Growth Slowdown Analysis by Income Thresholds and Annual Update of Competitiveness Analysis for 34 Greater China Economies
by Tan Khee Giap, Wang Peng & Xie Teleixi (Lee Kuan Yew School of Public Policy, NUS, Singapore)

Inaugural 2016 Ease of Doing Business Index on Attractiveness to Investors, Business Friendliness and Competitive Policies (EDB Index ABC) for 21 Sub-National Economies of India
by Tan Khee Giap, Sasidaran Gopalan, Jigyasa Sharma & Tan Kong Yam (Lee Kuan Yew School of Public Policy, NUS, Singapore)

2016 Annual Competitiveness and Growth Slowdown Analysis for Sub-National Economies of India
by Tan Khee Giap, Sasidaran Gopalan, Anuja Tandon & Tan Kong Yam (Lee Kuan Yew School of Public Policy, NUS, Singapore)

2016 Growth Slowdown Analysis, Ease of Doing Business Index, and Annual Competitiveness Studies of Indonesia's Sub-National Economies
by Tan Khee Giap, Mulya Amri, Nursyahida Ahmad & Tan Kong Yam (Lee Kuan Yew School of Public Policy, NUS, Singapore)

2016 Annual Competitiveness Analysis and Development Strategies for Indonesian Provinces
by Tan Khee Giap, Mulya Amri & Nursyahida Ahmad (Lee Kuan Yew School of Public Policy, NUS, Singapore)

2015

2015 Annual Competitiveness Analysis, Agricultural Productivity and Development Vision for ASEAN-10
by Tan Khee Giap, Nguyen Le Phuong Anh, Sasidaran Gopalan & Luu Nguyen Trieu Duong (Lee Kuan Yew School of Public Policy, NUS, Singapore)

*More information on this series can also be found at http://www.worldscientific.com/series/aciwss

(Continued at end of book)

Asia Competitiveness Institute - World Scientific Series

2016 Growth Slowdown Analysis, Ease of Doing Business Index, and Annual Competitiveness Studies of Indonesia's Sub-National Economies

Tan Khee Giap
Co-Director, Asia Competitiveness Institute
Lee Kuan Yew School of Public Policy, National University of Singapore

Mulya Amri
Research Fellow & Deputy Director (Research), Asia Competitiveness Institute
Lee Kuan Yew School of Public Policy, National University of Singapore

Nursyahida Ahmad
Research Assistant, Asia Competitiveness Institute
Lee Kuan Yew School of Public Policy, National University of Singapore

Tan Kong Yam
Co-Director, Asia Competitiveness Institute
Lee Kuan Yew School of Public Policy, National University of Singapore

Special Remarks

Darmin Nasution
Coordinating Minister for Economic Affairs, Republic of Indonesia

Reviewers

Kuntoro Mangkusubroto
Professor of Decision Analysis, School of Business and Management, Bandung Institute of Technology, Indonesia

Kirida Bhaopichitr
Research Director, Thailand Development Research Institute (TDRI), Thailand

Darwin Marcelo
Infrastructure Economist, The World Bank Group

Paramita Dasgupta
Practice Manager, Asia, Trade & Competitiveness, The World Bank Group

Kristy Tsun-Tzu Hsu
Director, Taiwan ASEAN Studies Center, Chung-Hua Institution for Economic Research, Taiwan

APINDO

Lee Kuan Yew School of Public Policy
Asia Competitiveness Institute

NUS National University of Singapore

World Scientific

Published by

World Scientific Publishing Co. Pte. Ltd.
5 Toh Tuck Link, Singapore 596224
USA office: 27 Warren Street, Suite 401-402, Hackensack, NJ 07601
UK office: 57 Shelton Street, Covent Garden, London WC2H 9HE

British Library Cataloguing-in-Publication Data
A catalogue record for this book is available from the British Library.

Cover photo: *The photo of the Kuala Namu, North Sumatra Airport Terminal is copyright and reproduced here with the kind permission of Dr Mulya Amri.*

Asia Competitiveness Institute – World Scientific Series
2016 GROWTH SLOWDOWN ANALYSIS, EASE OF DOING BUSINESS INDEX, AND ANNUAL COMPETITIVENESS STUDIES OF INDONESIA'S SUB-NATIONAL ECONOMIES

ISBN 978-981-3226-87-6

Desk Editor: Jiang Yulin

Typeset by Stallion Press
Email: enquiries@stallionpress.com

Printed in Singapore

Contents

Foreword

Indonesia continues to embark on extensive reforms to boost economic growth and attract more investment. Such efforts are coming to fruition, as affirmed by the country's steady improvement in the World Bank's Doing Business ranking. Over a short period of 5 years, Southeast Asia's largest economy has registered one of the biggest jumps in the international Doing Business ranking, up 38 places from 129th position in 2012 to 91st place in 2017. To further improve the investment climate in light of global economic slowdown, Indonesia has issued 14 economic reform packages (*Paket Kebijakan Ekonomi*) between September 2015 and November 2016.

Despite the aggressive reforms, foreign direct investment (FDI) inflows into the country are recently on the decline, due in part to external factors. Net FDI inflows fell from US$21.8 billion in 2014 to US$16.6 billion in 2015. However, investment within the country is increasingly expanding to other regions. In line with the national aspiration to enable broad-based development, the share of national FDI inflows to Java almost halved from 91% in 2009 to 53% in 2015, with the remainder being channelled to other parts in the country.

An increasingly diversified investment across all the regions in Indonesia attests to growing confidence in the economic landscape and potential of Indonesia as a whole. It is thus important for Indonesia to sustain its reform momentum despite the global slowdown and rising protectionist sentiments elsewhere in the world.

Asia Competitiveness Institute (ACI) consistently high quality research on Indonesia's sub-national economies allows us to see the variation of economic performance, potentials, and challenges across the country and helps policymakers and business leaders make more informed decisions. I hope ACI will continue its excellent work in providing empirical and evidenced-based insights for Indonesia as Southeast Asia's largest economy.

Mr Mahendra Siregar
Chairman of Indonesia Investment Coordinating Board, 2013–2014

Preface

The Asia Competitiveness Institute (ACI) aims to contribute to the understanding and enhancement of economic growth and living standards in Asia. Among the institute's most important research products are empirical analyses of sub-national level economies in Asia's largest countries. Indonesia has been at the forefront of these studies, along with China and India, as well as other countries in Southeast Asia.

Currently in its fourth edition, the 2016 annual competitiveness analysis of Indonesia's provinces and regions is constantly being updated and complemented with relevant research topics. This time, ACI has included results of its latest studies assessing the probability of growth slowdown and ease of doing business across Indonesian provinces. Indonesia as a commodity-exporting country has been hurt by the recent commodity price bust and weak international demand. Its Gross Domestic Product growth rate declined from 6.2% in 2011 to 4.8% in 2015, but the country is now picking up again, registering a 5.0% growth in 2016, thus attesting to a generally stable economic outlook.

A politically and economically stable Indonesia is good for the region. With the downturn caused by falling commodity prices, Indonesia is increasingly trying to diversify its economic output. Less reliance on quick riches from commodity sales, in turn, will support the development of a more meritocratic business environment. In this context, the set of reforms recently adopted by President Joko Widodo's government should raise the competitiveness of various economic sectors and regions in Indonesia.

As ACI continues to expand its evidenced-based assessments of economic policies in the ASEAN countries, China, and India, more insights will be generated to help policymakers raise governance standards and improve the lives of the people. This is in line with the vision and mission of the Lee Kuan Yew School of Public Policy. I hope this study contributes to the ongoing policy discussions in Indonesia on achieving a healthy, stable, and broad-based economic growth.

Professor Kishore Mahbubani
Dean
Lee Kuan Yew School of Public Policy
National University of Singapore

Acknowledgements

This book, *2016 Growth Slowdown Analysis, Ease of Doing Business Index, and Annual Competitiveness Studies of Indonesia's Sub-National Economies*, provides updates to our previous studies on provincial and regional competitiveness in Indonesia with the latest available data. On top of that, leveraging on Asia Competitiveness Institute's (ACI) rich database, we also conducted growth slowdown analysis by income thresholds and propose a new framework to analyse the ease of doing business in Indonesia's sub-national economies.

The research that we conducted benefited immensely from feedback and comments on our preliminary findings during a review seminar held at Lee Kuan Yew School of Public Policy (LKYSPP), National University of Singapore (NUS), on 9 September 2016, and during the 2016 Annual ACI Conference on 24 November 2016 in Singapore. For that, we would like to thank the following experts and reviewers, whose welcome notes are reproduced in this book:

- Professor Dr. Kuntoro Mangkusubroto
  Professor of Decision Analysis, School of Business and Management
  Bandung Institute of Technology, Indonesia
- Dr Kirida Bhaopichitr
  Research Director, Thailand Development Research Institute, Thailand
- Dr Darwin Marcelo
  Infrastructure Economist, The World Bank Group
- Ms Paramita Dasgupta
  Practice Manager, Trade & Competitiveness, Asia, The World Bank Group
- Ms Kristy Tsun-Tzu Hsu
  Director, Taiwan ASEAN Studies Center
  Chung-Hua Institution for Economic Research, Taiwan

We also would like to extend our deepest appreciation for the support and encouragement from the following Indonesian leaders:

- Dr Darmin Nasution, Coordinating Minister for Economic Affairs, Republic of Indonesia — for delivering the keynote speech on progress and development of Indonesia's economy during our Annual Conference on 24th September 2016 (Dr Nasution's speech is reproduced as special remarks in this book);
- Dr Luky Eko Wuryanto, Vice President and Chief Administration Officer, Asian Infrastructure Investment Bank; and former Deputy Minister for Infrastructure and Regional Development, Coordinating Ministry for Economic Affairs, Republic of Indonesia — for being a distinguished dinner speaker at the ACI 2016 Annual Conference;
- Mr Mahendra Siregar, former Chairman of BKPM (2013–2014), Vice Minister of Finance (2011–2013), and Vice Minister of Trade (2009–2011), Republic of Indonesia — for delivering a discussant note at the ACI 2016 Annual Conference;
- Dr Wahyu Utomo, Deputy Minister for Infrastructure and Regional Development, Coordinating Ministry for Economic Affairs, and Head of the Committee for Acceleration of Priority Infrastructure Delivery (KPPIP) Implementation Team, Republic of Indonesia — for delivering a discussant note at the ACI 2016 Annual Conference.

This report is the result of a strong partnership between ACI and the business sector, government, and academia in various Indonesian provinces. We are grateful for the continued strong partnership with the Indonesian Employers' Association (APINDO) in coordinating the business perception surveys across Indonesian provinces during 2015. We would also like to extend our gratitude to various provincial government institutions and universities throughout Indonesia for their cooperation in hosting discussions in their premises and participating in our surveys.

The coordination and execution of field trips would not have been possible without the excellent work by Nurina Merdikawati (ACI Research Associate, 2013–2016), Yap Xin Yi (ACI Manager & Special Assistant to Co-Directors), Tracy Cai (ACI Manager & Personal Assistant to Co-Director), Shanty Citra Eka Vebriani Yusup (ACI survey coordinator in Jakarta), as well as NUS students/research assistants Rizky Novrianto, Ririn Radiawati Kusuma, Noviandri Nurlaili Khairina, Yayat Budianto, Totar Maria Tambunan, Ryan H. Limawan, Karina Djati Prameswari, and Umaya Puri Khiranti who conducted the surveys in 2015.

We acknowledge important research contribution on growth slowdown by Luu Nguyen Trieu Duong and Lian Xiao (Chapter 4), on ease of doing business by Dr Sasidaran Gopalan (Chapter 5), and excellent research and writing support by Jenn Beh (Chapters 1, 5, and 6). We also extend our appreciation for the support and encouragement of all ACI researchers and administrative staff.

Finally, we are immensely grateful for the continued guidance and support of Dean Kishore Mahbubani, Associate Professor Eduardo Araral (Vice Dean, Research), Mr Donald Low (Associate Dean, Research and Executive Education) and Mr Thomas Chan Hean Boon (Associate Director, Research Support Unit) as well as other colleagues from the Lee Kuan Yew

School of Public Policy. Ultimately, a generous research funding from the Ministry of Trade and Industry, Singapore enables this great effort, without which, such an extensive book would not have been possible.

Tan Khee Giap, Mulya Amri, Nursyahida Ahmad, and Tan Kong Yam
Asia Competitiveness Institute
Lee Kuan Yew School of Public Policy
National University of Singapore

About the Authors

Tan Khee Giap is a Co-Director of the Asia Competitiveness Institute (ACI) and Associate Professor at the Lee Kuan Yew School of Public Policy, National University of Singapore. He is also the Chairman of the Singapore National Committee for Pacific Economic Cooperation. Upon graduating with a PhD from University of East Anglia, England, in 1987 under the Overseas Research Scheme awarded by the Committee of Vice-Chancellors and Principals of the Universities of the United Kingdom, he joined the banking sector as a treasury manager and served as secretary to the Assets and Liabilities Committee for three years, thereafter he taught at the Department of Economics and Statistics, National University of Singapore, 1990–1993. Dr Tan joined Nanyang Technological University in 1993 and was Associate Dean, Graduate Studies Office, 2007–2009. He is now with Lee Kuan Yew School of Public Policy, National University of Singapore.

Dr Tan has consulted extensively with the various government ministries, statutory boards and government-linked companies of Singapore government including Ministry of Finance, Ministry of Trade & Industry, Ministry of Manpower, Housing & Development Board, Civil Aviation Authority of Singapore, Singapore Tourism Board, Trade Development Board, Maritime Port Authority, Ministry of Information, Culture & Arts, Economic Development Board, Ministry of National Development, Media Development Authority, Ministry of Environment and Water Resources, Singapore Design Council, Ministry of Community Development, Youth & Sports, Singapore Press Holdings, Mendaki, StarHub, CapitaLand and Great Eastern Life on policies concerning financial, fiscal, trade, tourism, public housing, labour, telecommunication, tourism, liveable cities, creative industry, media, community development, airport and seaport activities. He has also served as a consultant to international agencies such as the Asian Development Bank, Asian Development Bank Institute, United Nations Industrial Development Group, World Gold Council, ASEAN Secretariat, Central Policy Unit of Hong Kong, Kerzner International, Las Vegas Sands and Marina Bay Sands.

Dr Tan is the lead author for 27 books, serving as journals editor and published widely in international refereed journals. His current research interests include econometric forecasting, Cost of Living Index, Global Liveable Cities Index and competitiveness analysis on 31 provinces in China, 35 states in India and ASEAN-10 economies.

Dr Tan was Deputy President of the Singapore Economic Society, 2004. He served in the 2002 Economic Review Committee (ERC). He has also served as Chairman of the Task Force on Portable Medical Benefits (PMB), as the Deputy Chairman of the IPS Forum for Economic Restructuring (IFER) in 2003 and served as a member of the Resource Panel of the Government Parliamentary Committee for Transport, Government Parliamentary Committee for Finance and Trade & Industry and Government Parliamentary Committee for Defence and Foreign Affairs since 2007.

Dr Tan has extensively advised and guided multinational corporations leading to public listings especially those companies from Mainland China and Taiwan. He is also currently an Independent Director of the publicly listed BreadTalk Group, Boustead Projects, TEE Land and Chengdu Rural Commercial Bank.

Mulya Amri is a Research Fellow and Deputy Director (Research) at the Asia Competitiveness Institute (ACI), Lee Kuan Yew School of Public Policy (LKYSPP), National University of Singapore (NUS). He has held a key role in ACI's research on Indonesian sub-national competitiveness since 2011, including co-writing three books on the topic, the latest one titled *2014 Annual Competitiveness Analysis and Development Strategies for Indonesian Provinces*. He is also closely involved in ACI's research on city liveability and competitiveness, and has written widely on the topic of urban development and city-level governance. Mulya has 15 years of working experience in the private, public, and non-profit sectors. Upon moving to Singapore in 2008, he worked with HOK (a global planning and architecture consultancy firm) on city planning projects throughout Asia and with Jurong Consultants (the consultancy arm of Singapore's JTC Corporation) on the planning of industrial zones in the Middle East. Prior to that, Mulya worked with international development agencies such as the World Bank, UNDP, and UN-HABITAT on projects related to urban and housing development, local governance, as well as community-driven development in various Indonesian regions. He is also a co-founder and sits on the advisory board of COMBINE Resource Institution, a non-profit organisation based in Yogyakarta, Indonesia. Mulya has a PhD degree in Public Policy from the National University of Singapore. Prior to that, he graduated with a bachelor's degree from Institut Teknologi Bandung, Indonesia, and was awarded the Fulbright scholarship to study for a Master's degree in Urban Planning at the University of California, Los Angeles, and a Chevening award to study at the London School of Economics and Political Science.

Nursyahida Ahmad is a Research Assistant at Asia Competitiveness Institute (ACI) at the Lee Kuan Yew School of Public Policy (LKYSPP), National University of Singapore (NUS). Nursyahida graduated from Nanyang Technological University in 2015, with a Bachelor of Arts in Economics (second upper). At ACI, Nursyahida is a member of the project on Indonesia's competitiveness analysis at the provincial and regional level. She is also a member of the research project on firm-level productivity, efficiency and competitiveness in the 16 Asian economies. Nursyahida has co-authored two books on provincial development and policy options for Indonesia. Her research interests include development economics and socioeconomic studies.

Tan Kong Yam is presently the Co-Director of the Asia Competitiveness Institute. He is also Professor of Economics at the Nanyang Technological University. From June 2002 to June 2005, he was a senior economist at the World Bank office in Beijing where he worked on issues of macro stabilization, integration of the fragmented domestic market, banking reform, international trade and investment, energy security as well as regional inequality. In 2004, he was a member of the World Bank expert group on the eleventh five-year plan (2006–10) for the State Council in China. The expert group provided analysis and policy recommendations on urbanization, regional inequality, innovation policy, energy and water policy as well as strategy on banking reform to the Chinese government.

Prior to that, he was the chief economist of the Singapore government (1999–2002), and Head, Department of Business Policy, Faculty of Business Administration at the National University of Singapore (NUS). He is a graduate of Princeton (1975–79, class of 1931 scholar, Paul Volcker Thesis prize) and Stanford University (1980–83), where he completed his Master's and PhD in three years. Prior to joining NUS, he worked at the Hoover Institution at Stanford University, World Bank, the Monetary Authority of Singapore, and was the Director of Research at the Ministry of Trade and Industry in Singapore.

His research interests are in international trade and finance, economic and business trends in the Asia Pacific region and economic reforms in China. He has published ten books and numerous articles in major international journals including the *American Economic Review*, *World Bank Economic Review*, *Long Range Planning*, and *Australian Journal of Management* among others on economic and business issues in the Asia Pacific region. He served as a board member at the Singapore Central Provident Fund Board (1984–96) and the National Productivity Board (1989–90). He has also consulted for many organizations including Temasek, GIC, Citigroup, IBM, ATT, BP, ABN-AMRO, Ikea, Bank of China, China Construction Bank, People's Bank of China, EDB, Areva, CapitaLand, Guangdong provincial government, Samsung, Mauritius government, Ministry of Trade and Industry, Mobil, Singapore Technology, etc.

List of Abbreviations

ACI	Asia Competitiveness Institute
ADB	Asian Development Bank
AEC	ASEAN Economic Community
AFI	Attractiveness to Foreign Investors
APINDO	Indonesian Employers' Association (*Asosiasi Pengusaha Indonesia*)
ASEAN	Association of Southeast Asian Nations
BAPPENAS	Indonesian Ministry of National Development Planning (*Badan Perencanaan Pembangunan Nasional*)
BBM	Bugis, Buton and Makassar
BKPM	Investment Coordinating Board (*Badan Koordinasi Penanaman Modal*)
BMA	Bayesian Model Averaging
BPS	Indonesia Statistics Agency (*Badan Pusat Statistik*)
BRICS	Brazil, Russia, India, China, and South Africa
CMEA	Coordinating Ministry of Economic Affairs
CMIE	Centre for Monitoring Indian Economy Pvt. Ltd
CRRL	Competition, Regulatory Standards, and Rule of Law
CUI	Catch-up Index
DAU	General Allocation Fund (*Dana Alokasi Umum*)
DB	Doing Business
DKI	Special Capital Region (*Daerah Khusus Ibukota*)
DNI	Investment Negative List (*Daftar Negatif Investasi*)
EDB Index ABC	Ease of Doing Business Index on Attractiveness to Investors, Business Friendliness and Competitive Policies
EU	European Union

FAQ	Frequently Asked Questions
FBMC	Financial, Businesses, and Manpower Conditions
FDBE	Financial Deepening and Business Efficiency
FDI	Foreign Direct Investment
FTA	Free Trade Agreement
GDP	Gross Domestic Product
GDPPC	Gross Domestic Product per Capita of Country
GIS	Government and Institutional Setting
GMID	Global Market Information Database
GPFS	Government Policies and Fiscal Sustainability
GNI	Gross National Income
GRDP	Gross Regional Domestic Product
GSP	Generalized System of Preferences
GVC	Global Value Chain
ICT	Information, Communications, and Technology
IGL	Institutions, Governance, and Leadership
IIGF	Indonesia Infrastructure Guarantee Fund
IMD	International Institute for Management Development
IMF	International Monetary Fund
INDO-DAPOER	Indonesia Database for Policy and Economic Research
ISDS	Investor–State Dispute Settlement
IP	Intellectual Property
KPPIP	Committee for Acceleration of Priority Infrastructure Delivery (*Komite Percepatan Penyediaan Infrastruktur Prioritas*)
KPPOD	Regional Autonomy Watch (*Komite Pemantauan Pelaksanaan Otonomi Daerah*)
LKYSPP	Lee Kuan Yew School of Public Policy
LMF	Labour Market Flexibility
MBTK	Maloy Batuta Trans Kalimantan
MIFEE	Merauke Integrated Food and Energy Estate
MINT	Mexico, Indonesia, Nigeria, Turkey
MNC	Multinational Companies
MOSPI	Ministry of Statistics and Programme Implementation
MOU	Memorandum of Understanding

MP3EI	Master Plan for Acceleration and Expansion of Indonesia's Economic Development (*Masterplan Percepatan dan Perluasan Pembangunan Indonesia*)
MRT	Mass Rapid Transit
MS	Macroeconomic Stability
NGO	Non-government Organisation
NUS	National University of Singapore
OECD	Organisation for Economic Co-operation and Development
OTS	Openness to Trade and Services
PDRB	Gross Regional Domestic Product (*Produk Domestik Regional Bruto*)
PI	Physical Infrastructure
PIP	Posterior Inclusion Probability
PP	Productivity Performance
PPP$	Purchasing Power Parity Dollar
PSTD	Posterior Standard Deviation
PTSP	Provincial One-Stop-Service Agency (*Pelayanan Terpadu Satu Pintu*)
PT SMI	PT Sarana Multi Infrastructure
QLID	Quality of Life and Infrastructure Development
RCA	Revealed Comparative Advantage
RCEP	Regional Comprehensive Economic Partnership
REER	Real Effective Exchange Rates
REV	Regional Economic Vibrancy
RPJMN	National Medium Term Development Plan (*Rencana Pembangunan Jangka Menengah Nasional*)
RSVI	'Ranked' Standardised Value of Indicator
SBY	Susilo Bambang Yudhoyono
SD	Standard Deviation
SEZ	Special Economic Zone
SLES	Standard of Living, Education, and Social Stability
SME	Small and Medium-sized Enterprise
SOE	State-owned Enterprise
SVI	Standardised Value of Indicator
TDRI	Thailand Development Research Institute
TI	Technological Infrastructure
TOT	Terms of Trade

TPP	Trans-Pacific Partnership
UNCTAD	The United Nations Conference on Trade and Development
UP4PB	Unit for Acceleration of Development in Papua and West Papua (*Unit Percepatan Pembangunan Papua dan Papua Barat*)
US	United States
VGF	Viability Gap Fund
VOC	Dutch East India Company (*Vereenigde Oost-Indische Compagnie*)
WEF	World Economic Forum
WEO	World Economic Outlook
WTO	World Trade Organisation

List of Provinces

	Region	Name of Province in English	Name of Province in Bahasa Indonesia
1	Sumatra	Aceh	Aceh
2	Bali–Nusa Tenggara	Bali	Bali
3	Java	Banten	Banten
4	Sumatra	Bengkulu	Bengkulu
5	Java	DI Yogyakarta	DI Yogyakarta
6	Java	DKI Jakarta	DKI Jakarta
7	Sulawesi	Gorontalo	Gorontalo
8	Sumatra	Jambi	Jambi
9	Java	West Java	Jawa Barat
10	Java	Central Java	Jawa Tengah
11	Java	East Java	Jawa Timur
12	Kalimantan	West Kalimantan	Kalimantan Barat
13	Kalimantan	South Kalimantan	Kalimantan Selatan
14	Kalimantan	Central Kalimantan	Kalimantan Tengah
15	Kalimantan	East Kalimantan (including North Kalimantan)	Kalimantan Timur (termasuk Kalimantan Utara)
16	Sumatra	Bangka Belitung Islands	Kepulauan Bangka Belitung
17	Sumatra	Riau Islands	Kepulauan Riau
18	Sumatra	Lampung	Lampung
19	Maluku–Papua	Maluku	Maluku
20	Maluku–Papua	North Maluku	Maluku Utara

(*Continued*)

(*Continued*)

	Region	Name of Province in English	Name of Province in Bahasa Indonesia
21	Bali–Nusa Tenggara	West Nusa Tenggara	Nusa Tenggara Barat
22	Bali–Nusa Tenggara	East Nusa Tenggara	Nusa Tenggara Timur
23	Maluku–Papua	Papua	Papua
24	Maluku–Papua	West Papua	Papua Barat
25	Sumatra	Riau	Riau
26	Sulawesi	West Sulawesi	Sulawesi Barat
27	Sulawesi	South Sulawesi	Sulawesi Selatan
28	Sulawesi	Central Sulawesi	Sulawesi Tengah
29	Sulawesi	Southeast Sulawesi	Sulawesi Tenggara
30	Sulawesi	North Sulawesi	Sulawesi Utara
31	Sumatra	West Sumatra	Sumatera Barat
32	Sumatra	South Sumatra	Sumatera Selatan
33	Sumatra	North Sumatra	Sumatera Utara

List of Tables and Figures

Chapter 1

Chapter 2

Chapter 3

Chapter 5

Chapter 6

Chapter 1
Introduction

1.1 Why This Book and for Whom

Geographically situated in the middle of a huge and rising Asia, Singapore's economy is directly linked with the dynamics of growth and development in surrounding regions. It is thus critical for the Asia Competitiveness Institute (ACI) at the Lee Kuan Yew School of Public Policy, National University of Singapore, to offer a substantial contribution to the development and exchange of knowledge about the competitiveness of various economies situated around Singapore.

There are several ways in which ACI's contributions to the competitiveness literature are distinctive. First, our work complements existing studies and literature (which mostly explores national-level conditions) by drilling down to analyses at the sub-national level. The states of India, as well as the provinces of China and Indonesia are especially notable because these sub-national economies are substantial. For example, in India, the states of Uttar Pradesh and Maharashtra had a population of 199.28 million and 112.37 million, respectively, as per the 2011 census. In China, Guangdong and Shandong provinces were home to 104.30 million and 95.73 million people, respectively, as of 2010. Meanwhile, the Indonesian provinces of West Java and East Java accommodate 43.05 million and 37.48 million people, respectively, in 2010. If each of these sub-national economies were to be compared against the world's countries, they would rank among the most populous. We agree that national-level policies and institutions matter, but we also believe that economic activities are not always tied down to country-level contexts, and we argue that each of these sub-national economies deserves to be analysed on their own.

Second, our work is based on a comprehensive and empirical methodology to regularly assess competitiveness at the sub-national level. The research findings presented in the following chapters of this book are the latest results of ACI's annual research on competitiveness and related issues pertaining to Indonesian provinces, using the latest available data. It complements our past publications on the competitiveness of Indonesian provinces (Tan *et al.*, 2013, 2015a, 2015b, 2017a, 2017b). And in developing a deeper understanding of the economies around Singapore, this volume also complements[1] our other publications on the competitiveness of the states and federal territories of India (Tan, Gopalan, and Tandon, 2017; Tan *et al.*, 2014a, 2015c), of the economies of Greater China (Tan, Yuan, and Xie, 2017; Tan, Yuan, and Yoong, 2015; Tan *et al.*, 2014b), and of the member countries of (ASEAN-10) (Tan *et al.*, 2016a, 2017c). Relatedly, these studies also complement our research on city-level economies, namely, on cost of living and purchasing power (Tan *et al.*, 2016b; Tan and Luu, 2016), as well as liveability (Tan *et al.*, 2012).

The objectives of this book, in particular, are: (1) to track the competitiveness landscape across Indonesia's provinces and regions, (2) to identify the strengths and weaknesses of each sub-national economy, and suggest development strategies based on empirical simulation studies, (3) to highlight specific challenges faced by each province and region that require urgent attention, (4) to spur intellectual debate among key stakeholders in order to lift Indonesia's competitiveness at the national and sub-national levels, and (5) to further attract collaboration with strategic partners and strengthen efforts to raise Indonesia's competitiveness through more outward-oriented policies (trade, foreign direct investment, technology transfer, etc.).

ACI's work is evidence-based and conducted through quantitative analyses which are subsequently presented in ways that are intuitively comprehensible to policymakers and business owners. The latter, together with academics and non-government organisations (NGOs) are among ACI's target audience. To facilitate multidisciplinary dialogue among the relevant stakeholders, ACI holds review seminars prior to any book publication, to seek comments and suggestions as peer review.

The rest of this chapter is organised as follows: First, Section 1.2 provides a brief overview of Indonesia's recent economic development in 2016 as a context for this publication. Subsequently, Section 1.3 outlines the structure of the book and provides brief summaries of each chapter as a roadmap for the reader in navigating this book.

1.2 Overview of Indonesia's Recent Economic Development

In 2013, Indonesia was named as an investment destination to watch, the "I" in the MINT bloc alongside Mexico, Nigeria, and Turkey (O'Neill, 2013).[2] Reports forecasted that if Indonesia were able to keep an annual GDP growth rate of 7.0%, the world's fourth most populous country would become the seventh largest economy in the world by 2030 (Oberman *et al.*, 2012).

The global commodity price bust coupled with weak international demand, however, have hurt many economies, especially commodity-exporting countries such as Indonesia. The fact that almost half of Indonesia's export basket in 2015 was made up of commodities (25% mineral products and 15% vegetable products) weakened the country's trade balance (OECD, 2017). Indonesia's Gross Domestic Product (GDP) growth gradually slowed from a high of 6.2% in

---

[1] There are currently 34 provinces in Indonesia. North Kalimantan, as Indonesia's newest province (carved out of East Kalimantan in 2012) is not yet analysed on its own due to lack of disaggregated data. North Kalimantan is therefore still analysed as part of East Kalimantan.

[2] The term 'MINT' was coined by Jim O'Neill, who earlier came up with the term 'BRICS' (Brazil, Russia, India, China, and South Africa).

Figure 1.1: GDP Growth Rate for Indonesia, BRICS Countries, and MINT Countries (2011–2015)

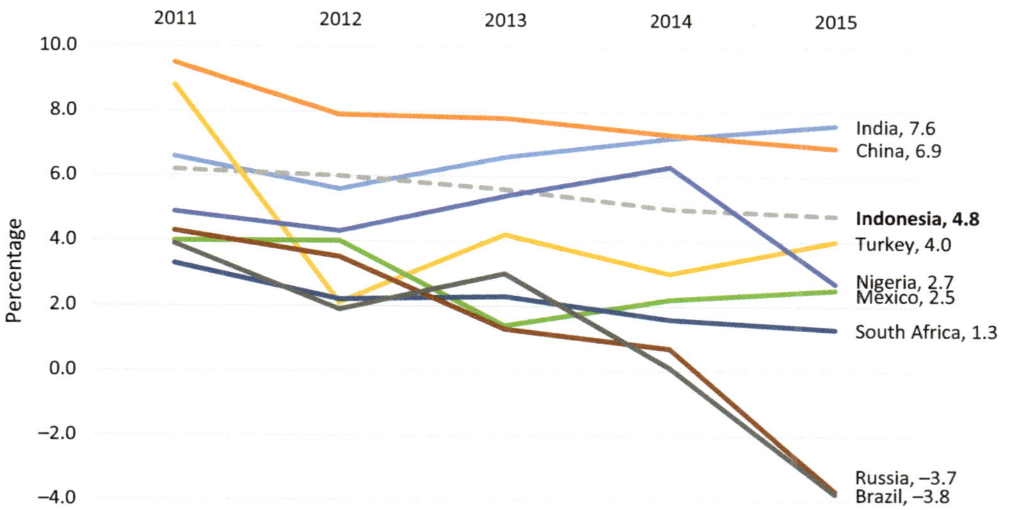

Note: Number after country name indicates GDP growth rate in 2015.
Source: World Development Indicators Data, compiled by Asia Competitiveness Institute.

2011 to 4.8% in 2015. This is lower than the rate originally targeted by the state budget (5.7%), and also below that achieved by neighbouring countries such as Vietnam (6.7%), the Philippines (5.8%), and Malaysia (5.0%).

In a wider perspective, the decline in Indonesia's growth is not as troubling as the situation in many other developing countries. Indonesia still registered a marginally higher growth than the average for 10 member countries of the Association of Southeast Asian Nations (ASEAN-10), which was 4.8% for 2015 (Asian Development Bank, 2016a). In the meantime, the remainder of the MINT countries, namely, Mexico, Nigeria, and Turkey registered a more disappointing GDP growth rate of 2.5%, 2.7%, and 4.0%, respectively (see Figure 1.1).

Nonetheless, we are left with the notion that Indonesia still has some way to go to fulfil its promise as the next economic powerhouse, especially when other developing ASEAN countries performed substantially better (see Figure 1.2). Two years into President Joko Widodo's (Jokowi) administration, whose election stirred much fanfare, Indonesia continues to face many structural challenges inherited from previous administrations.

Indonesia eventually emerged in 2016 in better shape than it did in 2015. The country's growth rate for 2016 is estimated to go up to 5.0%, (Asia Development Bank, (ABD)) or 5.1% (World Bank) by the end of the year, although this is slightly lower than the 5.2% projected at the beginning of 2016 (Asian Development Bank, 2016b). Part of the reason for improvement is an uptick that started in mid-2016 in the commodities-related sectors, namely, mining and quarrying, as well as oil and gas manufacturing. There was also a sharp pickup in wholesale and retail trade, as well as in the transportation and logistics sector. Manufacturing as a whole, however, continued to grow less, as did agriculture and construction (see Figure 1.3).

Figure 1.2: GDP Growth Rate for Indonesia and ASEAN-10 Countries (2011–2015)

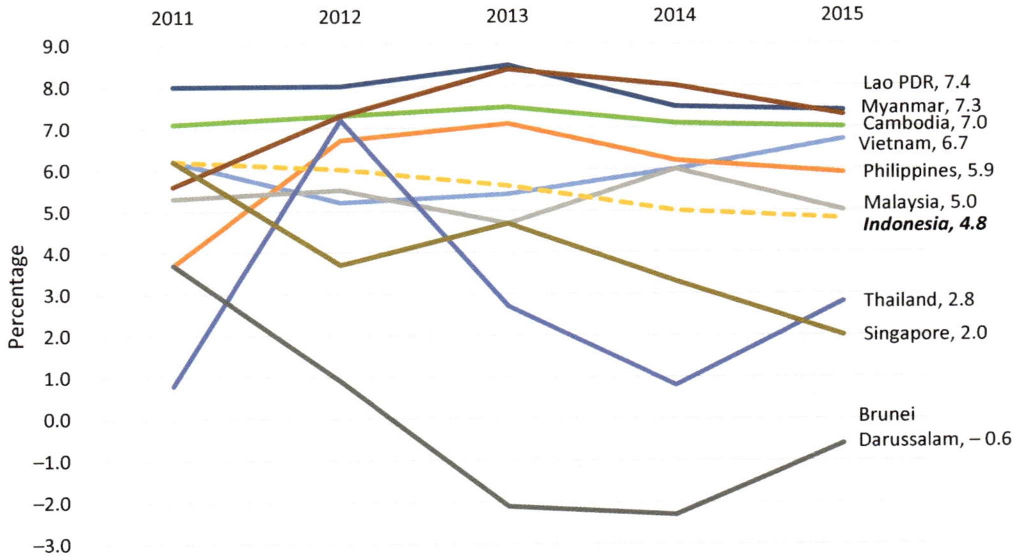

Note: Number after country name indicates GDP growth rate in 2015.
Source: World Development Indicators Data, compiled by Asia Competitiveness Institute.

Figure 1.3: GDP Growth Rate for Selected Industries, Indonesia (2014–2016)

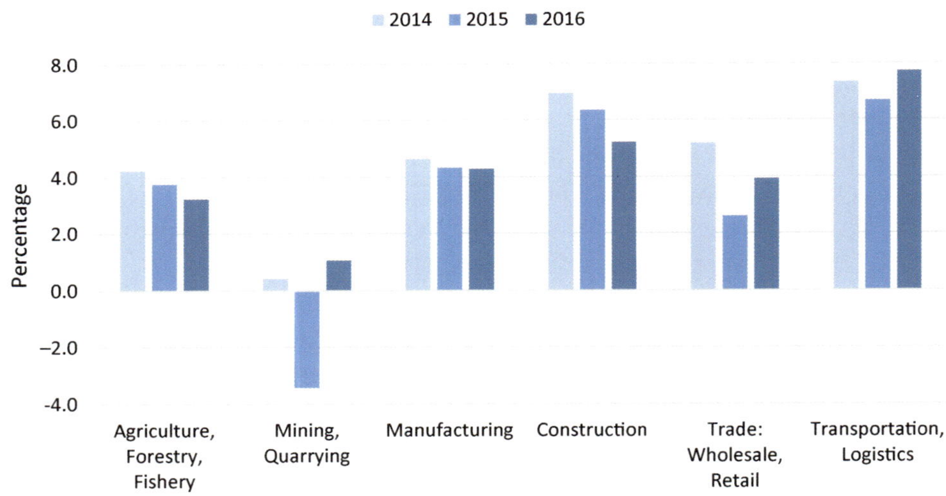

Source: Indonesia Statistics Agency (BPS), compiled by Asia Competitiveness Institute.

In terms of expenditure types, growth between mid-2015 and mid-2016 was primarily driven by fiscal stimulus; government consumption grew by 5.4% in 2015 as opposed to 1.2% in 2014, peaking at 7.1% in the third and fourth quarters of 2015, although it slowed down abruptly after the second quarter of 2016 (see Figure 1.4). Household consumption stayed on trend, growing

Figure 1.4: GDP Growth Rate by Expenditure, Indonesia (Q1-2014 to Q4-2016)

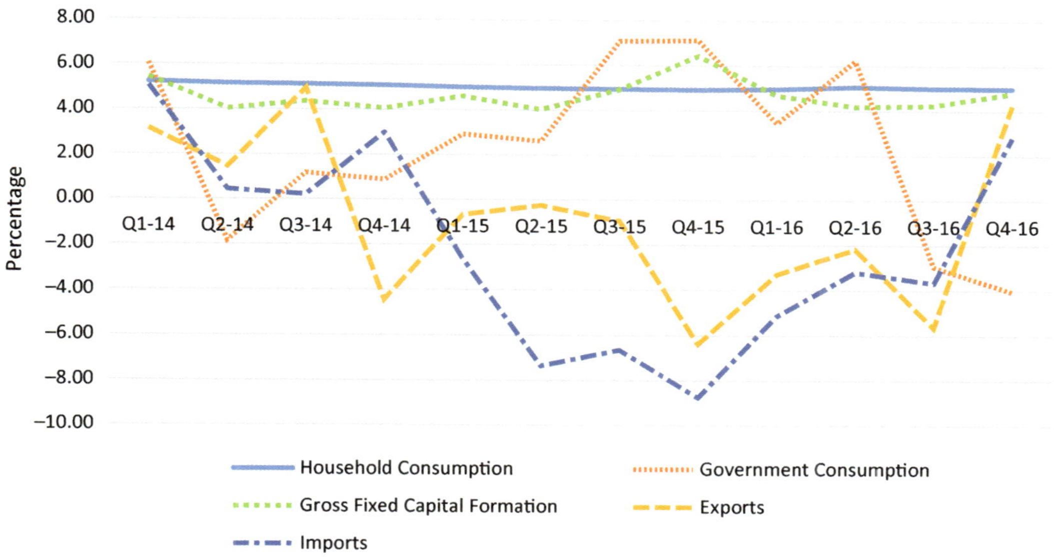

Source: Indonesia Statistics Agency (BPS), compiled by Asia Competitiveness Institute.

5.0% throughout 2014, 2015, and 2016. Gross fixed capital formation grew more strongly at 5.1% in 2015 compared to 4.6% in 2014 and started 2016 strong at 5.6% in the first quarter of 2016, but slowed to 4.1% in the third quarter.

The stabilisation of global financial markets starting late 2015 helped create a more conducive environment, but external demand remains unfavourable. Exports are still dampened by the external demand slowdown, while imports contracted from lower domestic demand. Both of Indonesia's exports and imports dropped steadily starting 2014 and stayed low throughout most of 2015 and 2016, with a steep increase taking place only in the last quarter of 2016 (see Figure 1.4).

Indonesia's current account deficit reduced from US$ 27.5 billion in 2014 to US$ 17.5 billion in 2015. These translate to 3.1% and 2.1% of the GDP in 2014 and 2015, respectively. The deficit reduced further to US$16.3 billion in 2016 (see Figure 1.5). Indonesia's exports and imports of goods declined, leaving a positive net balance in merchandise trade. Meanwhile, exports and imports of services remained relatively stable, with a negative balance in service trade.

With a substantial slowdown in trade starting 2014, Indonesia boosted GDP growth through government spending. An important policy decision to enable higher government spending was the fuel subsidy rationalisation programme that started under President Jokowi's watch, where energy subsidies fell by 65.2% from Rp 342 trillion in 2014 to Rp 119 trillion in 2015, freeing up funds for more productive use such as in infrastructure and healthcare (Negara, 2016). Infrastructure spending, which has historically stayed below 10% of the government expenditure, is earmarked at more than 15% for 2015 and also 2016. Regional transfers have also been budgeted to increase from 32% in 2014 to 37% in 2016 as part of the peripheral growth strategy (Negara, 2016). Various conditional cash transfer to individuals as programmes well as an increase in budget transfers to provincial,

Figure 1.5: Current Account Components of Indonesia (2014–2016)

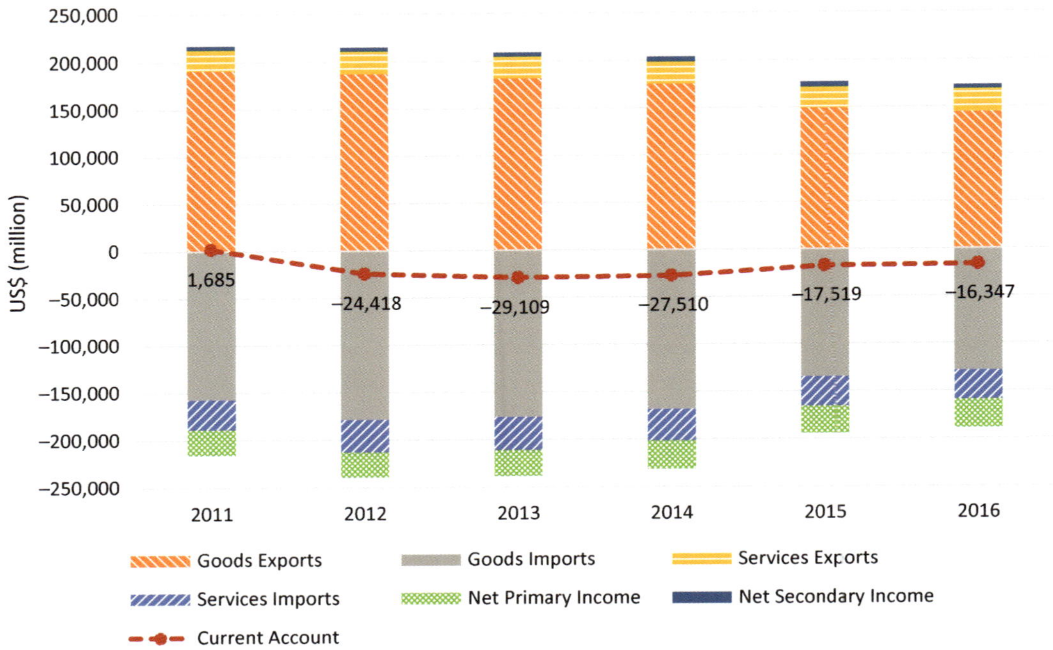

Source: Bank Indonesia, compiled by Asia Competitiveness Institute.

Figure 1.6: Components of Indonesia's Government Expenditure (Actual), 2014–2016

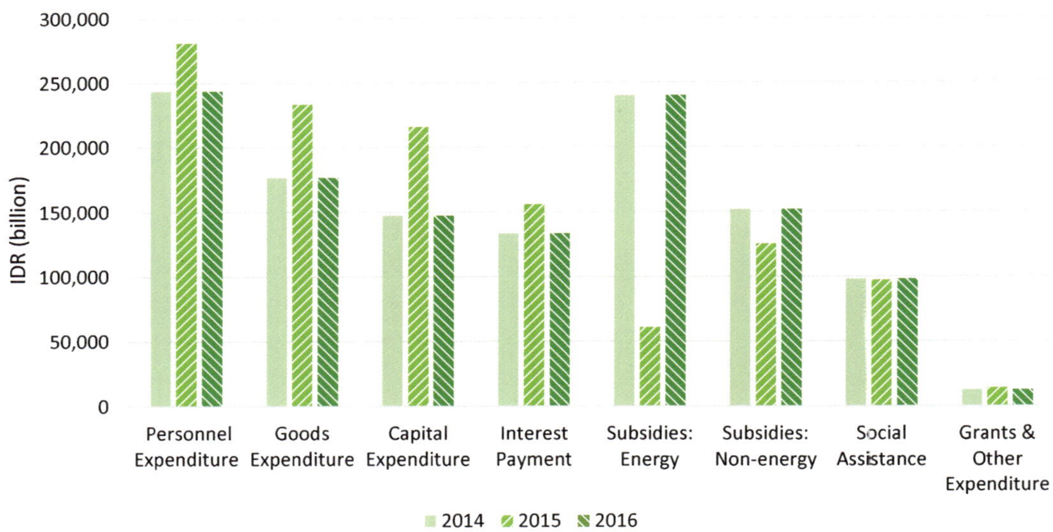

Source: BPS, compiled by Asia Competitiveness Institute.

local, and village governments in turn also helped provide the means to boost local consumption throughout the country. See Figure 1.6 for more details on how Indonesia expended its public finances from 2014 to 2016, focusing on a drop in subsidies and hike in expenditures in 2015.

Infrastructure development is of high priority on the government's agenda, with the creation of the inter-ministerial Committee for Acceleration of Priority Infrastructure Delivery (KPPIP) in late 2014. Infrastructure related to sea connectivity, such as the Kuala Tanjung Port in North Sumatra (close to Sei Mangkei Special Economic Zone (SEZ)) and Bitung Port in North Sulawesi (by the Bitung SEZ), are in line with President Jokowi's maritime highway vision. But land connectivity is also prioritised, including the Trans-Sumatra toll road, the Balikpapan–Samarinda toll road in East Kalimantan, the Manado–Bitung toll road in North Sulawesi, the East Kalimantan Railway, and the Mass Rapid Transit and Light Rail Transit in Jakarta. For energy, new power plants and transmission lines are being constructed across the country.

Policies to boost public spending help keep the economy running, but require substantial fiscal resources. To increase revenue, the government is pushing to boost tax collection and repatriate assets stored overseas, generate more private and foreign investment by improving the ease of doing business in the country, and increase foreign exchange revenue from exports and tourism receipts.

The 2016 budget is relatively optimistic. A 21% growth in revenue primarily from tax collection was projected to cover the development expenditures needed and to stay in line with the constitutionally mandated budget deficit ceiling of 3% (Asian Development Bank, 2016b). However, in 2015, only 83% of the domestic tax budget was realised. To plug Indonesia's leaky tax base, President Jokowi has taken measures to encourage asset revaluation and introduce the Tax Amnesty Law in 2016 to claw back unpaid taxes on assets and foreign funds (Brummitt, 2015).

Figures from actual government revenue in 2016 show marked increase in tax revenue (see Figure 1.7). The latest reports as of January 2017 register a commitment for repatriation amounting to Rp141 trillion, although the actual funds that have entered into the domestic banking system is merely 63.5%, indicating that not all the promised funds may eventually be realised (Wirayani and Sundaryani, 2017). As the programme comes to an end, an extension will be a negative indicator, showing a lack of bite and discipline, but what is clear is that the full target of one quadrillion rupiah is unlikely to be achieved, adding more pressure to expand future revenue sources.

With inflation unexpectedly low since the end of 2015 and throughout 2016, hovering around Bank Indonesia's 3–5% target for 2016–2017, the central bank shifted to a looser monetary policy. The policy rate was cut several times from 7.50% in December 2015 to 4.75% in October 2016 (see Figure 1.8), with the intention to boost investments, among others.

Since October of 2015, 14 economic reform packages (*Paket Kebijakan Ekonomi*) have been released with the objective to improve the investment climate (as measured by achieving investment grade rating[3]) and improve Indonesia's ranking on the World Bank's Ease of Doing Business from 109 to 40 in 2016 (see Table 1.1 for more details on the reform packages). The signalling provided by these policies were positive and involves various measures such as cutting red tape, increasing incentives for small and medium enterprises, and reducing foreign ownership restrictions in some sectors.

---

[3] Only Standard and Poor's is still holding Indonesia at a notch below investment grade, BB+ with a positive outlook. Fitch and Moody's has maintained Indonesia's ratings at Baa3 (stable) and BBB-(stable).

Figure 1.7: Sources of Indonesia's Government Revenue (Actual), 2014–2016

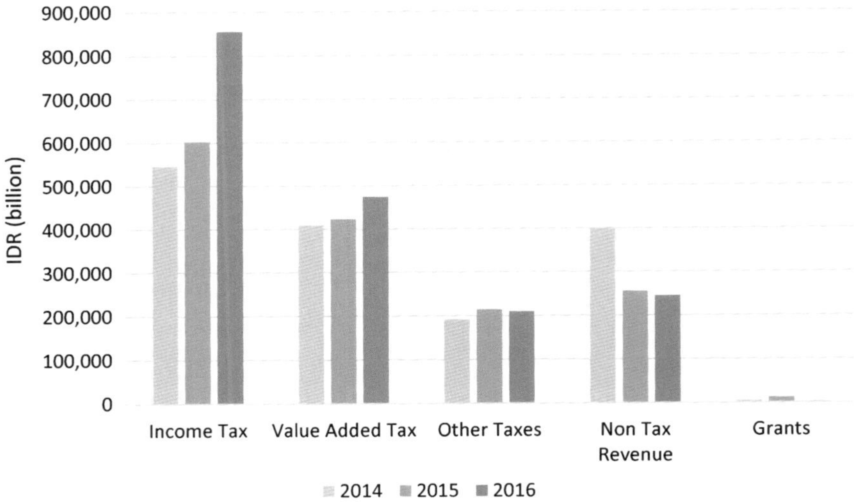

Source: BPS, compiled by Asia Competitiveness Institute.

Figure 1.8: Inflation and Central Bank Policy Rate, 2014–2016

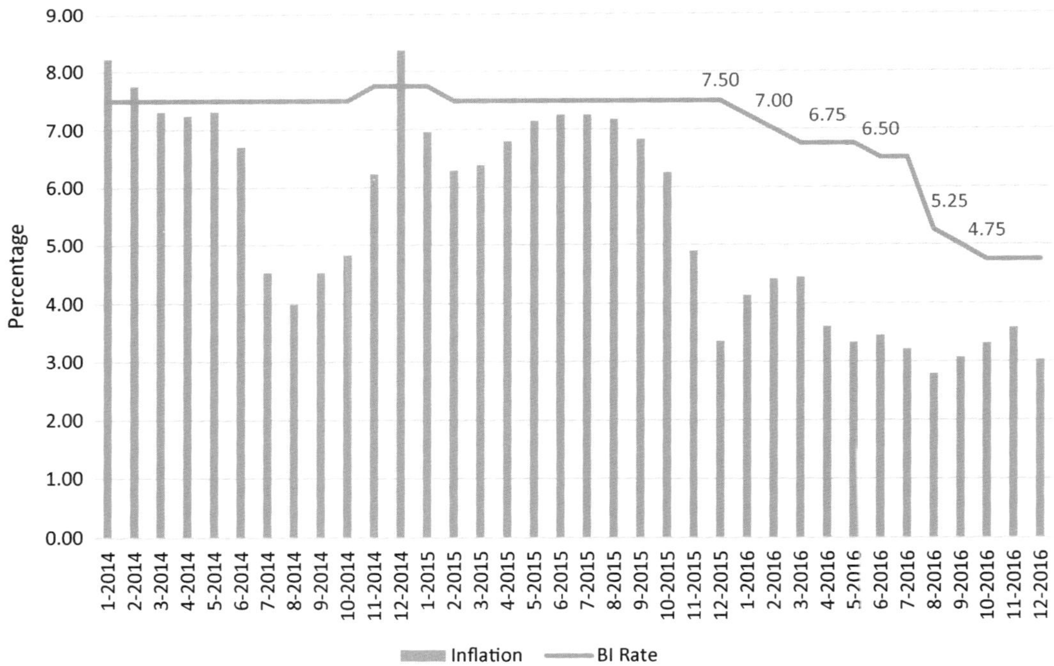

Source: Bank Indonesia, compiled by Asia Competitiveness Institute.

Table 1.1: Indonesia's Economic Reform Packages, 2015–2016

No.	Date	Key Reforms
1	9 Sept 2015	• Boost industrial competitiveness through deregulation and easing business licensing • Improve law enforcement and business certainty • Increase property investment
2	30 Sept 2015	• Cut interest rate tax for exporters • Speed licensing for investment in industrial estates • Relax import taxes on capital goods in industrial estates and aviation industry
3	7 Oct 2015	• Cut energy tariffs for labour-intensive industries and offer tariff discounts for off-peak use • Reduce interest rates for micro-loans to SMEs (*Kredit Usaha Rakyat*)
4	15 Oct 2015	• Introduce fixed formula to determine increases in labour wages and safety nets • Soft micro-loans for small and medium, export-oriented, labour-intensive businesses
5	22 Oct 2015	• Tax incentive for asset revaluation and scrap double taxation on real estate investment trusts • Deregulate Islamic banking
6	5 Nov 2015	• Expand SEZ to boost peripheral development • Tax incentives, simpler procedures, and foreign ownership of property in SEZs • Increase regulation on water resources and cut procedure time for import of pharmaceutical raw materials
7	4 Dec 2015	• Waive income tax for workers in labour-intensive industries (>5,000 workers) • Provide free leasehold certificates for street vendors operating in 34 state-owned designated areas
8	21 Dec 2015	• One-map policy to harmonise land utilisation • Scrap income tax for 21 categories of airplane spare parts • Incentives for development of oil refineries by the private sector
9	27 Jan 2016	• Single billing system for port services conducted by SOEs; integrate National Single Window system with "inaportnet" (port information system) • Mandatory use of IDR for transactions in transportation • Remove price difference between private, commercial, and state postal services
10	11 Feb 2016	• Revision of Investment Negative List (DNI) to remove foreign ownership cap on 35 businesses • Protect small and medium enterprises as well as cooperatives
11	29 Mar 2016	• Lower tax rate on property acquired by local real estate investment trusts • Harmonise customs checks at ports under the National Single Window • Loans for export-oriented SMEs under the *Kredit Usaha Rakyat* • Roadmap for the pharmaceutical industry
12	29 Apr 2016	• Per Ease of Doing Business indicators, shorten procedures for starting a business, reduce minimum paid-up capital, secure building permissions
13	10 Sept 2016	• Faster and simplified housing approvals and lower fees
14	10 Nov 2016	• Roadmap for the e-commerce industry • Increase access to funding and grants for startups • Lower tax rate and simpler licensing for local e-commerce startups

Source: BAPPENAS,[4] Coordinating Ministry for Economic Affairs,[5] Indonesia-Investments.com,[6] accessed January 2017; compiled by Asia Competitiveness Institute.

[4] http://www.bappenas.go.id/id/data-dan-informasi-utama/publikasi/paket-kebijakan-ekonomi

[5] https://www.ekon.go.id/ekliping/cat/paket1/

[6] http://www.indonesia-investments.com/news/todays-headlines/indonesia-unveils-11th-economic-stimulus-package-a-quick-look/item6650

Figure 1.9: FDI into Indonesia, 2011–2015

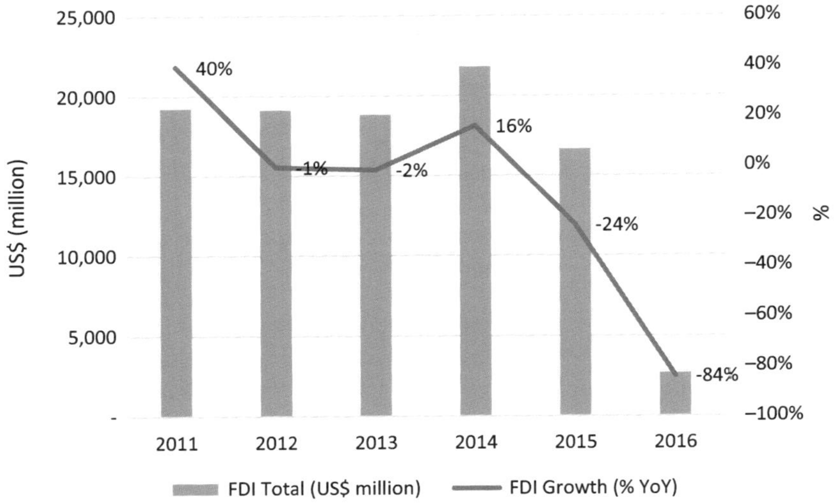

Source: Bank Indonesia, compiled by Asia Competitiveness Institute.

So far the efforts seem to have paid off: Indonesia is among countries that have made the most improvements in the Ease of Doing Business report of 2017 (World Bank, 2016), where the country's overall ranking improved to 91st position in 2017, up from 106th in 2016 to 114th in 2015.[7]

Improvements in ease of doing business are indeed welcome, but in this climate, Indonesia must count on improving foreign direct investment (FDI) and domestic private sector to generate more revenue for public spending and ultimately boost economic growth. This translates to an FDI target of IDR595 trillion or US$43.5 billion[8] between 2016 and 2019. Although President Jokowi has gone on roadshows abroad and focused on reforms to lure investors, external factors have also undermined investments into Indonesia. Net FDI inflows fell from US$ 21.8 billion in 2014 to US$16.6 billion in 2015 and potentially further dropping to US$2.6 billion amidst pull-out of about US$8.8 billion of foreign investment in the last quarter of 2016 (see Figure 1.9). FDI from top 10 source countries, most notably China and the US, have fallen. The pursuit for infrastructure investments has yet to result in any real inflows in the last two years too; instead, agriculture, manufacturing, mining, and quarrying are the biggest recipients of direct investments, attracting approximately two-thirds of the direct investments into the economy.

Stronger overtures to further open up Indonesia's economy have also been made, such as the indication to join the Regional Comprehensive Economic Partnership (RCEP), the revival

[7] More exploration on ease of doing business in Indonesia is presented in Chapter 5, where ACI presents the Inaugural Ease of Doing Business Index on Attractiveness to Investors, Business Friendliness and Competitive Policies (EDB Index ABC) for Indonesian Provinces.

[8] Based on an exchange rate of US$/Rp of 13,695.

of free trade agreement negotiations with Australia and European Union, and the ratification of the WTO Trade Facilitation Agreement (Hermansyah, 2015; Bernadette, 2015; Amindoni, 2016).

At the same time, despite reforms such as reduction in the negative investment list in the 10th Economic Package, new protectionist measures introduced by President Jokowi (such as foreign ownership restriction on e-commerce,[9] reduction in beef imports, and increased local content requirements for digital device manufacturing) are sending mixed signals to investors (Patunru and Rahardja, 2015; Maulani, 2016).

Investors are nervous about policy and legal uncertainties. To this end, both the Jokowi and past president Susilo Bambang Yudhoyono (SBY) administrations have treaded a similar path. Having been hauled to court by several multinational companies, Indonesia has terminated bilateral investment treaties, which include investor–state dispute settlement (ISDS) clauses that enable companies to sue countries. Recently, in January 2017, Indonesia eased the 2014 export ban of raw nickel ore and bauxite. The export ban on raw minerals was passed to move Indonesia up the value chain, thus encouraging companies to build smelter that processes raw minerals so they can be exported. A Chinese company, having invested US$525 million in building a smelter, is now considering legal action against the Indonesian government as this reversal means that companies that have built such facilities lose out (Asmarini and Jensen, 2017). Such policy uncertainties make Indonesia a relatively risky investment destination.

Aside from seeking investment, Indonesia is also looking to increase its foreign exchange revenue by boosting tourism receipts. As of March 2016, the number of countries whose citizens can visit Indonesia for 30 days without a visa has been expanded to 169 countries. Indonesia received 9.4 million foreign tourists in 2014, which is an increase compared to previous years, but still underwhelming compared to Malaysia and Thailand, which attracted 27 million and 24 million respectively in the same year (OECD, 2017). For 2016, Indonesia is aiming to attract 12 million foreign tourists and 260 million domestic tourists throughout the country, generating foreign exchange revenue equivalent to Rp 172 trillion and an additional Rp 223 trillion from domestic sources.

The ability of a country to attract investments and maintain them, lure in foreign and domestic tourists, resume a high level of economic growth as well as provide jobs and prosperity to its population depends on a well-orchestrated effort at both the national and sub-national levels. Although President Jokowi has introduced a slew of reforms, successful execution is highly dependent on the political will of central and local governments. The pace of implementation of these reforms varies as cooperation and coordination between ministries, local governments, and regulators, which are essential to embed these changes, greatly differ.

In this context, it is important to understand the dynamics of growth, development, and social conditions in each of Indonesia's sub-national (provincial) economies. The performance and potential of Indonesia as a whole will not be too far off from the sum of its parts. By

[9] In February 2016, the government announced 100% foreign ownership. However, in the 10th economic package, the Investment Negative List (DNI) reduced foreign ownership of e-commerce companies to 49% with the exception for venture capital companies.

understanding the profile of each province, we can better identify parts of Indonesia which act as growth engines and role models, as well as other parts which need to be further strengthened.

1.3 Structure and Content of the Book

This book presents results from ACI's latest series of research projects on Indonesia's sub-national economies. Aside from the annual competitiveness analysis and simulation studies on Indonesia's provinces and regions, in this edition, we also present results from two new thematic research projects analysing growth slowdown and ease of doing business at the provincial level.

The book comprises six chapters, inclusive of this introductory chapter which serves as a roadmap for readers. Chapter 2 details the 2016 annual update on provincial competitiveness ranking and simulation for Indonesian provinces. Chapter 3 features the same competitiveness analysis framework applied to six Indonesian regions, which are geographic aggregation of the provinces. Chapter 4 offers insights into the possibilities of growth slowdown for each province based on various income thresholds. Chapter 5 presents a novel framework to measure the ease of doing business at the sub-national level. Chapter 6 is the concluding chapter with a brief overview of ACI's future research agenda for Indonesia.

The 2016 annual update of Indonesia's provincial competitiveness analysis (Chapter 2) provides the latest iteration of one of ACI's flagship research projects. We measure competitiveness as a composite of four environments spanning: (i) Macroeconomic Stability, (ii) Government and Institutional Setting, (iii) Financial, Businesses, and Manpower Conditions, and (iv) Quality of Life and Infrastructure Development.

As seen in Table 1.2, the Special Capital Region (trans. Daerah Khusus Ibukota (DKI)) Jakarta occupies first place, as it has been for the past four years since the annual analysis was first published in 2013, while East Java remains as the second most competitive province after Jakarta.[10] Overall, we can see that provinces in the Java region tend to occupy the top of the ranking, while those in the Maluku–Papua region tend to occupy the bottom end. Meanwhile, the performance of provinces in Kalimantan, Sulawesi, as well as Bali–Nusa Tenggara regions tend to be mixed, and those in the Sumatra region tend to occupy the lower-middle part of the spectrum.

The 2016 update on competitiveness analysis of Indonesian regions (Chapter 3) applies the same framework used in Chapter 2, but on six regions of Indonesia. Each region is an aggregation of several provinces. Consistent with the findings at the provincial level presented in Chapter 2, we see that the Java region tops the performance on competitiveness, while the Maluku–Papua region holds the last place, as has been the case for the past years. However, while the top- and bottom-performing regions are of no surprise, the dynamics of performance among Kalimantan, Sulawesi, and Sumatra regions are interesting to follow. The result on

[10] See Tan and Amri (2016) for causality analysis of output growth in East Java.

Table 1.2: Highlights of ACI's 2016 Overall Competitiveness Ranking of Indonesian Provinces (Top-five and Bottom-five Provinces)

2016 Overall Competitiveness			
Rank	**Std. Scores**	**Province**	**Region**
1	3.2008	DKI Jakarta	Java
2	2.0817	East Java	Java
3	1.4636	Central Java	Java
4	1.3309	West Java	Java
5	0.9956	East Kalimantan	Kalimantan
...	...	...	...
29	–0.8476	Maluku	Maluku–Papua
30	–0.9933	West Sulawesi	Sulawesi
31	–1.3060	North Maluku	Maluku–Papua
32	–1.3927	East Nusa Tenggara	Bali–Nusa Tenggara
33	–1.5192	Papua	Maluku–Papua

Source: Asia Competitiveness Institute.

Sumatra deserves special attention as it shows that the conventional notion of Sumatra being a competitive region does not hold ground empirically. Instead, we see Kalimantan and Sulawesi regions surging ahead.

This chapter is immediately followed by a discussant note by Professor Dr Kuntoro Mangkusubroto, Professor of Decision Analysis at the School of Business and Management, Bandung Institute of Technology, Indonesia.

In 2015–2016, the ACI conducted an analysis on the probability of growth slowdown at the sub-national economies of Indonesia, China, India, as well as the countries of ASEAN-10. Chapter 4 presents the output of this research, focusing specifically on Indonesian provinces. The research was conducted as a response to the call for attention on 'middle income traps' brought forward by the World Bank and Asian Development Bank in 2012–2014. However, understanding that the income brackets of sub-national economies of Indonesia greatly vary, we decided not to focus only on 'traps' among the middle-income economies, but also on possibilities of growth slowdown across all income thresholds. Here, we define growth slowdown as episodes when the least square growth rate of GRDP per capita declines by at least 2% points, implying that the slowdown is non-negligible.

The research found that Indonesia's probability of experiencing growth slowdown in 2012–2017 is 0.10264 as a whole. Specifically for upper-middle income and high-income provinces, the average probability of slowdown is 0.22144. For lower-middle income provinces, it is 0.09026, while for low-income provinces, it is 0.04903. As seen in Table 1.3, two provinces with the highest probability of slowdown are Riau (probability: 0.39514) and East Kalimantan (probability: 0.31613).

Table 1.3: Highlights of Indonesian Provinces' Probability of Experiencing Growth Slowdown in 2012–2017 (Top-five and Bottom-five Provinces)

No.	Province	Income Group Which the Province Belongs to in 2012	Probability of Experiencing Growth Slowdown during 2012–2017
1	Riau	High-income	0.39514
2	East Kalimantan	High-income	0.31613
3	DKI Jakarta	High-income	0.20778
4	East Java	Lower-middle-income	0.20395
5	West Sulawesi	Low-income	0.15698
...	...	...	...
29	Gorontalo	Low-income	0.01767
30	Central Sulawesi	Lower-middle-income	0.00864
31	Banten	Lower-middle-income	0.00759
32	West Nusa Tenggara	Low-income	0.00042
33	North Maluku	Low-income	0.00007

Source: Asia Competitiveness Institute.

This chapter is immediately followed by discussant notes by Dr Kirida Bhaopichitr, Research Director of the Thailand Development Research Institute, Thailand, and Dr Darwin Marcelo, Infrastructure Economist at The World Bank Group.

Chapter 5 presents findings from ACI's inaugural study on Ease of Doing Business Index, which covers three major environments: Attractiveness to Investors, Business Friendliness and Competitive Policies (EDB Index ABC) for Indonesian Provinces. This research is a response to the need for a more comprehensive framework to understand the intricacies of conducting a business activity beyond that conducted annually by the World Bank at the country level. Through the EDB Index ABC, we argue that formal regulatory aspects should be considered together with economic factors (including macro- and micro-level variables), while the role of government in terms of managing competition is similarly paramount.

Findings from this study present an interesting comparison against the provincial competitiveness index as presented in Chapter 2. The top-performing province here is South Sulawesi (which ranks sixth in the competitiveness index), followed by DKI Jakarta and East Java (see Table 1.4). A scatterplot of the EDB Index ABC scores and the Overall Competitiveness scores show that provinces with high level of competitiveness also tend to show high levels of Ease of Doing Business, implying that a holistic approach to ease of doing business may be able to provide a better approximation of an economy's competitiveness level.

Immediately following chapter 5 is the discussant notes of Ms Paramita Dasgupta, Practice Manager of Trade & Competitiveness at The World Bank Group Asia, and Ms Kristy Tsun-Tzu Hsu, Director of the Taiwan-ASEAN Studies Center, Chung-Hua Institution for Economic Research, Taiwan.

Table 1.4: Highlights of ACI's Ease of Doing Business Index — ABC of Indonesian Provinces (Top-five and Bottom-five Provinces)

2016 EDB Index ABC			
Rank	**Std. Scores**	**Province**	**Region**
1	1.8570	South Sulawesi	Sulawesi
2	1.6182	DKI Jakarta	Java
3	1.5415	East Java	Java
4	1.4857	Central Java	Java
5	1.2494	West Java	Java
...	...	...	...
29	−1.2252	South Sumatra	Sumatra
30	−1.3921	Riau Islands	Sumatra
31	−1.4492	West Papua	Maluku–Papua
32	−1.8133	West Sumatra	Sumatra
33	−1.8458	Jambi	Sumatra

Source: Asia Competitiveness Institute.

Chapter 6 presents a concluding summary of our key findings in this book, which reiterates Indonesia's status as a rising middle power and the need to expand growth centres in the country, and ends off with a note on our future research agenda.

As Indonesia revives itself and tries to regain a healthy and more resilient growth level, we hope that this study can help policymakers, academics, and business practitioners alike to better understand the economic potentials of Indonesia, not just as a country but also as a collection of interesting and vibrant sub-national economies, each with their own strengths and challenges.

References

Amindoni, Ayomi. 2016. "Indonesia to ratify WTO trade facilitation agreement." *The Jakarta Post.* Apr 13, 2016. Retrieved from http://www.thejakartapost.com/news/2016/04/13/indonesia-to-ratify-wto-trade-facilitation-agreement.html.

Asian Development Bank. 2016a. *Basic Statistics 2016*. Asian Development Bank. Available at: http://www.adb.org/publications/basic-statistics-2016.

———. 2016b. "Asian Development Outlook 2016 Update: Meeting the Low-Carbon Growth Challenge." Asian Development Bank. Available at: http://www.adb.org/publications/asian-development-outlook-2016-update.

Asmarini, Wilda and Fergus Jensen. 2017. "Nickel smelters consider suing Indonesia after ore export ban U-turn." *Reuters*. Jan 13, 2017. Retrieved from http://www.reuters.com/article/us-indonesia-mining-idUSKBN14X12A.

Bernadette, Christina. 2015. "Indonesia's trade minister calls for TPP membership in 2 years." *Reuters*. Oct 9, 2015. Retrieved from http://www.reuters.com/article/us-trade-tpp-indonesia-idUSKCN0S312R20151009.

Brummitt, C. 2015. "Indonesia Plans Tax Shakeup as Widodo Renews Push for Investment." *Bloomberg*. Oct 27, 2015. Retrieved from http://www.bloomberg.com/news/articles/2015-10-27/indonesia-plans-tax-shakeup-as-widodo-renews-push-for-investment.

Hermansyah, Aation. 2015. "Indonesia eyes FTA with Australia in 2017, CEPA in 2018." *The Jakarta Post*. May 13, 2015. Retrieved from http://www.thejakartapost.com/news/2016/05/12/indonesia-eyes-fta-with-australia-in-2017-cepa-in-2018.html.

Negara, Siwage Dharma. 2016. "Indonesia's 2016 Budget: Optimism Amidst Global Uncertainties." 3. ISEAS Perspective. Singapore: ISEAS — Yusof Ishak Institute.

Oberman, Raoul, Richard Dobbs, Arief Budiman, Fraser Thompson, and Morten Rosse. 2012. "The Archipelago Economy: Unleashing Indonesia's Potential." McKinsey Global Institute. Available at: http://www.mckinsey.com/global-themes/asia-pacific/the-archipelago-economy.

OECD. 2017. "Economic Outlook for Southeast Asia, China and India 2017 — Addressing Energy Challenges." Available at: http://www.oecd.org/dev/economic-outlook-for-southeast-asia-china-and-india-23101113.htm.

Maulani, A. M. A. 2016. "Indonesia revises foreign ownership regulation for e-commerce: here's what you need to know." *e27*. May 27, 2016. Retrieved from https://e27.co/indonesia-just-revised-foreign-ownership-regulation-for-e-commerce-heres-what-you-need-to-know-20160527/.

O'Neill, Jim. 2013. "Who You Calling a BRIC?" *Bloomberg View*, November 12. Retrieved from: https://www.bloombergview.com/articles/2013-11-12/who-you-calling-a-bric-.

Patunru, Arianto. A. and Rahardja Sjamsu. 2015. "Trade protectionism in Indonesia: Bad times and bad policy." *Lowy Institute for International Policy*. July 2015. Retrieved from http://www.lowyinstitute.org/publications/trade-protectionism-indonesia-bad-times-and-bad-policy.

Tan, Khee Giap and Mulya Amri. 2016. "Economic Growth in East Java, Indonesia: A Geweke Causality Analysis." *International Journal of Business and Social Science*, Vol. 7, No. 7, September 2016 *[US]*.

Tan, Khee Giap, Mulya Amri, Linda Low, and Kong Yam Tan. 2013. *Competitiveness Analysis and Development Strategies for 33 Indonesian Provinces*. Singapore: World Scientific.

Tan, Khee Giap, Mulya Amri, Nurina Merdikawati, and Nursyahida Ahmad. 2017a. *2015 Annual Competitiveness Analysis and Development Strategies for Indonesian Provinces*. Asia Competitiveness Institute — World Scientific Series. Singapore: World Scientific. Available at: http://www.worldscientific.com/worldscibooks/10.1142/10246.

Tan, Khee Giap, Sasidaran Gopalan, and Anuja Tandon. 2017. *2015 Agricultural Total Factor Productivity and Competitiveness Analysis for States and Federal Territories and Five Regions of India*. Singapore: World Scientific. Available at: http://www.worldscientific.com/worldscibooks/10.1142/10231.

Tan, Khee Giap, Linda Low, Kartik Rao, and Kong Yam Tan. 2015c. *2014 Regional Competitiveness Analysis and a Master Plan on Regional Development Strategies for India: Annual Competitiveness Update and Evidence on Economic Development Model for Selected States of India*. Book, Whole. Singapore: World Scientific.

Tan, Khee Giap, Linda Low, Kong Yam Tan, and Kartik Rao. 2014a. *Annual Analysis of Competitiveness, Simulation Studies and Development Perspective for 35 States and Federal Territories of India: 2000–2010*. Book, Whole. Singapore: World Scientific.

Tan, Khee Giap, Nurina Merdikawati, Mulya Amri, and Blake Harley Berger. 2015a. *2014 Annual Competitiveness Analysis and Development Strategies for Indonesian Provinces*. Singapore: World Scientific.

Tan, Khee Giap, Nurina Merdikawati, Mulya Amri, and Kong Yam Tan. 2015b. *2014 Provincial and Inaugural Regional Competitiveness Analysis: Safeguarding Indonesia's Growth Momentum.* Singapore: World Scientific.

———. 2017b. *2015 Agricultural Productivity, Decentralisation, and Competitiveness Analysis for Provinces and Regions of Indonesia*. Asia Competitiveness Institute — World Scientific Series. Singapore: World Scientific. Available at: http://www.worldscientific.com/worldscibooks/10.1142/10245.

Tan, Khee Giap and Trieu Duong Luu Nguyen. 2016. "Measuring Cost of Living for Ordinary Residents in Cities: A New Index." *Business and Management Studies,* Vol. 2, No. 3, pp. 52–77, September 2016 [US]

Tan, Khee Giap, Le Phuong Anh Nguyen, Sasidaran Gopalan, and Nguyen Trieu Duong Luu. 2017c. *2015 Annual Competitiveness Analysis, Agricultural Productivity and Development Vision for ASEAN-10.* Singapore: World Scientific. Available at: http://www.worldscientific.com/worldscibooks/10.1142/10219.

Tan, Khee Giap, Kong Yam Tan, Randong Yuan, and Le Phuong Anh Nguyen. 2016b. *2014 Annual Indices for Expatriates and Ordinary Residents on Cost of Living, Wages and Purchasing Power for World's Major Cities*. Singapore: World Scientific. Available at: http://www.worldscientific.com/worldscibooks/10.1142/9087.

Tan, Khee Giap, Wing Thye Woo, Kong Yam Tan, and Grace Ee Ling Aw. 2012. *Ranking the Liveability of the World's Major Cities*. Singapore: World Scientific. Available at: http://www.worldscientific.com/worldscibooks/10.1142/8553.

Tan, Khee Giap, Sangiita Wei Cher Yoong Yoong, Sasidaran Gopalan, and Le Phuong Anh Nguyen. 2016a. *2014 Annual Competitiveness Ranking and Simulation Study for ASEAN-10 and Development Strategies to Enhance Asia Economic Connectivity*. Singapore: World Scientific. Available at: http://www.worldscientific.com/worldscibooks/10.1142/10004.

Tan, Khee Giap, Randong Yuan, and Teleixi Xie. 2017. *2015 Estimation of Agricultural Productivity and Annual Update of Competitiveness Analysis for Greater China*. Singapore: World Scientific. Available at: http://www.worldscientific.com/worldscibooks/10.1142/10244.

Tan, Khee Giap, Randong Yuan, and Sangiita Wei Cher Yoong. 2015. *2014 Annual Provincial and Regional Competitiveness Analysis for Greater China Economies: Development Strategies under the New Normal*. Book, Whole. Singapore: World Scientific.

Tan, Khee Giap, Randong Yuan, Sangiita Wei Cher Yoong, and Mu Yang. 2014b. *Annual Analysis of Competitiveness, Simulation Studies and Development Perspective for 34 Greater China Economies: 2000–2010*. Book, Whole. Singapore: World Scientific.

Wirayani, Prima and Sundaryani, Fedina. 2017. "Hole found in Indonesia tax amnesty." *The Jakarta Post.* Jan 5, 2017. Retrieved from http://www.thejakartapost.com/news/2017/01/05/hole-found-in-indonesia-tax-amnesty.html.

World Bank. 2016. "Doing Business 2017 — Equal Opportunity for All." World Bank. Available at: http://www.doingbusiness.org/reports/global-reports/doing-business-2017.

Special Remarks on Indonesia's Economy and Reforms in 2016[1]

Dr Darmin Nasution

Coordinating Minister for Economic Affairs
Republic of Indonesia

Bismillahirohmannirahim,
Assalamualaikum Warahmatullahi Wabarakatuh,

Ladies and Gentlemen,

The slowdown of the global economy for the past years has resulted in the reduction of GOP growth for developed and developing countries. Based on the World Bank economic outlook, the global growth is projected to slow down to 3.1% in 2016 before recovering to 3.4% in 2017. There are a number of factors causing the circumstances, including some new developments, such as the new U.S Government; Brexit-the U.K. referendums result in favour of leaving the European Union; ongoing realignments, such as rebalancing in China and the adjustment of commodity exporters to a protracted decline in the terms of trade; and slow-moving trends, such as demographics and the evolution of productivity growth; as well as noneconomic factors, such as geopolitical and policy uncertainty. Even with the optimistic prospect for 2017 and the expected stable price for commodities (including crude oil, copper, rubber, natural gas, nickel, coal, palm oil), the risk of the financial sector and the emerging market is still considered threatening.

Influenced by the global factors, I am pleased to say that Indonesia's economy remains at stable position. Indonesia's economy is supported by private sectors' consumption and the boost in government spending from the annual rate of 4.8% to 5% in the third quartile 2016.

Meanwhile, we managed to control the rate of inflation at around 3%, lower the poverty rate from time to time, improve the income distribution which is shown by Indonesia's Gini ratio

[1]The contents of this special remarks were delivered as the Coordinating Minister for Economic Affairs' keynote address during the 2016 Annual Asia Competitiveness Institute Conference on 24 November 2016, in Singapore.

at 0.397, and avoiding a huge rise in open unemployment rate, which demonstrates Indonesia's quality of growth.

As the result, our economic outlook is positive, with stronger and stricter efforts to manage deficit supported by higher tax income from the tax amnesty program. From all evidences that I explained earlier, I believe that we are in the right path to achieve a better quality of development.

In addition, Indonesia has just recently improved its Ease of Doing Business (EODB) rank from 106 to 91 which positioned Indonesia among the 10 top reforming countries. I would also like to inform you that Indonesia is ranked the third highest country of FDI in 2016. We are very committed to improve the investment climate by debottlenecking unnecessary procedures and bureaucracy in the central and regional governments. In order to achieve higher economic growth as already targeted by the President at around 6% in 2018, we would need three things which are: continuous spending, improvement of quality and effectiveness in government spending, and higher private sector investments in Indonesia. In addition, we must emphasize on advancing Information and Technology front for administering taxation in facilitating tax revenue for Government.

The Government has made several reforms with the issuance of 14 Economic Packages to encourage business deregulations. The reforms include Bureaucratic Simplification and Fiscal Incentive, Tax Allowance and Tax Holiday, Reduction of Oil Fuel, Electricity, and Gas Price, Tax incentives for revaluation of fixed assets, Development of Special Economic Zones, Acceleration of Land Certification Process, Revising Negative Investment List to protect SMEs and to increase foreign investments, Improving Ease of Doing Business, and others. The 14th package which was introduced last week is hoped to encourage e-commerce growth in Indonesia in its path to become the biggest digital based nation in South East Asia by 2020.

To support e-commerce, the government is looking at alternative funding schemes, including the Business Credit for the tenants, grants and business incubator for platform development, USO funds for small to medium platforms, angel capital for start-ups in commercialization phase, seed capital, and crowd-funding.

In infrastructure sector, the government has determined the 225 projects and 1 program in electricity as National Strategic Infrastructure Project. To implement those all projects, we need about Rp 2,900 Trillion (equivalent to USD 220 billion). This huge demand is impossible to be financed solely by the state budget and our state-owned enterprises (SOE). Thus, we are looking at massive progress of Public Private Partnerships (PPP) to work together with the government to build all infrastructure projects.

The Government has done significant reforms in fiscal, and institutional, and regulatory aspects to attract more investors.

On the fiscal side, the government is now able to provide Viability Gap Fund (VGF) to fund the constructions for parts of the project up to 49% of the total investment cost to reduce the CAPEX. Moreover, the government also has a risk sharing scheme to ensure fair and effective risk allocation to public and private sectors.

On the institutional side, has established the Committee for Acceleration of Priority Infrastructure Delivery (KPPIP) to coordinate and support the Project Owner on the preparation and delivery of priority projects and empowered PT Sarana Multi Infrastructure (PT SMI) with capital injection of IDR 20.3 Trillion, of which IDR 18.3 Trillion came from the merging of Pusat

Investasi Pemerintah to PT SMI. This injection will be used by PT SMI to fund more economic and social projects at national and regional level. Furthermore, the mandate of Indonesia Infrastructure Guarantee Fund (IIGF) will be expanded to include guarantee on direct lending to State Owned Enterprise to attract direct fund channelling to the SOEs and avoid the bureaucratic process of Government-to-Government loan. Last but not least, we have also established PPP Unit under Ministry of Finance which serves to provide the Project Development Facility and Transaction Advisory support for PPP projects, besides examining the provision of government support for the PPP project.

On the regulatory side, we have revised the regulations on PPP, availability payment, direct lending, land acquisition and other regulations as mentioned in the Economic Policy Packages.

I would like to inform you that this year we have achieved contract signings and financial close for various PPP projects such as Central Jawa Pover Plant 2x1,000 MW and Palapa Ring Broadband. We are closely monitoring other PPP projects and provide the necessary acceleration actions to have them ready for construction by 2018 or even faster.

We realized that there are still homework to be done by the government to make Indonesia more business friendly and attractive to investors and I would like to let you know that we are working hand in hand within the government, academics, and private sectors to find other means and initiatives to grow our economy.

Ladies and Gentlemen,

As a member of the G20, it is imperative that Indonesia needs to match its human, social, financial, and delivery capitals with the global best practices. Government puts importance to improve Human Capital quality, by championing various education provisions, including vocational education to engender ready-to-be-deployed workforce.

In order to achieve this, leveraging private sectors management and efficiency skills are highly important and this can be achieved with collaborations with both local and international firms.

There are plenty of opportunities for private investors to invest in Indonesia, whether in transportation, energy, and telecommunication factors to fulfil the Nawa Cita's targets.

I would like to show my appreciation to the organizer of the Asia Competitiveness Institute for their efforts to carry out comprehensive survey to list down the competitiveness index of the provinces for sustainable economic growth.

The ACI survey provides critical policy insights on competitiveness to lay the groundwork for Governments to frame and improve their competitiveness policies, and provides guidance for business seeking entities to enter the market.

Last but not least, we need to remember that the research and policy propositions that the ACI has helped developed and create must be in the best interest of development benefitting Indonesia. We wish through the previous and future cooperation will benefit both parties, particularly Indonesia in improving its competitiveness.

Wassalamualaikum Warahmatullahi Wabarakatuh.

Chapter 2
2016 Annual Update on Competitiveness Analysis of Indonesian Provinces

2.1 Introductory Notes

Indonesia's overall competitiveness is tied to its leaders' ability to corral support from the central and local governments in order to see bureaucratic reforms through and ensure growth is broad-based across regions. With the end of the commodity supercycle, Indonesia can no longer afford to tolerate the structural weaknesses in its economy. For economic growth to be sustainable, each province in Indonesia has a role to play in improving its own competitiveness from macroeconomic management, governance, financial, business and labour conditions to infrastructure development.

In line with the above objective, Asia Competitiveness Institute (ACI) has been tracking the competitiveness of Indonesia's provinces across the years, enabling policymakers to assess the competitiveness profile of each province in Indonesia *vis-à-vis* their peers (Tan and Amri 2013; Tan *et al.*, 2015a, 2017a).

This chapter is organised as follows. Section 2.1 provides a snapshot of Indonesia's recent economic development and competitiveness. Section 2.2 outlines the methodology comprising a broad sweep of competitiveness review, ACI's competitiveness framework, indicators, data sources, standardised score, and *what-if* competitiveness simulation. Section 2.3 discusses the empirical findings and Section 2.4 concludes by drawing some policy implications.

2.1.1 Broad Sweep of Competitiveness Review

Initially, the term 'competitiveness' was closely associated with firms' performance (Porter, 1980) based on a notion that it was primarily firms that competed with each other. Over time, the discourse expanded into the national level (Porter, 1990; Berger and Bristow, 2009), as also shown by the establishment of "Council on Competitiveness" and similar institution in various advanced industrialised countries. After all, the performances of those firms depend on various factors that are embedded in the firms' location. These include, but not limited to, quality of labour and infrastructure, governance, costs of doing business, as well as the performance of competing and complementary firms around the area (Bristow, 2009; Camagni, 2002; Kitson, Martin, and Tyler, 2004).

The more common approach to measure a country's competitiveness is by constructing a benchmarking index, as adopted by the two highly cited cross-country competitiveness studies: (i) Global Competitiveness Report published by the World Economic Forum (WEF), and (ii) World Competitiveness Yearbook by the International Institute for Management Development (IMD). The benchmarking index is effective at summarising complex and multidimensional factors in a user-friendly and easily digestible platform. The information from the ranking, score, and progress over time can facilitate discussion with general public to promote key reforms that often require multistakeholders efforts.

Beyond country-level competitiveness, there are more studies delving into the sub-national level, either at state/provincial level or district/city level. For instance, the Beacon Hill Institute at Suffolk University has been publishing the annual competitiveness report for 50 states in US since 2002. As previously mentioned in Chapter 1, the ACI has also been analysing the sub-national competitiveness not only in Indonesia but also in India (Tan, Gopalan, and Tandon, 2017; Tan *et al.*, 2015b) and China (Tan, Yuan, and Xie, 2017; Tan, Yuan, and Yoong, 2015). Going deeper into a smaller subset of economic entity allows us to suggest development strategy which are relevant to stimulate productive discussion among key stakeholders at the sub-national level in the first instance before engaging them at the national level.

2.1.2 Competitiveness Analyses on Indonesia

The competitiveness of Indonesia as a country is analysed regularly by a number of institutions, including the WEF, IMD, and ACI.

ACI's annual competitiveness analysis of the 10 member countries of Association of Southeast Asian Nations (ASEAN) found Indonesia at the fifth position since 2002 onwards, behind Singapore, Malaysia, Brunei, and Thailand (Tan *et al.*, 2017b, 2016) (see Figure 2.1). Indonesia competed closely with the Philippines for this fifth position in 2000–2002 as well as 2005, but surged ahead and maintained its position from 2006 onwards. The country's standardised scores for Overall Competitiveness peaked in 2010 at 0.115, but declined steadily to –0.014 in 2012 and 2013, in line with the negative impact of global growth slowdown and commodity price bust.

In similar light, the WEF's Global Competitiveness Report showed an improvement in Indonesia's global competitiveness ranking from 2012–2013 to 2014–2015, improving from 50th to 34th ranking (Schwab and Sala-i-Martin, 2016). Since then, however, Indonesia has slipped down to 41st place in 2016–2017 (see Figure 2.2). The IMD's World Competitiveness Yearbook also finds that Indonesia's competitiveness rose from 42nd in 2012 to 37th in 2014, but declined to 48th position in 2016 (see Figure 2.3) (IMD, 2015).

At the sub-national level, there remains a dearth of research, specifically on Indonesia's provinces. A study by Bank Indonesia and University of Padjadjaran measured the competitiveness of provinces, cities and regencies using an input–output framework to identify the productivity of a sub-national entity (PPSK Bank Indonesia and LP3E FE-UNPAD 2008). The Indonesia Governance Index for all provinces was published subsequently, with economic governance as one of the four main sub-indexes or "arenas" being analysed (Partnership for Governance Reform, 2013). Additionally, an analysis of economic governance in hundreds of cities and

Figure 2.1: Asia Competitiveness Institute Competitiveness Rankings for ASEAN-10 Countries, 2000–2014

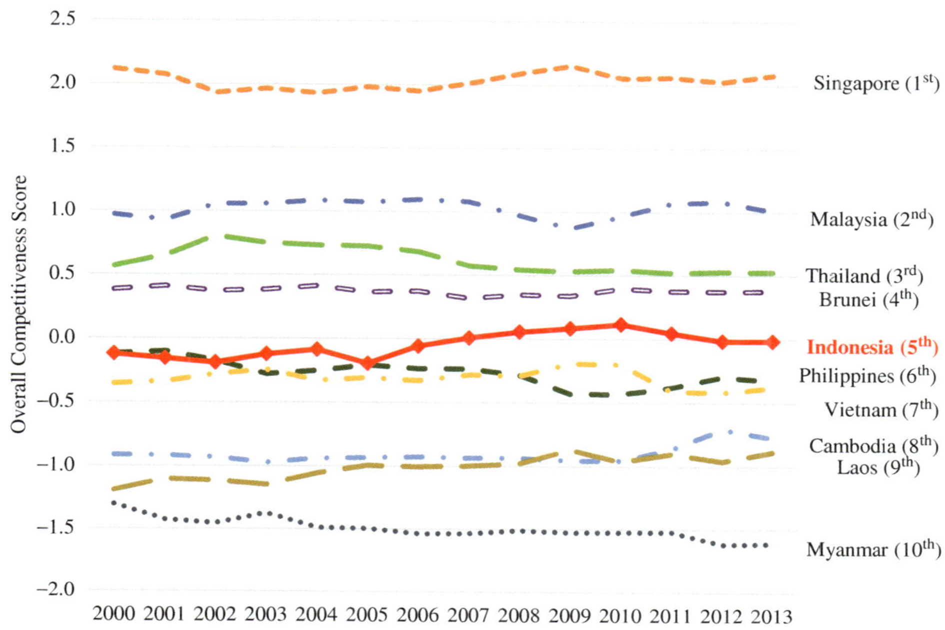

Source: Asia Competitiveness Institute.

Figure 2.2: World Economic Forum Global Competitiveness Rankings, 2013–2017 (Selected Countries)

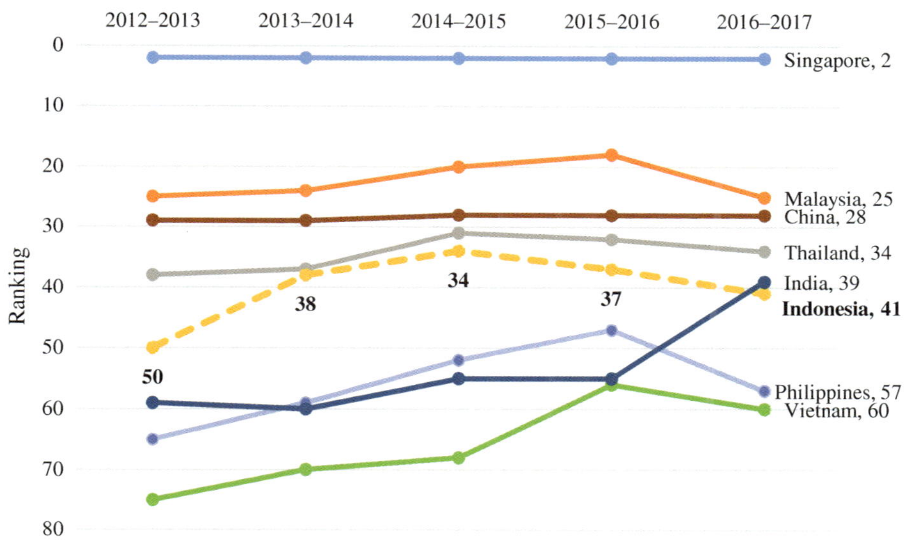

Source: WEF data, compiled by Asia Competitiveness Institute.

Figure 2.3: International Institute for Management Development World Competitiveness Rankings, 2012–2016 (Selected Countries)

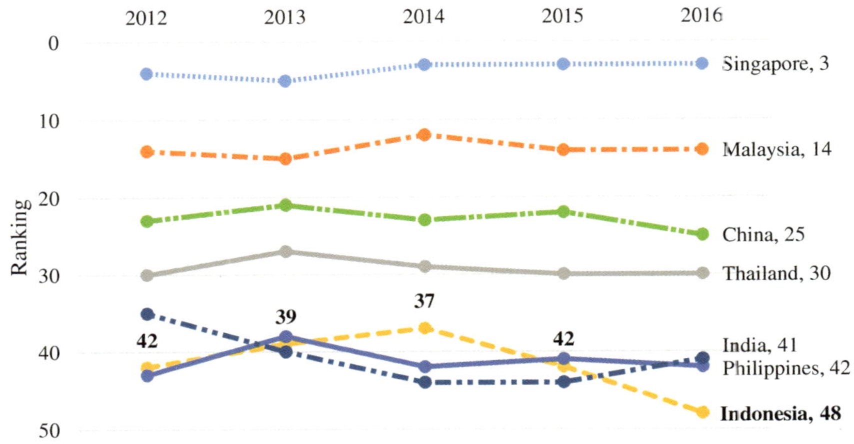

Source: IMD data, compiled by Asia Competitiveness Institute.

regencies in Indonesia were also conducted, first in 2006 and later in 2011 (KPPOD and The Asia Foundation, 2007; KPPOD and The Asia Foundation, 2011).

All these are efforts to measure, in one form or another, the competitiveness of Indonesia's sub-national entities and should be welcomed. However, these studies are not done on a regular basis as they depend on donor funding for a certain project. With this lack of regular analysis on the competitiveness of Indonesia's sub-national entities, it becomes difficult to track progress.

ACI intends to fill this gap in knowledge on the economic profile of Indonesian provinces. In this sense, we choose to explore competitiveness at the provincial level (as opposed to the city or regency level) because provinces are typically sizeable enough to function as an economy whereas cities and regencies may not. The following sections of this chapter present the methodology, empirical findings, and policy implications of the latest iteration of ACI's 2016 annual competitiveness analysis of Indonesian provinces.

2.2 Research Methodology

2.2.1 ACI's Competitiveness Framework

ACI's approach to competitiveness is a holistic one, encompassing different factors that collectively shape the ability of an economy to achieve substantial and inclusive economic development over a sustained period of time. In line with this comprehensive approach, the ACI defines competitiveness through four different environments and 12 sub-environments as follows (see Figure 2.4):

1 **Macroeconomic Stability**

This environment encompasses aggregated economic conditions that underline the comparative and competitive advantages of each province based on classical macroeconomic indicators.

Figure 2.4: ACI's Competitiveness Framework

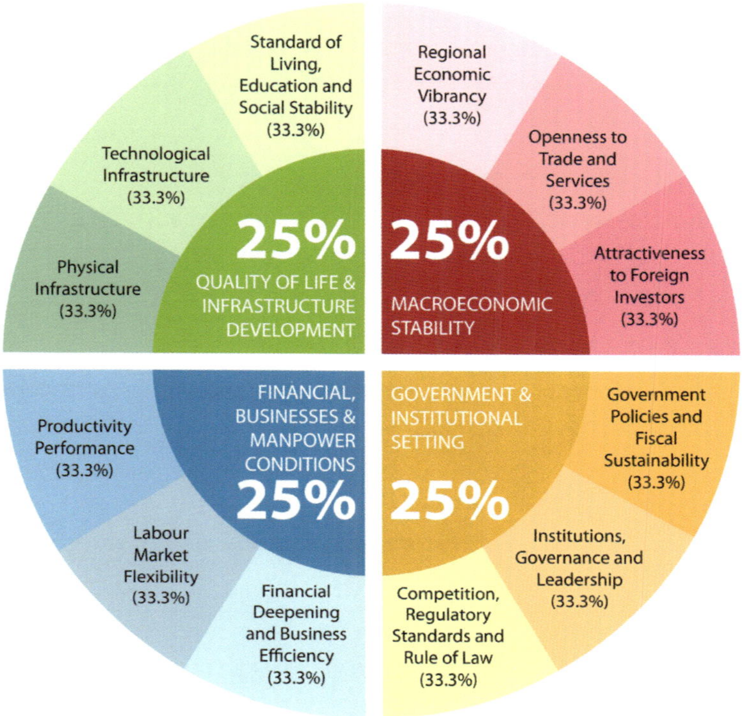

Source: Asia Competitiveness Institute.

(a) *Regional Economic Vibrancy*

This sub-environment captures the size of each province's economy and its growth trajectory according to different characteristics in their economic structure. Beyond gross regional domestic product (GRDP), this sub-environment also takes into account inflation rate as well as capital formation.

(b) *Openness to Trade and Services*

This sub-environment measures the degree of openness to international trade for each province. All indicators related to exports, imports, and the ratio of openness are included.

(c) *Attractiveness to Foreign Investors*

This sub-environment measures to what extent each province manages to attract both foreign and direct investment. Considering that both foreign and direct investment may fluctuate on a yearly basis, we use the average value of the last three years of investment for each province.

2 Government and Institutional Setting

This environment covers the efficacy of government institutions as well as expectations of progress in the public sector.

(a) *Government Policies and Fiscal Sustainability*

This sub-environment captures the financial capacity of each provincial government to ensure fiscal sustainability to undertake various policies under their jurisdiction. All fiscal-related indicators, such as provincial government's revenue, tax collections, expenditure and fiscal balance are included.

(b) *Institutions, Governance, and Leadership*

This sub-environment covers the broad spectrum of governance quality ranging from how prevalent the corruption practice to how well the provincial government coordinates among different layers of local governments.

(c) *Competition, Regulatory Standards, and Rule of Law*

This sub-environment covers to what extent each province is able to create and enforce consistent rule of law and regulation that allow competition and ease of doing business to thrive.

3 Financial, Businesses, and Manpower Conditions

This environment encompasses the performance and potential of firms as well as conditions that managers face in running their companies.

(a) *Financial Deepening and Business Efficiency*

This sub-environment captures the availability of sound financial system to support the growing firms. Additionally, wide-ranging assessments to firms' performance, strategy, human resource and equipment capacity, application of information technology, and innovation are included.

(b) *Labour Market Flexibility*

This sub-environment covers the size of each province's labour force, employment, and unemployment rate, as well as the stickiness of labour market as measured by minimum monthly wage, ease of recruiting managerial and technical workers, and relationship between labour unions and management.

(c) *Productivity Performance*

This sub-environment covers all indicators related to productivity as measured by the output per worker, both in general terms and specific to each economic structure.

4 Quality of Life and Infrastructure Development

This environment covers wide-ranging indicators related to physical and technological infrastructure as well as provision of basic social services.

(a) *Physical Infrastructure*

This sub-environment not only captures the market size as measured by population and urbanisation rate but also the physical infrastructure, including air, sea, and land connectivity as well as access to water and electricity services.

(b) *Technological Infrastructure*

This sub-environment captures the rate of information, communications, and technology (ICT) adoption in each province. All indicators related to telephone, hand phone, desktop, and laptop ownership as well as internet access at various location points are included.

(c) *Standard of Living, Education, and Social Stability*

This sub-environment encompasses access to education and healthcare, as well as broader set of measurements for quality of life such as equality of income distribution, environmental sustainability, and accessibility of goods and services.

As visualised in Figure 2.4, each environment contributes the same weight (25%) to the Overall Competitiveness Index. ACI's competitiveness framework further drills down to nested approach, wherein each of the four environments is further divided into three sub-environments. Therefore, there are 12 sub-environments altogether. Each sub-environment contributes the same weight (33.3%) towards its respective environment's index.

In aggregating sub-environments into environments and environments into an overall ranking, ACI uses a simple averaging mechanism with equal weights. While assigning different weights for different indicators with varying levels of importance may seem appropriate, the implementations are as controversial due to subjective value judgements. Thus, to achieve a balanced view towards the different factors that make up an overall notion of competitiveness, we use equal weights across all indicators.

2.2.2 Indicators and Data Sources

ACI's 2016 competitiveness index for Indonesian provinces[1] uses a combination of secondary and primary data, with a total of 103 indicators. Although the weights assigned to the four environments and 12 sub-environments are equal, some sub-environments have more indicators than others due to data availability. See Appendix 1 for the complete list of indicators.

Formal Government Statistics

Most of the indicators used in this analysis (78 out of 103 indicators) were formal secondary data drawn from various government agencies, such as Indonesia's Central Statistical Agency (BPS), Bank Indonesia, Ministry of Trade, Ministry of Health, and Ministry of Environment and Forestry. We also use data from World Bank's Indonesia Database for Policy and Economic Research (INDO-DAPOER) as well as CEIC Indonesia Premium Database which cited BPS as

[1] There are currently 34 provinces in Indonesia. North Kalimantan, as Indonesia's newest province (carved out of East Kalimantan in 2012), is not yet analysed on its own due to lack of disaggregated data. North Kalimantan is therefore still analysed as part of East Kalimantan.

their original sources. Due to a lag in data availability, the latest available data at the time of collection in mid-2015 was data for the year 2013.

Surveys in Each Province

A smaller portion of the data (25 out of 103 indicators) was based on primary data obtained through perception surveys conducted in each province in the second half of 2015. This allows us to capture the more recent dynamics of competitiveness to complement the time-lags from the secondary data.

Three categories of stakeholders were involved separately in each province: (a) business owners and operators, (b) provincial government officials, and (c) academicians. Responses from the three stakeholders were aggregated at the province level with the intention that one stakeholder group provides a balancing view for the others.

The survey relied on purposive sampling method, where the ACI collaborated with local partners representing the three stakeholders:

(a) For business owners and operators, surveys were done in collaboration with the Indonesian Employers' Association (APINDO), which has chapters in each province and invited their members to participate.
(b) For the provincial governments, surveys were supported by the Coordinating Ministry for Economic Affairs, which provided reference letters to the governors. The provincial government, in turn, invited representatives from various departments to participate.
(c) For academics, the ACI collaborated with universities in each province, most often with the faculty of economics and business. The university then invited their lecturers, researchers, and graduate students to participate.

Figure 2.5 illustrates the characteristics of our survey respondents in 2015. One-fifth (20.8%) of our academic respondents were senior lecturers with more than 20 years of teaching experience. This proportion doubles for respondents from the provincial government, with more than one-third (40.0%) having over 20 years of experience in public service. For business owners and operators, there is a balanced representation of micro, small, medium, and large businesses.

The surveys were conducted using an electronic response system, where questions were presented on a computer projector, and participants keyed in their answers using keypads. Facilitators from ACI were present at each survey to read the questions and give clarifications when needed.

A total of 2,278 respondents participated in the surveys. Of these, 847 were business owners and operators (37.2%), 741 were academics (32.5%), and 690 were provincial government officials (30.3%). The number of respondents is about 69 per province on average (2,278 respondents divided by 33 provinces). Out of the 69 respondents, typically 26 were business owners and operators, 22 were academics, and 21 were provincial government officials.

Figure 2.5: Characteristics of Respondents of ACI's 2015 Survey

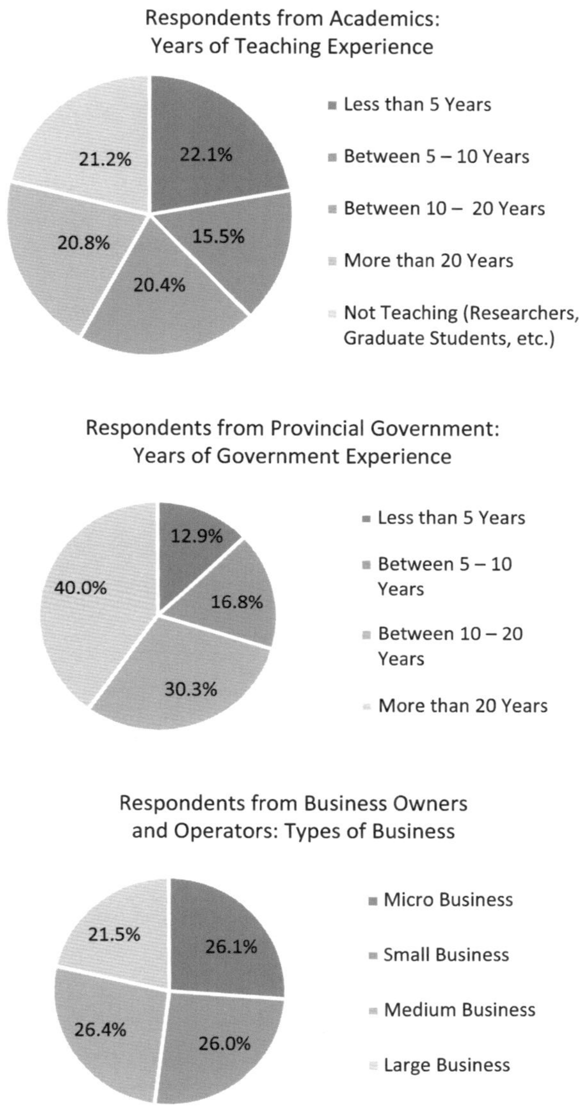

Source: Asia Competitiveness Institute.

2.2.3 The Standardised Score

After data collection, we aggregated the different types of data into a coherent dataset where the value of one indicator is comparable to the value of another. However, each indicator is measured in different units. For example, government revenue is measured in thousands of Rupiah, while Cargo at International Seaport is measured in tonnes. To resolve these differences, we use the statistical method of 'standardised score'.

The standardised score has no unit of measurement because it simply measures how well a certain province performs in comparison to the average province. In statistical terms, it measures how many standard deviations away each province is from the average province. See Appendix 2 for a detailed, technical explanation.

If a province has a standardised score of zero, it is basically an average performer in terms of that particular indicator. Having a negative score means the province performs below average. Having a positive score means above-average performance. The farther the score is from zero, the farther the performance of said province from the national average.

2.2.4 *What-if* Simulation Analysis

A competitiveness ranking in itself identifies which provinces are doing well and which ones are facing challenges. However, it stops short of giving constructive advice on improving the rankings.

ACI's *what-if* competitiveness simulation allows us to answer the question: "if a particular province improves on its weakest indicators while assuming that other provinces remained constant, how would that province's ranking improve?" It is conducted based on the improvement of each province's top-20% weakest indicators, and a recalculation of the standardised score based on such improvement.

To conduct the simulation, (1) first, we sorted the different indicators for each province based on the standardised score. This allows us to identify the top-20% weakest indicators for each province. (2) Next, we raised the scores of these indicators moderately to match the average score. This means that the scores of these indicators are raised to zero if previously negative. If they were already zero or positive, no changes were made. (3) Once the scores have been raised, we recalculated the ranking with the assumption that the scores of other provinces remained constant. Therefore, this policy simulation was done one-by-one for each province.

2.3 Competitiveness Analysis Results

Using the methodology introduced in Section 2, the rankings are derived by sorting the standardised scores of each province as shown in Tables 2.1–2.5. Additionally, the rankings are illustrated on maps to gain insights on the geographical spread of performance across provinces.

2.3.1 Ranking and Scores for Overall Competitiveness

Provinces in the Java region remain dominant at the top-10 (see Table 2.1). DKI Jakarta as the nation's capital is much more competitive than the rest, given its substantially high score (std. score: 3.201) compared to the runner-up, East Java (2.082). Most top performers stay at the top with minimal change in ranking. Compared to previous year's 2015 research results, Central Java (third) switches spot with East Kalimantan (fifth), whereas North Sulawesi (ninth) exchanges position with Banten (11th). Among the top-10 provinces, Bali records the highest

Table 2.1: 2016 Overall Competitiveness: Ranking and Scores

2016 Rank	2015 Rank	Province	2016 Std. Score
1	1	DKI Jakarta	3.201
2	2	East Java	2.082
3	5	Central Java	1.464
4	4	West Java	1.331
5	3	East Kalimantan	0.996
6	10	South Sulawesi	0.966
7	12	Bali	0.670
8	8	South Kalimantan	0.648
9	11	North Sulawesi	0.549
10	6	DI Yogyakarta	0.397
11	9	Banten	0.258
12	7	Riau Islands	0.093
13	13	Central Kalimantan	-0.002
14	20	Central Sulawesi	-0.077
15	16	Riau	-0.184
16	21	Southeast Sulawesi	-0.195
17	19	West Kalimantan	-0.280
18	25	Lampung	-0.306
19	26	West Nusa Tenggara	-0.336
20	30	Bangka Belitung Islands	-0.434
21	27	Gorontalo	-0.447
22	17	South Sumatra	-0.449
23	22	West Sumatra	-0.488
24	15	North Sumatra	-0.558
25	23	Bengkulu	-0.651
26	24	Aceh	-0.691
27	28	West Papua	-0.729
28	14	Jambi	-0.767
29	29	Maluku	-0.848
30	18	West Sulawesi	-0.993
31	31	North Maluku	-1.306
32	32	East Nusa Tenggara	-1.393
33	33	Papua	-1.519

Source: Asia Competitiveness Institute.

jump, from 12th to seventh place, followed by South Sulawesi, which climbs four positions to sixth place. These provinces, together with East Kalimantan (fifth) and South Kalimantan (eighth) remain in the top-10. Meanwhile, some provinces dropped out of the top-10, namely Banten (from ninth to 11th) and Riau Islands (from seventh to 12th).

At the lower end of the table, North Maluku (31st), East Nusa Tenggara (32nd), and Papua (33rd) remain as the bottom-three. Provinces such as Bengkulu (25th), Aceh (26th), West Papua (27th) and Maluku (29th) remain at the bottom-10. Those that observe substantial decline in

Figure 2.6: 2016 Map of Overall Competitiveness Ranking

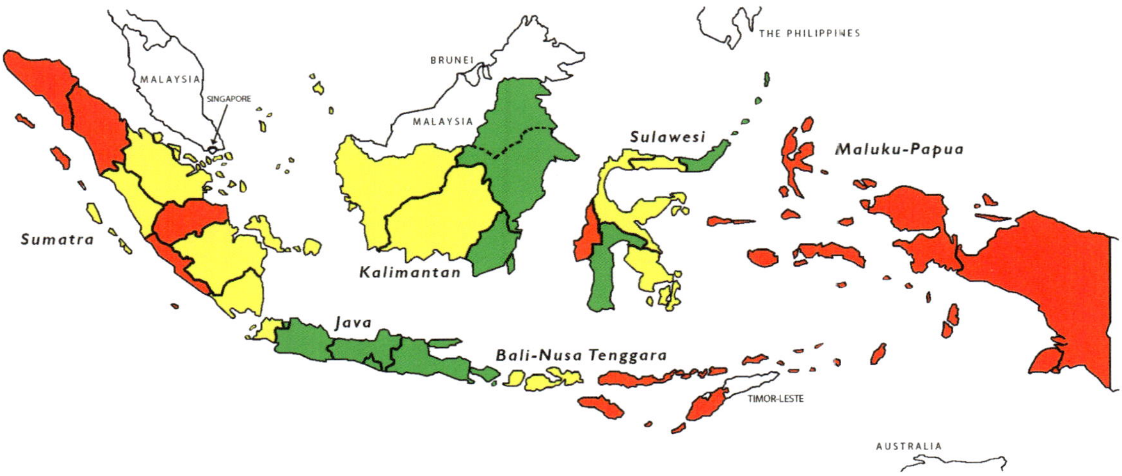

Source: Asia Competitiveness Institute.

ranking include North Sumatra (24th), which drops by nine positions, as well as Jambi (28th) and West Sulawesi (30th), which fall by 14 and 12 positions respectively.

DKI Jakarta's high score skews the distribution of standardised score among 33 provinces. The average-performing province (standardised score of zero) is positioned between 12th and 13th positions, while the median province (that occupying the 17th position) has a negative score of −0.280.

The Overall Competitiveness ranking can also be viewed on a map of Indonesian provinces, as seen in Figure 2.6. On the map, provinces are colour-coded based on three groups: top-10 positions (green), bottom-10 positions (red), and middle-13 positions (yellow). The map shows a noticeable geographic concentration of high, mediocre, and low competitiveness provinces. Six of the top-10 provinces are located in Java, while the remaining four are spread across Kalimantan (East Kalimantan and South Kalimantan), Bali–Nusa Tenggara (Bali) and Sulawesi (South Sulawesi and North Sulawesi). The bottom-10 provinces are mostly part of the eastern region, highlighting continued disparity between eastern region *vis-à-vis* the rest of Indonesia. More provinces in western Indonesia are also found in the bottom-10 compared to previous findings in 2015 ranking (Tan *et al.*, 2017a, 2017c).

Interestingly, provinces in the country's western area (Sumatra) are not as competitive as what conventional wisdom holds. The low-performing provinces from western Indonesia are Aceh (26th), North Sumatra (24th), Bengkulu (25th) and Jambi (28th), all of which are located in Sumatra. The remaining Sumatra provinces, half of Sulawesi provinces, and West Nusa Tenggara province belong to the middle-13 group. Hence, we can infer that for Overall Competitiveness, (i) provinces in Java (sans Banten) are highly competitive, (ii) provinces in Kalimantan are either competitive or mediocre, (iii) provinces in (1) Sulawesi and (2) Bali–Nusa Tenggara have either high, mediocre or low competitiveness, (iv) mediocre and low competitiveness provinces are mostly found in Sumatra, and (iv) provinces in the eastern regions of Indonesia tend to perform poorly in overall competitiveness.

2.3.2 Ranking and Scores by Four Environments

Macroeconomic Stability

DKI Jakarta (std. score: 4.154) tops the Macroeconomic Stability ranking table, further strengthening its position as the epicentre of Indonesia's economic growth (see Table 2.2). The score gap

Table 2.2: 2016 Macroeconomic Stability: Ranking and Scores

2016 Rank	2015 Rank	Province	2016 Std. Score	Sub-environment Scores REV	OTS	AFI
1	1	DKI Jakarta	4.154	4.018	4.811	2.175
2	2	East Java	2.325	2.264	0.940	2.956
3	3	West Java	1.578	1.950	–0.422	2.653
4	4	East Kalimantan	0.692	0.449	0.834	0.549
5	7	Central Java	0.663	0.853	0.115	0.789
6	5	Riau Islands	0.627	0.386	1.959	–0.685
7	6	Banten	0.235	–0.114	0.011	0.725
8	11	South Kalimantan	0.169	–0.307	0.574	0.180
9	8	South Sulawesi	0.128	0.137	–0.382	0.585
10	9	Riau	0.068	0.291	–0.020	–0.091
11	16	Central Sulawesi	–0.021	–0.185	–0.497	0.628
12	10	North Sumatra	–0.090	0.348	0.159	–0.744
13	12	South Sumatra	–0.136	0.089	–0.296	–0.152
14	13	North Sulawesi	–0.172	–0.348	–0.441	0.334
15	22	Papua	–0.212	0.073	–0.113	–0.522
16	14	Central Kalimantan	–0.217	–0.347	–0.458	0.230
17	18	Bali	–0.260	–0.434	–0.498	0.243
18	23	West Kalimantan	–0.314	–0.374	–0.375	–0.082
19	20	DI Yogyakarta	–0.349	–0.633	–0.548	0.256
20	15	Southeast Sulawesi	–0.388	–0.325	–0.356	–0.346
21	30	Gorontalo	–0.475	–0.399	–0.530	–0.330
22	25	Lampung	–0.494	–0.419	–0.182	–0.708
23	19	West Papua	–0.497	–0.211	–0.269	–0.835
24	27	West Nusa Tenggara	–0.506	–0.771	–0.483	–0.086
25	21	Jambi	–0.521	–0.529	–0.421	–0.430
26	17	West Sulawesi	–0.550	–0.428	–0.549	–0.480
27	28	Maluku	–0.672	–0.782	–0.362	–0.636
28	26	Aceh	–0.677	–0.237	–0.487	–1.068
29	29	North Maluku	–0.684	–0.842	–0.118	–0.852
30	24	West Sumatra	–0.762	–0.596	–0.325	–1.098
31	31	Bangka Belitung Islands	–0.809	–0.816	–0.233	–1.094
32	33	East Nusa Tenggara	–0.904	–0.807	–0.521	–1.067
33	32	Bengkulu	–0.931	–0.953	–0.516	–0.997

Note: REV: Regional Economic Vibrancy; OTS: Openness to Trade and Services; AFI: Attractiveness to Foreign Investors.
Source: Asia Competitiveness Institute.

with the runner-up, East Java (2.325), is even more profound. Again, DKI Jakarta and East Java skew the distribution, as we see that the average province is positioned between 10th and 11th places, while the median (Bali at the 17th place) has a negative standardised score of –0.260.

By delving into sub-environment scores, we can identify the underlying driver(s) behind each province's performance in Macroeconomic Stability. Most provinces at the top-10 excel in all three sub-environments, although several fall short in certain sub-environments. For instance, despite scoring well for overall Macroeconomic Stability environment, West Java (ranked third) falls short in terms of Openness to Trade and Services, while Riau Islands (ranked sixth) struggled in Attractiveness to Foreign Investors.

On the other hand, the bottom-10 provinces tend to underperform in all three sub-environments. Bangka Belitung Islands (31st) and West Sumatra (30th) score particularly low in Attractiveness to Foreign Investors. Meanwhile, Bengkulu (33rd) and North Maluku (29th) fall behind in terms of Regional Economic Vibrancy.

The map for Macroeconomic Stability (Figure 2.7) shows less apparent geographic concentration among high, mediocre, and low competitiveness provinces. Although half of the top-10 provinces are from Java, the remaining five are scattered across Sumatra (Riau Islands at sixth and Riau at 10th), Kalimantan (East Kalimantan at fourth and South Kalimantan at eighth), and Sulawesi (South Sulawesi at ninth). The middle-13 and bottom-10 provinces are even more spread out. Kalimantan mirrors Java region in that there is no province in both regions which are in the bottom-10.

We can infer that for Macroeconomic Stability, (i) provinces in Java are highly competitive with the exception of DI Yogyakarta at 19th, (ii) provinces in Kalimantan are either competitive or mediocre, (iii) provinces in Sumatra and Sulawesi show mixed performance as they host a range of high, mediocre, and low competitiveness provinces, and (iv) provinces in Bali–Nusa Tenggara and Maluku–Papua regions exhibit either low or mediocre performance.

Figure 2.7: 2016 Map of Macroeconomic Stability Ranking

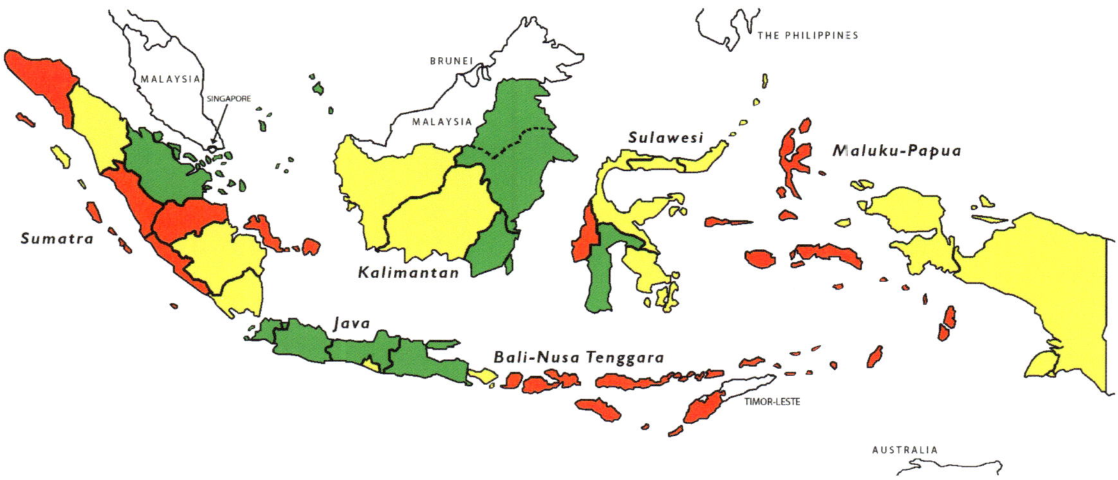

Source: Asia Competitiveness Institute.

Government and Institutional Setting

In Table 2.3 for Government and Institutional Setting environment, the top-10 provinces are relatively more diverse, with more provinces from Sulawesi being represented among the upper end of the ranking table. There are five provinces from Java, three from Sulawesi, and one each from Kalimantan and Bali–Nusa Tenggara. South Sulawesi (std. score: 1.927) shows marked improvement by 11 positions to second place, closely trailing DKI Jakarta (2.388). Likewise, West Java (sixth), Bali (eighth) and Central Sulawesi (ninth) all improve substantially. The spread of the scores between the top- and bottom-performing provinces is more symmetrical compared to the

Table 2.3: 2016 Government and Institutional Setting: Ranking and Scores

2016 Rank	2015 Rank	Province	2016 Std. Score	Sub-environment Scores		
				GPFS	IGL	CRRL
1	1	DKI Jakarta	2.388	4.548	0.158	0.841
2	13	South Sulawesi	1.927	0.019	1.764	2.693
3	4	Central Java	1.671	0.948	1.299	1.633
4	6	North Sulawesi	1.617	−0.384	1.705	2.435
5	5	East Java	1.252	1.418	0.822	0.667
6	12	West Java	1.060	1.789	0.083	0.591
7	7	South Kalimantan	0.836	0.109	0.961	0.873
8	19	Bali	0.688	0.111	0.562	0.925
9	15	Central Sulawesi	0.578	−0.493	1.123	0.712
10	3	DI Yogyakarta	0.528	−0.226	0.881	0.573
11	22	Gorontalo	0.298	−0.626	1.008	0.309
12	14	West Kalimantan	0.115	−0.242	0.175	0.334
13	20	West Nusa Tenggara	0.115	−0.430	0.648	0.048
14	26	Maluku	0.112	−0.724	0.878	0.107
15	16	Banten	0.030	0.657	−0.466	−0.121
16	8	Central Kalimantan	0.009	−0.333	0.433	−0.079
17	10	Southeast Sulawesi	−0.118	−0.583	0.499	−0.191
18	2	East Kalimantan	−0.152	0.391	−0.293	−0.451
19	28	Lampung	−0.182	−0.211	−0.393	0.182
20	32	Bangka Belitung Islands	−0.393	−0.537	0.118	−0.494
21	9	West Sulawesi	−0.442	−0.783	0.216	−0.460
22	30	Riau	−0.447	−0.306	−0.389	−0.344
23	29	Aceh	−0.649	−0.083	−0.524	−0.900
24	11	Jambi	−0.699	−0.476	−0.099	−1.048
25	23	Bengkulu	−0.767	−0.585	−0.469	−0.727
26	24	West Sumatra	−0.863	−0.289	−1.208	−0.507
27	17	South Sumatra	−0.922	−0.148	−1.091	−0.903
28	25	Papua	−0.945	−0.533	−0.616	−1.045
29	21	East Nusa Tenggara	−1.210	−0.647	−0.878	−1.286
30	31	West Papua	−1.215	−0.597	−2.006	−0.219
31	33	North Maluku	−1.221	−0.778	−0.688	−1.371
32	18	Riau Islands	−1.377	−0.271	−1.723	−1.205
33	27	North Sumatra	−1.622	0.295	−2.490	−1.572

Note: GPFS: Government Policies and Fiscal Sustainability; IGL: Institutions, Governance, and Leadership; CRRL: Competition, Regulatory Standards, and Rule of Law.
Source: Asia Competitiveness Institute.

other environments (see Tables 2.2, 2.4 and 2.5 for comparison), where the average province is positioned similar to the median province.

Further analysing performance in more detail, the top-10 provinces tend to do well across the three sub-environments. However, North Sulawesi (fourth), Central Sulawesi (ninth) and DI Yogyakarta (10th) fare below average in the Government Policies and Fiscal Sustainability sub-environment, while DKI Jakarta scores proportionately higher due to its large budget. This shows that despite having smaller public budget, provinces such as North Sulawesi and DI Yogyakarta still have a favourable environment of Government and Institutional Setting, due to good performance in other sub-environments, namely, (i) Institutions, Governance, and Leadership as well as (ii) Competition, Regulatory Standards, and Rule of Law.

Provinces in the bottom-10 perform poorly in all three sub-environments, faring worst either in Institutions, Governance, and Leadership or Competition, Regulatory Standards, and Rule of Law. These are observed in provinces which have substantial decline in ranking, such as Riau Islands (32nd), Jambi (24th) and South Sumatra (27th) which drop 14, 13 and 10 positions, respectively, compared to previous year.

The map in Figure 2.8 shows a noticeable geographical concentration of high and low competitiveness provinces in terms of Government and Institutional Setting. The top-10 provinces tend to be located in Java, Kalimantan, and Sulawesi. In fact, it is only in this environment that we can see more representations of non-Java provinces in the top-10. The Sulawesi region deserves a special mention as half of its six provinces are ranked among the top-10 while none are in the bottom-10. On the other hand, mediocre- and low-performing provinces tend to be found in the Maluku–Papua and Sumatra regions.

Figure 2.8: 2016 Map of Government and Institutional Setting Ranking

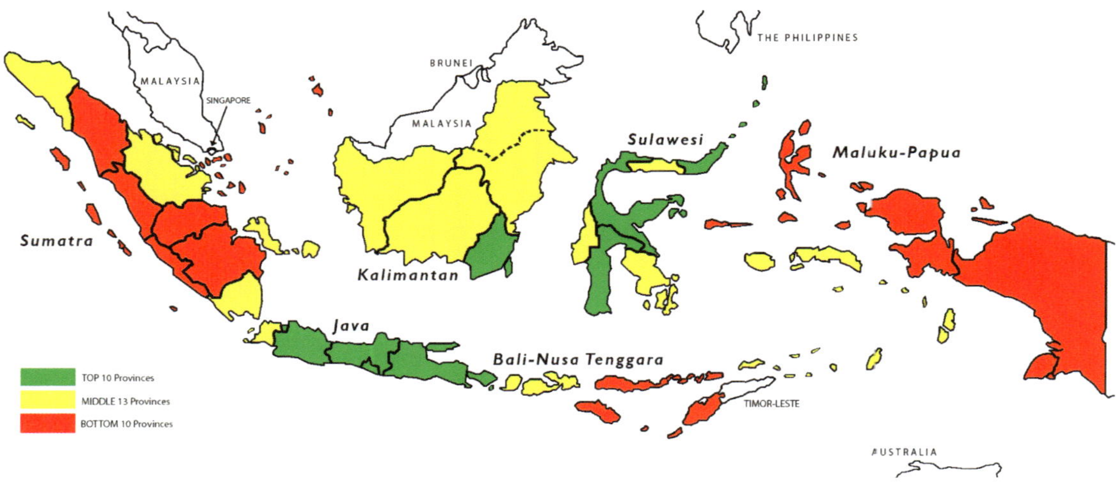

Source: Asia Competitiveness Institute.

Financial, Businesses, and Manpower Conditions

The top-10 provinces in Financial, Businesses, and Manpower Conditions (Table 2.4) largely consists of incumbents with two newcomers: South Sulawesi (currently eighth place, up from 14th last year) and South Kalimantan (10th, up from 15th in 2015). It is encouraging to have one of Indonesia's easternmost provinces, West Papua, consistently remaining among the top-10 in this environment, despite the lagging performance of its neighbours. In this environment, we also see the standardised score skewed upwards towards DKI Jakarta's significantly high score (std. score: 3.032).

Table 2.4: 2016 Financial, Businesses, and Manpower Conditions: Ranking and Scores

2016 Rank	2015 Rank	Province	2016 Std. Score	Sub-environment Scores: FDBE	LMF	PP
1	1	DKI Jakarta	3.032	2.684	–0.079	3.775
2	2	East Java	2.207	1.436	3.342	–0.135
3	3	Central Java	1.807	1.565	2.846	–0.608
4	5	West Java	1.285	0.488	2.492	–0.275
5	4	East Kalimantan	0.945	–0.088	–0.631	2.707
6	7	West Papua	0.940	1.498	–0.843	1.325
7	8	Bali	0.711	1.171	0.805	–0.481
8	14	South Sulawesi	0.334	0.807	0.137	–0.242
9	6	Riau Islands	0.229	–0.448	–0.701	1.632
10	15	South Kalimantan	0.116	0.518	–0.054	–0.221
11	12	West Kalimantan	0.104	0.368	0.024	–0.174
12	11	Central Kalimantan	0.042	0.393	–0.292	–0.013
13	28	Bangka Belitung Islands	0.039	0.499	–0.353	–0.064
14	9	DI Yogyakarta	0.004	0.085	0.538	–0.615
15	13	North Sumatra	–0.007	–0.161	0.071	0.076
16	21	Lampung	–0.028	0.322	0.141	–0.523
17	25	South Sumatra	–0.047	0.124	–0.202	–0.021
18	17	Banten	–0.120	0.063	–0.113	–0.203
19	30	Southeast Sulawesi	–0.205	0.430	–0.397	–0.465
20	18	North Sulawesi	–0.208	0.187	–0.618	–0.007
21	24	West Sumatra	–0.245	0.092	–0.630	0.022
22	19	Bengkulu	–0.331	0.185	–0.301	–0.581
23	10	Riau	–0.340	–1.124	–0.452	0.860
24	32	West Nusa Tenggara	–0.636	–0.589	0.004	–0.753
25	22	Central Sulawesi	–0.748	–0.814	–0.513	–0.248
26	27	Gorontalo	–0.829	–0.570	–0.289	–0.886
27	20	Jambi	–0.890	–1.028	–0.458	–0.389
28	29	Papua	–0.940	–1.708	–0.084	–0.185
29	16	West Sulawesi	–1.110	–1.446	–0.237	–0.654
30	26	Aceh	–1.140	–1.225	–1.050	–0.124
31	31	East Nusa Tenggara	–1.225	–1.302	–0.410	–0.867
32	33	Maluku	–1.228	–0.670	–1.076	–0.838
33	23	North Maluku	–1.514	–1.743	–0.618	–0.826

Note: FDBE: Financial Deepening and Business Efficiency; LMF: Labour Market Flexibility; PP: Productivity Performance.
Source: Asia Competitiveness Institute.

This environment offers interesting insight as all of the top-10 provinces fare below average in at least one of the sub-environments. Provinces located in Java tend to excel in Labour Market Flexibility, owing to a large pool of workforce. But DKI Jakarta is behind in this sub-environment as its unemployment rate and minimum wage are among the highest in the country. Provinces with heavy reliance on labour-intensive sectors, including those in Java (but not DKI Jakarta), tend to perform poorly in Productivity Performance, which is determined by value added per worker. Those with high scores in this sub-environment tend to be very productive relative to other provinces in Indonesia, either in the service industries (DKI Jakarta, ranked first), primary resources (East Kalimantan at fifth, West Papua at sixth), or manufacturing (Riau Islands at ninth).

The bottom-10 provinces are mostly laggards in one or two sub-environment(s) and mediocre performers in the remaining sub-environment(s). For example, North Maluku (33rd) and Papua (28th) scored particularly low in terms of Financial Deepening and Business Efficiency. Meanwhile, Maluku (32nd) and Aceh (30th) are struggling in Labour Market Flexibility, while Gorontalo (26th) and East Nusa Tenggara (31st) need to catch up in Productivity Performance.

According to the map in Figure 2.9, the top-10 provinces are still dominated by those in Java. There are however representations from all regions except for Sumatra, which observe provinces that are mediocre or low-performing. South Sulawesi (eighth place) is a new entrant into the top-10 (previously at 14th place), while West Papua has been part of the top-10 provinces in terms of Financial, Businesses, and Manpower Conditions for several years. Both provinces are known to offer vibrant business opportunities and host a large number of migrants from other regions.

Figure 2.9: 2016 Map of Financial, Businesses, and Manpower Conditions Ranking

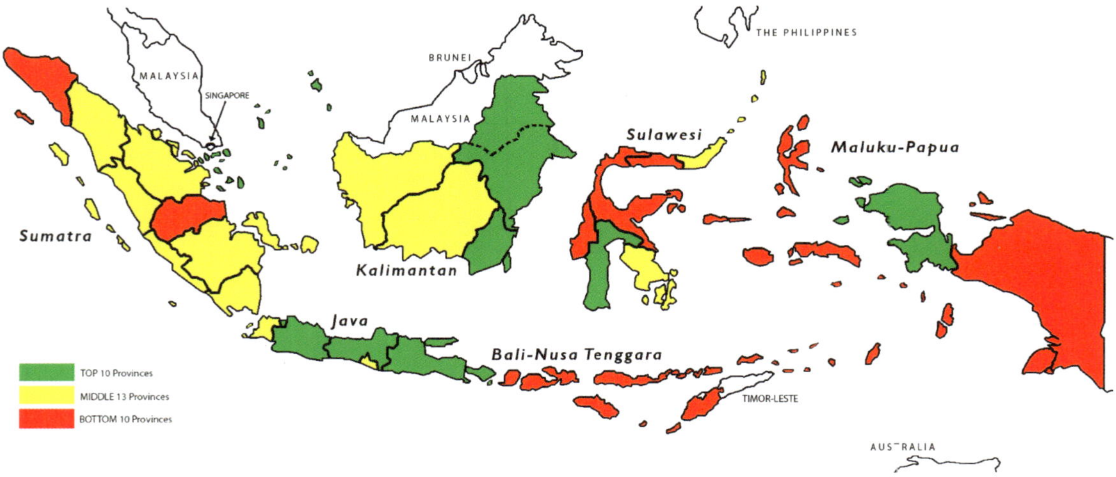

Source: Asia Competitiveness Institute.

In general, we observe that (i) provinces in Java tend to be competitive, (ii) provinces in Kalimantan show mediocre performance, except in East Kalimantan and South Kalimantan which belong in the top-10, (iii) Sulawesi and Maluku–Papua show mixed performance, (iv) provinces in Sumatra are mostly mediocre, except Jambi and Aceh which belong to the bottom-10, and (v) provinces in the Bali–Nusa Tenggara region tend to be struggling, except Bali which maintains its top-10 position.

Quality of Life and Infrastructure Development

Table 2.5 shows East Kalimantan (std. score: 1.877) maintains its top ranking, followed closely by East Java (1.243) and DKI Jakarta (1.231). It is notable to mention here that DKI Jakarta has consistently been ranked in the third place for this environment for the past three years. Overall, we see less dramatic changes in the composition of provinces occupying the top-10, middle-13, and bottom-10, implying that it takes time to observe the impacts of policy reforms related to Quality of Life and Infrastructure Development. However, we do see some shifts in position among provinces that are already in the top-10. For example, East Java jumped three spots and claimed the second place this year, while DI Yogyakarta slid down two spots from runner-up to fourth place. Meanwhile, South Sulawesi (currently seventh) and Central Java (ninth) are newcomers to the top-10, having ranked 11th and 14th, respectively, in 2015.

In general, the scores tend to be distributed more evenly, but with a large gap observed between the scores of West Papua (–1.690) at 32nd and Papua (–3.032) at 33rd. For this environment, the scores tend to be skewed downwards towards Papua's extremely low score, in contrast to the situation in previous environments (compare against Tables 2.2–2.4).

Some provinces in the top-10 score below or just slightly above average in the sub-environment of Standard of Living, Education, and Social Stability. These include provinces with dense population where social services are being strained, such as DKI Jakarta, Banten, and Central Java. Interestingly, some provinces in the bottom-10 have favourable scores for this sub-environment, such as Maluku, Jambi, and Gorontalo.

Papua's position as the bottom-performing province in terms of Quality of Life and Infrastructure Development for three consecutive years is worrying. Papua is far behind the rest of Indonesia particularly in Standard of Living, Education, and Social Stability (–3.841). Although the Special Autonomy Law provided substantial resources for Papua to improve its people's living standards, progress has been less than expected.

The geographical concentration of low-performing provinces is even more apparent in the map in Figure 2.10. All provinces from the easternmost region are part of the bottom-10 group, while provinces belonging to middle-13 group are more spread out. Hence, in general, (i) provinces in Java tend to be competitive, (ii) provinces in Sumatra, Kalimantan, Sulawesi, and Bali–Nusa Tenggara islands show mixed performance, and (iii) provinces in Maluku–Papua tend to show low performance.

Table 2.5: 2016 Quality of Life and Infrastructure Development: Ranking and Scores

2016 Rank	2015 Rank	Province	2016 Std. Score	Sub-environment Scores PI	TI	SLES
1	1	East Kalimantan	1.877	1.754	1.128	1.083
2	5	East Java	1.243	2.326	0.209	0.091
3	3	DKI Jakarta	1.231	0.050	3.226	-0.675
4	2	DI Yogyakarta	1.156	-0.413	1.230	1.627
5	7	Bali	1.122	0.884	0.903	0.583
6	8	South Kalimantan	1.067	1.858	0.520	-0.124
7	11	South Sulawesi	0.871	0.628	0.279	0.933
8	4	Riau Islands	0.837	0.085	1.526	0.158
9	14	Central Java	0.800	1.403	0.198	0.090
10	6	Banten	0.726	2.213	1.225	-1.905
11	13	North Sulawesi	0.615	0.016	0.182	1.101
12	9	West Java	0.569	1.157	0.698	-0.653
13	12	West Sumatra	0.224	-0.493	-0.030	0.996
14	18	Central Kalimantan	0.160	-0.367	-0.079	0.784
15	15	Aceh	0.133	-0.061	-0.503	0.847
16	16	Riau	0.100	-0.435	0.147	0.499
17	23	Southeast Sulawesi	0.053	-0.319	0.079	0.352
18	21	Central Sulawesi	-0.069	-0.163	-0.567	0.585
19	22	West Nusa Tenggara	-0.106	-0.180	-0.238	0.194
20	10	North Sumatra	-0.165	0.525	-0.737	-0.136
21	19	Bengkulu	-0.170	-0.788	-0.143	0.572
22	25	Bangka Belitung Islands	-0.302	-0.205	0.115	-0.548
23	24	Lampung	-0.330	-0.802	-0.117	0.223
24	20	South Sumatra	-0.412	-0.408	-0.084	-0.378
25	17	Jambi	-0.478	-0.838	-0.413	0.241
26	26	Gorontalo	-0.503	-0.369	-0.894	0.200
27	29	West Kalimantan	-0.852	-1.276	0.219	-0.742
28	28	North Maluku	-0.989	-0.533	-1.745	0.188
29	27	Maluku	-1.074	-0.556	-2.083	0.369
30	30	West Sulawesi	-1.250	-0.935	-1.201	-0.506
31	31	East Nusa Tenggara	-1.362	-0.758	-0.959	-1.162
32	32	West Papua	-1.690	-1.429	-1.095	-1.047
33	33	Papua	-3.032	-1.570	-0.996	-3.841

Note: QLID: Quality of Life and Infrastructure Development; PI: Physical Infrastructure; TI: Technological Infrastructure; SLES: Standard of Living, Education, and Social Stability.
Source: Asia Competitiveness Institute.

2.3.3 *What-if* Simulation Analysis on Overall Competitiveness

The methodology for *what-if* competitiveness simulation has been explained earlier in Section 2.2.4. The scenario is to raise each province's top-20% weakest indicators to the average score. Afterwards, the standardised score is recalculated based on such an improvement, one at a time with the assumption that all other provinces' scores remain constant.

Figure 2.10: 2016 Map of Quality of Life and Infrastructure Development Ranking

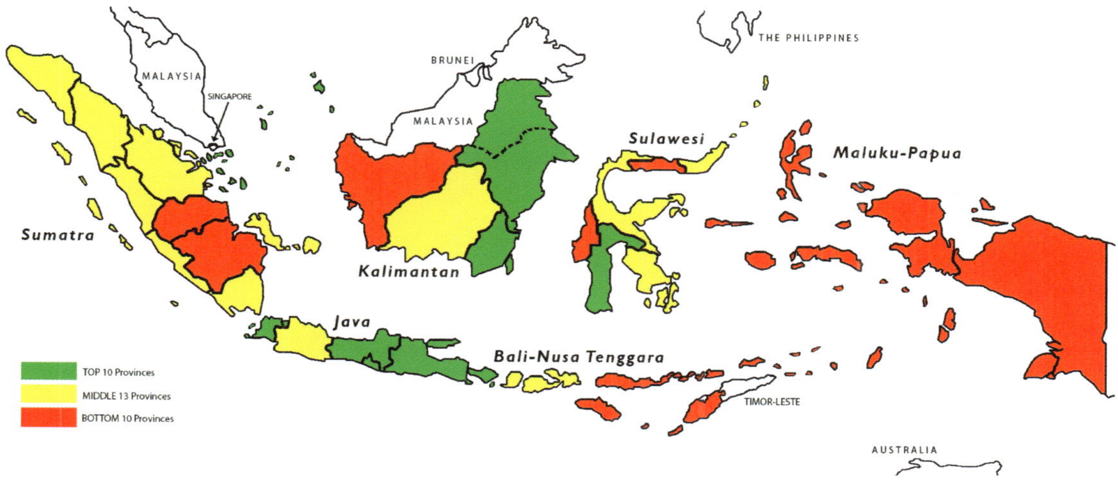

Source: Asia Competitiveness Institute.

The complete simulation results are shown in Tables 2.6–2.10, comparing the ranking and score for each province before and after the simulation. The simulation hopes to assist the provinces in prioritising key areas which will increase their competitiveness.

For Overall Competitiveness (Table 2.6), the pattern shows that significant changes in ranking are less likely to occur among the top-10 as the competition is already intense to begin with. Nevertheless, after policy simulation, their standardised scores increase, indicating that even low-hanging fruits exist for the top performers.

After the simulation, some provinces end up improving their ranking to a position that is similar to what other provinces would have attained. For instance, there are five provinces which eventually sit at the 11th position after the simulation, namely, Central Kalimantan, Central Sulawesi, North Sumatra, Riau and Southeast Sulawesi provinces. This is also commonly observed for provinces currently positioned at middle-13, wherein their rankings after simulation range from 11th to 13th positions.

Some provinces emerge with much better ranking, demonstrating their potential to improve competitiveness. These provinces are largely in the bottom-10 and belong to the Papua–Maluku and Sumatra regions. Papua and West Papua's rankings increase by 15 positions (to 18th and 12th, respectively), the highest increment among all provinces. In fact, Papua also observes the largest increase in standardised scores from –1.519 to –0.379 after the simulation.

Substantial increases can also be observed in Aceh and North Sumatra (up by 13 positions), North Sumatra (up by 13 positions), as well as Maluku and Jambi (up by 12 positions). By identifying their top-20% weakest indicators and lifting them to the average values, they have transformed from the bottom-10 provinces to the middle-13 provinces.

2.3.4 *What-if* Simulation Analysis on Four Environments

The *what-if* competitiveness simulation is also conducted for each of the four environments, allowing us to focus on the improvements that each province could attain in more specific areas. In Table 2.7, minimal changes to ranking in the Macroeconomic Stability environment

Table 2.6: 2016 *What-if* Competitiveness Simulation on Overall Competitiveness

	Rank		Std. Score	
Province (in alphabetical order)	**Before**	**After**	**Before**	**After**
Aceh	26	**13**	–0.691	**0.015**
Bali	7	**7**	0.670	**0.943**
Bangka Belitung Islands	20	**13**	–0.434	**0.061**
Banten	11	**7**	0.258	**0.785**
Bengkulu	25	**15**	–0.651	**–0.193**
Central Java	3	**3**	1.464	**1.779**
Central Kalimantan	13	**11**	–0.002	**0.320**
Central Sulawesi	14	**11**	–0.077	**0.360**
DI Yogyakarta	10	**7**	0.397	**0.797**
DKI Jakarta	1	**1**	3.201	**3.720**
East Java	2	**2**	2.082	**2.342**
East Kalimantan	5	**4**	0.996	**1.357**
East Nusa Tenggara	32	**24**	–1.393	**–0.605**
Gorontalo	21	**13**	–0.447	**0.014**
Jambi	28	**17**	–0.767	**–0.231**
Lampung	18	**12**	–0.306	**0.145**
Maluku	29	**17**	–0.848	**–0.258**
North Maluku	31	**23**	–1.306	**–0.525**
North Sulawesi	9	**7**	0.549	**0.922**
North Sumatra	24	**11**	–0.558	**0.272**
Papua	33	**18**	–1.519	**–0.379**
Riau	15	**11**	–0.184	**0.326**
Riau Islands	12	**7**	0.093	**0.743**
South Kalimantan	8	**7**	0.648	**0.885**
South Sulawesi	6	**5**	0.966	**1.207**
South Sumatra	22	**13**	–0.449	**–0.011**
Southeast Sulawesi	16	**11**	–0.195	**0.269**
West Java	4	**3**	1.331	**1.749**
West Kalimantan	17	**13**	–0.280	**0.076**
West Nusa Tenggara	19	**12**	–0.336	**0.103**
West Papua	27	**12**	–0.729	**0.140**
West Sulawesi	30	**20**	–0.993	**–0.384**
West Sumatra	23	**12**	–0.488	**0.124**

Source: Asia Competitiveness Institute.

Table 2.7: 2016 *What-if* Competitiveness Simulation on Macroeconomic Stability

Province (in alphabetical order)	Rank		Std. Score	
	Before	After	Before	After
Aceh	28	**20**	−0.677	**−0.375**
Bali	17	**12**	−0.260	**−0.050**
Bangka Belitung Islands	31	**21**	−0.809	**−0.472**
Banten	7	**7**	0.235	**0.304**
Bengkulu	33	**19**	−0.931	**−0.354**
Central Java	5	**4**	0.663	**0.787**
Central Kalimantan	16	**13**	−0.217	**−0.117**
Central Sulawesi	11	**9**	−0.021	**0.129**
DI Yogyakarta	19	**12**	−0.349	**−0.040**
DKI Jakarta	1	**1**	4.154	**4.173**
East Java	2	**2**	2.325	**2.350**
East Kalimantan	4	**4**	0.692	**0.913**
East Nusa Tenggara	32	**30**	−0.904	**−0.723**
Gorontalo	21	**19**	−0.475	**−0.341**
Jambi	25	**21**	−0.521	**−0.412**
Lampung	22	**15**	−0.494	**−0.205**
Maluku	27	**26**	−0.672	**−0.537**
North Maluku	29	**26**	−0.684	**−0.530**
North Sulawesi	14	**10**	−0.172	**0.074**
North Sumatra	12	**7**	−0.090	**0.232**
Papua	15	**15**	−0.212	**−0.212**
Riau	10	**8**	0.068	**0.169**
Riau Islands	6	**4**	0.627	**0.746**
South Kalimantan	8	**7**	0.169	**0.366**
South Sulawesi	9	**7**	0.128	**0.350**
South Sumatra	13	**13**	−0.136	**−0.136**
Southeast Sulawesi	20	**17**	−0.388	**−0.255**
West Java	3	**3**	1.578	**1.712**
West Kalimantan	18	**18**	−0.314	**−0.292**
West Nusa Tenggara	24	**17**	−0.506	**−0.262**
West Papua	23	**18**	−0.497	**−0.294**
West Sulawesi	26	**22**	−0.550	**−0.487**
West Sumatra	30	**17**	−0.762	**−0.254**

Source: Asia Competitiveness Institute.

Table 2.8: 2016 *What-if* Competitiveness Simulation on Government and Institutional Setting

Province (in alphabetical order)	Rank		Std. Score	
	Before	After	Before	After
Aceh	23	**12**	−0.649	**0.099**
Bali	8	**8**	0.688	**0.688**
Bangka Belitung Islands	20	**15**	−0.393	**0.036**
Banten	15	**11**	0.030	**0.364**
Bengkulu	25	**20**	−0.767	**−0.350**
Central Java	3	**3**	1.671	**1.671**
Central Kalimantan	16	**12**	0.009	**0.198**
Central Sulawesi	9	**7**	0.578	**0.876**
DI Yogyakarta	10	**10**	0.528	**0.528**
DKI Jakarta	1	**1**	2.388	**2.473**
East Java	5	**5**	1.252	**1.257**
East Kalimantan	18	**12**	−0.152	**0.145**
East Nusa Tenggara	29	**19**	−1.210	**−0.202**
Gorontalo	11	**11**	0.298	**0.425**
Jambi	24	**17**	−0.699	**−0.130**
Lampung	19	**15**	−0.182	**0.048**
Maluku	14	**12**	0.112	**0.216**
North Maluku	31	**20**	−1.221	**−0.363**
North Sulawesi	4	**4**	1.617	**1.659**
North Sumatra	33	**15**	−1.622	**0.031**
Papua	28	**20**	−0.945	**−0.406**
Riau	22	**17**	−0.447	**−0.022**
Riau Islands	32	**19**	−1.377	**−0.207**
South Kalimantan	7	**7**	0.836	**0.836**
South Sulawesi	2	**2**	1.927	**1.966**
South Sumatra	27	**17**	−0.922	**−0.089**
Southeast Sulawesi	17	**11**	−0.118	**0.322**
West Java	6	**6**	1.060	**1.148**
West Kalimantan	12	**12**	0.115	**0.153**
West Nusa Tenggara	13	**13**	0.115	**0.115**
West Papua	30	**17**	−1.215	**−0.076**
West Sulawesi	21	**20**	−0.442	**−0.190**
West Sumatra	26	**17**	−0.863	**−0.022**

Source: Asia Competitiveness Institute.

Table 2.9: 2016 *What-if* Competitiveness Simulation on Financial, Businesses, and Manpower Conditions

Province (in alphabetical order)	Rank		Std. Score	
	Before	**After**	**Before**	**After**
Aceh	30	**22**	−1.140	**−0.320**
Bali	7	**5**	0.711	**1.048**
Bangka Belitung Islands	13	**9**	0.039	**0.257**
Banten	18	**9**	−0.120	**0.281**
Bengkulu	22	**19**	−0.331	**−0.132**
Central Java	3	**2**	1.807	**2.192**
Central Kalimantan	12	**8**	0.042	**0.336**
Central Sulawesi	25	**18**	−0.748	**−0.090**
DI Yogyakarta	14	**8**	0.004	**0.467**
DKI Jakarta	1	**1**	3.032	**3.693**
East Java	2	**2**	2.207	**2.423**
East Kalimantan	5	**4**	0.945	**1.516**
East Nusa Tenggara	31	**25**	−1.225	**−0.684**
Gorontalo	26	**22**	−0.829	**−0.317**
Jambi	27	**23**	−0.890	**−0.365**
Lampung	16	**9**	−0.028	**0.313**
Maluku	32	**24**	−1.228	**−0.490**
North Maluku	33	**26**	−1.514	**−0.842**
North Sulawesi	20	**8**	−0.208	**0.389**
North Sumatra	15	**9**	−0.007	**0.218**
Papua	28	**15**	−0.940	**−0.018**
Riau	23	**9**	−0.340	**0.310**
Riau Islands	9	**8**	0.229	**0.582**
South Kalimantan	10	**9**	0.116	**0.309**
South Sulawesi	8	**8**	0.334	**0.571**
South Sumatra	17	**10**	−0.047	**0.202**
Southeast Sulawesi	19	**10**	−0.205	**0.121**
West Java	4	**3**	1.285	**1.922**
West Kalimantan	11	**9**	0.104	**0.314**
West Nusa Tenggara	24	**19**	−0.636	**−0.180**
West Papua	6	**5**	0.940	**1.041**
West Sulawesi	29	**24**	−1.110	**−0.534**
West Sumatra	21	**16**	−0.245	**−0.019**

Source: Asia Competitiveness Institute.

Table 2.10: 2016 *What-if* Competitiveness Simulation on Quality of Life and Infrastructure Development

Province (in alphabetical order)	Rank		Std. Score	
	Before	**After**	**Before**	**After**
Aceh	15	**11**	0.133	**0.646**
Bali	5	**2**	1.122	**1.499**
Bangka Belitung Islands	22	**13**	−0.302	**0.385**
Banten	10	**2**	0.726	**1.688**
Bengkulu	21	**14**	−0.170	**0.183**
Central Java	9	**2**	0.800	**1.383**
Central Kalimantan	14	**11**	0.160	**0.665**
Central Sulawesi	18	**13**	−0.069	**0.303**
DI Yogyakarta	4	**2**	1.156	**1.735**
DKI Jakarta	3	**1**	1.231	**2.604**
East Java	2	**1**	1.243	**1.927**
East Kalimantan	1	**1**	1.877	**2.024**
East Nusa Tenggara	31	**24**	−1.362	**−0.417**
Gorontalo	26	**13**	−0.503	**0.280**
Jambi	25	**15**	−0.478	**0.129**
Lampung	23	**13**	−0.330	**0.334**
Maluku	29	**18**	−1.074	**−0.062**
North Maluku	28	**18**	−0.989	**−0.028**
North Sulawesi	11	**7**	0.615	**1.007**
North Sumatra	20	**13**	−0.165	**0.438**
Papua	33	**27**	−3.032	**−0.638**
Riau	16	**11**	0.100	**0.643**
Riau Islands	8	**2**	0.837	**1.407**
South Kalimantan	6	**2**	1.067	**1.478**
South Sulawesi	7	**4**	0.871	**1.204**
South Sumatra	24	**18**	−0.412	**−0.016**
Southeast Sulawesi	17	**10**	0.053	**0.719**
West Java	12	**4**	0.569	**1.148**
West Kalimantan	27	**16**	−0.852	**0.081**
West Nusa Tenggara	19	**11**	−0.106	**0.676**
West Papua	32	**20**	−1.690	**−0.194**
West Sulawesi	30	**18**	−1.250	**−0.084**
West Sumatra	13	**11**	0.224	**0.712**

Source: Asia Competitiveness Institute.

are common, highlighting that most of the provinces' top-20% weakest indicators are not dominated by those from the Macroeconomic Stability environment. The biggest improvement is mostly found among the bottom-10 provinces, such as Bengkulu (from 33rd to 19th), West Sumatra (from 30th to 17th), and Bangka Belitung Islands (from 31st to 21st).

Interestingly, other provinces in the bottom-10 only improved by a smaller margin after simulation. For example, the following provinces go up by one to three positions: Maluku (from 27th to 26th), East Nusa Tenggara (from 32nd to 30th), and North Maluku (from 29th to 26th).

Table 2.8 on Government and Institutional Setting shows plenty of opportunities for provinces to increase its competitiveness by prioritising governance reforms. The environment's lowest-performing province, North Sumatra (33rd), increases by 18 positions, indicating notable potential for improvement. The same can be observed for Riau Islands (from 32nd to 19th), North Maluku (from 31st to 20th), West Papua (from 30th to 17th), and East Nusa Tenggara (from 29th to 19th) all of which see their rankings increase by more than 10 positions. Nonetheless, most of the scores have yet to reach average performance after simulation, indicating that improvements in these top-20% weakest indicators should be sizeable, above and beyond reaching average values (or the standardised score of zero).

The Government and Institutional Setting environment offers more opportunity for improvement. After simulation, the lowest attainable position is 20th, as opposed to 30th in the Macroeconomic Stability environment (compare against Table 2.7). Also, we identify provinces that have more potential to improve. For example, look at two of Sumatra's largest provinces: North Sumatra and Riau. Without the *What-if* competitiveness simulation, Riau is better than North Sumatra in Government and Institutional Setting. But the simulation allows North Sumatra to jump 18 spots up to 15th position. Meanwhile, the same simulation would bring Riau up by only five places up to 17th position.

Table 2.9 shows provinces in middle-13 registering largest increases in rankings, indicating there is ample opportunity for improvement in all provinces, beyond those which are bottom-ranked. Riau (23rd), Papua (28th) and North Sulawesi (20th) increase by 14, 13 and 12 positions, respectively. Other middle-ranked provinces with considerable increase include Banten (18th) and Southeast Sulawesi (19th) which increase by 9 positions.

Again, we see some variation in potential for improvement. The competitiveness ranking table on Financial, Businesses, and Manpower Conditions places Papua at 28th place, below Jambi (27th) and Gorontalo (26th). But after simulation, Papua jumps 13 places to attain 15th ranking, while Jambi and Gorontalo only improved by four places, up to 23rd and 22nd ranking, respectively. Similarly, Riau was ranked 23rd under Bengkulu (22nd) and West Sumatra (21st). But after simulation, Riau jumps 14 places to ninth ranking, while West Sumatra and Bengkulu went up by five and three positions, respectively.

In Table 2.10, most provinces in the bottom-10 register the largest increases and improve to enter the middle-13 group. Gorontalo, and West Papua and West Sulawesi register the biggest leap, with an increase of 13 and 12 positions, respectively.

The exceptions are East Nusa Tenggara and Papua. Papua jumps only by six spots (from 33rd to 27th), rendering it to remain within the bottom-10 ranks, even after improvement by simulation. Meanwhile, West Papua jumps 12 spots (from 32nd to 20th). This, again, highlights the need for attention on Papua, especially in terms of its Quality of Life and Infrastructure Development.

This is also the only environment where it is feasible — after simulation — to have three provinces (DKI Jakarta, East Java and East Kalimantan) achieve the first rank while six other provinces potentially occupying the second position. This implies that these provinces have similar improvement gaps to overcome in this particular environment.

It is also worth noting that provinces experience more movements in their rankings and scores before and after simulation in this environment, thereby indicating that for many provinces, their top-20% weakest indicators generally pertain to Quality of Life and Infrastructure Development.

2.3.5 Median and Maximum Web Analysis

The median competitiveness web analysis in Figure 2.11 plots the attained scores across the 12 sub-environments for DKI Jakarta (ranked first) and Papua (ranked last), along with the median scores of the 33 provinces of Indonesia.

DKI Jakarta fares far above the median province's scores in most sub-environments, with the largest difference found in (i) Openness to Trade and Services, (ii) Government Policies and Fiscal Sustainability and (iii) Regional Economic Vibrancy. Against this backdrop, however, DKI Jakarta performs relatively worse than the median score in Standard of Living, Education, and Social Sustainability. Other indicators, namely, (i) Labour Market Flexibility, (ii) Physical Infrastructure and (iii) Institutions, Governance, and Leadership are also among the sub-environments which require further progress given that DKI Jakarta scores just minimally above the median score.

For Papua, most of its sub-environment scores are below the median, particularly so in Standard of Living, Education, and Social Stability. Exceptions are found in (i) Regional

Figure 2.11: 2016 Median Competitiveness Web Analysis: Top- and Bottom-performing Provinces

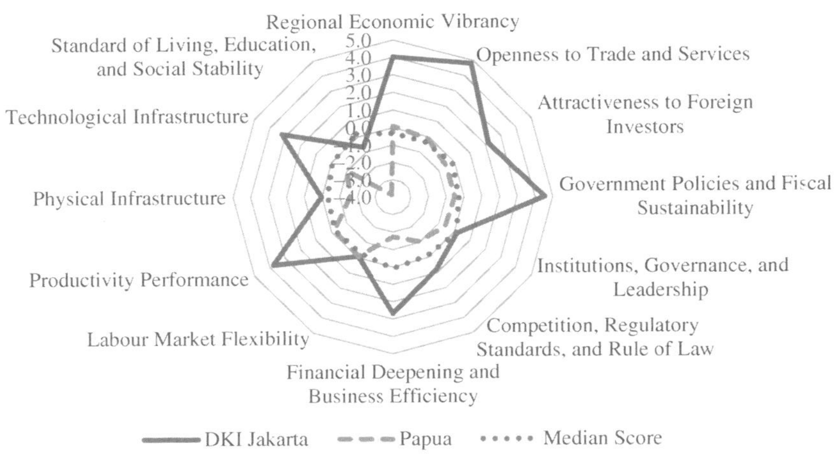

Source: Asia Competitiveness Institute.

Figure 2.12: 2016 Maximum Competitiveness Web Analysis: Top- and Bottom-performing Provinces

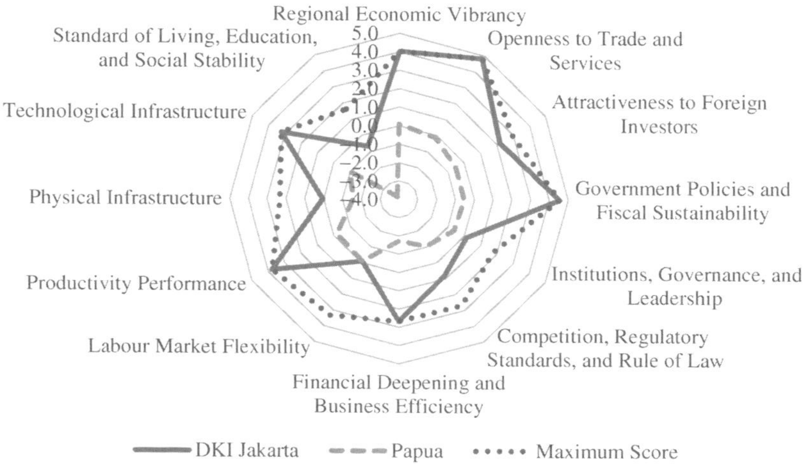

Source: Asia Competitiveness Institute.

Economic Vibrancy, (ii) Openness to Trade and Services, (iii) Labour Market Flexibility and (iv) Productivity Performance, which scores above the median, albeit with marginal differences.

With the exception of (i) Institutions, Governance, and Leadership, (ii) Financial Deepening and Business Efficiency and (iii) Standard of Living, Education and Social Stability, the median scores for 33 provinces in all other sub-environments are negative, suggesting that at least half of these provinces are performing below the national average in many of these aspects.

In Figure 2.12, the scores for DKI Jakarta and Papua are also plotted along with the maximum scores for the 33 provinces of Indonesia. As the number one province, DKI Jakarta achieves maximum scores in six out of 12 sub-environments. The province becomes the nation's benchmark in (i) Regional Economic Vibrancy, (ii) Openness to Trade and Services, (iii) Government Policies and Fiscal Sustainability, (iv) Financial Deepening and Business Efficiency, (v) Productivity Performance and (vi) Technological Infrastructure.

In contrast, Papua's scores are quite distant from the maximum scores. The widest gaps are found in (i) Standard of Living, Education, and Social Stability, (ii) Government Policies and Fiscal Sustainability and (iii) Openness to Trade and Services.

It is also worth noting that despite DKI Jakarta's dominance, there are other provinces which perform better in certain sub-environments. East Java achieves the maximum scores in (i) Attractiveness to Foreign Investors, (ii) Labour Market Flexibility and (iii) Physical Infrastructure. South Sulawesi tops in governance, particularly in (i) Institutions, Governance, and Leadership and (ii) Competition, Regulatory Standards, and Rule of Law. Meanwhile, DI Yogyakarta scores the maximum in Standard of living, Education, and Social Stability. This highlights that DKI Jakarta's competitiveness is not all-encompassing, and more importantly, good standards of competitiveness can be exemplified from various provinces which have the best practices.

2.4 Policy Implications and Concluding Notes

In general, the results from our 2016 competitiveness analysis still highlight the high competitiveness of six provinces in Java Island. DKI Jakarta tops most environments, though the province still struggles to perform equally well in ensuring a continuous improvement in quality of life. East Java, Central Java, and West Java also perform consistently well across four environments. Meanwhile, DI Yogyakarta and Banten face challenges in maintaining competitiveness as they slip in rankings in almost all environments. Compared to other islands, Java's road connectivity is the most advanced, making it possible for growth to spill over from DKI Jakarta to neighbouring provinces, further advancing the pivotal role of provinces in Java as the nation's primary manufacturing and service hubs.

The performance of resource-rich provinces remains varied, indicating differing capabilities in optimising the benefits of having natural resources. East Kalimantan still remains an exemplar of a province with positive investments in both people and infrastructure, maintaining its lead in Quality of Life and Infrastructure Development. However, its extensive decline in performance for Institutions, Governance, and Leadership warrants more attention and improvement to its governing aspects, particularly pertaining to crime rate and government efficiency and accountability.

East Kalimantan's neighbouring province, South Kalimantan, has demonstrated steady development by improving and becoming among the top-10 provinces in (i) Macroeconomic Stability, (ii) Financial, Businesses, and Manpower Conditions, and (iii) Quality of Life and Infrastructure Development. It is perhaps worth noting that the impact of fallen commodity prices have yet to affect the performance of these provinces this year, considering that most of the indicators in this analysis are based on 2013 secondary data.

Several other resource-rich provinces like Papua and South Sumatra are less successful in turning natural wealth into sustained economic growth and better living standards. These provinces have persisted with sub-par scores and low or declining rankings in all the environments.

Against this backdrop, our findings capture notable observations — the prevailing disparity between the easternmost provinces and rest of Indonesia, and the increasingly lagging competitiveness of provinces in the Sumatra region against their neighbouring islands.

Papua, East Nusa Tenggara, and North Maluku remain as the bottom three provinces in Overall Competitiveness for two consecutive years. Other provinces in the eastern part of Indonesia, especially archipelagic provinces, also perform poorly as in the case of East Nusa Tenggara, North Maluku, Maluku, and West Nusa Tenggara, which score below average in almost all aspects of competitiveness.

Meanwhile, with the exception of Riau, Lampung, and Bangka Belitung Islands, all provinces in Sumatra have declined in overall competitiveness. Despite having relative proximity to the Java region, provinces in Sumatra have yet to benefit from spillover effects. Such effects may not take place anytime soon, especially with the withdrawal of the Sunda Strait Bridge construction, which would have connected these two large islands.

Such varying successes and failures of provinces to maintain competitiveness suggest that there are plenty of opportunities for peer learning to identify the areas that can be adopted from the experience of high-performing provinces and learn from the less successful policies (or the lack thereof) of provinces which are relatively worse off.

Benefits can be attained from neighbouring economies through trade of goods, manpower and market if intra- and inter-regional connectivity are established. Hence, further efforts to strengthen connectivity not only within the provinces but also across provinces are the way forward to revitalise Indonesia's competitiveness as a whole.

While infrastructure development has been a priority of central government for years, it is yet to seamlessly connect Indonesia's vast archipelago. A number of projects related to port construction and upgrading in various locations are in the pipeline, with varying degrees of progress. Concurrently, highway projects are being undertaken to improve intraregional connectivity, such as the Trans Sumatra toll road, albeit with delays and funding challenges. Building connectivity is hard work, but it is not an impossible task. To make it feasible, strong and long-term commitment is required.

Beyond improving connectivity, it is necessary that provinces continue to improve their own competitiveness, tapping and optimising their own resources while finding the solutions in others.

ACI's competitiveness analysis provides insights into the competitiveness profile of each province. Such mapping of potential, strengths, and weaknesses can provide a roadmap for central and local government officials to review their past policies, fine-tune their ongoing policies, and plan their future policies in advance. The competitiveness framework should not be viewed as merely promoting competition with one another, but more as a platform to track each province's performance, which offer fresh perspectives to learn from one another's success story.

References

Berger, Thomas, and Gillian Bristow. 2009. "Competitiveness and the Benchmarking of Nations — A Critical Reflection." *International Advances in Economic Research* 15 (4): 378. doi:10.1007/s11294-009-9231-x.

Bristow, Gillian. 2009. *Critical Reflections on Regional Competitiveness: Theory, Policy and Practice*. Vol. 31;31; Book, Whole. Abingdon, Oxon; New York, NY; Routledge.

Camagni, Roberto. 2002. "On the Concept of Territorial Competitiveness: Sound or Misleading?" *Urban Studies* 39 (13): 2395–2411. doi:10.1080/0042098022000027022.

IMD. 2015. "IMD World Competitiveness Yearbook 2016." Switzerland: Institute of Management and Development.

Kitson, Michael, Ron Martin, and Peter Tyler. 2004. "Regional Competitiveness: An Elusive yet Key Concept?" *Regional Studies* 38 (9): 991–999. doi:10.1080/0034340042000320816.

KPPOD, and The Asia Foundation. 2007. "Local Economic Governance: A Survey of Business Operators in 243 Districts/Municipalities in Indonesia, 2007." Jakarta, Indonesia: KPPOD, The Asia Foundation, supported by USAID.

KPPOD. 2011. "Local Economic Governance: A Survey of Business Operators in 245 Districts/Municipalities in Indonesia, 2011." Jakarta, Indonesia: KPPOD, The Asia Foundation, supported by Australian AID.

Partnership for Governance Reform. 2013. *Indonesia Governance Index 2012*. Jakarta: Partnership for Governance Reform and Australian Agency for International Development.

Porter, Michael E. 1980. *Competitive Strategy: Techniques for Analyzing Industries and Competitors*. Book, Whole. New York: Free Press.

Porter, Michael E. 1990. *The Competitive Advantage of Nations*. Book, Whole. New York: Free Press.

PPSK Bank Indonesia, and LP3E FE-UNPAD. 2008. *Profil Dan Pemetaan Daya Saing Ekonomi Daerah Kabupaten/Kota Di Indonesia*. Jakarta: Rajawali Pers.

Schwab, Klaus, and Xavier Sala-i-Martin. 2016. "The Global Competitiveness Report 2016–2017." Geneva: World Economic Forum. https://www.weforum.org/reports/the-global-competitiveness-report-2016-2017-1.

Tan, Khee Giap, and Mulya Amri. 2013. "Subnational Competitiveness and National Performance: Analysis and Simulation for Indonesia." *Journal of CENTRUM Cathedra: The Business and Economics Research Journal* 6 (2): 173–192.

Tan, Khee Giap, Mulya Amri, Nurina Merdikawati, and Nursyahida Ahmad. 2017a. *2015 Annual Competitiveness Analysis and Development Strategies for Indonesian Provinces*. Asia Competitiveness Institute — World Scientific Series. Singapore: World Scientific. Available at http://www.worldscientific.com/worldscibooks/10.1142/10246.

Tan, Khee Giap, Sasidaran Gopalan, and Anuja Tandon. 2017. *2015 Agricultural Total Factor Productivity and Competitiveness Analysis for States and Federal Territories and Five Regions of India*. Singapore: World Scientific. Available at http://www.worldscientific.com/worldscibooks/10.1142/10231.

Tan, Khee Giap, Linda Low, Kartik Rao, and Kong Yam Tan. 2015b. *2014 Regional Competitiveness Analysis and a Master Plan on Regional Development Strategies for India: Annual Competitiveness Update and Evidence on Economic Development Model for Selected States of India*. Book, Whole. Singapore: World Scientific.

Tan, Khee Giap, Nurina Merdikawati, Mulya Amri, and Blake Harley Berger. 2015a. *2014 Annual Competitiveness Analysis and Development Strategies for Indonesian Provinces*. World Scientific.

Tan, Khee Giap, Nurina Merdikawati, Mulya Amri, and Kong Yam Tan. 2017c. *2015 Agricultural Productivity, Decentralisation, and Competitiveness Analysis for Provinces and Regions of Indonesia*. Asia Competitiveness Institute — World Scientific Series. Singapore: World Scientific. http://www.worldscientific.com/worldscibooks/10.1142/10245.

Tan, Khee Giap, Le Phuong Anh Nguyen, Sasidaran Gopalan, and Nguyen Trieu Duong Luu. 2017b. *2015 Annual Competitiveness Analysis, Agricultural Productivity and Development Vision for ASEAN-10*. Singapore: World Scientific. http://www.worldscientific.com/worldscibooks/10.1142/10219.

Tan, Khee Giap, Sangiita Wei Cher Yoong Yoong, Sasidaran Gopalan, and Le Phuong Anh Nguyen. 2016. *2014 Annual Competitiveness Ranking and Simulation Study for ASEAN-10 and Development Strategies to Enhance Asia Economic Connectivity*. Singapore: World Scientific. http://www.worldscientific.com/worldscibooks/10.1142/10004.

Tan, Khee Giap, Randong Yuan, and Teleixi Xie. 2017. *2015 Estimation of Agricultural Productivity and Annual Update of Competitiveness Analysis for Greater China*. Singapore: World Scientific. http://www.worldscientific.com/worldscibooks/10.1142/10244.

Tan, Khee Giap, Randong Yuan, and Sangiita Wei Cher Yoong. 2015. *2014 Annual Provincial and Regional Competitiveness Analysis for Greater China Economies: Development Strategies under the New Normal*. Book, Whole. Singapore: World Scientific.

Chapter 3
2016 Annual Update on Competitiveness Analysis of Indonesian Regions

3.1 Introductory Notes

Geographically, Indonesia is a vast archipelagic country spanning 5,150 kilometres east to west. It consists of five large islands, namely, Sumatra, Java, Kalimantan, Sulawesi, and Papua, and many thousands of medium- and smaller-sized ones, where the sea area is larger than the land area. Historically, Java has been the epicentre of Indonesia's economic growth and political clout even long before Indonesia's independence in 1945. During the Dutch colonisation era, Jakarta (then Batavia) was the heart of Dutch East India Company's (VOC) operations, monopolising spice trading in the 16th and 17th centuries. Post-independence, Java continues to play a strategic role with Jakarta named as the capital of the new nation, continuing its role as the centre of government and of economic activities.

As early as in 1975, Java contributed to 50% of Indonesia's gross domestic product (GDP) and was home to 63% of Indonesia's population. Following the pivot to industrialisation in the 1980s after the fall in oil prices, Java continued to assume a more dominant role in Indonesia's economy as most labour-intensive manufacturing sites were first developed in the island. By 1993, Java's contribution to Indonesia's GDP went up to 59% (Garcia and Soelistianingsih, 1998).

Such disparity persists with Java's contribution to Indonesia's GDP still hovering around 60% in 2014 (Figure 3.1). Java's long standing advancement in generating economic output attracted substantial investment, as seen from its three-year average of foreign domestic investment (FDI) in 2012–2014 which reached 58.6% of Indonesia's total FDI. Despite earlier efforts to redistribute Indonesia's population through government-led transmigration programme, Java was still home to 56.9% of Indonesia's population in 2014. The region's supremacy contrasts with its relatively small size, with a land size that accounted only for 6.8% of total land in Indonesia.

The issue of regional disparity also takes place in other countries, emerging and developed countries alike. China's initial strategy to open up the country focused on development of eastern coastal area as shown by establishment of the first four special economic zones (SEZs) in Shenzhen, Zhuhai, Shantou, and Xiamen. Hence, its coastal areas, dotted with seaports and

Figure 3.1: Regional Share of GDP, FDI, Population, and Land Area

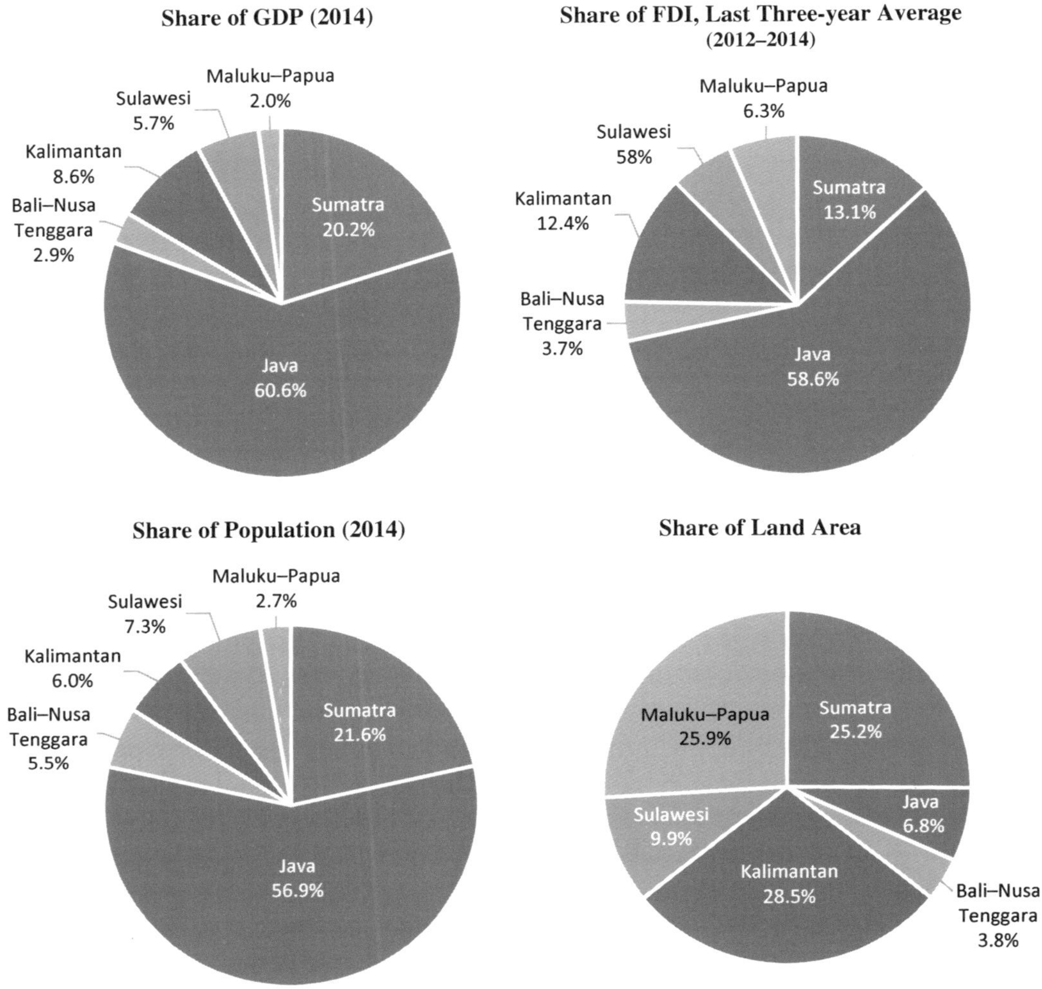

Source: Indonesia's Statistical Agency (BPS), compiled by Asia Competitiveness Institute.

blessed with accessibility are far more developed than the rest of the country (Tan, Yuan, and Yoong, 2015). In the case of Germany, even after reunification between East and West German territories in 1989, regional disparity remains with former West German territories charting higher per capita income and worker productivity (Matthews, 2014).

The OECD (2010) summed up three categories of policy responses to address regional disparity: (i) ensuring that the main policy focuses on reducing regional disparities, (ii) giving support to the lagging regions though this is not the main policy focus, and (iii) prioritising on 'national' economic growth despite the disparities within the country. In the case of Indonesia, in a highly centralised system under the leadership of President Soeharto during the New Order era of 1966–1998, policies were geared towards the third category to spur 'national' economic growth which relied heavily on development in Java at the expense of regional disparity.

Political turmoil following the downfall of repressive New Order regime gave birth to decentralisation,[1] which delegated substantial powers and resources to district and city levels, instead of provincial level to pre-empt emergence of large administrative unit disintegrating from the country (Mietzner, 2013). Such devolution of power also eased and mitigated growing discontent among locals regarding natural resources taken out from their areas to fund the central government with little return for the locals. Decentralisation has its own merits in that it broadens and spreads decision-making power, providing incentives for the local officials to attract investment to spur economic growth in their respective localities.

The Papua region, which consists of Papua and West Papua province, is granted a special autonomy status based on Law No. 21/2001, providing the region with greater revenue streams that can be used to finance their local development.[2] Additionally, the region also received special revenues amounting to 2% of the ceiling of general allocation fund (DAU) intended to finance education and health and another additional funding from the central government for infrastructure development. More policies considered to be part of the second category to support lagging regions were reflected in President Susilo Bambang Yudhoyono's term (2004–2014) aiming to address wide-ranging issues in Papua related to poverty, education, and health. In 2011, the unit for acceleration of development in Papua and West Papua (UP4PB) was launched to build a basis for sustainable development, aligned with the local aspirations.

Consistent with the shift in regional policies adopted by OECD countries, ranging from top-down interventions targeted at providing aid to lagging regions to broader aims to enhance regional competitiveness (OECD, 2010), the central government of Indonesia created Master Plan for Acceleration and Expansion of Indonesia's Economic Development 2011–2025 (MP3EI). The MP3EI intended to be all region-focussed to tap underutilised regional potential and integrate development projects with wider policy area coverage by identifying six economic corridors (Figure 3.2) and their corresponding themes for their role in mobilising national economic development (Coordinating Ministry of Economic Affairs, 2011).

The aim to spread growth centres across Indonesia is a step in the right direction as heavy reliance on Java that only accounts for 6.8% of land area in Indonesia but attract 56.9% of people gave rise to pollution and traffic congestion. Outmigration of able, young generation into Java further aggravates the situation and leaves lagging regions without adequate capable human resources to drive their economic development. While the MP3EI puts more emphasis on infrastructure development, investments in education and healthcare are equally important to reduce the regional imbalance. Garcia and Soelistianingsih (1998) found that lagging regions reaped the most benefits from improvement in education and healthcare that allowed them to catch up with other regions.

Spreading of growth to other regions can also take place as a result of the invisible hand of market forces as in the case of China (Tan, Yuan, and Yoong, 2015). With rising wages in the more developed eastern coastal area, more labour-intensive manufacturing shifted to the less

---

[1] Based on Law No. 22/1999 on local government and Law No. 25/1999 on intergovernmental fiscal relationship.

[2] The special autonomy law granted higher provincial share of natural resource revenues; 70% of gas oil and revenues and 80% of forestry, fishery, and mining revenues are allocated to the province.

Figure 3.2: Map of Six Economic Corridors

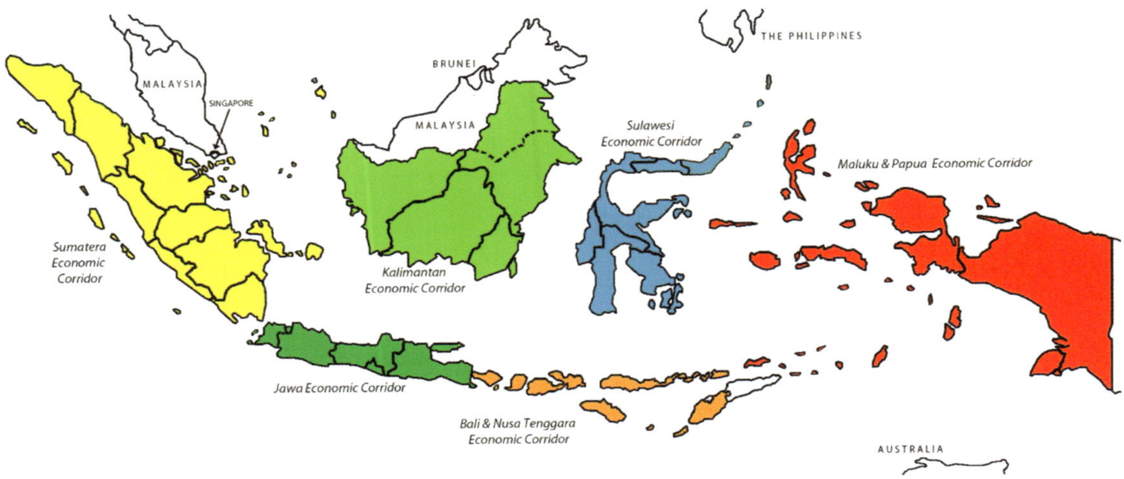

Source: Asia Competitiveness Institute based on regional classification adopted in the MP3EI.

developed western China. Such spillover was made possible due to well-developed infrastructure connecting the two regions. This phenomenon also takes place in Indonesia, but the effect is somewhat limited to Java Island, spreading from Jakarta to nearby provinces (Banten and West Java), and further to Central Java and East Java where minimum wage is the lowest nationally. Indonesia's archipelagic landscape provides a distinct challenge compared to China as a landmass. For growth to organically spill over to other regions, a seamless connectivity across regions is imperative.

Under President Joko Widodo (Jokowi)'s leadership, maritime infrastructure emerged as the main policy focus which can play a significant role for spreading the growth across Indonesia. This is to avoid a situation where Java becomes more self-sufficient and less involved in inter-regional trade (Sonis *et al.*, 1997), while regions outside Java and Sumatra lose out (Nazara, Sonis, and Hewings, 2000). Ideally, regional development should not be a zero-sum game but more a matter of ensuring that growth in each region would eventually support overall national that growth. All regions have the potential to engage in extensive exchange of production inputs and activities, instead of limited exchange in consumption goods.

Much of the anecdotal evidence reveal how the easternmost provinces such as Papua and West Papua merely become consumers of goods shipped from Java, and the cargos are left behind empty and stacked in their ports with no return goods bound to Java. If the Merauke Integrated Food and Energy Estate (MIFEE) in Papua came to realisation, considering the needs of the local, indigenous population, more goods will be shipped out of Papua Region that will incentivise more frequent shipment and trade between the western and eastern parts of Indonesia.

Given such dynamics of regional development policies in Indonesia, it is timely to evaluate regional competitiveness by adopting the country's regional classification (currently based on the MP3EI). The MP3EI was drafted in 2011 during the leadership of Susilo Bambang

Yudhoyono. Since Jokowi rose to presidency in 2014, there have been some concerns raised towards the master plan. One of the criticisms is that MP3EI tend to be top-down in nature and focuses on established industries and big businesses, as opposed to SMEs and the creative economy. The MP3EI was also criticized for being land-based, where the 'economic corridors' are drawn based on land connectivity instead of maritime connectivity (the latter being one of Jokowi's priority programmes).

Despite the healthy debate on the relevancy of MP3EI going forward, the fact remains that there are no other formal and current policy document that identifies Indonesia's sub-national but supra-provincial regions. In this condition, we choose to remain consistent with the regional grouping as specified in MP3EI, which we had adopted in our earlier works (Tan *et al.*, 2015, 2016).

Our study contributes to the literature by shedding light on regional disparity from a competitiveness perspective. This builds up from our forte to track competitiveness of Indonesia over time.[3] The results and analysis spur further intellectual debates among key stakeholders to lift the competitiveness of Indonesia as a whole.

The structure of the chapter is as follows. Section 3.1 provides a snapshot of regional disparity and efforts to balance regional growth and development in Indonesia. Section 3.2 lays out research methodology for data aggregation. Section 3.3 gives details on the empirical findings, including rankings and scores for six regions based on Overall Competitiveness and four environments. Discussions on sub-environment spread as well as median and maximum competitiveness web analysis are also provided. Section 3.4 concludes.

3.2 Research Methodology: A Note on Regional Data Aggregation

Our methodology to analyse regional competitiveness is based on the competitiveness framework as applied to provinces in Chapter 2, but with aggregation of data at the regional level.[4] For the current 2016 results, the data are based on 2013 for secondary data collected from official sources and 2015 for primary data collected from Asia Competitiveness Institute's (ACI) perception survey.

As each region consists of a number of provinces, the main issue in extending the competitiveness ranking and analysis from the provincial to the regional level is data aggregation. We adopt three approaches to data aggregation, as explained in the following.

First, many of the indicators used for the provincial ranking can be directly aggregated to obtain the indicator values for a region by summing across all the constituent provinces in that region, as long as those indicators are based on absolute quantities, such as 1.1.01 Gross Regional Domestic Product (GRDP) and 4.1.01 Population. The approach to data aggregation in this context is simple summation, applicable for indicator 1.1.01 GRDP (as an example). Since

[3] See previous Asia Competitiveness Institute's (ACI) publication on Indonesia's competitiveness in Tan *et al.* (2013, 2015a, 2015b).

[4] For the provincial analysis, the ACI uses a total of 103 indicators that cover 33 provinces. North Kalimantan, the newly created province being carved out of East Kalimantan in 2012, is not yet included pending availability of data.

it is based on absolute quantity, the regional value can be obtained by summing the data across all the provinces within this region.

Approach 1: Simple Sum

Example: Indicator 1.1.01 GRDP (Unit: Million Rupiah, 2000 Constant Prices)
For Region A with *n* provinces at time *t*,

$$GRDP_{A,t} = \sum_{i=1}^{n} \text{Real } GRDP_{i,t}$$

Second, for those indicators defined as ratios or proportions, the aggregation can be computed according to their definition by firstly aggregating the absolute quantities upon which they are defined (e.g. first by aggregating the numerator and denominator). The approach to data aggregation in this case is the sum of proportions, applicable to indicator 2.1.03 Tax Revenue/Government Revenue, for example. According to its definition, this indicator is calculated as the ratio between tax revenue and government revenue for a particular region. Since both the numerator and denominator are absolute quantities, they are firstly aggregated across all the provinces within the region and then divided to obtain the regional value.

Approach 2: Sum of Proportions

Example: Indicator 2.1.03 Tax Revenue/Government Revenue (Unit: Ratio)
For Region A with *n* provinces at time *t*,

$$Tax\ Revenue\ /\ Government\ Revenue_{A,t} = \frac{\sum_{i=1}^{n} Tax\ Revenue}{\sum_{i=1}^{n} Government\ Revenue_{i,t}}$$

The third approach is when the calculation is average-weighted at the regional level by population of the province. This applies to indicators collected from ACI surveys and also from indicators that are calculated as percentage of households at the original province, as provided in the following example for 4.2.01 Telephone Ownership.

Approach 3: Sum of Percentages

Example: Indicator 4.2.01 Telephone Ownership (Unit: Percentage of Households)
For Region A with *n* provinces at time *t*,

$$\text{Telephone Ownership}_{A,t} = \sum_{i=t}^{n} \left(Telephone\ Ownership_{i,t}\ x \frac{\text{Population}_{i,t}}{\sum_{i=1}^{n} \text{Population}_{i,t}} \right)$$

For a complete list of indicators used for the regional competitiveness analysis (also used for the provincial analysis in Chapter 2), please refer to Appendix 1. For explanatory notes on how to derive regional indicator data from provincial data, please refer to Appendix 3. Once the data aggregation is completed for all relevant indicators, the competitiveness ranking analysis is performed by following the computational procedure as explained in Chapter 2, for which the technical explanation of the algorithm to compute ACI's competitiveness ranking is provided in Appendix 2.

3.3 Competitiveness Analysis Results

3.3.1 Ranking and Scores for Overall Competitiveness

Table 3.1 shows the Overall Competitiveness ranking and score for the six regions in Indonesia. Consistent with the results from provincial competitiveness analysis in Chapter 2, Java region attains the top position with a score of 1.805 while the Maluku–Papua region is ranked last with a score of –1.404. The difference in scores between the top-performing region and bottom-performing region is 3.209, as compared to 4.720 for the difference in score between the first and bottom-ranked province (DKI Jakarta and Papua, respectively). This indicates that DKI Jakarta's score is very high in the provincial competitiveness ranking. When DKI Jakarta is grouped with the remaining five Java provinces to form a region, the score for Java Region is not as high.

Despite Sumatra Region's proximity to Java Region as the engine of Indonesia's growth, its competitiveness is lagging, occupying the fourth position consistently in the past three years. Its score difference with Sulawesi Region is rather substantial (0.557). Interregional friendly rivalry can be a catalyst to strengthen the Overall Competitiveness of Indonesia as a whole.

Table 3.2 provides a list of top and bottom-performing provinces in each region in terms of its Overall Competitiveness ranking. The numbers in brackets refer to their respective provincial ranking which can be found in greater detail in Chapter 2. Within region, the performance across provinces can be quite diverse. In Bali–Nusa Tenggara Region, this disparity is manifested by a 25-point difference in ranking between Bali, which ranks seventh and East Nusa Tenggara at 32nd

Table 3.1: 2016 Overall Competitiveness: Ranking and Scores

2016 Rank	2015 Rank	Region	2016 Std. Score
1	1	Java	1.805
2	2	Kalimantan	0.392
3	3	Sulawesi	0.220
4	4	Sumatra	–0.337
5	5	Bali–Nusa Tenggara	–0.676
6	6	Maluku–Papua	–1.404

Source: Asia Competitiveness Institute.

Table 3.2: 2016 Overall Competitiveness: Top and Bottom Provinces in Each Region

	Region					
	Sumatra	**Java**	**Kalimantan**	**Sulawesi**	**Bali–Nusa Tenggara**	**Maluku–Papua**
Top Province	Riau Islands (12)	DKI Jakarta (1)	East Kalimantan (5)	South Sulawesi (6)	Bali (7)	West Papua (27)
Bottom Province	Jambi (28)	Banten (11)	West Kalimantan (17)	Gorontalo (21)	East Nusa Tenggara (32)	Papua (33)

Source: Asia Competitiveness Institute.

position. Given its thriving tourism industry, Bali's strengths lie in good business and financial conditions, as well as infrastructure. On the other hand, East Nusa Tenggara still has to struggle with inadequate infrastructure that becomes a stumbling block to generate growth or attract foreign investments into the province. Several other regions such as Sumatra and Sulawesi also show substantial diversity in performances of their provinces. In Sumatra for instance, Riau Islands as an industrialised province performs fairly well in all aspects, save its governance, and is ranked 12th in the Overall Competitiveness. By contrast, Jambi performs below average in all environments and ranks 28th.

It is also worth noting that there is minimal disparity in the performance of provinces in Maluku–Papua Region, wherein all provinces are ranked among the bottom-10 provinces. This further confirms the lagging performance of Maluku–Papua as a region and a collection of provinces.

The map in Figure 3.3 illustrates the geographical spread of Overall Competitiveness rankings in six regions in Indonesia. The regions are colour-coded according to their competitiveness performance, with darker shade for more competitive regions and lighter shade for least competitive regions. Less competitive regions are mostly found to the east of Java Region, where Bali–Nusa Tenggara and Maluku–Papua Regions are at the bottom of Overall Competitiveness ranking.

Using data aggregation methodology in Section 3.2 and adopting competitiveness methodology described in Chapter 2, the following section shows the results of regional ranking for Overall Competitiveness and each of the four competitiveness environments. Additional tables are included to outline the top- and bottom-performing provinces in each region to give an insight on disparity within the region. The discussion on the relative performance of each region at the sub-environment level will also be provided. The results are based on 2013 data from official sources and data from ACI's perception survey in 2015, collated and analysed in 2016.[5]

[5] As of 2016, there are 34 provinces in Indonesia. North Kalimantan, the newly created province being carved out of East Kalimantan in 2012, is not yet included pending availability of data.

Figure 3.3: 2016 Overall Competitiveness: Geographical Spread

Source: Asia Competitiveness Institute.

3.3.2 Ranking and Scores by Four Environments

Macroeconomic Stability

For Macroeconomic Stability, Kalimantan surpasses Sumatra to take second position (Table 3.3). Java remains the top-performing region, with the spread of scores illustrating the dichotomy between Java region and the other parts of Indonesia in terms of macroeconomic prowess. The difference between the top- and bottom-performing regions in Macroeconomic Stability (3.084) is fairly comparable to the finding from Overall Competitiveness (std. score: 3.209). However, more substantial gap is found between Java region (2.085) and Kalimantan region (0.013). This is not unusual as Java contributed to about 62% of Indonesia's GDP in 2013, a factor which is heavily considered in this environment.

The smallest difference in score is found between Sumatra and Kalimantan (0.031), underlining more intense competition between the two regions. However, in terms of GRDP size, share of Indonesia's GDP from Sumatra Region was 20.8%, more than twice the GDP contribution of Kalimantan Region (8.2%) in 2013. Kalimantan Region is able to maintain its second position as the region consists of only high- and mediocre-performing provinces (East Kalimantan at fourth; South Kalimantan at eighth; Central Kalimantan at 16th; and West Kalimantan at 18th), and no low-performing provinces. On the other hand, Sumatra Region faces more diverse competitiveness among its provinces, ranging from Riau Islands at sixth to Bengkulu at 33rd in terms of Macroeconomic Stability.

While Java Region is ranked first in the Macroeconomic Stability environment, one of its respective provinces, DI Yogyakarta, performs below average and ranks at 19th (Table 3.4). Unlike its peers, industrialisation does not take off in DI Yogyakarta as the province puts more emphasis on its tertiary sector to drive its tourism and culturally oriented economy. Even so,

Table 3.3: 2016 Macroeconomic Stability: Ranking and Scores

2016 Rank	2015 Rank	Province	2016 Std. Score	Sub-environment Scores		
				REV	OTS	AFI
1	1	Java	2.085	1.996	1.884	2.068
2	3	Kalimantan	0.013	–0.098	0.204	–0.070
3	2	Sumatra	–0.018	0.240	0.400	–0.693
4	4	Sulawesi	–0.349	–0.266	–0.935	0.207
5	5	Maluku and Papua	–0.732	–0.686	–0.484	–0.918
6	6	Bali and Nusa Tenggara	–0.999	–1.186	–1.069	–0.594

Source: Asia Competitiveness Institute.

Table 3.4: 2016 Macroeconomic Stability: Top and Bottom Provinces in Each Region

	Region					
	Sumatra	**Java**	**Kalimantan**	**Sulawesi**	**Bali–Nusa Tenggara**	**Maluku–Papua**
Top Province	Riau Islands (6)	DKI Jakarta (1)	East Kalimantan (4)	South Sulawesi (9)	Bali (17)	Papua (15)
Bottom Province	Bengkulu (33)	DI Yogyakarta (19)	West Kalimantan (18)	West Sulawesi (26)	East Nusa Tenggara (32)	North Maluku (29)

Source: Asia Competitiveness Institute.

GRDP across all industries (primary, secondary and tertiary) for DI Yogyakarta has not been substantial to command better scores relative to its neighbouring provinces. Notwithstanding its low growth, DI Yogyakarta still attracts foreign investment and scores favourably in investment promotion and management.

For Kalimantan Region, the stark difference in terms of the ranking of its top province (East Kalimantan) and bottom province (West Kalimantan) can be traced to their natural resource endowment. East Kalimantan has richer oil, gas, and mining than the remaining provinces in Kalimantan. Such greater endowment, coupled with operational and investing activities of big multinational companies (MNCs) help East Kalimantan generate higher income and foreign investments. In Sulawesi Region, the more established provinces such as South Sulawesi and North Sulawesi perform much better in Macroeconomic Stability environment as compared to newly created provinces such as Gorontalo and West Sulawesi. Meanwhile, Papua earns higher rank at 15th as compared to North Maluku (29th) in Papua-Maluku region.

As illustrated in Figure 3.4, every region has varying performance in each of the sub-environments that makes up the Macroeconomic Stability environment. Java is the only region performing consistently well in all three sub-environments. Sumatra lags behind in Attractiveness to Foreign Investors with a standardised score that resembles Bali–Nusa Tenggara's. This highlights the need for Sumatra to review its policies towards creating a conducive business

Figure 3.4: 2016 Macroeconomic Stability: Sub-environment Spread

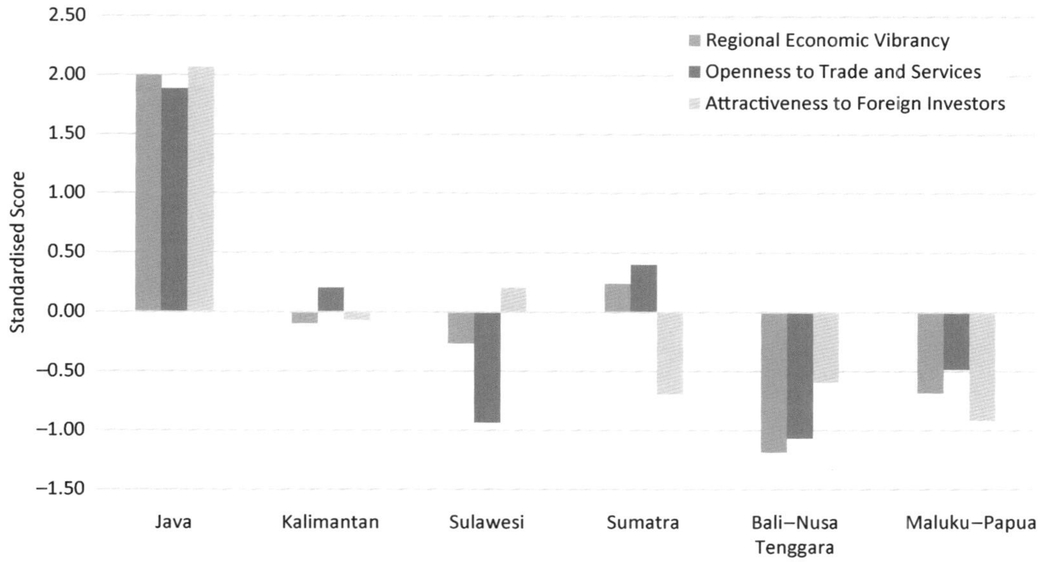

Source: Asia Competitiveness Institute.

environment for investment to thrive, taking cues from Java and Sulawesi which fare better in this aspect. Kalimantan also performs below average in Regional Economic Vibrancy and Attractiveness to Foreign Investors, despite being ranked second in the environment. Meanwhile, Sulawesi registers low volumes in exports and imports, a consequence of poor trading facilities found in the region. Both Bali–Nusa Tenggara and Maluku–Papua Regions perform far below average in all sub-environments.

Government and Institutional Setting

Table 3.5 shows a relatively symmetrical distribution for the standardised scores of all six regions in Government and Institutional Setting. With a score difference of 2.574, the gap between top-performing Java Region (1.453) and bottom-performing Sumatra Region (−1.121) is smaller compared to other environments (Tables 3.3, 3.7, and 3.9). Sulawesi Region surpasses Kalimantan Region to attain second position and obtains a standardised score that is fairly close to Java, thereby indicating similar performance in overall governance. Maluku–Papua Region have also surpassed Sumatra Region to achieve fifth position, albeit with minimal difference in scores. Sumatra's declining performance in this environment is also manifested in the findings from provincial competitiveness ranking in Chapter 2, where all provinces from Sumatra score below average and six out of 10 provinces belong to the bottom-10 category. As illustrated in Table 3.6, Lampung is ranked 19th despite being at the top among Sumatra provinces. This indicates that provincial-level governance in Sumatra Region is generally sub-par compared to other regions.

Table 3.5: 2016 Government and Institutional Setting: Ranking and Scores

2016 Rank	2015 Rank	Province	2016 Std. Score	Sub-environment Scores		
				GPFS	IGL	CRRL
1	1	Java	1.453	2.146	0.557	0.839
2	3	Sulawesi	1.118	–0.505	1.568	1.662
3	2	Kalimantan	0.024	–0.214	0.238	0.034
4	4	Bali and Nusa Tenggara	–0.353	–0.521	–0.007	–0.333
5	6	Maluku and Papua	–1.121	–0.907	–0.731	–1.094
6	5	Sumatra	–1.121	0.000	–1.625	–1.107

Source: Asia Competitiveness Institute.

Table 3.6: 2016 Government and Institutional Setting: Top and Bottom Provinces in Each Region

	Region					
	Sumatra	**Java**	**Kalimantan**	**Sulawesi**	**Bali–Nusa Tenggara**	**Maluku–Papua**
Top Province	Lampung (19)	DKI Jakarta (1)	South Kalimantan (7)	South Sulawesi (2)	Bali (8)	Maluku (14)
Bottom Province	North Sumatra (33)	Banten (15)	East Kalimantan (18)	West Sulawesi (21)	East Nusa Tenggara (29)	North Maluku (31)

Source: Asia Competitiveness Institute.

Similar to the analysis on Overall Competitiveness, the disparity between top- and bottom-performing provinces in Bali–Nusa Tenggara Region is the highest. Bali ranks eighth, while East Nusa Tenggara ranks 29th. In Java, DKI Jakarta is first. Five out of six provinces in Java region are placed in the top-10, with the exception of Banten, which ranks 15th, hampered by low standardised score in Institutions, Governance, and Leadership.

A similar observation can be seen in the Sulawesi region, where three out of five provinces, South Sulawesi (second), North Sulawesi (fourth) and Central Sulawesi (ninth) rank among the top-10. Meanwhile, Southeast Sulawesi and West Sulawesi decline substantially to 17th and 21st positions, respectively.

In the Maluku–Papua Region, more resources should be directed to build the governance capacity and capability of the young provinces of West Papua and North Maluku, which are lagging in Government and Institutional Setting.

Analysing the scores from each sub-environment allows us to pinpoint the driver for each region's performance in Government and Institutional Setting. Based on Figure 3.5, Java remains the only region with favourable Government Policies and Fiscal Sustainability, due largely to its government's sizeable financial resources. Sulawesi scores the highest amongst all regions in (i) Institutions, Governance, and Leadership and (ii) Competition, Regulatory Standards, and Rule of Law. With improvements to Government Policies and Fiscal Sustainability, Sulawesi may have the potential to surpass Java in this environment.

Figure 3.5: 2016 Government and Institutional Setting: Sub-environment Spread

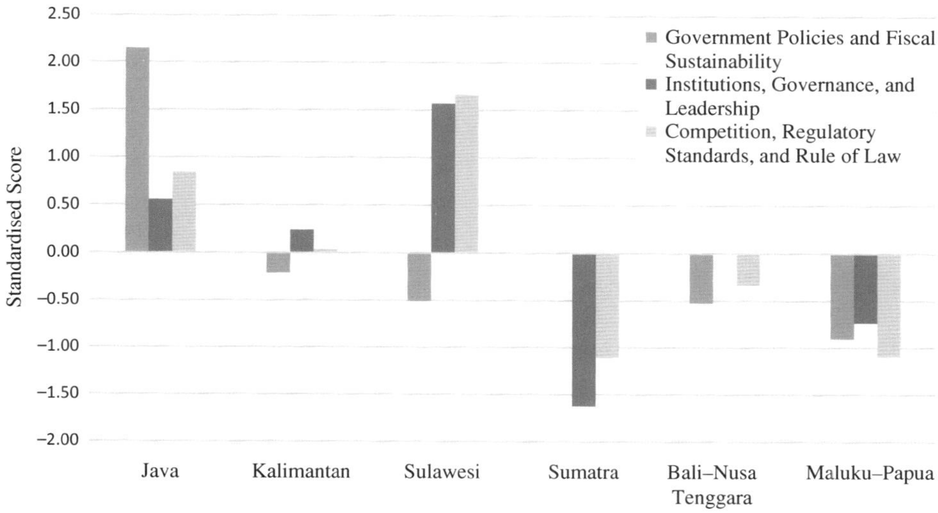

Source: Asia Competitiveness Institute.

For the same environments which Sulawesi tops, Sumatra ranks last. Government coordination, efficiency and regulatory governance are among issues that hamper the Sumatra region. The Maluku–Papua resion scores the lowest in Government Policies and Fiscal Sustainability, owing to poor tax to government revenue ratio, thereby indicating disproportionate income generated from taxation. It is apparent that both Sumatra and Maluku–Papua regions have plenty to catch up to be on par with the quality of governance in the other regions.

Financial, Businesses, and Manpower Conditions

Regions, which excel in macroeconomic indicators as captured in Table 3.3, also perform equally well in the microeconomic indicators as reflected in their Financial, Businesses, and Manpower Conditions ranking in Table 3.7. Java Region still leads as the most competitive region in this environment, while Maluku–Papua remains at the bottom with a score difference of 2.969. This difference is much lower than the gap between the environment's top- and bottom-performing provinces of DKI Jakarta (3.032) and North Maluku (–1.514), suggesting that variation in performance is larger when comparing among provinces. All regions maintain their standing for two consecutive years. Given Sumatra's near-average score, there is opportunity for the region to make progress and join the ranks of Java and Kalimantan as top-performing regions.

Disparity within region is most striking in the case of Maluku–Papua Region, where West Papua as the top province ranks sixth while Maluku as the bottom province sits at 33rd (Table 3.8), rendering a 27-position difference. West Papua remains a role model for its peers,

Table 3.7: 2016 Financial, Businesses, and Manpower Conditions: Ranking and Scores

2016 Rank	2015 Rank	Province	2016 Std. Score	Sub-environment Scores FDBE	LMF	PP
1	1	Java	1.866	1.906	2.170	0.366
2	2	Kalimantan	0.612	0.260	–0.458	1.656
3	3	Sumatra	–0.103	–0.331	–0.379	0.464
4	4	Sulawesi	–0.401	0.049	–0.490	–0.514
5	5	Bali and Nusa Tenggara	–0.871	–0.486	–0.010	–1.578
6	6	Maluku and Papua	–1.103	–1.397	–0.834	–0.394

Source: Asia Competitiveness Institute.

Table 3.8: 2016 Financial, Businesses, and Manpower Conditions: Top and Bottom Provinces in Each Region

	Region					
	Sumatra	Java	Kalimantan	Sulawesi	Bali–Nusa Tenggara	Maluku–Papua
Top Province	Riau Islands (9)	DKI Jakarta (1)	East Kalimantan (5)	South Sulawesi (8)	Bali (7)	West Papua (6)
Bottom Province	Aceh (30)	Banten (18)	Central Kalimantan (12)	West Sulawesi (29)	East Nusa Tenggara (31)	North Maluku (33)

Source: Asia Competitiveness Institute.

particularly for its performance in (i) Financial Deepening and Business Efficiency, and (ii) Productivity Performance sub-environments. Other notable gaps can also be observed in the Bali–Nusa Tenggara Region (Bali at seventh; East Nusa Tenggara at 31st), Sumatra Region (Riau Islands at ninth; Aceh at 30th) and Sulawesi Region (South Sulawesi at eighth; West Sulawesi at 29th). Kalimantan Region registers the lowest disparity, with all its provinces scoring above average. Meanwhile in Java, DI Yogyakarta and Banten lag behind their peers and becomes the only two provinces in Java that are not part of the top-10 provinces for Financial, Business, and Manpower Conditions.

To get a more detailed picture of each region's performance in Financial, Businesses, and Manpower Conditions, Figure 3.6 presents the score breakdown for each sub-environment. Java at the top becomes the only region which consistently scores above average in all three sub-environments. In fact, it is the only region that scores a positive value in Labour Market Flexibility, given its abundant pool of manpower. Despite the nationwide trend of rising minimum wages, East Java, Central Java, and West Java still emerged as provinces with the lowest minimum wage in 2013. Meanwhile, outside of Java, Labour Market Flexibility remains an important issue. Kalimantan's positive performance is mostly driven by its high productivity, which scores higher than Java Island. Kalimantan's economic structure that relies on oil and gas extraction and its related processing activities is relatively more capital-intensive, hence, driving

Figure 3.6: 2016 Financial, Businesses, and Manpower Conditions: Sub-environment Spread

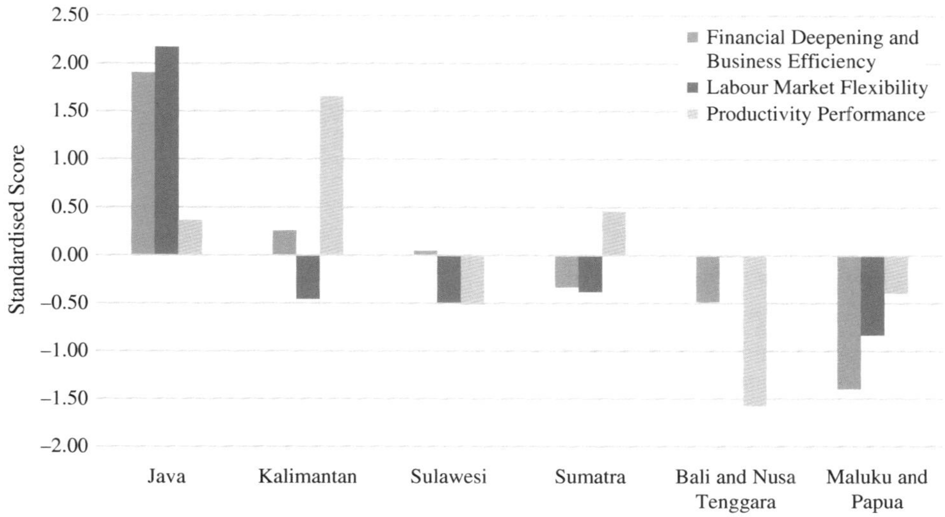

Source: Asia Competitiveness Institute.

its score in this sub-environment. For instance, East Kalimantan has the highest primary industry productivity among provinces in Indonesia.

In contrast, the bottom two regions are riddled with sub-par scores in all three sub-environments. Nonetheless, Bali–Nusa Tenggara Region's score in Labour Market Flexibility is just below average, due largely to Bali's favourable performance in employment, unemployment rate and labour relations. In contrast, its score in Productivity Performance is the lowest among all six regions. Meanwhile, Maluku–Papua Region has the lowest scores in both (i) Financial Deepening and Business Efficiency and (ii) Labour Market Flexibility. The region has highest minimum wage, and firms' capacity and innovation remain low.

Quality of Life and Infrastructure Development

For Quality of Life and Infrastructure Development, four out of six regions obtain positive standardised scores, reflecting their above-average performance, and also highlighting extremely low scores obtained by the Maluku–Papua region, which skews the distribution of scores downwards (Table 3.9). The score difference between Java and Kalimantan (0.276), and Kalimantan and Sulawesi (0.336) are fairly small, underlining ample opportunity for these regions to surpass one another. Given that Bali–Nusa Tenggara Region scores slightly below average, there is possibility for the region to improve further and perform positively. Meanwhile, a wide gap still exists between Maluku–Papua Region (–2.045) and the rest of Indonesia. At the provincial level, Papua (–3.032) and West Papua (–1.690) remain as the bottom two provinces, while North Maluku (–0.989) and Maluku (–1.074) sit at 28th and 29th positions, respectively.

Table 3.9: 2016 Quality of Life and Infrastructure Development: Ranking and Scores

2016 Rank	2015 Rank	Province	2016 Std Score	Sub-environment Scores PI	TI	SLES
1	1	Java	1.025	1.687	1.298	–0.333
2	2	Kalimantan	0.749	0.521	1.070	0.346
3	4	Sulawesi	0.413	–0.127	–0.090	1.287
4	3	Sumatra	0.044	–0.032	–0.464	0.609
5	5	Bali–Nusa Tenggara	–0.186	–0.406	–0.101	0.025
6	6	Maluku–Papua	–2.045	–1.643	–1.714	–1.935

Source: Asia Competitiveness Institute.

Table 3.10: 2016 Quality of Life and Infrastructure Development: Top and Bottom Provinces in Each Region

	Region: Sumatra	Java	Kalimantan	Sulawesi	Bali–Nusa Tenggara	Maluku–Papua
Top Province	Riau Islands (8)	East Java (2)	East Kalimantan (1)	South Sulawesi (7)	Bali (5)	North Maluku (28)
Bottom Province	Jambi (25)	West Java (12)	West Kalimantan (27)	West Sulawesi (30)	East Nusa Tenggara (31)	Papua (33)

Source: Asia Competitiveness Institute.

In Kalimantan Region, performance among provinces in Quality of Life and Infrastructure Development vary widely, as can be seen from East Kalimantan's top position while West Kalimantan consistently remains near to the bottom (Table 3.10). The poor performance for the latter is largely driven by its quality of physical infrastructure and living standards. Such diversity is also observed in Bali–Nusa Tenggara Region, where Bali ranks fifth and East Nusa Tenggara maintains its position at 31st. Meanwhile, East Java ranks first among provinces in Java for Quality of Life and infrastructure Development, unlike all other environments where DKI Jakarta holds the leading position.

DKI Jakarta scores slightly above average for Physical Infrastructure, suggesting that its infrastructure has not been adequate to support its large population. Its living standards have also been compromised and cannot keep up with the population's demand, scoring well below average. In Sumatra, the performance among provinces is less varied, but six out of 10 provinces perform below average. Riau Islands remains the top-performing among its neighbouring provinces, scoring substantially well in its Technological Infrastructure. As mentioned, all provinces in Maluku–Papua Region perform poorly. The living standards in Maluku and North Maluku are however scored above average.

Even among the top four regions, each region performs differently in each sub-environment, as illustrated in Figure 3.7. For instance, Java Region is set to become a benchmark and attains the highest scores in Physical and Technological Infrastructure sub-environments. Nonetheless,

Figure 3.7: 2016 Quality of Life and Infrastructure Development: Sub-environment Spread

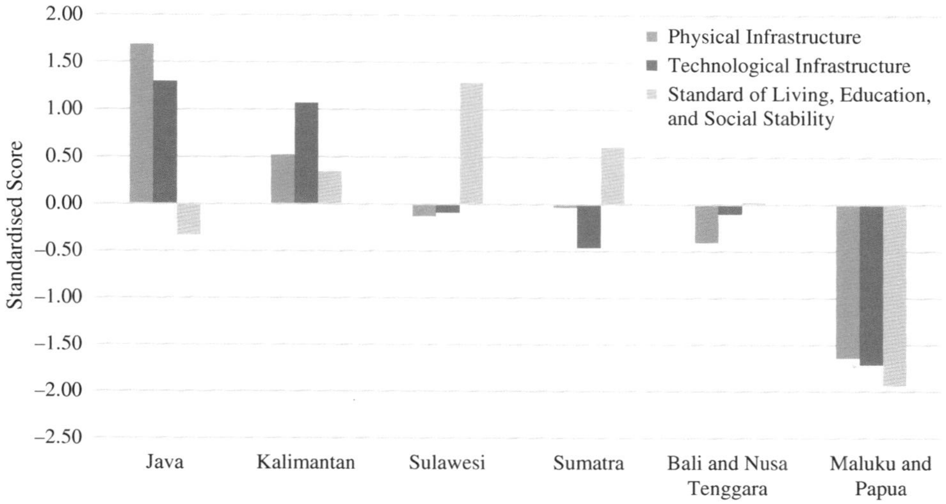

Source: Asia Competitiveness Institute.

Java scores below average in Standard of Living, Education, and Social Stability, far below Sulawesi, Sumatra, and Kalimantan regions. Java scores the lowest in several indicators, including Population per Health Facility and Medical Worker, Environmental Quality Index and number of Fatalities due to Natural Disaster. Much can be achieved from adopting best practices from Sulawesi, which performed better in the aforementioned areas.

Meanwhile, Maluku–Papua Region faces tough challenges to catchup with the rest of Indonesia. Much improvement needs to be made to upgrade not only its physical and technological infrastructure but also its provisions of necessities like healthcare, education, and basic goods and services.

3.3.3 Median and Maximum Web Analysis

The spread of sub-environment scores as illustrated in Figures 3.4–3.7 allows us to pinpoint the source of each region's performance in each environment. The following median and maximum competitiveness web charts will allow us to compare and contrast attainment of each region not only in three sub-environments under their respective environment but also in all 12 sub-environments. Figure 3.8 provides a snapshot for comparison between the top- and bottom-performing regions against the median score while Figure 3.9 provides the comparison with the maximum score.

As a top-performing region, Java attains higher scores than the median in all sub-environments except Standard of Living, Education, and Social Stability. The widest gaps between Java's scores and the median are found in (i) Labour Market Flexibility, (ii) Government Policies and Fiscal Sustainability, and (iii) Attractiveness to Foreign Investors, further attesting Java's

Figure 3.8: 2016 Median Competitiveness Web Analysis: Top- and Bottom-performing Regions

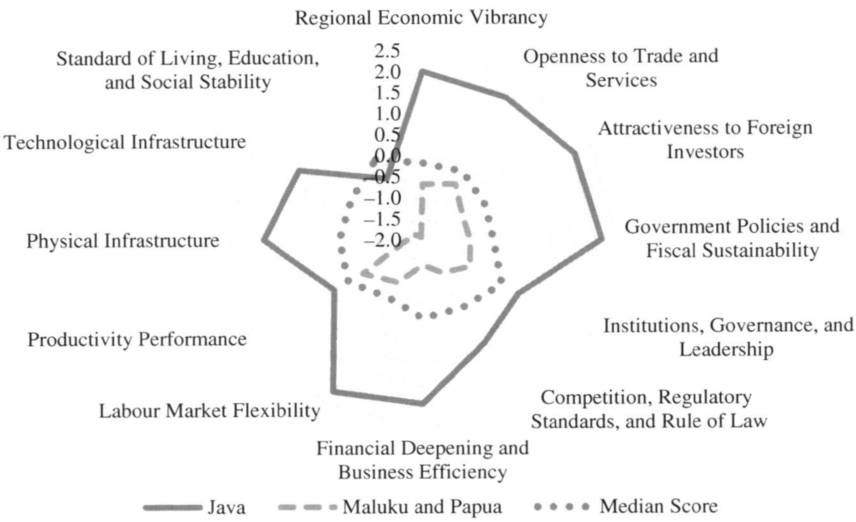

Source: Asia Competitiveness Institute.

Figure 3.9: 2016 Maximum Competitiveness Web Analysis: Top- and Bottom-performing Regions

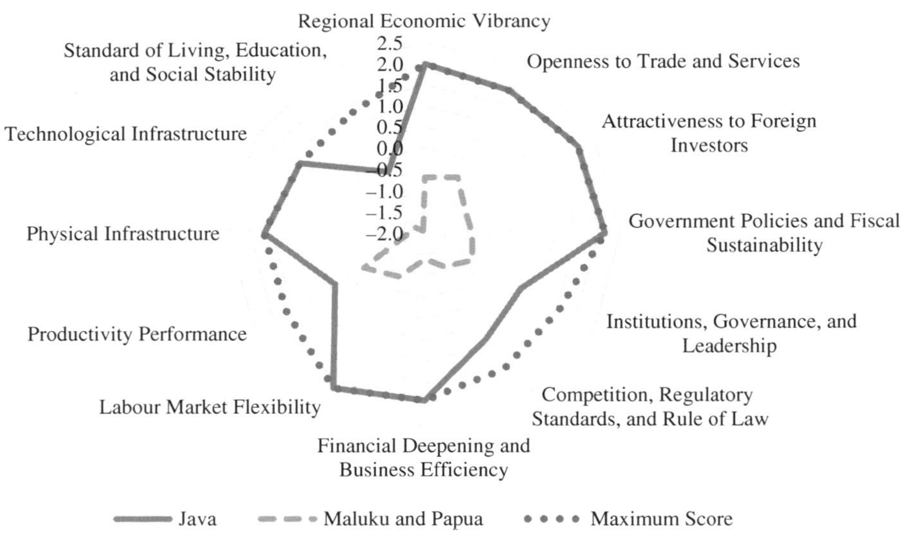

Source: Asia Competitiveness Institute.

position as the main economic driver for Indonesia. For Maluku–Papua Region, its scores in all 12 sub-environments are well below the median, with the widest gap found in Standard of Living, Education, and Social Stability, particularly due to low provision and poor quality of education.

From Figure 3.9, it is observed that Java Region tops in eight out 12 sub-environments. Sulawesi also shows favourable competitiveness, topping three sub-environments (i) Institutions, Governance, and Leadership, (ii) Competition, Regulatory Standards, and Rule of Law, and (iii) Standard of Living, Education, and Social Stability. Meanwhile, Kalimantan tops in Productivity Performance. These essentially show that beyond Java, other regions of Indonesia have the potential to achieve in various aspects of competitiveness.

3.4 Policy Implications and Concluding Notes

In line with a paradigm shift in regional policy (from providing subsidies to lagging regions to unleashing the competitiveness of each region), the central government of Indonesia launched a master plan for economic development in 2011, where growth is to be spread out through six economic corridors. Despite the more recent debate around the master plan, it is nonetheless useful to adopt its regional classification to conduct a regional competitiveness analysis for Indonesia.

By adopting such regional classification, our research found that Java Region is still lauded as the most competitive region, leading in all four environments. The dichotomy between western and eastern parts of Indonesia is less profound as Sumatra Region, which is often coined as Java's peer in the domination of western areas, stays at fourth position below Kalimantan and Sulawesi regions.

The sub-environment spread allows us to dig deeper into factors enhancing or impending each region's competitiveness. For instance, despite Sumatra's runner-up position in Macroeconomic Stability, the region suffers from lagging Attractiveness to Foreign Investors. Given ACI's strength to drill deeper into provincial level, more direct impact and tangible policymaking can be done. The results also help us to infer which region can be a benchmark for best practice policies as in the case of Kalimantan and Sulawesi regions for Institutions, Governance, and Leadership. All in all, this provides abundant learning opportunities from inter-regional friendly rivalry to unleash the potential of each region that eventually improve national competitiveness.

Disparity within a region is also prevalent in multiple instances. For example, in Sumatra Region, Riau Islands often leads in the top-10 while its peers, which are less industrialised and relying on extractive industries, fall behind in the bottom-10. Such differences also persist between oil-rich provinces, and not so well-endowed provinces as in the case of East Kalimantan which holds first position in terms of Quality of Life and Infrastructure Development while its neighbour, West Kalimantan, ranks 27th. This signals that even the gaps between soft and hard infrastructure within region still exist, while such gaps across the regions remain a perennial challenge.

The performance of Indonesia's easternmost region, Maluku–Papua, continues to fall behind, particularly in Quality of Life and Infrastructure Development environment with extremely low standardised score. As the least developed region, Maluku–Papua stands to benefit the most, especially from improvement in education and health outcomes. Improvement in human resources is key for the region to achieve higher competitiveness. The existing national agenda for Indonesia to enhance its maritime infrastructure gives a promising outlook for Maluku–Papua Region to be more involved in the interregional trade that may increase complementarity among Indonesia's regions. Committed government, both at central and local levels, is an important aspect to strengthen the impetus for higher competitiveness for Indonesia as a whole. Starting from a low base, getting results quickly by reaping the low-lying fruits also boosts confidence to tackle more difficult issues.

References

Coordinating Ministry for Economic Affairs. 2011. *Master Plan for Acceleration and Expansion of Indonesia's Economic Development 2011–2025 (MP3EI).* Jakarta: Coordinating Ministry for Economic Affairs.

Garcia, Jorge and Lana Soelistianingsih. 1998. "Why Do Differences in Provincial Incomes Persist in Indonesia?" *Bulletin of Indonesian Economic Studies* 34 (1): 95–120.

Matthews, Chris. 2014. "Poor Germany: Why the east will never catch up to the west." *Fortune*, November 9. Accessed on July 28, 2015. http://fortune.com/2014/11/09/germany-east-west-economy/.

Mietzner, Marcus. 2013. "Indonesia's Decentralisation: The Rise of Local Identities and the Survival of the Nation-State." Paper presented at the Indonesia Update Conference 2013, Canberra, Australia, September 20.

Nazara, Suahasil, Michael Sonis, and Geoffrey J.D. Hewings. 2000. "Interregional Competition and Complementarity in Indonesia." *The Regional Economics Applications Laboratory (REAL) Discussion Paper REAL 01-T-2*: 1–22.

OECD. 2010. Regional Development Policy Trends in OECD Member Countries. Paris: OECD Publishing.

Sonis, Michael, Geoffrey J.D. Hewings, Jiemin Guo, and Edison Hulu. 1997. "Interpreting spatial economic structure: feedback loops in the Indonesian interregional economy, 1980, 1985." *Regional Science and Urban Economics* 27: 325–342.

Tan, Khee Giap, Mulya Amri, Linda Low, and Tan Kong Yam. 2013. *Competitiveness Analysis and Development Strategies for 33 Indonesian Provinces.* Singapore: World Scientific.

Tan Khee Giap, Nurina Merdikawati, Mulya Amri, and Blake Harley Berger. 2015a. *2014 Annual Competitiveness Analysis and Development Strategies for Indonesian Provinces.* Singapore: World Scientific.

Tan, Khee Giap, Nurina Merdikawati, Mulya Amri, and Tan Kong Yam. 2015b. *2014 Provincial and Inaugural Regional Competitiveness Analysis: Safeguarding Indonesia's Growth Momentum.* Singapore: World Scientific.

Tan, Khee Giap, Yuan Randong, and Sangiita Yoong Wei Cher. 2015. *2014 Annual Provincial and Regional Competitiveness Analysis for Greater China Economies: Development Strategies under the New Normal.* Singapore: World Scientific.

Discussant Note 3.1[1]

2016 Annual Update of Competitiveness Ranking and Simulation of Indonesian Provinces and Regions

Professor Dr. Kuntoro Mangkusubroto

School of Business and Management
Bandung Institute of Technology, Indonesia

It is always a pleasure to be at ACI, especially at this conference. I have been involved with ACI for many years, and have seen how they have been so productive and supportive. Thank you ACI for organising this conference. It is important for Indonesia's development, especially for competitiveness among regions. Thank you for all your effort, and after reading (the research), I can say that this is a world-class research output. I was really surprised that ACI's ranking is 13th in the world. I expected ACI to be number two or number three in the world, but I am looking forward to ACI reaching such high ranks in the very near of future.

Having read very carefully the research output sent to me a week ago, I can say that the findings and the methodology of the research is excellent. I do not see any critical issues that needs to be addressed in this report. Regarding the methodology, I will give some minor comments. It took me a few hours to read and analyse this (research). There are surprises even for an Indonesian, and I live in Indonesia, and know Indonesia maybe better than Prof Tan and my friends from ACI. Maybe they know Indonesia better than I do, I do not know. There is no surprise that Java is the factor for growth in Indonesia. It is also no surprise that Papua is left behind, still at the bottom.

However, there is something intriguing, and that is a problem. Why is North Sulawesi and South Sulawesi ranked the highest in institutional measures? And, why is West Sumatra together with North Sumatra among the lowest ranked provinces in Indonesia? There needs to be more

[1]The contents of this discussion note were delivered during the 2016 Annual Asia Competitiveness Institute Conference on 24 November 2016, in Singapore.

in-depth analysis. Perhaps I am reading the summary and cannot see the details in the research assumptions, the factors that lead to the results in survey. Maybe later, the researcher can provide some explanations.

One thing that is surprising, or unsurprising for some, is that almost all the archipelagic provinces — Maluku, North Maluku, East Nusa Tenggara, West Nusa Tenggara, and Riau Islands — have low rankings and/or did poorly in the indicators compared to other provinces. It is very logical because in archipelagic provinces like these, it is much more difficult in terms of manufacturing, transportation, and mobilization of people. This is what makes things more difficult. But if we expand the logic, Indonesia is basically an archipelagic country. This is an important point.

I have often criticized my fellow ministers and technocrats in Indonesia, who are usually economists, and some of them engineers. They are actually the brains behind the development of Indonesia, having graduated from some of the best universities in the US. But when they develop a policy, perhaps Indonesia is seen as the same as the US, as a landmass. We have always assumed Indonesia to be landmass nation. They forget, or perhaps not forgetting because textbooks do not mention, how to develop an archipelago like Indonesia. There are intrinsic problems we face in developing an archipelago like Indonesia. So the next time, please share with me how to develop the archipelagic provinces in Indonesia like Sumatra, Java and Kalimantan if you find it.

I have a few comments on the research from a macro perspective, and I do not want to go into details because it will be distracting. Firstly, this research is based on perceptions, and there is nothing wrong with that. However, we have to be very careful in capturing perceptions. Again, Indonesia is an archipelago country. The farther east you go, the more you will see that, and I believe our friends from APINDO will agree with this, more businessmen are likely to come either from the island or outside the island. In Maluku, the 'BBM' people are more advanced. BBM is in reference to the Bugis, Buton, and Makassar peoples. Going further east to Papua, again there are more BBM. In North Maluku, again more 'BBM'. If you ask their perceptions of the province, they would have different perspective compared to the native businessmen. This is an issue when we consider the sample of people included in the surveys. I will be happy if this survey is done for five or six years, and we have enough data points for a longitudinal study to compare statistics from the bureau, the data ACI collects and data from the national or regional statistical offices. Through this comparison, for instance the ease of doing business, if the deviation between statistics and perception is not large, then the perception approach is acceptable. But if there is a big deviation, it means that there are other factors that may distort the result of ACI's research.

Secondly, the issue with local and provincial policy is that it is highly dependent on central government policy. For example, natural resources especially oil and gas. It is not surprising to see Riau as one of the lowest ranked in Indonesia. Why is that so? A province rich with oil and gas is one of the lowest in Indonesia. Well, I can say openly it is because oil and gas policy is from the central government. The regional government has no say in oil and gas, so we have to be very careful because some policies are not the result of the provincial government process or recommendation. It is solely dependent on the policy coming from the central government. That is the Papua and Aceh effect, the only two special provinces in Indonesia with special autonomy. On top of special autonomy, they have the freedom to develop, but their ranking is one of the lowest. Not only one of the lowest, Papua is the lowest amongst all the provinces, despite the freedom to manage the funds coming from Jakarta. They have not been able to improve the wellbeing of the people. Is it because of this effect? Does it mean that there is something implicitly wrong with the central government policy with regards to special autonomy of these two provinces? It is important for these factors to be addressed before we continue this research.

Lastly, as I have mentioned several times, this research is very important for Indonesia. It cannot remain as a research result but it should be followed up. I recommend that this research result be disseminated to all Indonesian bureaucrats of the central government as well as the provincial level. However, give them the tools to improve things. ACI uses a certain approach like simulation and explains the key elements that are very strategic to improve other dimensions. But make it more operational, such that we can have certain policy approaches in Indonesia from the provincial level as well from the central government. By disseminating the result of the research and equipping them with the tools, this research can be made use of as the basis to further develop their research.

I would like to congratulate ACI again with high appreciation. I am so proud of being a member of the panel of ACI this morning, I can see a world class research.

Chapter 4
Growth Slowdown Analysis by Income Thresholds for Indonesia's Sub-national Economies[1]

4.1 Introductory Notes

4.1.1 Background

Indonesia is confidently claiming its place as one of the world's rising "middle powers".[2] It is the fourth most populous country in the world, the 10th largest economy in terms of purchasing power parity and a member of the G-20.[3] Robust economic growth has lifted millions out of poverty. Over the period of 2000–2014, the compound annual growth rate of real GDP in Indonesia was a respectable 5.5%.[4]

Notwithstanding the positive growth performance of the country over the past two decades, pundits and policymakers alike have expressed concerns on whether growth will be derailed in the future. According to the World Bank, Indonesia will face very real risk of a growth slowdown if structural reforms are not carried out.[5] Meanwhile, the Asian Development Bank (ADB) has warned about the possibility that the country would fall into the "middle-income trap".[6] This sentiment was echoed by Indonesian policymakers. Speaking in December 2013 during an international seminar in Bali, Mr. Chatib Basri, the previous Minister of Finance of Indonesia, noted that Indonesia has not graduated from the middle-income group despite attaining middle-income status in the 1990s, which was a worrying sign.[7]

---

[1]In this chapter, we use the term "sub-national economies" to refer to Indonesian provinces, because this is part of a larger study that encompasses various economies in the region, including provinces of Indonesia, states and federal territories of India, provinces and economies of Greater China, and ASEAN-10 economies.

[2]See Cooper and Mo (2013).

[3]See http://www.worldbank.org/en/country/indonesia/overview (accessed February 5, 2016).

[4]Asia Competitiveness Institute, based on data from the International Monetary Fund, World Economic Outlook database.

[5]See The World Bank Office Jakarta (2014).

[6]See Rhee (2012).

[7]See Sambijantoro (2013).

There are many challenges to future economic growth in Indonesia. Low commodity prices, especially low oil, coal and natural rubber prices, have hurt Indonesia's exports. Exports from Indonesia fell for the fourth year in a row to US$150.2 billion, down 15%.[8] To compound the difficulties, the ongoing slowdown of the Chinese economy is expected to have significant negative impacts on the economic performances of Indonesia and other ASEAN economies.[9] Domestically, timely disbursement of budget for infrastructure projects still falls short, creating uncertainties for investors and potentially hampering infrastructure development. Furthermore, Indonesia is still overly reliant on the concentration of economic activities in Java. While more special economic zones are planned outside Java, their operationalisation remains a challenge in terms of efficient logistics and transportation cost as well as capable human resources. Another challenge is the steadily weakening of the rupiah against the US dollar. Finally, it remains to be seen whether Indonesia can effectively cope with the risk of terrorist attacks in order to ensure that economic development will not be derailed by security concerns.

The outlook for Indonesia is not entirely bleak. There are also great potentials for future growth. Though indeed Indonesia is likely to be buffeted by economic slowdown in China, it also stands to benefit from China's ailments. With China's eroding competitiveness due to rising wages, Indonesia stands to regain its comparative advantage in labour-intensive export sector. Furthermore, Indonesia will also gain from the establishment of the ASEAN Economic Community (AEC). Though far from being fully realised,[10] the AEC can be expected to create more opportunities for growth, as it liberalises intra-ASEAN trade and investment, thus further opening up the ASEAN market for Indonesia's access while making the entire region more attractive for investors outside ASEAN. Meanwhile, President Joko Widodo's administration has tackled some of the most pressing issues in the country. In particular, fuel subsidies have been greatly reduced, providing fiscal space for government to embark on much-needed infrastructure projects. In addition, the ongoing bureaucracy reform has streamlined the business permits and licenses, with the Investment Coordinating Board (BKPM) launching one-stop service centres in January 2015. Also, the President's call to transform Indonesia into a global maritime axis has been translated into various projects to improve existing ports and build new ones to strengthen sea-based connectivity. This effort will become very crucial to connect Indonesia's vast archipelago. At the same time, it will facilitate further integration into other regional connectivity master plans, such as the 21st Century Maritime Silk Road, Master Plan on ASEAN Connectivity, and Asia Competitiveness Institute's Asia Economic Connectivity Vision 2030.[11]

Through the Master Plan for Acceleration and Expansion of Indonesia's Economic Development (MP3EI), Indonesia has firmly stated its goal to progress into the high-income group by 2025, hence, succeeding in avoiding the "middle-income trap". It is thus timely for us to assess the risk of growth slowdown in Indonesia and identify potential determinants of slowdown for policy interventions. Up until now, works on whether Indonesia will fall into the

[8]See Kyozuka (2016).

[9]See Wei (2015).

[10]See Tan *et al.* (2017).

[11]See Tan *et al.* (2016).

middle-income trap or experience economic slowdown have focused on the country as a whole. Given Indonesia's regional diversity and variation in terms of Gross Regional Domestic Product (GRDP) per capita,[12] it is more appropriate if one analyses growth slowdown at the sub-national level. Our research therefore attempts to fill this gap.

This chapter provides a comprehensive analysis of growth slowdown for the Indonesia sub-national economies against the backdrop of other developing Asian economies, including ASEAN economies,[13] Greater China economies, and India sub-national economies,[14] to inform policy directions. In other words, we investigate episodes where growth had hitherto been fast but has then slowed substantially. Our analysis covers economies at all levels of development, including low-, lower-middle-, upper-middle- and high-income economies. For each income group, we construct a specific logistic model in order to identify the relevant determinants of growth slowdown. In doing so, we aim to answer two research questions. First, are determinants of economic slowdown likely to differ across income groups? Second, what are the probabilities that Indonesia's sub-national economies will experience a growth slowdown in the near future?

4.1.2 Understanding Growth Slowdowns and "Income Traps"

Economists have expended great efforts to understand the challenges to continued economic growth at different levels of development. Many have conceptualised the problems to growth through the idea of income traps. "Poverty trap" and, more recently, "middle-income trap" are common parlances in the development policy community. This section provides a brief review on existing research on poverty trap and "middle-income trap", and seeks to distinguish our study on growth slowdown from these literature.

Much has been written about poverty trap. The literature on poverty trap is motivated by the observation that the very rich and very poor countries do not seem to converge in GDP per capita over time. Several studies in this literature have pointed out that the cross-country income distribution has become increasingly bimodal, with probability mass concentrated at the two extremes.[15] In other words, while a handful of countries have grown to achieve high GDP per capita, many others have continued to be stuck in poverty. Poverty trap is one of the arguments proposed to explain this phenomenon. According to the poverty trap theory, economies clustering around the lower end of the income distribution are beset with self-reinforcing mechanisms which causes the persistence of poverty. These self-reinforcing mechanisms are the so-called traps.[16]

[12]In this chapter, we use the term "Gross Regional Domestic Product" to refer to the gross domestic product of the Indonesian provinces, the Indian states and union territories as well as the Greater China economies.

[13]See Tan, Luu, and Lian (2017) for analysis of growth slowdown on ASEAN economies.

[14]The Greater China economies include the mainland China provinces, Taiwan, Hong Kong and Macau while the India sub-national economies refer to the states and union territories of India. We exclude certain economies from the analysis because of data constraints. In total, our study covers 107 Asian developing economies (See Section 4.5 for more details).

[15]See, for example, Azariadis and Stachurski (2005) and Quah (1993).

[16]Definition is adopted from Azariadis and Stachurski (2005).

Both the theoretical and empirical literatures about poverty trap are well developed. The theoretical models for poverty trap suggest the existence of multiple equilibria and elaborate the ways in which "bad" equilibria of low growth and low income may be selected. According to Azariadis and Stachurski (2005), there are in general two "canonical" classes of models. The first model is called *historical* self-reinforcement, a process whereby initial conditions of the endogenous variables, such as the stocks of physical and human capital or technological progress, can shape long-run outcomes. The second is the *inertial* self-reinforcement hypothesis which emphasises the role of beliefs and expectations in selecting "bad" equilibria and the role of societal conventions, norms and institutions in perpetuating poverty by preserving expectations and beliefs. In terms of the empirics, there have been efforts to test for the existence of poverty trap.[17] There have also been many studies which empirically examine specific trap mechanisms[18] or traps which occur at the individual or the group level.[19]

In contrast to poverty trap, the term middle-income trap has only gained currency in academic and policy discourses in recent years. Over the past few years, a debate has arisen around the observation that there are countries which have attained middle-income status for an extended period of time but have not yet been able to catch up to the high-income economies. Some authors, such as Gill and Kharas (2007), Felipe (2012a) and Aiyar *et al.* (2013) claimed that these economies have fallen into a "middle-income trap" while others, such as Im and Rosenblatt (2013) and Bulman, Eden, and Nguyen (2014) disputed the existence of such trap. More recently, Ye and Robertson (2016) concluded that if middle-income traps do exist, they are not very common. In fact, much remains to be clarified about the concept. As Gill and Kharas (2015) have noted, different authors define "middle-income traps" in various ways. Despite the lack of consensus about the definition and existence of middle-income traps in the academic literature, policymakers tend to be concerned about them nonetheless. This has motivated a rich body of research into factors which are key in helping an economy avoid being trapped at the middle-income level.[20]

Our research has important differences with both the poverty trap and middle-income trap literature. We focus on growth slowdown at different levels of development.[21] In other words, unlike the poverty trap literature, we do not investigate mechanisms and factors which hamper the ability of low-income economies to generate growth. Instead, we are interested in episodes of reversals in growth rate *after the economy has enjoyed extended periods of fast growth.* We feel that the focus on growth slowdown is more relevant for low-income economies of our interest in ASEAN and Greater China, India, and Indonesia as the main challenge for these economies is not so much how to generate but how to sustain growth. Meanwhile, in contrast to most

[17] See Bloom, Canning, and Sevilla (2003).

[18] See Azariadis and Stachurski (2005, 339–340) for a comprehensive review.

[19] For instance, Jalan and Ravallion (2002) investigates geographical poverty traps arising from factor endowments among rural households from post-reform rural China.

[20] See, for example, Yusuf and Nabeshima (2009), Felipe (2012b), Bulman, Eden, and Nguyen (2014), Zhang (2014), Kasenda (2015), Agenor (2015) and Gill and Kharas (2015).

[21] Our study classifies economies into low-, lower-middle-, upper-middle- and high-income economies. See Section 4.3 for details.

of the middle-income trap literature, we do not wade into the debate on the trap existence. Instead, our research sharply focuses on factors which may make growth slowdown more likely at the middle-income level. Regardless of whether the middle-income trap exists, policymakers in middle-income economies should be concerned with potential weaknesses which may cause their economies to slow down.

In essence, our study is in line with the budding literature focusing on growth dynamics which has emerged in the wake of Pritchett (2000). Pritchett (2000) observed that instability is a fundamental property of the growth series of developing countries as there are many upturns and downturns over time. Because of this instability, argued Pritchett, studies which focus on the long-term growth rates are unlikely to be able to offer any useful insights. Instead, it is far more important to examine the "hills, plateaus, mountains and plains" — the various growth patterns — in the data series. In recent years, an increasing number of empirical research have emerged to chart this territory.[22] Works which are most similar to ours include Eichengreen, Park, and Shin (2012), Eichengreen, Park, and Shin (2013), Aiyar *et al.* (2013) and Zhang and Puy (2015). The first three examined episodes of growth slowdown in middle-income economies while the fourth analysed growth slowdown in low-income economies. As compared to these studies, ours is more comprehensive as we analyse economies at all levels of development, including low-, lower-middle-, upper-middle- and high-income economies.

4.1.3 Motivation and Expected Contributions

Our study makes several significant contributions. We are among the first, if not the first, to provide a systematic quantitative analysis on the issue of growth slowdown at the high-income level, on top of investigating growth slowdown for economies in other income groups. The subject of high-income slowdown has only begun to garner attention in public and policy discourses in recent years.[23] Nevertheless, it is highly relevant. As Japan's anaemic economic performance over the past 20 years demonstrates, further development after an economy attains high-income status is hardly assured and the failure to address the impediments to growth can be costly. As such, high-income economies, as well as those that are about to progress into this income group, also need to be mindful of the risk of growth slowdown.

In addition, our research enhances the understanding of growth dynamics of Indonesia sub-national economies. Current research and most of the empirical literature on growth slowdown, have focused on Indonesia as a whole in their analyses. However, national aggregates may mask the remarkable diversity between the different provinces. The Indonesia sub-national economies are very different from each other in terms of their levels of development,

[22]Examples of these researches include Hausmann, Pritchett, and Rodrik (2005) which studied factors that trigger growth accelerations; Hausmann, Rodríguez, and Wagner (2006) which studied growth collapses; Jerzmanowski (2006) which highlighted the importance of institutions in determining the probability of economies switching between different regimes of growth; Reddy and Minoiu (2008) which investigated real income stagnations; Aiyar *et al.* (2013), L. Zhang and Puy (2015), Eichengreen, Park, and Shin (2012) and Eichengreen, Park, and Shin (2013) which examined growth slowdowns.

[23]For example, see Neumann (2015) and Dehn (2014).

as reflected by the great variations in their GRDP per capita.[24] As a result, they are likely to face dissimilar growth problems and challenges, which need to be highlighted and discussed.

Furthermore, as mentioned in Section 4.1.1, we benchmark Indonesia sub-national economies against ASEAN economies, Greater China economies and the India sub-national economies. We track their development progress and assess the risk of these economies experiencing growth slowdown. In doing so, we have created a dataset of internationally comparable data on real GRDP per capita for Greater China economies and sub-national economies of India and Indonesia. To the best of our knowledge, we are the pioneers in this respect given that such data are not available elsewhere in the literature. Our dataset presents GRDP per capita in 1990 constant prices Purchasing Power Parity dollar (PPP$) data for 33 Greater China economies, 32 Indian states and union territories and 33 Indonesian provinces from the early 1990s to the present. The dataset is reported in Section 4.2[25] while the method to obtain it is detailed in Section 4.4.1. The method can easily be applied to calculate the GRDP per capita in 1990 PPP$ for sub-national economies in any of the other countries, leaving great potentials to expand our unique dataset.

Finally, our research has important policy implications. The empirical findings from our model specifications enable us to perform statistical predictions on the probability of each economy in our study experiencing growth slowdown in the near future. This probability can be interpreted as a preliminary caution for national and local governments so that they can take targeted actions in order to minimise the risks of economic slowdown. Meanwhile, variables identified as determinants of growth slowdown by our models indicate areas where policy actions and supportive reforms are needed.

The rest of the chapter is organised as follows. Section 4.2 provides some stylised facts about the economic growth landscape of the Indonesia sub-national economies. Section 4.3 summarises existing literatures on income thresholds classification, identification of growth slowdown, as well as drivers of growth and determinants of growth slowdown. Section 4.4 details the methodology adopted by our study while Section 4.5 discusses data description, statistical computation and sources. Section 4.6 reveals our empirical findings, followed by Section 4.7 which indicates the relative strengths and weaknesses for the economies. Lastly, Section 4.8 concludes the chapter by drawing relevant policy implications for each Indonesia sub-national economy based on our results.

4.2 Stylised Facts on the Economic Growth Landscape of the Indonesia Sub-national Economies

We classify the Indonesia sub-national economies into four income groups based on the level of GRDP per capita measured in 1990 PPP$ of each economy. We adopt the classification

---

[24] See Section 4.2 for more details.

[25] See Tan, Lian, and Xie (2016) and Tan, Luu, and Yoong (2016) for the datasets of China and India sub-national economies respectively.

thresholds proposed by Felipe (2012a) which were derived from the World Bank's Gross National Income (GNI) per capita thresholds.[26] Accordingly, an economy is categorised as low-income if its GRDP per capita (in 1990 PPP$) is less than $2,000; lower-middle-income if its GRDP per capita is at least $2,000 but less than $7,250; upper-middle-income if its GRDP per capita is at least $7,250 but less than $11,750 and high-income if its GRDP per capita is $11,750 or higher. These thresholds are held constant over time.[27] As the GRDP per capita for all Indonesia sub-national economies are available in current values of local currency unit (i.e. rupiahs), we convert the original data into the required 1990 PPP$. The conversion methodology is discussed in detail in Section 4.4.1.

Tables 4.1 and 4.2 display the GRDP per capita (in 1990 PPP$) of each Indonesia sub-national economy throughout the 1990–2013 period. For the seven new economies created after 1990, namely North Maluku, Banten, Bangka Belitung Islands, Gorontalo, West Papua, Riau Islands, and West Sulawesi, we have estimated their GRDP per capita data back to 1990.[28] As North Kalimantan was formed fairly recently in 2012, data limitations restrict our analysis to treating North Kalimantan and East Kalimantan as a single economy. The distribution of the economies by income group over time is shown in Figures 4.1 and 4.2. We use red to denote the low-income group, yellow for the lower-middle-income group, green for the upper-middle-income group and blue for the high-income group.

According to the classification criteria we employ, as many as 20 economies (around 61% of the total) were categorised as low-income in 1990. At the same time, 11 economies (around 33% of the total) belonged to the lower-middle-income group and the remaining two economies (around 6% of the total), namely East Kalimantan and Riau Islands, were in the high-income group.

The early and mid-1990s witnessed robust growth of the Indonesia sub-national economies. The number of low-income economies greatly decreased between 1990 and 1995, which is reflected in the steep decline of the red area in Figure 4.1 over the period. In total, 12 economies graduated into the lower-middle-income group during these years. In addition, the more developed economies also registered strong growth performance. DKI Jakarta, for example, experienced a rapid transition from the lower-middle-income group to the upper-middle-income group and eventually to the high-income group in the short time span of seven years from 1990 to 1996.

However, the 1997 Asian Financial Crisis halted the healthy growth momentums of the Indonesia sub-national economies. Almost all economies experienced decline in their GRDP per capita during the crisis. For instance, DKI Jakarta fell back into the upper-middle-income group in 1998 as its GRDP per capita declined from $12,107 to $9,772 before climbing back to the high-income group in 2000 (See Tables 4.1 and 4.2). At the lower end of the spectrum, a handful of economies which had graduated into the lower-middle-income group regressed into the

---

[26]The World Bank's GNI thresholds take into account both income and non-income measures of well-being. Since they are based on the World Bank's classification, the thresholds proposed by Felipe also retain the same underlying information. See Felipe (2012a, 6).

[27]As noted in Felipe (2012a), World Bank's GNI thresholds are adjusted for inflation annually and therefore remain constant in real terms. Thus, using constant thresholds of GRDP per capita measured in real terms (1990 PPP$) is in principle equivalent to the World Bank's income classification method. See Felipe (2012a, 7).

[28]See Section 4.5 for further details.

Table 4.1: GRDP per Capita (in 1990 PPP$) for Indonesia Sub-national Economies, 1990–1999

Economy	1990	1991	1992	1993	1994	1995	1996	1997	1998	1999
Aceh	4,494	4,439	4,439	5,042	4,722	4,890	4,910	4,970	4,060	3,759
Bali	2,310	2,445	2,613	3,405	3,573	3,687	3,902	4,003	3,051	2,848
Bangka Belitung Islands	3,223	3,289	3,395	3,294	3,378	3,613	3,786	3,905	3,450	3,266
Banten	2,303	2,371	2,429	2,927	3,113	3,093	3,363	3,273	2,438	2,260
Bengkulu	1,438	1,491	1,576	1,802	1,978	2,033	1,994	1,970	1,543	1,463
Central Java	1,617	1,767	1,934	1,984	2,113	2,264	2,326	2,355	1,573	1,955
Central Kalimantan	2,103	2,191	2,417	3,399	3,647	3,853	4,087	4,024	3,228	3,043
Central Sulawesi	1,191	1,201	1,263	1,621	1,779	1,868	2,004	2,006	2,115	1,976
DI Yogyakarta	1,389	1,478	1,601	2,422	2,700	2,820	2,953	2,917	2,270	2,372
DKI Jakarta	5,888	6,122	6,684	9,930	10,376	11,017	11,806	12,107	9,772	10,016
East Java	1,907	2,033	2,169	2,518	2,693	2,805	2,970	3,034	2,628	2,535
East Kalimantan	12,058	12,158	12,604	12,521	13,395	13,460	13,139	12,668	13,077	11,920
East Nusa Tenggara	778	819	892	1,036	1,106	1,158	1,212	1,297	868	863
Gorontalo	416	449	495	674	723	796	945	996	968	986
Jambi	1,466	1,474	1,555	1,882	1,997	2,102	2,166	2,127	1,756	1,728
Lampung	1,137	1,155	1,309	1,439	1,580	1,757	1,797	1,791	1,753	1,764
Maluku	2,749	2,857	2,910	3,212	3,293	3,339	3,312	3,245	2,346	1,727
North Maluku	1,088	1,152	1,196	1,406	1,453	1,474	1,484	1,460	1,064	693
North Sulawesi	1,648	1,714	1,814	2,339	2,425	2,582	2,959	3,008	2,840	2,788
North Sumatra	2,231	2,267	2,523	2,879	3,132	3,193	3,298	3,483	2,921	3,083
Papua	3,167	3,493	3,620	4,951	5,017	5,917	6,040	5,929	6,734	5,468
Riau	6,624	7,338	6,523	6,341	5,990	6,182	6,178	6,067	5,649	5,506
Riau Islands	17,226	18,859	17,279	21,421	20,944	21,885	22,125	21,150	16,722	15,877

(Continued)

Table 4.1: (*Continued*)

Economy	1990	1991	1992	1993	1994	1995	1996	1997	1998	1999
South Kalimantan	1,910	2,108	2,233	2,807	2,954	3,093	3,261	3,125	2,659	2,740
South Sulawesi	1,410	1,499	1,604	1,814	1,925	2,052	2,111	2,114	1,919	1,815
South Sumatra	2,568	2,618	2,697	2,579	2,615	2,800	2,923	3,007	2,763	2,567
Southeast Sulawesi	1,289	1,342	1,358	1,471	1,549	1,652	1,693	1,655	1,679	1,543
West Java	1,848	1,925	2,017	2,372	2,556	2,735	2,860	2,860	2,290	2,211
West Kalimantan	1,799	1,907	2,020	2,521	2,685	2,829	2,998	3,139	2,516	2,404
West Nusa Tenggara	840	896	996	1,229	1,303	1,370	1,423	1,416	1,326	1,256
West Papua	1,879	2,012	2,070	2,934	2,985	3,440	3,561	3,623	3,594	2,942
West Sulawesi	930	995	1,065	1,156	1,232	1,324	1,364	1,366	1,299	1,231
West Sumatra	1,754	1,795	1,921	2,451	2,682	2,755	2,869	2,834	2,617	2,627

Low-Income (y_t < \$2,000) **Low-Middle-Income (\$2,000 ≤ y_t < \$7,250)**
Upper-Middle-Income (\$7,250 ≤ y_t < \$11,750) **High-Income (\$11,750 ≤ y_t)**

Note: y_t denotes GRDP per capita (in 1990 PPP$) of an economy in year *t*.
Source: Asia Competitiveness Institute based on data from Central Statistical Bureau and the World Bank.

Table 4.2: GRDP per Capita (in 1990 PPP$) for Indonesia Sub-national Economies, 2000–2013

Economy	2000	2001	2002	2003	2004	2005	2006	2007	2008	2009	2010	2011	2012	2013
Aceh	4,408	4,003	4,303	4,475	4,296	4,306	4,468	4,050	3,491	3,108	2,920	2,939	3,026	3,083
Bali	2,694	2,682	2,924	2,887	2,895	2,916	2,788	2,790	2,848	3,008	2,864	2,902	3,144	3,355
Bangka Belitung Islands	2,979	3,138	3,491	3,862	3,947	3,986	3,801	3,770	3,751	3,655	3,621	3,758	4,020	4,262
Banten	2,731	2,718	2,861	2,841	2,759	2,704	2,746	2,648	2,849	2,805	2,679	2,727	2,857	3,074
Bengkulu	1,513	1,452	1,516	1,802	1,825	1,936	1,916	1,916	1,851	1,851	1,798	1,880	2,029	2,173
Central Java	1,771	1,784	1,913	2,038	2,103	2,213	2,400	2,380	2,360	2,355	2,277	2,364	2,533	2,699
Central Kalimantan	2,599	2,533	2,717	2,774	3,370	3,311	3,215	3,241	3,164	3,262	3,192	3,344	3,600	3,834
Central Sulawesi	2,033	2,085	2,189	2,327	2,243	2,252	2,156	2,237	2,344	2,399	2,348	2,552	2,800	3,030
DI Yogyakarta	2,097	2,062	2,230	2,356	2,418	2,401	2,366	2,365	2,304	2,301	2,188	2,288	2,409	2,550
DKI Jakarta	13,235	13,185	13,945	18,554	18,637	18,591	14,784	14,839	14,860	15,214	14,884	15,628	16,796	18,133
East Java	2,786	2,788	2,983	3,159	3,280	3,379	3,473	3,536	3,452	3,513	3,445	3,626	3,943	4,264
East Kalimantan	16,289	15,115	13,855	14,213	16,319	18,794	17,208	16,733	19,436	15,814	15,018	16,540	16,691	15,820
East Nusa Tenggara	982	983	1,028	1,072	1,100	1,082	1,048	1,048	988	1,002	982	1,011	1,086	1,164
Gorontalo	851	906	1,003	938	937	979	1,126	1,168	1,209	1,317	1,285	1,336	1,441	1,541
Jambi	1,930	1,973	2,185	2,296	2,400	2,509	2,498	2,703	2,865	2,785	2,888	3,105	3,378	3,748
Lampung	1,697	1,625	1,717	1,796	1,787	1,753	1,842	2,028	2,052	2,260	2,363	2,565	2,771	2,983
Maluku	1,650	1,627	1,744	1,680	1,597	1,549	1,434	1,419	1,297	1,326	1,292	1,395	1,578	1,710
North Maluku	760	672	639	626	635	592	550	541	546	599	583	596	649	683
North Sulawesi	2,599	2,490	2,549	2,601	2,547	2,631	2,629	2,658	2,658	2,803	2,688	2,814	3,036	3,257

(*Continued*)

Table 4.2: *(Continued)*

Economy	2000	2001	2002	2003	2004	2005	2006	2007	2008	2009	2010	2011	2012	2013
North Sumatra	2,916	2,904	3,077	3,335	3,466	3,544	3,501	3,529	3,478	3,513	3,514	3,688	3,930	4,278
Papua	6,879	6,169	4,726	4,435	4,116	6,150	5,362	5,439	4,893	5,410	5,135	4,070	3,906	4,421
Riau	12,250	11,800	11,670	9,040	8,799	9,175	8,997	9,927	10,808	10,497	10,354	11,206	11,975	12,460
Riau Islands	12,259	11,013	10,334	10,310	10,546	9,581	9,003	8,659	7,909	7,611	7,073	7,117	7,530	7,757
South Kalimantan	2,809	2,716	2,992	2,998	3,019	2,982	2,758	2,777	2,692	2,751	2,736	2,848	3,009	3,113
South Sulawesi	2,176	2,164	2,240	2,307	2,302	2,120	2,160	2,181	2,243	2,404	2,433	2,615	2,908	3,188
South Sumatra	3,173	3,116	3,051	3,225	3,381	3,678	3,703	3,758	3,814	3,571	3,511	3,723	4,014	4,260
Southeast Sulawesi	1,582	1,600	1,673	1,750	1,849	2,004	2,032	2,099	2,149	2,245	2,108	2,171	2,342	2,449
West Java	2,660	2,550	2,594	2,746	2,752	3,028	3,169	3,120	3,132	3,106	2,972	3,044	3,193	3,398
West Kalimantan	2,501	2,382	2,475	2,516	2,586	2,538	2,536	2,529	2,380	2,394	2,284	2,312	2,464	2,635
West Nusa Tenggara	1,531	1,651	1,644	1,651	1,903	1,906	1,829	1,898	1,669	1,895	1,829	1,661	1,605	1,720
West Papua	2,907	3,213	3,342	3,649	3,586	3,777	3,431	3,510	3,934	4,638	5,861	7,139	8,035	8,847
West Sulawesi	1,401	1,343	1,382	1,332	1,340	1,304	1,311	1,393	1,545	1,584	1,572	1,683	1,786	1,887
West Sumatra	2,623	2,598	2,756	2,857	2,901	3,003	3,106	3,113	3,093	3,058	2,985	3,112	3,307	3,611

Low-Income ($y_t < \$2,000$) **Low-Middle-Income ($\$2,000 \le y_t < \$7,250$)**
Upper-Middle-Income ($\$7,250 \le y_t < \$11,750$) **High-Income ($\$11,750 \le y_t$)**

Note: y_t denotes GRDP per capita (in 1990 PPP$) of an economy in year *t*.
Source: Asia Competitiveness Institute based on data from Central Statistical Bureau and the World Bank.

Figure 4.1: Area Chart for Distribution of Indonesia Sub-national Economies by Income Categories, 1990–2013

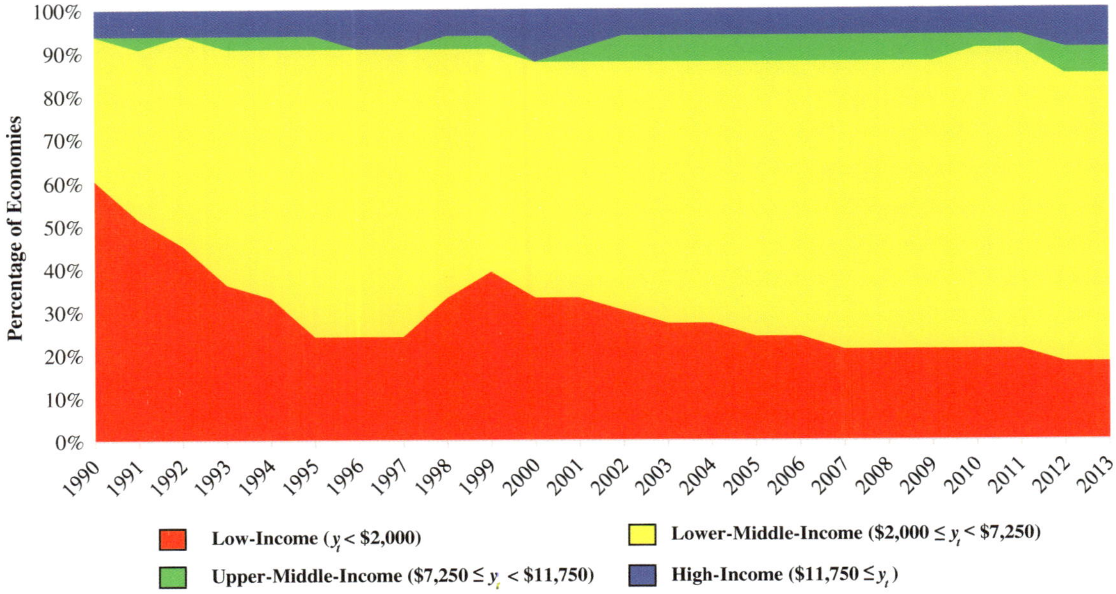

Note: y_t denotes GRDP per capita (in 1990 PPP$) of an economy in year t.
Source: Asia Competitiveness Institute based on data from Central Statistical Bureau and the World Bank.

Figure 4.2: Bar Chart for Distribution of Indonesia Sub-national Economies by Income Categories, 1990–2013

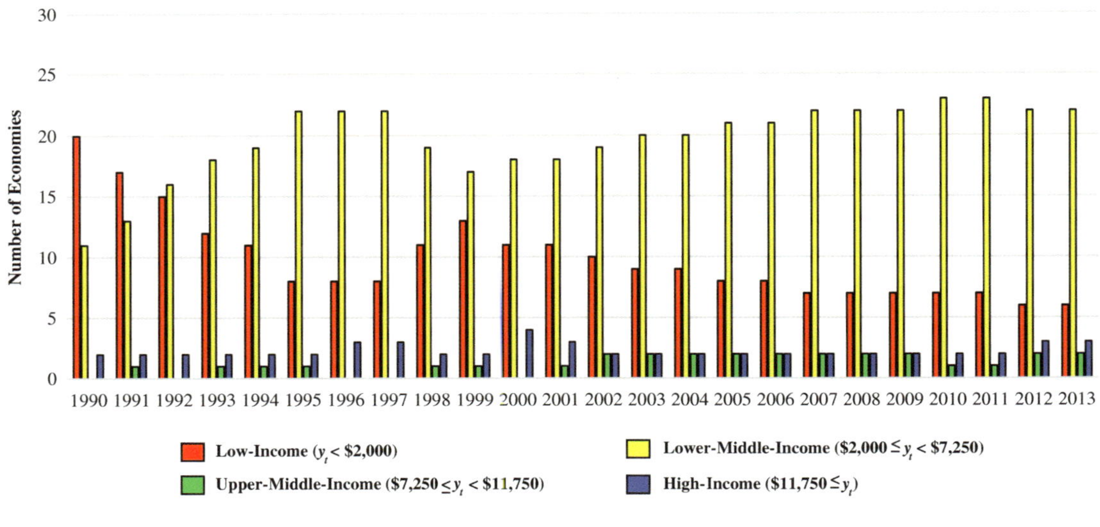

Note: y_t denotes GRDP per capita (in 1990 PPP$) of an economy in year t.
Source: Asia Competitiveness Institute based on data from Central Statistical Bureau and the World Bank.

low-income group. As shown in Figure 4.2, the number of low-income economies rose from eight in 1997 to 13 in 1999. The economies which fell back to low-income group included Jambi, Central Java, Maluku, South Sulawesi, and Central Sulawesi.

The pace at which these economies recovered varied. South Sulawesi and Central Sulawesi, which dropped to the low-income group in 1998 and 1999 respectively, rebounded quickly to become lower-middle-income economies again in 2000. In contrast, Maluku has not managed to make another upward transition after falling back into the low-income group in 1999. Meanwhile, Jambi and Central Java, which both regressed in 1998, took 4 and 5 years, respectively, to resume lower-middle-income status in 2002 and 2003.

After the Asian Financial Crisis, growth momentums of most Indonesia sub-national economies have not reached the levels observed in the early and mid-1990s. Graduation from the low-income group happened much more slowly. From 2003 to 2013, only three more economies, namely Bengkulu, Lampung, and Southeast Sulawesi, made the transition from the low- to the lower-middle-income group. Further upward movements into higher income groups were also scarce and only happened in more recent years. As a result, the green and blue areas in Figure 4.1 are relatively stable from 2001 onwards.

In recent years, Indonesia sub-national economies have achieved decent economic growth. Table 4.3 shows the compound annual growth rates of GRDP per capita (in 1990 PPP$) of the economies for the period 2009–2013. On average, over these five years, the Indonesia sub-national economies have managed to grow their real GRDP per capita by about 3.81% annually. However, growth performances varied greatly. The standard deviation of the growth rates is 3.59%, almost as high as the average.

By 2013, there were six economies (around 18% of the total) which were still mired in the low-income group. These included Gorontalo, Maluku, North Maluku, West Nusa Tenggara, East Nusa Tenggara, and West Sulawesi. Aside from Maluku, the other five economies have stagnated in the low-income group since the start of the study period in 1990. Almost 67% of the Indonesian economies, or 22 in total, were lower-middle-income economies. Eight among these, namely Aceh, Bali, Banten, Central Kalimantan, Bangka Belitung Islands, Papua, South Sumatra, and North Sumatra, have remained in this group since 1990. There were only two upper-middle-income economies (around 6% of the total), namely Riau Islands and West Papua, and three high-income economies (around 9% of the total), namely DKI Jakarta, East Kalimantan, and Riau.

4.3 Literature Review

In this section, we review existing literature on works related to growth slowdown, including various ways of classifying economies into income groups and defining a growth slowdown episode. We will also discuss drivers of growth and determinants of growth slowdown used in other similar studies.

4.3.1 Income Thresholds Classification

In current literature, there are two main approaches to income classification. The first is based on absolute levels of income. The World Bank's categorisation of economies into

Table 4.3: Compound Annual Growth Rate of GRDP per Capita (in 1990 PPP$) for Indonesia Sub-national Economies, 2009–2013

Economy	Compound Annual Growth Rate of GRDP per Capita (in 1990 PPP$) for Indonesia Sub-national Economies, 2009–2013
Aceh	–0.20%
Bali	2.77%
Bangka Belitung Islands	3.91%
Banten	2.31%
Bengkulu	4.08%
Central Java	3.47%
Central Kalimantan	4.12%
Central Sulawesi	6.01%
DI Yogyakarta	2.61%
DKI Jakarta	4.48%
East Java	4.96%
East Kalimantan	0.01%
East Nusa Tenggara	3.81%
Gorontalo	4.00%
Jambi	7.71%
Lampung	7.19%
Maluku	6.57%
North Maluku	3.35%
North Sulawesi	3.82%
North Sumatra	5.05%
Papua	–4.92%
Riau	4.38%
Riau Islands	0.48%
South Kalimantan	3.14%
South Sulawesi	7.31%
South Sumatra	4.51%
Southeast Sulawesi	2.20%
West Java	2.27%
West Kalimantan	2.43%
West Nusa Tenggara	–2.39%
West Papua	17.52%
West Sulawesi	4.48%
West Sumatra	4.24%
Average	**3.81%**
Standard Deviation	**3.59%**

Note: Average reported is simple average.
Source: Asia Competitiveness Institute based on data from Central Statistical Bureau and the World Bank.

low-, lower-middle-, upper-middle-, and high-income economies based on the economies' nominal Gross National Income (GNI) per capita exemplifies this approach. The World Bank adopts GNI per capita as a classification criterion because it is a useful and readily available indicator. It is also correlated with other, non-income measures of welfare such as life expectancy at birth, mortality rates of children and enrolment rates in school. As of 2016, the World Bank defined low-income economies as those with GNI per capita of US$1,045 or less in 2014; lower-middle-income economies as those whose GNI per capita lies between US$1,045 and US$4,125; upper-middle-income economies as those with GNI per capita lies between US$4,125 and US$12,736 and high-income economies as those with GNI per capita of US$12,736 or more.[29] The GNI thresholds are adjusted for inflation and thus remain constant in real terms over time.

Felipe (2012a) also followed the absolute income-level approach. However, the author proposed thresholds of GDP per capita in constant 1990 PPP$. He first defined different sets of GDP per capita in 1990 PPP$ thresholds, where each set was made up of three different thresholds $t_0 < t_1 < t_2$. The t_0 distinguished low-income and lower-middle-income economies; t_1 separated lower-middle-income economies from upper-middle-income economies; while t_2 differentiated the upper-middle-income group from the high-income group. The three thresholds t_0, t_1 and t_2 could take different values at $250 intervals, where $\$1,500 \leq t_0 \leq \$4,750$; $\$5,000 \leq t_1 \leq \$8,750$; and $\$9,000 \leq t_2 \leq \$20,000$. Thus, for example, a set of thresholds might contain $t_0 = \$1,500$; $t_1 = \$5,000$; and $t_2 = \$9,000$ and another set may contain $t_0 = \$1,750$; $t_1 = \$5,000$; $t_2 = \$9,000$. In total, 10,080 sets were produced. Felipe used these sets of thresholds to classify all economies, which the World Bank also classified, over the period of 1987–2010. He then calculated the pairwise correlation between the World Bank's classification and the 10,080 classifications using polychoric correlation. The set which yielded the highest correlation was selected, as each income group classified according to these criteria was likely to retain the same underlying information (both income and non-income measures of well-being) encapsulated in the corresponding World Bank's income category. The author eventually selected the set with $t_0 = \$2,000$, $t_1 = \$7,250$ and $t_2 = \$11,750$.

Employing similar methodology as Felipe (2012a), Aiyar *et al.* (2013) also used the World Bank's GNI per capita thresholds as benchmarks to create income thresholds measured in GDP per capita in 2005 PPP$. However, unlike Felipe (2012a), each potential set of thresholds in Aiyar *et al.* (2013) consisted of only two thresholds t_1 and t_2 ($t_1 < t_2$) where t_1 separated low-income from middle-income while t_2 distinguished middle-income from high-income. Both t_1 and t_2 could take a set of values at $1,000 intervals, where $\$1,000 \leq t_1 \leq \$3,000$ and $\$12,000 \leq t_2 \leq \$16,000$, creating 15 combinations in total. The authors eventually selected the set with $t_1 = \$2,000$ and $t_2 = \$15,000$ as the classification resulted from this set overlapped the most with the World Bank's classification. Clearly, as compared to Aiyar *et al.* (2013), the set of classification criteria in Felipe (2012a) provided a finer differentiation of the economies as it distinguished the lower-middle-income group from the upper-middle-income group. Furthermore, Felipe's (2012a) thresholds were more precisely defined as the gap between each threshold was much smaller.

[29] See http://data.worldbank.org/about/country-and-lending-groups (accessed on February 22, 2016).

The second approach to income classification is based on relative levels of income. The Catch-up Index (CUI) proposed by Woo (2012) exemplifies this approach. The CUI of an economy was expressed as the percentage of the economy's income level relative to that of the United States (US) in the same year. Countries were classified as high-income if their CUIs were more than 55%; middle-income if their CUIs were between 55% and 20%; and low-income if their CUIs were less than 20% (Woo, 2012). Fundamentally, classification based on relative level of income is problematic as it is subjected to economic fluctuations in the benchmark economy. For example, the CUI values of the ASEAN economies during the 2008 Global Financial Crisis and its aftermaths could have been artificially inflated. This is because, on the one hand, the US experienced severe contractions in output and could only manage a slow recovery while on the other hand, ASEAN economies were much less affected and also recovered faster. As such, using CUI values to classify the ASEAN economies during this period risks mischaracterising (with an upward bias) their levels of development.

4.3.2 Growth Slowdown Identification

There are several definitions for growth slowdown in the existing literature. Aiyar *et al.* (2013) and Zhang and Puy (2015) characterised growth slowdown as "large, sudden and sustained deviations from the predicted growth path". These authors identified a country i as experiencing a growth slowdown in period t if the following two conditions were fulfilled simultaneously: (i) $res_t^i - res_{t-1}^i < p(0.20)$ and (ii) $res_{t+1}^i - res_{t-1}^i < p(0.20)$, where res_t^i is the residual of the country i in period t and $p(0.20)$ denotes the 20th percentile of the empirical distribution of differences in residuals from one time period to another. Both authors defined $t = 5$. The residual res_t^i was defined as the gap between the actual growth rate and the predicted growth rate of economy i which was estimated based on a regression of per capita GDP growth against lagged income level and measures of human and physical capital. Condition (i) thus requires the difference of residual between period t and period $t-1$ to be smaller than the 20th percentile of the empirical distribution, indicating that the actual performance of the economy falls substantially below expectation. Condition (ii) requires the difference of residual between period $t+1$ and period $t-1$ to be smaller than the 20th percentile of the empirical distribution, thereby ensuring that the slowdown is sustained over a prolonged duration. This definition of growth slowdown requires estimation of predicted growth rates, which are difficult to be implemented in our context due to data constraints.

On the other hand, Eichengreen, Park, and Shin (2012) defined growth slowdown as an episode where growth has hitherto been fast but has now slowed non-negligibly. The methodology, which was also adopted in Eichengreen, Park, and Shin (2013), was based on the analysis of growth accelerations by Hausmann, Pritchett, and Rodrik (2005). Formally, the authors identified a slowdown when three conditions were satisfied: (i) $g_{t,t-n} \geq 0.035$, (ii) $g_{t,t-n} - g_{t,t+n} \geq 0.02$ and (iii) $y_t > \$10,000$, where y_t is the GDP per capita in constant 2005 PPP$ in year t, while $g_{t,t-n}$ and $g_{t,t+n}$ are the average growth rate of the GDP per capita from year $t - n$ to t and the average growth rate of the GDP per capita from year t to $t + n$, respectively. In both Eichengreen, Park, and Shin (2012) and Eichengreen, Park, and Shin (2013), $n = 7$. Intuitively, the three conditions can be interpreted as follows. First, condition (i) requires the average growth rates of GDP per capita of an economy to be at least 3.5% or greater before the slowdown. Next, condition (ii) identifies slowdown episodes when the average growth rate of GDP per capita declines by at least 2% points, implying that the slowdown is non-negligible. Lastly, condition (iii) restricts identification of slowdown to those economies with GDP per capita that is larger than $10,000 (in 2005 PPP$) as the authors wanted to rule out crises in not yet successful developing economies.

4.3.3 Drivers of Growth and Determinants of Growth Slowdown

Table 4.4 lists potential drivers of growth and determinants of growth slowdown based on various existing literatures. The papers referred to in this table have empirically investigated the causes of growth slowdowns and key growth drivers of economies which might be income group-specific. Notable references include Aiyar *et al.* (2013), Eichengreen, Park, and Shin (2012), Flaaen, Ghani, and Mishra (2013), Bloom, Canning, and Sevilla (2003), Jalan and Ravallion (2002).

4.4 Methodological Approach

In this section, we discuss our methodology. Section 4.4.1 describes the method through which we obtain GRDP per capita in 1990 PPP$ data for the economies in our sample. Next, Section 4.4.2 discusses the set of thresholds used to divide economies into income groups. Section 4.4.3 then describes what constitutes an episode of growth slowdown. Section 4.4.4 discusses the income group-specific regression analysis that we use to identify factors associated with the occurrences of growth slowdown at each level of development. When studying economies in the upper-middle-income and high-income groups, we also employ the Bayesian Model Averaging (BMA) technique which is outlined in Section 4.4.5. Lastly, Section 4.4.6 presents the approach taken to obtain predictive probability for each economy on its likelihood of experiencing growth slowdown in the near future.

4.4.1 Obtaining Gross Regional Domestic Product per Capita in 1990 Purchasing Power Parity Dollars (PPP$)

GRDP per capita of all economies in our study is measured in 1990 PPP$. For the ASEAN economies, GRDP per capita in 1990 PPP$ is calculated by dividing GRDP in 1990 PPP$ data from the Total Economy Database, May 2015 version and Maddison (2010) to total population statistics reported by the World Bank. Meanwhile, GDRP per capita in 1990 PPP$ data for Hong Kong and Taiwan are obtained directly from the Total Economy Database.

However, data for the sub-national economies of mainland China, India, and Indonesia are only reported in their respective local currency units. There is no existing database which compiles GRDP per capita in 1990 PPP$ for sub-national economies. Furthermore, there is no readily available conversion factor for 1990 PPP$. Therefore, we take the following steps to obtain GRDP per capita data measured in 1990 PPP$ for the sub-national economies in mainland China, India, and Indonesia.

Table 4.4: List of Potential Drivers of Growth and Determinants of Growth Slowdown

No.	Variable	Definition and Explanation of the Variable	Authors Who Use the Variable
1	Size of Government index	This index measures the involvement of government in the economy. The index is made up of component indicators such as government investment and consumption spending, subsidies and transfers as a Percentage of GDP, top marginal income tax rate and government ownership of enterprises.	Aiyar *et al.* (2013)
2	Rule of Law index	The index is made up of indicators for judicial independence, military interference in the rule of law, contract enforcement, the protection of property rights and regulatory restrictions on the sale of real property.	Aiyar *et al.* (2013)
3	Freedom to Trade Internationally index	The index is constructed from measures of trade taxes, non-tariff barriers, black market exchange rates and international capital market controls.	Aiyar *et al.* (2013)
4	Regulation index	The index measures the extent of credit market regulations, labour regulations and business regulations.	Aiyar *et al.* (2013)
5	Chinn–Ito Index for financial openness	The index is based on binary dummy variables codifying the tabulation of restrictions on cross-border financial transactions.	Aiyar *et al.* (2013); Eichengreen, Park, and Shin (2012)
6	Total dependency ratio	Ratio of the number of old people (ages 65 and above) and young people (ages 15 and below) to the number of people of working age (ages between 15 and 64).	Aiyar *et al.* (2013); Eichengreen, Park, and Shin (2012)
7	Old dependency ratio	Ratio of the number of old people (ages 65 and above) to the number of people of working age (ages between 15 and 64).	Eichengreen, Park, and Shin (2012, 2013)
8	Young dependency ratio	Ratio of the number of young people (ages 15 and below) to the number of people of working age (ages between 15 and 64).	Eichengreen, Park, and Shin (2012, 2013)
9	Fertility rate	Average number of births per woman.	Aiyar *et al.* (2013); Eichengreen, Park, and Shin (2012)
10	Sex ratio	Ratio of total number of males in the population to the total number of females.	Aiyar *et al.* (2013)
11	Telephone lines per 100 people	Self-explanatory.	Aiyar *et al.* (2013)
12	Gigawatts of power generating capacity per 100 people	Self-explanatory.	Aiyar *et al.* (2013)

(Continued)

Table 4.4: ***(Continued)***

No.	Variable	Definition and Explanation of the Variable	Authors Who Use the Variable
13	Length of road network per 100 people	Self-explanatory.	Aiyar *et al.* (2013)
14	Gross Domestic Product (GDP) per capita	Self-explanatory.	Eichengreen, Park, and Shin (2012, 2013)
15	Pre-slowdown growth rate of GDP per capita	Growth rate of GDP per capita in the years preceding the slowdown.	Eichengreen, Park, and Shin (2012, 2013)
16	Openness to trade	Ratio of the sum of imports and exports to GDP.	Aiyar *et al.* (2013); Eichengreen, Park, and Shin (2012, 2013)
17	Terms of trade (TOT) shocks	Terms of trade is defined as the ratio of export price index to import price index. The specification of "shock" is based on the difference between the current value of the TOT and past values.	Aiyar *et al.* (2013); Eichengreen, Park, and Shin (2012, 2013)
18	Commodity price shocks	Shocks in world oil price and food price.	Aiyar *et al.* (2013)
19	Ratio of gross capital inflows to gross domestic product	Self-explanatory.	Aiyar *et al.* (2013)
20	Ratio of public debt to gross domestic product	Self-explanatory.	Aiyar *et al.* (2013)
21	Banking crisis dummy	A binary variable which identifies if the economy has experienced at least one banking crisis (=1 if yes, = 0 if no) in recent times.	Aiyar *et al.* (2013)
22	Financial crisis dummy	A binary variable which identifies if the economy has experienced at least one financial crisis, of any kind (banking crisis, currency crisis, etc.) in recent times; variable =1 if yes, = 0 if no.	Eichengreen, Park, and Shin (2012, 2013)
23	Inflation rate	Self-explanatory.	Aiyar *et al.* (2013); Eichengreen, Park, and Shin (2012, 2013)
24	Nominal exchange rate	Standard deviation of past nominal exchange rate over a certain past period (e.g. seven periods preceding the current one).	Eichengreen, Park, and Shin (2012, 2013)
25	Real exchange rate	Self-explanatory.	Aiyar *et al.* (2013); Eichengreen, Park, and Shin (2012, 2013)
26	Share of employment in manufacturing in total employment	Self-explanatory.	Eichengreen, Park, and Shin (2012)

(Continued)

Table 4.4: (*Continued*)

No.	Variable	Definition and Explanation of the Variable	Authors Who Use the Variable
27	Share of total value added from agriculture sector in gross domestic product	Self-explanatory.	Aiyar *et al.* (2013)
28	Share of total value added from services sector in gross domestic product	Self-explanatory.	Aiyar *et al.* (2013)
29	Government share in gross domestic product per capita	Self-explanatory.	Eichengreen, Park, and Shin (2012, 2013)
30	Investment share in gross domestic product per capita	Self-explanatory.	Eichengreen, Park, and Shin (2012, 2013)
31	Consumption share in gross domestic product per capita	Self-explanatory.	Eichengreen, Park, and Shin (2012, 2013)
32	Variables measuring the extent of diversification of the export basket	The extent of diversification is measured either by an index or the number of exports with revealed comparative advantage ratio (RCA)[30] ≥ 1.	Aiyar *et al.* (2013); Felipe (2012b)
33	Variables related to the sophistication of goods exports:		
	33.1 Share of high-tech exports in total manufactured exports	Definition of "high-tech exports" follows the World Bank. "High-tech exports" are products with high research and development intensity, such as aerospace, computers, pharmaceuticals, scientific instruments and electrical machinery.	Eichengreen, Park, and Shin (2013)

(*Continued*)

[30] Formally, the RCA ratio is given by:

$$RCA = \left(\frac{xval_{ci}}{\Sigma_i\, xval_{ci}}\right) \Big/ \left(\frac{\Sigma_c\, xval_{ci}}{\Sigma_i \Sigma_c\, xval_{ci}}\right)$$

where $xval_{ci}$ is the value of country c's export of product i. 30

Table 4.4: (*Continued*)

No.		Variable	Definition and Explanation of the Variable	Authors Who Use the Variable
	33.2	Index of sophistication of goods exports[31]	The index is proposed by Hausmann, Hwang, and Rodrik (2005). The index is a weighted average of the sophistication level of each good in the export basket. The sophistication level of the good, in turn, is determined based on the assumption that goods exported by rich country are sophisticated.	Flaaen, Ghani, and Mishra (2013); Felipe (2012b)
34	Variables related to the sophistication of service exports			
	34.1	Share of modern service exports in total service exports	"Modern services" are supposedly impersonal, hence less labour-intensive and therefore more productive. The authors pick out five among 11 service categories reported in the International Monetary Fund's Balance of Payments data to be modern services: communications, insurance, financial, computer and information and other business services.	Flaaen, Ghani, and Mishra (2013)
	34.2	Index of sophistication of service exports	An imitation of the index of sophistication of goods exports.	Flaaen, Ghani, and Mishra (2013)
35	Variables related to FDI:			
	35.1	Ratio of total foreign direct investment inflow to gross domestic product	Self-explanatory.	Zhang (2014)
	35.2	Foreign Direct Investment Regulatory Restrictiveness index	The index is constructed by the OECD, at the sectorial (e.g. manufacturing, tertiary) and sub-sectorial (e.g. business services, communication) levels for national economies. The higher the index value, the more restrictive to foreign direct investment the country is.	Flaaen, Ghani, and Mishra (2013)

(*Continued*)

[31] Formally, the export sophistication index for country c is given by:

$$index_c = \sum_i \frac{xval_{ci}}{\Sigma_i\, xval_{ci}} * \mathrm{PRODY}_i$$

where $xval_{ci}$ is the value of country c's export of product i, and

$$\mathrm{PRODY}_i = \sum_c \left[\left(\frac{xval_{ci}}{\Sigma_i\, xval_{ci}} \right) \Big/ \sum_c \left(\frac{xval_{ci}}{\Sigma_i\, xval_{ci}} \right) \right] * \mathrm{GDPPC}_c$$

with $GDPPC_c$ = gross domestic product per capita of country c.

Table 4.4: *(Continued)*

No.	Variable	Definition and Explanation of the Variable	Authors Who Use the Variable
36	Growth rate of real gross domestic product of the world	Self-explanatory.	Eichengreen, Park, and Shin (2013)
37	Gross domestic product weighted distance to other countries	Weighted sum of distance from the country in question to the rest in the sample. The weight is the percentage of the destination country in global GDP.	Aiyar *et al.* (2013)
38	Total amount of intra-regional trade (exports and imports to economies in the same region)	Self-explanatory.	Aiyar *et al.* (2013)
39	Variables related to the political conditions:		
	39.1 "Positive changes" — from authoritarian to more democratic	A binary variable which identifies if the country became more democratic in the preceding periods (= 1 if yes, = 0 if no). This is done by observing the change in the value of the Polity index, an index constructed by the Centre for Systemic Peace to measure the degree of authority of a political regime.	Eichengreen, Park, and Shin (2012, 2013)
	39.2 "Negative changes" — from democratic to more authoritarian	A binary variable which identifies if the country became more authoritarian in the preceding periods (= 1 if yes, = 0 if no). This is the counterpart to the "positive changes" variable.	Eichengreen, Park, and Shin (2012, 2013)
40	Wars and civil conflicts dummy	A binary variable which identifies if the country has experienced wars or civil conflicts in recent times (=1 if yes, = 0 if no).	Aiyar *et al.* (2013)
41	Natural disaster dummy	A binary variable which identifies if the country has experienced natural disaster in recent times (=1 if yes, = 0 if no).	Aiyar *et al.* (2013)
42	Fraction of country's land area in the tropic zone	Self-explanatory.	Aiyar *et al.* (2013)
43	Ethno-linguistic fractionalization index	Index measuring the probability of two random people in a country speaking different languages.	Aiyar *et al.* (2013)

(Continued)

Table 4.4: (*Continued*)

No.	Variable	Definition and Explanation of the Variable	Authors Who Use the Variable
44	Fraction of Buddhist population in total population	Self-explanatory.	Aiyar *et al.* (2013)
45	Spanish colony dummy	Variable = 1 if country was a Spanish colony in the past, = 0 if not.	Aiyar *et al.* (2013)
46	Variables related to the education level of the population:		
	46.1 Years of schooling	Average number of years of schooling for population aged 15 and above.	Eichengreen, Park, and Shin (2013)
	46.2 Years of schooling at secondary and higher level	Average number of years of schooling at secondary and higher levels for population aged 15 and above.	Eichengreen, Park, and Shin (2013)
47	Scientific journal articles per 10,000 people	Self-explanatory.	Zhang (2014)
48	Latitude	Absolute value of latitude of approximate centre of country.	Bloom, Canning, and Sevilla (2003)
49	Landlocked	Dummy variable = 1 for landlocked countries and = 0 for all others.	Bloom, Canning, and Sevilla (2003)
50	% Land coastal	Percentage of land within 100 km of coast.	Bloom, Canning, and Sevilla (2003)
51	Maximum temperature	Average maximum temperature of capital city in degrees centigrade.	Bloom, Canning, and Sevilla (2003)
52	Rainfall	Average annual rainfall in capital city in centimetres.	Bloom, Canning, and Sevilla (2003)
53	Homogeneity	Percentage of population in largest single group that shares the same ethnic, linguistic, and religious characteristics.	Bloom, Canning, and Sevilla (2003)
54	Proportion of villages that have a mountainous terrain	Self-explanatory.	Jalan and Ravallion (2002)
55	Cultivated area per 10,000 persons per km^2	Self-explanatory.	Jalan and Ravallion (2002)
56	Infant mortality rate	Infant mortality rate per 1,000 live births.	Jalan and Ravallion (2002)
57	Medical personnel per 10,000 persons	Self-explanatory.	Jalan and Ravallion (2002)
58	Proportion of population living in the urban areas	Self-explanatory.	Jalan and Ravallion (2002)

Source: Compiled by Asia Competitiveness Institute.

First, GRDP data in current prices of local currency are collected and divided by the corresponding population data. All data sources are listed in Section 4.5. The resultant nominal GRDP per capita in local currency is then converted to constant 1990 PPP$ by multiplying them with a year-specific conversion factor, which is calculated as follows:

$$\text{Conversion factor for Country } C \text{ in year } t = \frac{\text{Country } C\text{'s GDP per capita in 1990 PPP\$ in year } t}{\text{Country } C\text{'s GDP per capita in Current prices of local currency unit in year } t},$$

where country C can be either China, India, or Indonesia, depending on the sub-national economy concerned and year t spans between 1993 and 2013 which is the study period.

All sub-national economies of the same country, therefore, share a common conversion factor for each year. By doing so, we assume that the ratio of GRDP per capita expressed in 1990 PPP$ to that in the current prices of local currency unit for a sub-national economy is the same as that at country level. All data for national GDP per capita in 1990 PPP$ are retrieved from the Total Economy Database, May 2015 version while national GDP per capita in current prices of local currency units are collected from the World Bank World Development Indicator.

4.4.2 Classification of Income Thresholds

To classify the economies into different income groups, we adopt the classification criteria based on absolute level of GRDP per capita in 1990 PPP$ as proposed by Felipe (2012a). The classification thresholds are outlined in Table 4.5 and are held constant over time.

Felipe's (2012a) thresholds are ideal for our study for at least two reasons. Firstly, the income thresholds proposed are defined based on GDP per capita rather than the GNI per capita. Although the World Bank's income classification, measured in current GNI per capita, is the most widely used to divide economies into income groups, it cannot be applied directly to our work as most of the economies included in our study are sub-national economies for which GNI per capita data are not available. Secondly, income thresholds by Felipe are obtained through finding the closest threshold values defined in terms of GDP per capita (in 1990 PPP$) to those

Table 4.5: Income Thresholds Classification Adopted

Income Group	Classification Thresholds
Low-income	GRDP per capita < PPP$2,000
Lower-middle-income	PPP$2,000 ≤ GRDP per capita < PPP$7,250
Upper-middle-income	PPP$7,250 ≤ GRDP per capita < PPP$11,750
High-income	GRDP per capita ≥ PPP$11,750

Source: Asia Competitiveness Institute, based on Felipe (2012a).

of the World Bank. This ensures that each income category still retains the same underlying information as their World Bank's counterparts.

Due to data constraint whereby we have insufficient observations to run separate regression analyses for the upper-middle-income and high-income economies, we have merged economies from these two groups into a single category, namely the combined group of upper-middle-income and high-income economies, when investigating potential determinants that are associated with growth slowdowns.

4.4.3 Identification of Growth Slowdowns

Following Eichengreen, Park, and Shin (2012), which is based on the analysis of growth accelerations by Hausmann, Pritchett, and Rodrik (2005), we define an episode as a growth slowdown if growth has hitherto been fast but has slowed non-negligibly. Episodes of slowdown are isolated according to income groups because we suspect that determinants of growth slowdown at various stages of development may be different from each other. Other empirical works, such as Aiyar *et al.* (2013) and Bulman, Eden, and Nguyen (2014), offer evidence supporting this hypothesis.

Formally, a slowdown is identified when conditions (1) and (2) below are fulfilled along with one of the conditions (3), depending on whether the economy at time t is in the low-income group (i.e. condition (3a)), lower-middle-income group (i.e. condition (3b)), or combined group of upper-middle-income and high-income economies (i.e. condition (3c)). The three conditions are as follows:

$$g_{t,t-n} \geq 0.035 \tag{1}$$

$$g_{t,t-n} - g_{t,t}+_{n} \geq 0.02 \tag{2}$$

$$y_t < \text{PPP\$2,000} \tag{3a}$$

$$\text{PPP\$2,000} \leq y_t < \text{PPP\$7,250} \tag{3b}$$

$$y_t \geq \text{PPP\$7,250} \tag{3c}$$

where y_t is the GRDP per capita in 1990 PPP\$ in year t, while g_t,$t-n$ and g_t,$t+n$ are the least square growth rate of the GRDP per capita from year $t-n$ to t and the least square growth rate of the GRDP per capita from year t to $t+n$, respectively. Mathematically, $g_{t,t-n}$ takes the following form:

$$ln\ (y_{t-n+i}) = a + ln\ (1 + g_{t,t-n})*\ i \quad \text{where } i = 0, 1, ..., n$$

In this paper, we set $n = 5$. Due to the structures of conditions (1) and (2), this means that growth slowdown cannot be identified for the first and last 5 years of the study period. As our analysis covers the period 1993–2013, slowdown episodes between 1998 and 2008 are identified.

The intuitive interpretations of the conditions are as follows. First, condition (1) requires that the least square growth rate of GRDP per capita of an economy to be at least 3.5% or greater before the slowdown. Economies satisfying this condition are those with high initial growth rates. Next, condition (2) identifies slowdown episodes when the least square growth rate of GRDP per capita declines by at least two percent, implying that the slowdown is non-negligible. Lastly, conditions (3a), (3b) and (3c) separate the occurrences of slowdown by their income groups. For instance, if GRDP per capita for an economy satisfies conditions (1), (2) and (3a), the economy is said to have experienced growth slowdown as a low-income economy. On the other hand, if another economy's GRDP per capita satisfies conditions (1), (2) and (3b) instead, that economy is deemed to undergo growth slowdown as a lower-middle-income economy.

In any particular year *t*, we assign the value 1 to economies for which a slowdown episode is identified. Economies which belong to the same income group but do not experience slowdown are coded as 0. In this way, we create income group-specific dummy variables representing the occurrence (or lack thereof) of growth slowdown. These dummies will serve as the dependent variables in the regression analysis.

Generally, economies in our sample do not stay within a single income group over the entire study period. As a result, the slowdown dummies generated for an economy over the years may be treated as observations for analyses of different income groups. For example, during the period 1993–2002, Thailand was a lower-middle-income economy. It subsequently graduated to the upper-middle-income group in 2003 and continued to stay in that group until the end of the study period. In this case, the slowdown dummies generated using data between 1993 and 2002 contribute to the analysis of growth slowdown in the lower-middle-income group while those generated using data from 2003 onwards are part of the analysis for the combined group of upper-middle-income and high-income economies.

Figure 4.3 shows the frequency of growth slowdown in each income group in the sample as identified by our approach. As the economies move across the income groups from low-income to lower-middle-income to upper-middle-income and lastly high-income group, the frequency of slowdown increases.

4.4.4 Regression Analysis on Determinants of Growth Slowdown

Having identified growth slowdown episodes, we now turn to studying their determinants. We specify income group-specific logistic regression models using the slowdown dummy created as the dependent variable to examine the impact of various determinants on the probability of an economy experiencing growth slowdown. We are guided by economic theories when picking potential independent variables. In other words, we specify three models of growth slowdown: one for the low-income economies, another for the lower-middle-income economies and a third for the combined group of upper-middle-income and high-income economies. Regressors in our model include GRDP per capita (in 1990 PPP$) as well as measures for demographic, infrastructure, human capital, macroeconomic conditions, and exogenous factors. As robustness check, we have also performed probit regressions on the same set of determinants as those by logistic models.

Figure 4.3: Frequency of Growth Slowdown in Each Income Group for ASEAN, Greater China, India, and Indonesia Economies

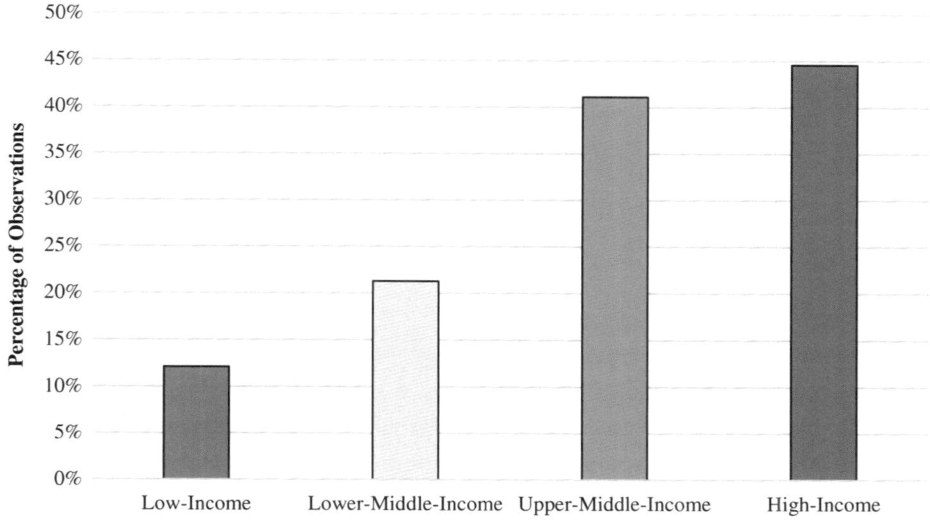

Note: Frequency of growth slowdown in each income group is calculated by dividing the number of slowdown occurrences by the total number of observations in that particular income group.
Source: Asia Competitiveness Institute.

When conducting the regressions, we also pool all the observations of the same income group from economies in ASEAN, Greater China, India, and Indonesia together. Although the regional traits are omitted as a result, this approach provides substantially more observations for each income group. Consequently, more precise estimates tend to be produced coupled with better probability predictive power of the regressions. Combining observations for economies from different geographical regions when running regressions to identify determinants of growth slowdowns is a common approach in the literature. For instance, Aiyar *et al.* (2013) used annual data of 138 countries and segregated them according to income groups when performing separate regressions. Meanwhile, Eichengreen, Park, and Shin (2012) estimated a single regression using annual data of countries with GDP per capita that are greater than $10,000 in 2005 PPP$.

Since a relatively large number of potential regressors are examined in our study, model uncertainty is one major problem that we have to contend with. In an attempt to tackle this issue, we employ the Bayesian Model Averaging (BMA) technique which is discussed in Section 4.4.5.

4.4.5 Bayesian Model Averaging as Robustness Check

The BMA technique is mainly employed to solve the "open-endedness of theories" problem. This is a fundamental challenge with growth regressions, in particular, when determining which variables to be included in the analysis (Brock and Durlauf, 2001). Open-endedness means that with the validation of one economic theory or model of growth, it does not simply imply that the others are false. BMA offers an alternative by considering all possible combinations of variables and assigns each combination a posterior model probability of being the "true" model based on Bayesian inference (Benkovskis *et al.*, 2015). BMA techniques will not generate a "best model". Instead, it generates a posterior inclusion probability (PIP) attached to each variable which can be interpreted as the probability of that variable belonging to the true empirical model. In other words, variables with high PIPs are considered robust determinants of growth slowdown (González-Aguado and Moral-Benito, 2013).

We mainly refer to the work by González-Aguado and Moral-Benito (2013) to develop the theoretical foundation for performing BMA techniques. In particular, the following equation shows a generic form of an empirical model:

$$\Psi = \theta X + \varepsilon$$

where Ψ is the dependent variable which in our case is the slowdown dummy, X represents a set of independent variables, θ is the vector of parameters, and ε is the error term. Suppose we have K possible independent variables to be selected. In this case, there will be 2^K different potential models which seek to explain the data, y, or 2^K different choices of X, indexed by $j = 1, 2, \ldots, 2^K$.

Next, we specify a prior mean model size $\bar{k}$ excluding the dependent variable. This is the prior belief of the right model size before seeing the data. In our case, we set $\bar{k}$ =3. Each variable then has a prior inclusion probability $\bar{k}/K$, and for a model, M_j, with m variables ($0 \leq m \leq K$), its prior model probability is calculated as follows:

$$p(M_j) = \left(\frac{\bar{k}}{K}\right)^m \left(1 - \frac{\bar{k}}{K}\right)^{K-m}$$

By Bayes' Rule, we can calculate the posterior model probability as follows:

$$p(M_j \mid \mathrm{y}) = \frac{f(y \mid M_j) p(M_j)}{f(y)}$$

Here, $f(y|M_j)$ is usually called the marginal likelihood. It can be calculated using the following equation:

$$g(\theta^j \mid y, M_i) = \frac{f(y \mid \theta^j, M_j) g(\theta^j \mid M_j)}{f(y \mid M_j)}$$

where θ^j is the parameter set for the model M_j. If we integrate both sides of the equation above with respect to θ^j and use the fact that $\int g(\theta^j|y, M_j)\, \mathrm{d}\, \theta^j = 1$ since g is a probability density function, we can obtain the following equation:

$$f(y \mid M_j) = \int f(y \mid \theta^j, M_j) g(\theta^j \mid M_j) d\theta^j$$

Moreover, considering θ is a function of θ^j over $j = 1, \ldots, 2^K$, then the posterior density of the parameters for all the models is as follows:

$$g(\theta \mid y) = \sum_{j=1}^{2^K} P(M_j \mid y) g(\theta \mid y, M_j)$$

By taking expectations on both sides, we obtain the estimation of the parameters,

$$E(\theta \mid y) = \sum_{j=1}^{2^K} P(M_j \mid y) E(\theta \mid y, M_j)$$

and the posterior variance is as follows:

$$var(\theta \mid y) = \sum_{j=1}^{2^K} P(M_j \mid y) var(\theta \mid y, M_j) + \sum_{j=1}^{2^K} P(M_j \mid y)(E(\theta \mid y, M_j) - E(\theta \mid y))^2$$

Lastly, we can compute the posterior inclusion probability, or robustness, of each variable x by

$$\text{posterior inclusion probability} = P(\theta_x \neq 0 \mid y) = \sum_{\theta_h \neq 0} P(M_j \mid y)$$

Following Benkovskis *et al.* (2015), we identify variables as robust if two criteria are met. First, the posterior inclusion probability (PIP) should exceed the prior inclusion probability. For example, if the total number of variables considered is $K = 17$ and the prior mean model size is $\bar{k} = 3$, the prior inclusion probability $\bar{k}/K = 3/17$. So, in order for a variable to be deemed as robust determinant of growth slowdown, its posterior inclusion probability should be at least 3/17. Second, the ratio of conditional posterior mean to conditional posterior standard deviation is larger than 1.65 in absolute value, which corresponds to a 90% coverage interval under Gaussian posterior parameter distribution. The mathematical representation is as follows:

$$\left| \frac{E(\theta \mid y)}{\sqrt{var(\theta \mid y)}} \right| > 1.65$$

The two criteria need to be simultaneously satisfied for a variable to be considered robust.

In our study, we apply BMA techniques to the combined group of the upper-middle-income and high-income economies after logistic and probit estimations are conducted. The issue of model uncertainty is most acute in this case as growth slowdown in high-income economies is relatively unexplored in the literature. The BMA results are presented in Section 4.6.2.[32]

---

[32]The Asia Competitiveness Institute expresses heartfelt gratitude to Dr Carlos Gonzalez-Aguado and Dr Enrique Moral-Benito for sharing their BMA programme.

4.4.6 Obtaining Predictive Probability of an Economy Falling into a Slowdown

Based on the income group-specific models which link the probability of growth slowdown with the various determinants, we can compute the predictive probability of a particular economy experiencing growth slowdown in the near future by applying the relevant estimated logistic regression coefficients to the latest available data for that economy. This exercise enables us to identify high-risk economies which may require urgent policy intervention to help avert the prospect of slowing down. Since we set $n = 5$, the predictive probability of growth slowdown generated covers the next five-year period starting from the year which the data represents.

Formally, suppose the logistic regression model for a particular income group includes the variables X_1, X_2, X_3, and X_4 with their respective coefficient estimates being $\widehat{\beta_1}, \widehat{\beta_2}, \widehat{\beta_3}$, and $\widehat{\beta_4}$ and the constant is estimated to be $\widehat{\beta_0}$. If the values of the four variables for an economy in that income group in year t are x_1, x_2, x_3, and x_4, the probability p of this economy experiencing growth slowdown during the period from year t to year $t + 5$ is given by:

$$p = \frac{\delta}{1+\delta}$$

where

$$\delta = \exp(\widehat{\beta_0} - \widehat{\beta_1}x_1 + \widehat{\beta_2}x_2 + \widehat{\beta_3}x_3 + \widehat{\beta_4}x_4)$$

Since δ is positive, p is strictly between 0 and 1. As the latest year with available data for all determinants in the logistic models is 2012, we are able to generate predictive probabilities reflecting the likelihood of growth slowdown during the 2012–2017 period. Economies with higher probabilities face greater risks of growth slowdown over these years.

The interpretation of a low probability number is less straightforward. Low predictive probability does not necessarily imply a bright prospect for the economy. For a slowdown to be defined in our methodological framework, we first require the least square growth rate of GDP per capita (in 1990 PPP$) to be at least 3.5% in the 5 years preceding the slowdown period (condition 1 presented in Section 4.4.3). Thus, low predictive probability may reflect either of the two following scenarios: the economy is indeed a fast growing economy which is likely to sustain its growth momentums or the economy's growth rate is low to begin with and is therefore not identified as experiencing slowdown by definition. In other words, it is possible that economies with low predictive probability suffer from stagnation, which is beyond the scope of this paper.

4.5 Data Description, Statistical Computation, and Sources

Our dataset covers 107 economies, containing nine ASEAN countries, 33 Greater China economies, 32 sub-national economies of India, and 33 sub-national economies of Indonesia[33], which

[33]The nine ASEAN economies included in our study are Cambodia, Indonesia, Laos, Malaysia, Myanmar, Philippines, Singapore, Thailand, and Vietnam (Brunei data are unavailable). The 33 Greater China economies covered in our study are the 31 mainland China provinces, Hong Kong and Taiwan (Macau data are unavailable). The 32 sub-national

spans the 1993–2013 period[34]. Following the methods outlined in Sections 4.4.1–4.4.3, we generate the growth slowdown dummy using data on GRDP and population. Various potential determinants of growth slowdown, such as demographic, infrastructure, human capital, macro-economic conditions, and exogenous factors, are also collected for each economy as the independent variables. Regression analysis is then conducted based on the independent and dependent variables collected in order to identify potential determinants of growth slowdowns for economies in each income group. Annual data are used in this study.

As mentioned in the previous sections, our analysis is conducted based on GRDP per capita data denoted in 1990 PPP$. For ASEAN economies, which include Cambodia, Indonesia, Laos, Malaysia, Myanmar, Philippines, Singapore, Thailand, and Vietnam, we are able to collect the data on GRDP in 1990 PPP$ directly from the Total Economy Database, May 2015 version.[35] GRDP per capita in 1990 PPP$ is therefore obtained by dividing the GRDP (in 1990 PPP$) for each economy in each year with the corresponding total population number for the year. We use the population statistics published in the World Bank World Development Indicator.

For Hong Kong and Taiwan, we collect GRDP per capita in 1990 PPP$ directly from the Total Economy Database, May 2015 version. As for the 31 mainland China economies, we first collect nominal GRDP in yuan and then divide the GRDP data by the total population in order to obtain each economy's nominal GRDP per capita in yuan. The nominal GRDP data (in yuan) are collected from various provincial statistical yearbooks and from the website of the National Bureau of Statistics of China, while the population data are from the China Population & Employment Statistics Yearbook 2013, the China Statistical Yearbook 2014 and from the website of the National Bureau of Statistics of China. GRDP per capita in 1990 PPP$ is then calculated using the method described in Section 4.4.1.

Likewise, for the sub-national economies of India, we first collect nominal GRDP in current rupees and then divide the data by the total population to obtain each economy's nominal GRDP per capita (in rupee). The nominal GRDP data (in rupees) for the economies in India are retrieved from the website of the Ministry of Statistics and Programme Implementation (MOSPI), Central Statistics Office, while the population data in census years (1991, 2001, and 2011) are collected from the Census of India. Population data for all other years during the 1993–2013 period are estimated based on census data. The conversion of nominal GRDP per capita data in rupees to that in 1990 PPP$ follows the procedure outlined in Section 4.4.1.

For the sub-national economies of Indonesia, the GRDP per capita in 1990 PPP$ data is prepared in a similar way as that for the 31 mainland China economies and the sub-national

---

economies of India included in our study are all the states and union territories of India excluding Dadra & Nagar Haveli, Daman & Diu, and Lakshadweep. Andhra Pradesh and Telangana are treated as a single economy using the name Andhra Pradesh. The 33 sub-national economies of Indonesia refer to all the provinces of Indonesia. North Kalimantan and East Kalimantan are treated as a single economy using the name East Kalimantan.

[34] Unlike the rest of the economies, data for Laos are available from 1993 to 2008 only.

[35] All GRDP data for the economies listed above are obtained from the Total Economy Database, May 2015 version (The Conference Board 2015) except for Laos, which are unavailable in the database and are therefore retrieved from the Maddison (2010).

economies of India. The nominal GRDP data (in rupiahs) are collected from the World Bank Indo-Dapoer and PDRB Menurut Penggunaan while the population data are from the World Bank Indo-Dapoer. For the seven new Indonesian provinces created after 1993, namely North Maluku, West Papua, Banten, Bangka Belitung Islands, Gorontalo, Riau Islands and West Sulawesi, we have backtracked their GRDP and population data until 1990.[36] We first calculate the ratios of the data between the newly created province and the province from which it was formed and then fit an exponential trend on the ratios. The GRDP and population data between 1993 and the year of bifurcation are then estimated based on the fitted exponential trend.

Our study examines different potential determinants of growth slowdowns for economies in the context of different income groups, ranging from dependency ratios, openness to trade, exchange rates, world's GDP growth rate, employment structure, literacy rate, economic structure, productivity, infrastructure, and government consumption expenditure. Ideally, many other explanatory variables should be considered as reviewed in Section 4.3.3. However, working on sub-national economies in Greater China, India, and Indonesia and the countries of ASEAN over the span of two decades demands consistency in the definition of indicators, which implies inevitable data gaps. We have also included some other potential determinants of growth slowdown which are important but not used in the existing works, including productivity measures of the primary, secondary, and tertiary industries. Table 4.6 summarises the list of potential independent variables we consider, with details on the units and sources of data for economies in the various regions.

For certain independent variables which have a few years of missing data and display a clear linear trend, we employ linear interpolation or extrapolation to fill in the missing data. In the case whereby all the economies of the same region do not have data for the earlier years of the study period, we conduct estimation based on the exponential trend of available data.

In our dataset, there are a few sub-national economies which are created during the study period. For mainland China, Chongqing was separated from Sichuan on 14th March 1997. We obtain backdated Chongqing's data for the 1993–1997 period from the National Bureau of Statistics of China and the Chongqing Municipal Statistics Bureau. For the case of India, three bifurcations occurred during the study period: Chhattisgarh was separated from Madhya Pradesh on 1 November 2000, Uttarakhand (formerly known as Uttaranchal) was created from Uttar Pradesh on 9 November 2000, and Jharkhand was carved out of Bihar on 15 November 2000. Data for these three newly created economies are missing before 2000 for a few independent variables. For these missing data, we first calculate the ratios of the data between the newly created economy and the economy from which it was formed, and then fit an exponential trend on the ratios. Data between 1993 and 2000 are then estimated based on the fitted exponential trend.

[36]North Maluku was created out of Maluku on 4 October 1999; West Papua was created out of Papua on 4 October 1999; Banten was created out of West Java on 17 October 2000; Bangka Belitung Islands was created out of South Sumatra on 4 December 2000; Gorontalo was created out of North Sulawesi on 22 December 2000; Riau Islands was created out of Riau on 25 October 2002; and West Sulawesi was created out of South Sulawesi on 5 October 2004, based on official Indonesian laws.

Table 4.6: Unit and Data Sources for Independent Variables

No.	Independent Variables	Unit	Data Sources: ASEAN	Data Sources: Greater China	Data Sources: India	Data Sources: Indonesia
1	Total Dependency Ratio	Percentage	• Abbas *et al.* (2010) • Barro and Lee (2013) • Bluedorn *et al.* (2013) • Centre for Research on the Epidemiology of Disaster, The International Disaster Database • Euromonitor International, Global Market Information Database • Fraser Institute, Economic Freedom of the World database • International Labour Organisation, Key Indicators of the Labour Market, 8th Edition • International Monetary Fund, World Economic Outlook Database, April 2015 • Maddison (2010)	• Almanac of China's Population • China Compendium of Statistics 1949–2008 • China Energy Statistical Yearbook • China Population & Employment Statistical Yearbook • China Statistical Yearbook • China Statistical Yearbook on Science and Technology • Global Market Information Database (GMID) • Hong Kong Annual Digest • Provincial Statistical Yearbook • Statistical Yearbook of the Chinese Investment in Fixed Assets • Taiwan Statistical Yearbook • Taiwan Statistical Data Book	• CEIC Database • Census of India: 1991, 2001 and 2011 • Centre for Monitoring Indian Economy Pvt. Ltd (CMIE): States of India database • Indiastat • Ministry of Statistics and Programme Implementation (MOSPI), Central Statistics Office • Ministry of Statistics and Programme Implementation (MOSPI), National Sample Survey Office • The Conference Board, Total Economy Database, May 2015 version	• CEIC Database • Indikator Kesejahteraan Rakyat • Investment Coordinating Board (BKPM) • Keuangan Pemerintah Provinsi • PDRB Menurut Penggunaan • PDRB Provinsi Menurut Lapangan Usaha • Proyeksi Penduduk Indonesia • Statistik Indonesia • Statistik Kesejahteraan Rakyat • Statistik Keuangan Pemerintah Provinsi • Statistik Perhubungan • Statistik Perhubungan • Statistik Transportasi
2	Old Dependency Ratio	Percentage				
3	Young Dependency Ratio	Percentage				
4	Openness To Trade	Percentage of GRDP				
5	Percentage Change in Nominal Exchange Rate	Percentage				
6	World Gross Domestic Product Real Growth Rate	Percentage				
7	Foreign Direct Investment Inflows as Percentage of GRDP	Percentage of GRDP				
8	Employment in Primary Industry as Percentage of Total Employment	Percentage of Total Employment				
9	Employment in Secondary Industry as Percentage of Total Employment	Percentage of Total Employment				
10	Employment in Tertiary Industry as Percentage of Total Employment	Percentage of Total Employment				
11	Literacy Rate	Percentage				
12	Overall Productivity	Constant 1990 PPP$				
13	Primary Industry Value added per Worker	Constant 1990 PPP$				
14	Secondary Industry Value added per Worker	Constant 1990 PPP$				

(*Continued*)

Table 4.6: (*Continued*)

No.	Independent Variables	Unit	Data Sources: ASEAN	Data Sources: Greater China	Data Sources: India	Data Sources: Indonesia
15	Tertiary Industry Value added per Worker	Constant 1990 PPP$	• The Conference Board, Total Economy Database, May 2015 version • United Nations Conference on Trade and Development • World Bank World Development Indicators	• The Conference Board, Total Economy Database, May 2015 version • World Bank World Development Indicators	• World Bank World Development Indicators	• The Conference Board, Total Economy Database, May 2015 version • World Bank Indo-Dapoer • World Bank World Development Indicators
16	Length of Road	Kilometre				
17	Road Density	Kilometre per Square Kilometre				
18	Length of Road per Capita	Kilometer per 10000 People				
19	Primary Industry Value added as Percentage of GRDP	Percentage of GRDP				
20	Secondary Industry Value added as Percentage of GRDP	Percentage of GRDP				
21	Tertiary Industry Value added as Percentage of GRDP	Percentage of GRDP				
22	Government Consumption Expenditure as Percentage of GRDP	Percentage of GRDP				

Source: Asia Competitiveness Institute.

For the case of Indonesia whereby seven economies were created during our study period, we employ the same technique to estimate missing data.

4.6 Empirical Findings

4.6.1 Determinants of Growth Slowdown by Income Thresholds

Table 4.7 summarises our research findings on determinants that are strongly associated with growth slowdown in the low-income group, lower-middle-income group and combined group of upper-middle-income and high-income economies. These results are generated by employing logistic regression model. In all three models, we employ GRDP per capita (in 1990 PPP$) as a control variable to guard against omitted variable bias.

As illustrated in Table 4.7, growth slowdown in low-income group is mainly associated with the level of GRDP per capita, Literacy Rate, Foreign Direct Investment Inflows as Percentage of GRDP and Length of Road per capita, with the first two determinants being significant at the 5% level while the last two at 10% level.

On the other hand, growth slowdown in the lower-middle-income group is associated with the level of GRDP per capita, Foreign Direct Investment Inflows as Percentage of GRDP, Old Dependency Ratio, Employment in Tertiary Industry as Percentage of Total Employment, and Literacy Rate with the first three determinants being significant at 1% level, Employment in Tertiary Industry as Percentage of Total Employment at 5% level, and Literacy Rate at 10% level.

Meanwhile, growth slowdown in the combined group of upper-middle-income and high-income economies is associated with GRDP per capita, Openness To Trade, Literacy Rate, Employment in Tertiary Industry as Percentage of Total Employment and Secondary Industry Value added per Worker, with the first two determinants being significant at 1% level while the last three determinants are significant at 5% level.

The next few paragraphs discuss each determinant in the three models, with the exception of the control variable GRDP per capita, in further detail. It is worth noting that some determinants are associated with the occurrence of growth slowdown in more than one income group.

Literacy Rate appears as a significant variable in growth slowdown models for all three income groups. The signs of the coefficients are consistently negative, indicating that literacy is negatively associated with the probability of slowdown in all income groups. Basic literacy is the prerequisite for further educational attainment, and it facilitates and enables learning throughout a person's lifecycle after becoming literate. Thus, high literacy rate is necessary for an economy to achieve a high degree of human capital accumulation which is important for sustaining growth.

Foreign Direct Investment Inflows as Percentage of GRDP is a significant variable in the slowdown model for the low-income and lower-middle-income economies. The signs of the coefficients in both models are negative, indicating an inverse relation between foreign direct investment inflows and the probability of slowdown for economies in the low- and

Table 4.7: Determinants of Growth Slowdown for the Low-income Group, Lower-middle-income Group and the Combined Group of Upper-middle-income and High-income Economies, Logistic Model

	Growth Slowdown Models		
Income Groups	**Low-income**	**Lower-middle-income**	**Combined Group of Upper-middle-income and High-income Economies**
GRDP per capita	0.0013**	0.0005***	0.0003***
	(0.0005)	(0.0001)	(0.0001)
Literacy Rate	–0.0304**	–0.0197*	–0.1481**
	(0.0133)	(0.0114)	(0.0597)
Foreign Direct Investment Inflows as Percentage of GRDP	–0.5082*	–0.1935***	
	(0.2629)	(0.0523)	
Length of Road per capita	–0.0126*		
	(0.0072)		
Employment in Tertiary Industry as Percentage of Total Employment		–0.0287**	–0.0426**
		(0.0115)	(0.0172)
Old Dependency Ratio		0.0750***	
		(0.0287)	
Openness to Trade			–0.0091***
			(0.0030)
Secondary Industry Value added per Worker			–0.00002**
			($7.89e^{-6}$)
Constant	–1.0075	–0.9246	14.5001***
	(1.0799)	(1.0452)	(5.5816)
No. of observations	358	667	147
Pseudo R^2	0.0680	0.0876	0.1215

Note: Numbers in the parentheses are standard errors. *, ** and *** denote the coefficient is significant at 10% level, 5% level and 1% level, respectively.
Source: Asia Competitiveness Institute.

lower-middle-income groups. The result is intuitive. The influx of capital through foreign direct investment increases capital accumulation in the host economy. More importantly, foreign direct investment promotes technological development through technological transfer and diffusion. It may also help to augment managerial expertise in the host economy. Thus, foreign direct investment is an important driver of continued growth in low- and lower-middle-income economies, as growth in these economies is usually hampered by capital inadequacies and technological backwardness.

Length of Road per capita appears as a significant determinant of growth slowdown for the low-income group. The negative sign of the coefficient points to an inverse relation between road per capita and the probability of low-income economies experiencing growth slowdown. This result suggests that basic infrastructure development is important for low-income economies to sustain growth. Improving road networks and transport infrastructure in general grants producers in low-income economies access to new markets. At the same time, it also connects firms from more developed regions to labour in low-income economies, thus creating more opportunities for growth.

Employment in Tertiary Industry as Percentage of Total Employment is a significant variable in the slowdown models for lower-middle-income economies as well as the upper-middle- and high-income economies. The sign of the coefficients is consistently negative, indicating an inverse relation between employment in tertiary industry and the probability of slowdown for these economies. As an economy progresses, it becomes increasingly hard to sustain growth through exporting manufacturing products. This is because the economy slowly loses its cost advantage to less developed competitors. Thus, it is important for more advanced economies to diversify into the tertiary sector so that they can move up the value chain and create more opportunities for sustainable growth. Furthermore, certain high value-added industries such as research and development, financial services and consultancy services also help to boost the potentials, productivity and performance of other sectors and industries of the economy.

Old Age Dependency Ratio is positively associated with the probability of growth slowdown for lower-middle-income economies. A high old dependency ratio means that the labour force has to support a higher number of elderlies. With fewer people of working age, the pool of productive labour shrinks. Furthermore, a smaller working-age population also means less domestic resources for productive investments as this group tends to save while the older population tends to dissave. Economies with high old dependency ratio are thus more prone to slowdowns.

Openness to Trade is negatively associated with the probability of slowdown for the upper-middle-income and high-income economies. Having access to foreign markets provides the economy with more opportunities for growth. Trade with multiple international partners might also help diversify the demand risks from sole reliance on domestic market demand to a mix between domestic and external consumers. Furthermore, the exposure to global competition provides the impetus for domestic economic restructuring and other reform initiatives to address existing weaknesses and inefficiencies in the domestic economy which may otherwise hamper growth.

Finally, Secondary Industry Value added per Worker is negatively associated with the probability of slowdown for upper-middle-income and high-income economies. The result underscores the importance of improving productivity for continued growth in upper-middle-income and high-income economies. As an economy matures, it becomes increasingly difficult to grow by expanding industrial production as idle or underemployed factors of production become scarcer. Thus, productivity enhancement is necessary for sustaining growth; economies with lower productivity are more prone to slowdown.

As a robustness check, we have also performed probit regressions using the same set of determinants as shown in Table 4.7 for the three income groups. The results are included in Appendix 4. In short, these two sets of results are similar to each other.

4.6.2 Bayesian Model Averaging Results

In this section, we present three sets of BMA results for the combined group of upper-middle-income and high-income economies. This is because among the list of possible determinants for growth slowdown considered in our study (see Table 4.6), we have variables related to the employment structure of the primary, secondary, and tertiary industries, the contribution of each sector to the economy's GRDP as well as value added per worker for each sector. Considering these three types of data are highly correlated, they may pose multicollinearity problem in a single BMA estimation.

We have therefore conducted three rounds of BMA estimations for the combined group of upper-middle-income and high-income economies. For the first round of BMA estimation, we include only variables related to employment structure and value added per worker while leaving out variables on economic structure. All the other potential determinants such as dependency ratios, openness to trade, exchange rates, etc. still remain in our BMA estimation. The second round of BMA estimation is similar to that of the first with the only difference being that variables related to economic structure are used in place of those on value added per worker. As for the third round of BMA estimation, economic structure-related variables and value added per worker variables are used while employment structure-related variables are omitted. The results for these three rounds of BMA estimations are thus labelled as Result (I), Result (II) and Result (III) respectively in Tables 4.8–4.10.

Common to these three results, GRDP per capita, Overall Productivity, Employment in Tertiary Industry as Percentage of Total Employment, Road Density, Tertiary Industry Value added per Worker and Government Consumption Expenditure as Percentage of GRDP are regarded as robust determinants of growth slowdown. Moreover, Secondary Industry Value added per Worker is considered a robust determinant in Results (I) (see Table 4.8). Note that three robust determinants identified through this BMA exercise are also in our logistic model for growth slowdown in the combined group of upper-middle-income and high-income economies, namely GRDP per capita, Employment in Tertiary Industry as Percentage of Total Employment, and Secondary Industry Value added per Worker.

Table 4.8: BMA Result (I) for the Combined Group of Upper-middle-income and High-income Economies

Determinants	Posterior Inclusion Probability (PIP)	Posterior Mean	Posterior Standard Deviation (PSTD)	Posterior Mean / PSTD
GRDP per Capita	0.99999	0.00064	0.00015	4.12338
Total Dependency Ratio	0.09732	–0.05030	0.02734	1.83994
Openness to Trade	0.06949	–0.00504	0.00337	1.49807
Percentage Change in Nominal Exchange Rate	0.04596	–0.02867	0.02289	1.25274
World Gross Domestic Product Real Growth Rate	0.04583	0.20967	0.15319	1.36868
Foreign Direct Investment Inflows as Percentage of GRDP	0.02444	0.01589	0.03105	0.51174
Employment in Secondary Industry as Percentage of Total Employment	0.03662	0.02284	0.02063	1.10711
Employment in Tertiary Industry as Percentage of Total Employment	1.00000	–0.15190	0.03097	4.90544
Literacy Rate	0.03494	0.06195	0.06056	1.02297
Overall Productivity	0.21863	–0.00009	0.00004	2.35135

(Continued)

Table 4.8: *(Continued)*

Determinants	**Posterior Inclusion Probability (PIP)**	**Posterior Mean**	**Posterior Standard Deviation (PSTD)**	**Posterior Mean / PSTD**
Primary Industry Value added per Worker	0.07917	–0.00004	0.00002	1.71429
Secondary Industry Value added per Worker	0.18367	–0.00002	0.00001	2.00000
Tertiary Industry Value added per Worker	0.99996	–0.00015	0.00003	4.38235
Road Density	1.00000	0.72957	0.13929	5.23795
Length of Road per Capita	0.02424	–0.00521	0.01203	0.43301
Government Consumption Expenditure as Percentage of GRDP	0.99996	0.41966	0.08587	4.88716
Old Dependency Ratio	0.02482	0.04029	0.05927	0.67980

Note: Cells highlighted in grey are considered robust determinants for growth slowdown in the combined group of upper-middle-income and high-income economies as they satisfy the two criteria simultaneously: (i) The posterior inclusion probability (PIP) exceeds the prior inclusion probability (i.e. $\frac{3}{17}$ = 0.17647) and (ii) The ratio of conditional posterior mean to conditional posterior standard deviation is larger than 1.65 in absolute value, which corresponds to a 90% coverage interval under Gaussian posterior parameter distribution.
Source: Asia Competitiveness Institute.

Table 4.9: BMA Result (II) for the Combined Group of Upper-middle-income and High-income Economies

Determinants	**Posterior Inclusion Probability (PIP)**	**Posterior Mean**	**Posterior Standard Deviation (PSTD)**	**Posterior Mean / PSTD**
GRDP per Capita	0.99998	0.00078	0.00014	5.63309
Total Dependency Ratio	0.05467	–0.04782	0.03672	1.30227
Openness to Trade	0.02569	–0.00181	0.00230	0.78472
Percentage Change in Nominal Exchange Rate	0.16702	–0.01240	0.00726	1.70756
World Gross Domestic Product Real Growth Rate	0.04764	0.19307	0.14079	1.37131
Foreign Direct Investment Inflows as Percentage of GRDP	0.03552	–0.02699	0.02568	1.05081
Employment in Secondary Industry as Percentage of Total Employment	0.02115	–0.00380	0.02091	0.18150
Employment in Tertiary Industry as Percentage of Total Employment	0.20822	–0.05732	0.02624	2.18438
Literacy Rate	0.02056	–0.00564	0.06622	0.08515
Overall Productivity	0.99953	–0.00024	0.00005	5.22222
Road Density	1.00000	0.55152	0.10345	5.33114
Length of Road per Capita	0.02133	–0.00254	0.01219	0.20866
Secondary Industry Value added as Percentage of GRDP	0.06572	–0.02682	0.01872	1.43279
Tertiary Industry Value added as Percentage of GRDP	0.99937	–0.10876	0.02273	4.78558

(Continued)

Table 4.9: *(Continued)*

Determinants	Posterior Inclusion Probability (PIP)	Posterior Mean	Posterior Standard Deviation (PSTD)	Posterior Mean / PSTD
Government Consumption Expenditure as Percentage of GRDP	0.99939	0.37034	0.07734	4.78842
Old Dependency Ratio	0.02357	0.03587	0.05495	0.65280

Note: Cells highlighted in grey are considered robust determinants for growth slowdown in the combined group of upper-middle-income and high-income economies as they satisfy the two criteria simultaneously: (i) The posterior inclusion probability (PIP) exceeds the prior inclusion probability (i.e. $\frac{3}{16}$ = 0.18750) and (ii) The ratio of conditional posterior mean to conditional posterior standard deviation is larger than 1.65 in absolute value, which corresponds to a 90% coverage interval under Gaussian posterior parameter distribution.
Source: Asia Competitiveness Institute.

Table 4.10: BMA Result (III) for the Combined Group of Upper-middle-income and High-income Economies

Determinants	Posterior Inclusion Probability (PIP)	Posterior Mean	Posterior Standard Deviation (PSTD)	Posterior Mean / PSTD
GRDP per Capita	0.99876	0.00071	0.00014	4.93056
Total Dependency Ratio	0.10938	–0.06037	0.03222	1.87374
Openness to Trade	0.02969	–0.00237	0.00241	0.98218
Percentage Change in Nominal Exchange Rate	0.09032	–0.01107	0.00782	1.41635
World Gross Domestic Product Real Growth Rate	0.03916	0.18080	0.14454	1.25085
Foreign Direct Investment Inflows as Percentage of GRDP	0.05383	–0.03809	0.02627	1.44978
Literacy Rate	0.02926	0.05384	0.06011	0.89569
Overall Productivity	0.99686	–0.00022	0.00005	4.71739
Primary Industry Value added per Worker	0.01876	0.00000	0.00002	0.20000
Secondary Industry Value added per Worker	0.01938	0.00000	0.00001	0.16667
Tertiary Industry Value added per Worker	0.01988	0.00002	0.00004	0.41026
Road Density	1.00000	0.58675	0.11090	5.29069
Length of Road per Capita	0.03187	–0.01070	0.01042	1.02707
Secondary Industry Value added as Percentage of GRDP	0.02545	–0.01341	0.01715	0.78177
Tertiary Industry Value added as Percentage of GRDP	0.99999	–0.12373	0.02311	5.35436
Government Consumption Expenditure as Percentage of GRDP	0.99990	0.41049	0.08471	4.84605
Old Dependency Ratio	0.01877	0.01127	0.05695	0.19795

Note: Cells highlighted in grey are considered robust determinants for growth slowdown in the combined group of upper-middle-income and high-income economies as they satisfy the two criteria simultaneously: (i) The posterior inclusion probability (PIP) exceeds the prior inclusion probability (i.e. $\frac{3}{17}$ = 0.17647) and (ii) The ratio of conditional posterior mean to conditional posterior standard deviation is larger than 1.65 in absolute value, which corresponds to a 90% coverage interval under Gaussian posterior parameter distribution.
Source: Asia Competitiveness Institute.

4.6.3 Predictive Probability of Growth Slowdown

Using the income group specific logistic models, we compute predictive probabilities of near-future slowdown for the economies in ASEAN, Greater China, India, and Indonesia. The predictive probability for an economy is computed using its 2012 data for the relevant determinants (see Section 4.4.6 for details). It is illustrative of the risk that an economy will experience growth slowdown in the 5 years following 2012, or the period 2012–2017: the higher the probability, the higher the likelihood of growth slowdown.

Figure 4.4 shows the scatterplot of the predictive probabilities for 107 economies in ASEAN, Greater China, India, and Indonesia against the initial level of GRDP per capita in 1990 PPP$ of each economy at the start of the prediction period in 2012. In general, upper-middle-income and high-income economies have higher probabilities of slowdown than lower-middle-income economies, which in turn are more likely to slow down than economies in the low-income group. In addition, within each income group, the likelihood of slowdown seems to increase with GRDP per capita level, as evident in the upward sloping trend line. Interestingly, the rate of increase is not uniform across income groups. The likelihood of slowdown seems to increase at decreasing rates as an economy graduates from one income group to another.

The section which follows discusses in detail the predictive probabilities of growth slowdown for Indonesia's sub-national economies. For completeness, we have also calculated the predictive probabilities, provided in Appendix 5, using the probit specifications reported in Appendix 4.

By 2012, there are six low-income economies, 22 lower-middle-income economies, two upper-middle-income economies and three high-income economies in Indonesia. Figure 4.5 provides an optimistic outlook on the near-future prospects of the Indonesia sub-national economies. The average predictive probability of growth slowdown is 0.10264, indicating that on average, Indonesia sub-national economies have only a 10% chance of experiencing growth slowdown in the 2012–2017 period. The average probability for the low-income economies is even lower at 0.04903; the average for the lower-middle-income economies is 0.09026 while the average for the combined group of upper-middle-income and high-income economies is 0.22144, which is still rather low. Riau is the economy most likely to slow down among all Indonesia sub-national economies, yet its probability of slowdown is still smaller than 0.5.

The specific predictive probability for each Indonesia sub-national economy is displayed in Table 4.11. Among the low-income economies, North Maluku has the lowest probability of experiencing growth slowdown in the period 2012–2017 at 0.00007, while West Sulawesi has the highest probability at 0.15698. Meanwhile, among the lower-middle-income economies, Banten's predictive probability at 0.00759 is the lowest while East Java's probability is the highest at 0.20395. Finally, among the combined group of upper-middle-income and high-income economies, Riau Islands has the lowest probability at 0.05495 while Riau has the highest probability at 0.39514.

The low overall-average probability of the Indonesia sub-national economies is impressive as compared to the prospects of economies in Greater China and India. The average predictive probability for the Greater China economies is 0.56872 while the average for the India

Figure 4.4: Scatterplot Showing Predictive Probabilities of Growth Slowdown for Economies in ASEAN, Greater China, Indonesia and India for the Period 2012–2017 (Based on Income Group-specific Logistic Models)

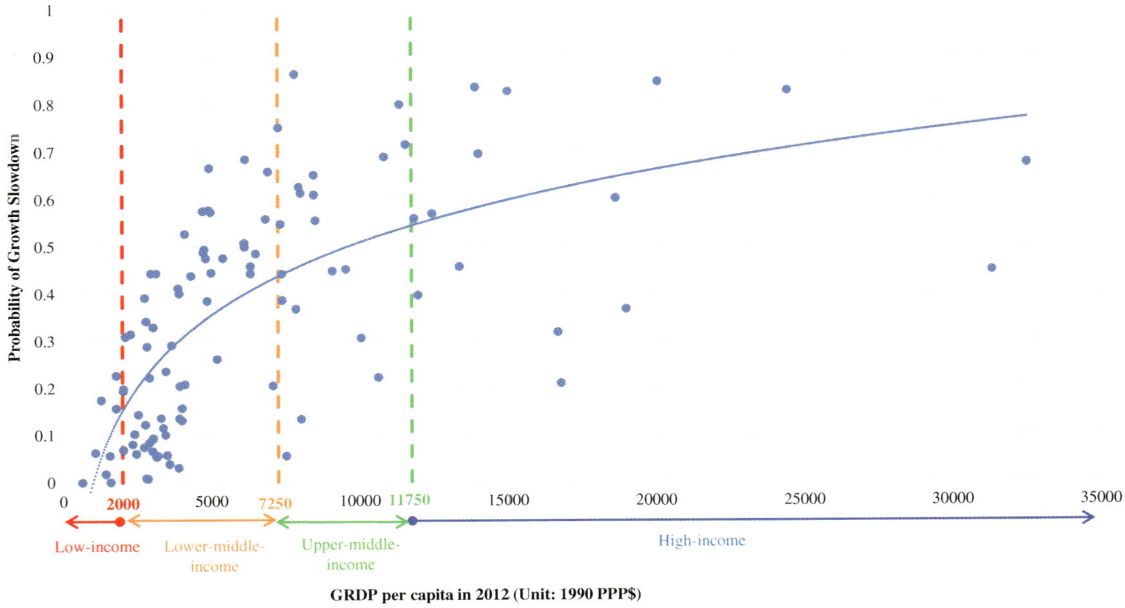

Source: Asia Competitiveness Institute.

sub-national economies is 0.43071.[37] One interpretation of this result is that on average, Indonesia sub-national economies are less at risk of experiencing growth slowdown than the two giants. However, as noted in Section 4.4.6, low probability may also indicate stagnation.

4.7 Relative Strengths and Weaknesses of Indonesia's Sub-national Economies

Equipped with the knowledge of the general risk level of each economy experiencing growth slowdown at its respective level of development, as illustrated by the predictive probability results in Section 4.6.3, it would be meaningful if we could pinpoint the relative strengths and weaknesses of each economy, thereby aiding policymakers to identify areas in which further improvement could be made to reduce the risks of growth slowdown. To this end, we compute the standardised score for each economy in terms of the determinants of growth slowdown for the income groups they belong to. Standardised scores are calculated for all determinants of growth slowdown with the exception of the control variable GRDP per capita.

Formally, the standardised score for determinant D of economy E which is in income group I is defined as $\textit{Standardised score}_{D,E,I} = \frac{X_{D,E,I} - \bar{X}_{D,I}}{SD_{D,I}}$, where $X_{D,E,I}$ is the value of determinant D of economy E which is in income group I, $\bar{X}_{D,I}$ is the mean value of determinant D for all economies

[37] See Tan, Lian, and Xie, (2016), Tan, Luu, and Yoong (2016).

Figure 4.5: Bar Chart Showing Predictive Probabilities of Growth Slowdown for Indonesia Sub-national Economies for the Period 2012–2017 (Based on Income Group-specific Logistic Models)

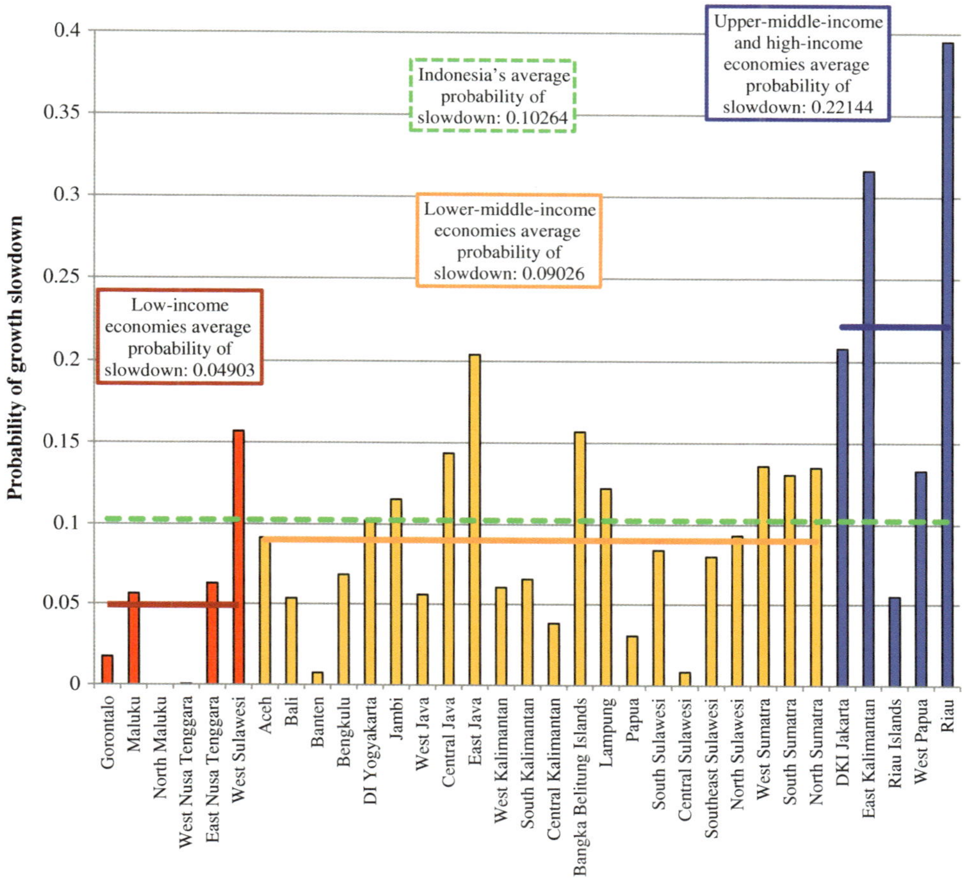

Note: Averages reported are simple averages.
Source: Asia Competitiveness Institute.

within the income group I, and $SD_{D,I}$ is the standard deviation of determinant D for all economies within the income group I. The mean value of determinant D for all economies within the income group I is defined as $\overline{X}_{D,I} = \frac{1}{N}\sum_{e=1}^{N} X_{D,e,I}$, where D is the total number of economies within the income group I. The standard deviation of determinant D for all economies within the income group I is defined as $SD_{D,I} = \sqrt{\frac{1}{N}\sum_{i=1}^{N}(X_{D,E,I} - \overline{X}_{D,I})^2}$. For all determinants except for old dependency ratio, a high value of $X_{D,E,I}$ would indicate a high *Standardised score*$_{D,E,I}$. In contrast, we reverse the score of old dependency ratio so that the standardised score is low if the original value of the ratio is high. This is because unlike the other determinants, high old dependency ratio is associated with increasing likelihood of growth slowdown.

Constructed in the manner described above, the standardised scores reflect the gaps between the economy's performance and the average performance of other economies in the same income

Table 4.11: Predictive Probabilities of Growth Slowdown for Indonesia Sub-national Economies for the Period 2012–2017 (Based on Income Group-specific Logistic Models)

Economy	Income Group Which Economy Belongs to in 2012	Probability of Experiencing Growth Slowdown during 2012–2017
Aceh	Lower-Middle-Income	0.09171
Bali	Lower-Middle-Income	0.05357
Bangka Belitung Islands	Lower-Middle-Income	0.15694
Banten	Lower-Middle-Income	0.00759
Bengkulu	Lower-Middle-Income	0.06825
Central Java	Lower-Middle-Income	0.14385
Central Kalimantan	Lower-Middle-Income	0.03835
Central Sulawesi	Lower-Middle-Income	0.00864
DI Yogyakarta	Lower-Middle-Income	0.10231
DKI Jakarta	High-Income	0.20778
East Java	Lower-Middle-Income	0.20395
East Kalimantan	High-Income	0.31613
East Nusa Tenggara	Low-Income	0.06271
Gorontalo	Low-Income	0.01767
Jambi	Lower-Middle-Income	0.11535
Lampung	Lower-Middle-Income	0.12226
Maluku	Low-Income	0.05630
North Maluku	Low-Income	0.00007
North Sulawesi	Lower-Middle-Income	0.09342
North Sumatra	Lower-Middle-Income	0.13513
Papua	Lower-Middle-Income	0.03061
Riau	High-Income	0.39514
Riau Islands	Upper-Middle-Income	0.05495
South Kalimantan	Lower-Middle-Income	0.06556
South Sulawesi	Lower-Middle-Income	0.08439
South Sumatra	Lower-Middle-Income	0.13094
Southeast Sulawesi	Lower-Middle-Income	0.08052
West Java	Lower-Middle-Income	0.05590
West Kalimantan	Lower-Middle-Income	0.06040
West Nusa Tenggara	Low-Income	0.00042
West Papua	Upper-Middle-Income	0.13319
West Sulawesi	Low-Income	0.15698
West Sumatra	Lower-Middle-Income	0.13616

Source: Asia Competitiveness Institute.

group. If the standardised score of an economy is zero, it means that the economy is an average performer within its income group. On the other hand, if the standardised score is negative, it implies that the economy is performing more poorly than others, while positive standardised score indicates better than average performance. The farther the standardised score is from zero, the farther the performance of said economy from the average of that particular income group. For instance, a large negative standardised score means very poor performance, while a large positive standardised score denotes very strong performance.

Figures 4.6–4.38 are web charts displaying the standardised scores of Indonesia sub-national economies in terms of the determinants of growth slowdown (with the exception of GRDP per capita). The larger the area under each economy's line, the better its performance in the particular dimension considered. To provide a better sense of the relative strengths and weaknesses of each economy, we also benchmark their standardised scores against the median scores and maximum scores of the income group they belong to. All data used in generating these web charts are as of 2012. The dimensions/determinants chosen to be considered for each economy depend on the income group in which the economy belongs to in the same year.

Aceh, Indonesia

Lower-middle-income economy

Figure 4.6 shows the relative strengths and weaknesses of Aceh, which was a lower-middle-income economy in 2012 according to the income classification we adopt. As discussed in Section 4.6.1, we found four determinants which are associated with growth slowdown in this particular income group, namely Old Dependency Ratio, Literacy Rate, Foreign Direct

Figure 4.6: Aceh's Strengths and Weaknesses

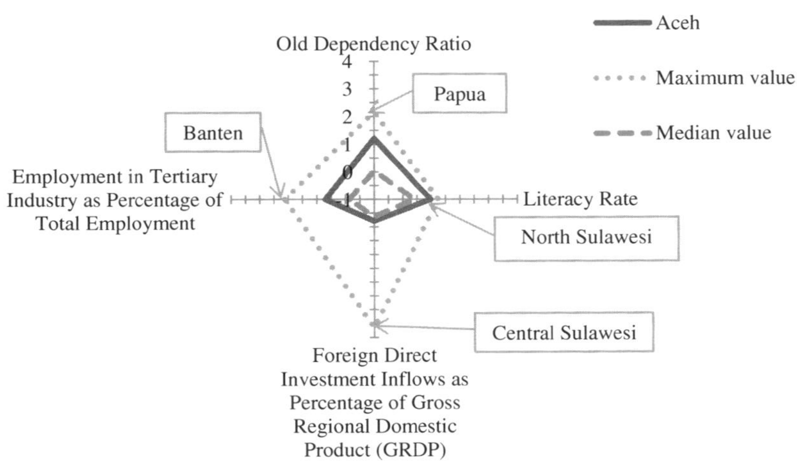

Source: Asia Competitiveness Institute.

Investment Inflows as Percentage of GRDP and Employment in Tertiary Industry as Percentage of Total Employment. The solid line shows the standardised score for Aceh. The dashed line represents the median score for all economies in the lower-middle-income group across ASEAN, Greater China, India, and Indonesia, while the dotted line denotes the maximum score for those economies.

In general, Aceh performed better than the median scores of the lower-middle-income group in all determinants considered. However, Aceh could consider attracting more foreign direct investment to its economy, bringing in the needed capital, managerial expertise and technology for continued economic growth, as its standardised score for the Foreign Direct Investment Inflows as Percentage of GRDP is only marginally above the median score. Relatively high Literacy Rate is Aceh's strength with its standardised score of 0.9709, rather close to the maximum value of 1.2460 as achieved by North Sulawesi. Aceh could tap on its high literacy rate to increase its Employment in Tertiary Industry as Percentage of Total Employment, where Aceh's score is far below the median of the lower-middle-income group.

Bali, Indonesia

Lower-middle-income economy

Figure 4.7 shows the relative strengths and weaknesses of Bali, which was a lower-middle-income economy in 2012 according to the income classification we adopt. As discussed in Section 4.6.1, we found four determinants which are associated with growth slowdown in this particular income group namely, Old Dependency Ratio, Literacy Rate, Foreign Direct Investment Inflows as Percentage of GRDP and Employment in Tertiary Industry as Percentage of Total Employment. The solid line shows the standardised score for Bali. The dashed line

Figure 4.7: Bali's Strengths and Weaknesses

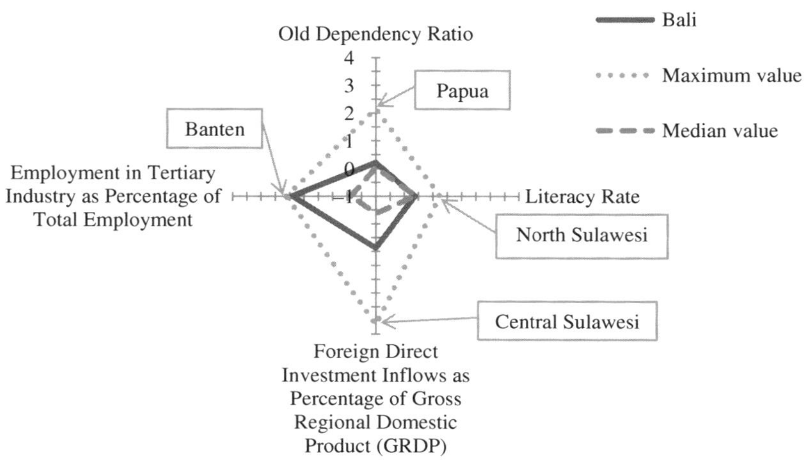

Source: Asia Competitiveness Institute.

represents the median score for all economies in the lower-middle-income group across ASEAN, Greater China, India, and Indonesia, while the dotted line denotes the maximum score for those economies.

In general, Bali performed better than the median scores of the lower-middle-income group in all determinants considered except for Literacy Rate. Bali's standardised score for Literacy Rate was a tad lower than the median score, signalling a possible area for improvement by widening access to basic education. Relatively high Employment in Tertiary Industry as Percentage of Total Employment is Bali's strength with its standardised score of 1.9120, which was rather close to the maximum value of 2.1165 as achieved by Banten. Bali could consider improving its Literacy Rate and thereby unleash its human capital potential to contribute in higher value-added activities within the service sector.

Bangka Belitung Islands, Indonesia

Lower-middle-income economy

Figure 4.8 shows the relative strengths and weaknesses of Bangka Belitung Islands, which was a lower-middle-income economy in 2012 according to the income classification we adopt. As discussed in Section 4.6.1, we found four determinants which are associated with growth slowdown in this particular income group, namely Old Dependency Ratio, Literacy Rate, Foreign Direct Investment Inflows as Percentage of GRDP, and Employment in Tertiary Industry as Percentage of Total Employment. The solid line shows the standardised score for Bangka Belitung Islands. The dashed line represents the median score for all economies in the lower-middle-income group across ASEAN, Greater China, India, and Indonesia, while the dotted line denotes the maximum score for those economies.

Figure 4.8: Bangka Belitung Islands' Strengths and Weaknesses

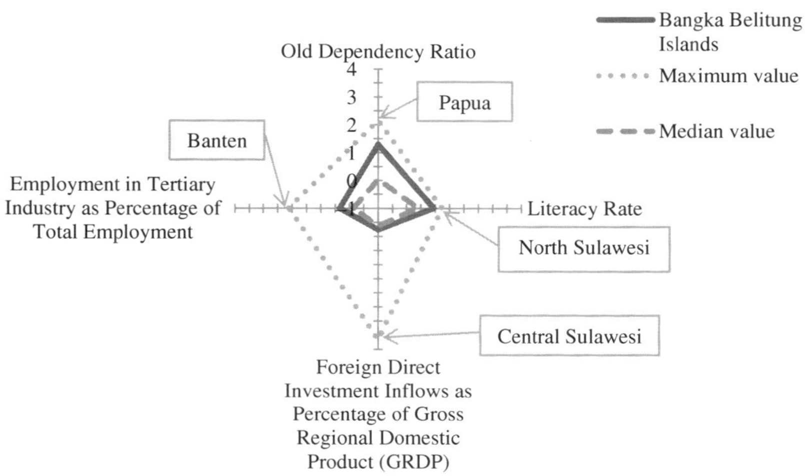

Source: Asia Competitiveness Institute.

In general, Bangka Belitung Islands performed better than the median scores of the lower-middle-income group in all determinants considered, but it could consider attracting more foreign direct investment to its economy, bringing in the needed capital, managerial expertise and technology for continued economic growth, as its standardised score for the Foreign Direct Investment Inflows as Percentage of GRDP was only slightly above the median score and still far from the maximum score. Relatively high Literacy Rate and low Old Dependency Ratio are Bangka Belitung Islands' strengths with their standardised scores of 0.9478 and 1.2974, respectively, which were rather close to the maximum values of 1.2460 and 2.1489, respectively.

Banten, Indonesia

Lower-middle-income economy

Figure 4.9 shows the relative strengths and weaknesses of Banten, which was a lower-middle-income economy in 2012 according to the income classification we adopt. As discussed in Section 4.6.1, we found four determinants which are associated with growth slowdown in this particular income group, namely Old Dependency Ratio, Literacy Rate, Foreign Direct Investment Inflows as Percentage of GRDP, and Employment in Tertiary Industry as Percentage of Total Employment. The solid line shows the standardised score for Banten. The dashed line represents the median score for all economies in the lower-middle-income group across ASEAN, Greater China, India, and Indonesia, while the dotted line denotes the maximum score for those economies.

Banten has demonstrated outstanding achievement in all of the four determinants considered, with their standardised scores close to the maximum scores of the lower-middle-income group. Moreover, its standardised score for Employment in Tertiary Industry as Percentage of Total Employment at 2.1165 was the maximum score. In order to further minimise the risk of

Figure 4.9: Banten's Strengths and Weaknesses

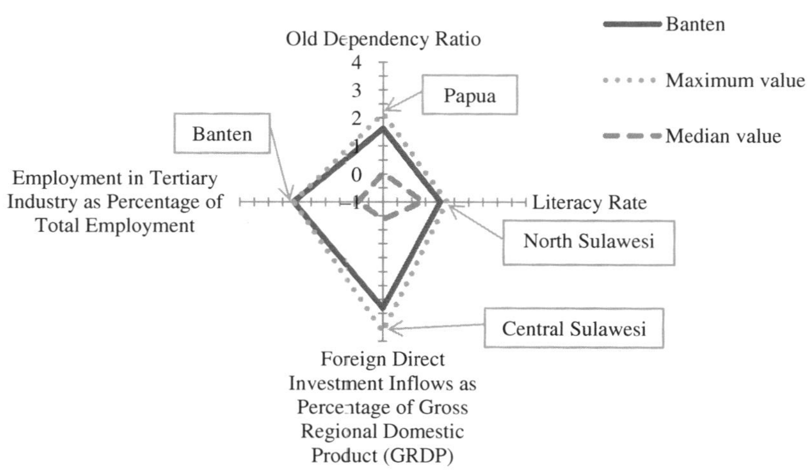

Source: Asia Competitiveness Institute.

experiencing growth slowdown in this particular income group, Banten could consider improving its Foreign Direct Investment Inflows as Percentage of GRDP, which is still slightly below the maximum score as achieved by Central Sulawesi. This will thus bring in the capital, managerial expertise and technology to ensure continued economic growth for Banten.

Bengkulu, Indonesia

Lower-middle-income economy

Figure 4.10 shows the relative strengths and weaknesses of Bengkulu, which was a lower-middle-income economy in 2012 according to the income classification we adopt. As discussed in Section 4.6.1, we found four determinants which are associated with growth slowdown in this particular income group, namely Old Dependency Ratio, Literacy Rate, Foreign Direct Investment Inflows as Percentage of GRDP, and Employment in Tertiary Industry as Percentage of Total Employment. The solid line shows the standardised score for Bengkulu. The dashed line represents the median score for all economies in the lower-middle-income group across ASEAN, Greater China, India, and Indonesia, while the dotted line denotes the maximum score for those economies.

In general, Bengkulu performed better than the median scores of the lower-middle-income group in most of the determinants considered. However, Bengkulu could consider attracting more foreign direct investment to its economy, bringing in the needed capital, managerial expertise and technology for continued economic growth, as its standardised score for the Foreign Direct Investment Inflows as Percentage of GRDP was slightly below the median score. Relatively high Literacy Rate is Bengkulu's strength, with its standardised score of 0.9287 which was rather close to the maximum value of 1.2460 as achieved by North Sulawesi. Bengkulu

Figure 4.10: Bengkulu's Strengths and Weaknesses

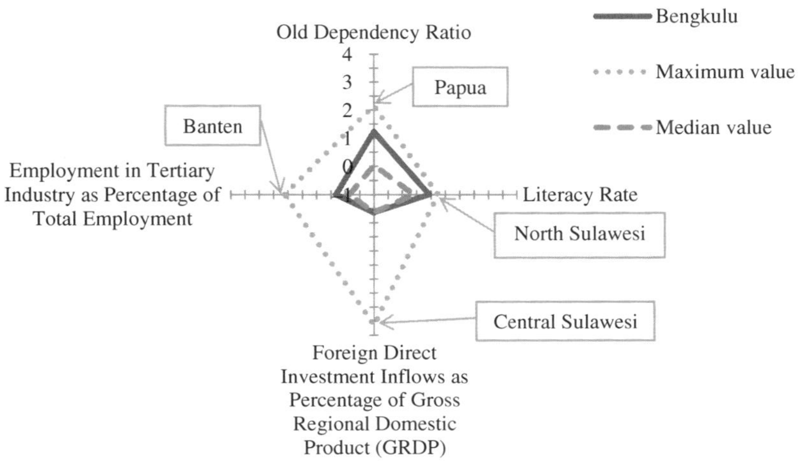

Source: Asia Competitiveness Institute.

could tap on its high literacy rate to increase its Employment in Tertiary Industry as Percentage of Total Employment where its score still lagged behind the median.

Central Java, Indonesia

Lower-middle-income economy

Figure 4.11 shows the relative strengths and weaknesses of Central Java, which was a lower-middle-income economy in 2012 according to the income classification we adopt. As discussed in Section 4.6.1, we found four determinants which are associated with growth slowdown in this particular income group, namely Old Dependency Ratio, Literacy Rate, Foreign Direct Investment Inflows as Percentage of GRDP, and Employment in Tertiary Industry as Percentage of Total Employment. The solid line shows the standardised score for Central Java. The dashed line represents the median score for all economies in the lower-middle-income group across ASEAN, Greater China, India, and Indonesia, while the dotted line denotes the maximum score for those economies.

In general, Central Java's standardised scores for the various determinants considered were rather close to the median scores of the lower-middle-income group. The only determinant in which Central Java performed noticeably better than the median was Employment in Tertiary Industry as Percentage of Total Employment, even though Central Java's standardised score was still lower than the maximum score. By tapping on its strength in the relatively high employment in tertiary industry, Central Java could consider attracting more foreign direct investment to its economy, bringing in the needed capital, managerial expertise

Figure 4.11: Central Java's Strengths and Weaknesses

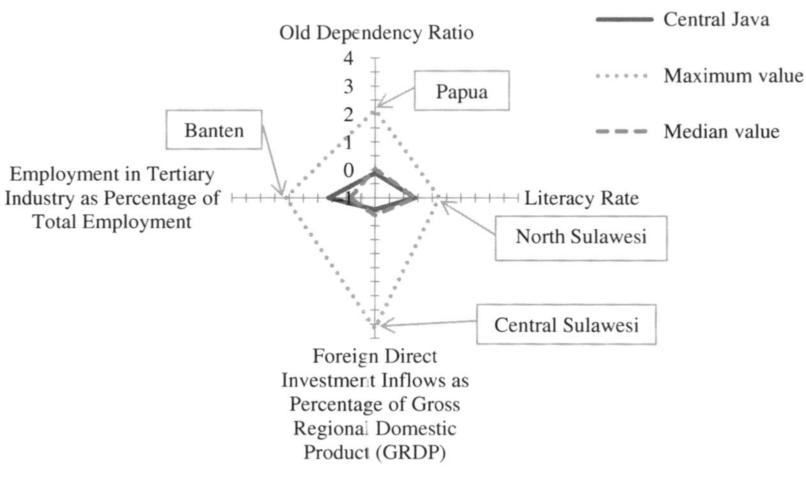

Source: Asia Competitiveness Institute.

and technology for continued economic growth, while widening its people's access to basic education.

Central Kalimantan, Indonesia

Lower-middle-income economy

Figure 4.12 shows the relative strengths and weaknesses of Central Kalimantan, which was a lower-middle-income economy in 2012 according to the income classification we adopt. As discussed in Section 4.6.1, we found four determinants which are associated with growth slowdown in this particular income group, namely Old Dependency Ratio, Literacy Rate, Foreign Direct Investment Inflows as Percentage of GRDP, and Employment in Tertiary Industry as Percentage of Total Employment. The solid line shows the standardised score for Central Kalimantan. The dashed line represents the median score for all economies in the lower-middle-income group across ASEAN, Greater China, India, and Indonesia, while the dotted line denotes the maximum score for those economies.

In general, Central Kalimantan performed remarkably well in most determinants, with standardised scores that are close to the maximum scores of the determinants in lower-middle-income group, except for Employment in Tertiary Industry as Percentage of Total Employment (score of –0.3483, lower than the median score of –0.1334). By tapping on its strength in Foreign Direct Investment Inflows as Percentage of GRDP, Central Kalimantan could consider diversifying its economy into the tertiary sector so that it can move up the value chain and create more opportunities for sustainable growth.

Figure 4.12: Central Kalimantan's Strengths and Weaknesses

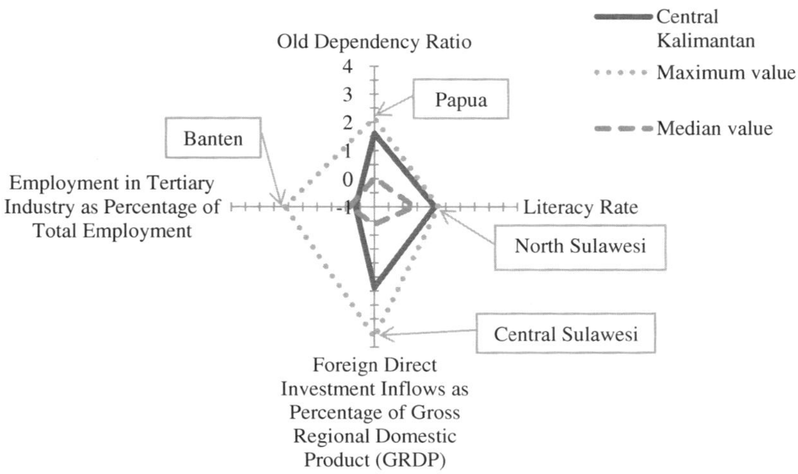

Source: Asia Competitiveness Institute.

Figure 4.13: Central Sulawesi's Strengths and Weaknesses

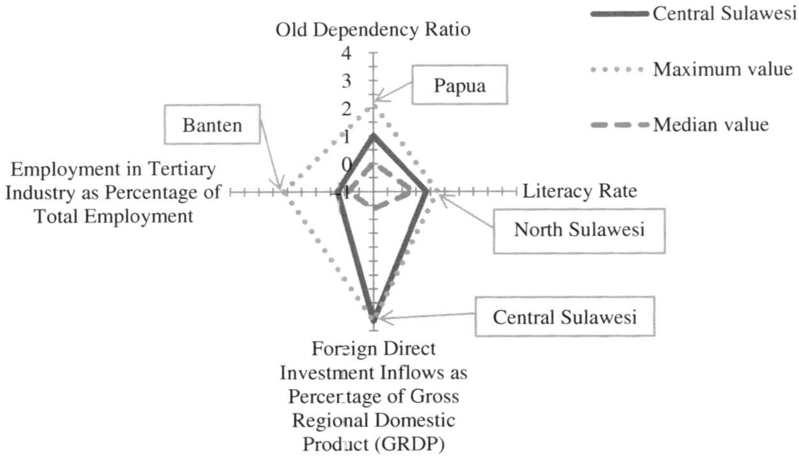

Source: Asia Competitiveness Institute.

Central Sulawesi, Indonesia

Lower-middle-income economy

Figure 4.13 shows the relative strengths and weaknesses of Central Sulawesi, which was a lower-middle-income economy in 2012 according to the income classification we adopt. As discussed in Section 4.6.1, we found four determinants which are associated with growth slowdown in this particular income group, namely Old Dependency Ratio, Literacy Rate, Foreign Direct Investment Inflows as Percentage of GRDP, and Employment in Tertiary Industry as Percentage of Total Employment. The solid line shows the standardised score for Central Sulawesi. The dashed line represents the median score for all economies in the lower-middle-income group across ASEAN, Greater China, India, and Indonesia, while the dotted line denotes the maximum score for those economies.

In general, Central Sulawesi performed better than the median scores of the lower-middle-income group in all the determinants considered. Favourable demographic landscape along with majority of the population being equipped with basic education, as demonstrated in the relatively high standardised scores of Central Sulawesi in Old Dependency Ratio and Literacy Rate, respectively, are Central Sulawesi's strengths. In addition, Central Sulawesi's Foreign Direct Investment Inflows as Percentage of GRDP was the maximum score at 3.6549. In order to ensure continued economic growth, Central Sulawesi could tap on its high literacy rate to increase its Employment in Tertiary Industry as Percentage of Total Employment.

DI Yogyakarta, Indonesia

Lower-middle-income economy

Figure 4.14 shows the relative strengths and weaknesses of DI Yogyakarta, which was a lower-middle-income economy in 2012 according to the income classification we adopt. As discussed

Figure 4.14: DI Yogyakarta's Strengths and Weaknesses

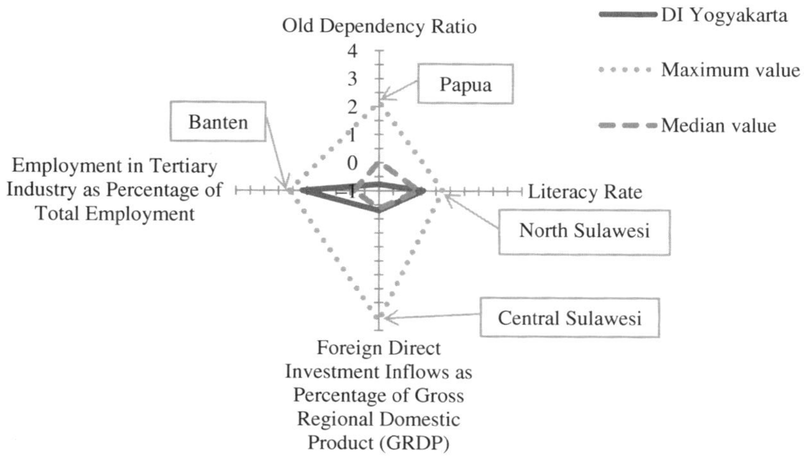

Source: Asia Competitiveness Institute.

in Section 4.6.1, we found four determinants which are associated with growth slowdown in this particular income group, namely Old Dependency Ratio, Literacy Rate, Foreign Direct Investment Inflows as Percentage of GRDP, and Employment in Tertiary Industry as Percentage of Total Employment. The solid line shows the standardised score for DI Yogyakarta. The dashed line represents the median score for all economies in the lower-middle-income group across ASEAN, Greater China, India, and Indonesia, while the dotted line denotes the maximum score for those economies.

The performances of DI Yogyakarta in the various determinants were rather mixed. The standardised scores for DI Yogyakarta's Literacy Rate and Foreign Direct Investment Inflows as Percentage of GRDP were close to the median scores of the lower-middle-income group, suggesting that there are much room for improvements in these aspects. On the other hand, relatively high Employment in Tertiary Industry as Percentage of Total Employment is DI Yogyakarta's strength with standardised score of 1.6733 which was rather close to the maximum value of 2.1165 in Banten. However, DI Yogyakarta needs to take note of the demographic challenge posed by a higher proportion of elderly people in the working population, given that its standardised score for Old Dependency Ratio was much lower than the median score. Policymakers may want to explore ways to increase productivity so that greying will not dampen economic growth for DI Yogyakarta.

DKI Jakarta, Indonesia

High-income economy

Figure 4.15 shows the relative strengths and weaknesses of DKI Jakarta, which was a high-income economy in 2012 according to the income classification we adopt. As mentioned in Section 4.4.2, due to data constraint, we have combined the analysis of high-income economies with that of the upper-middle-income economies. As discussed in Section 4.6.1, we found four

Figure 4.15: DKI Jakarta's Strengths and Weaknesses

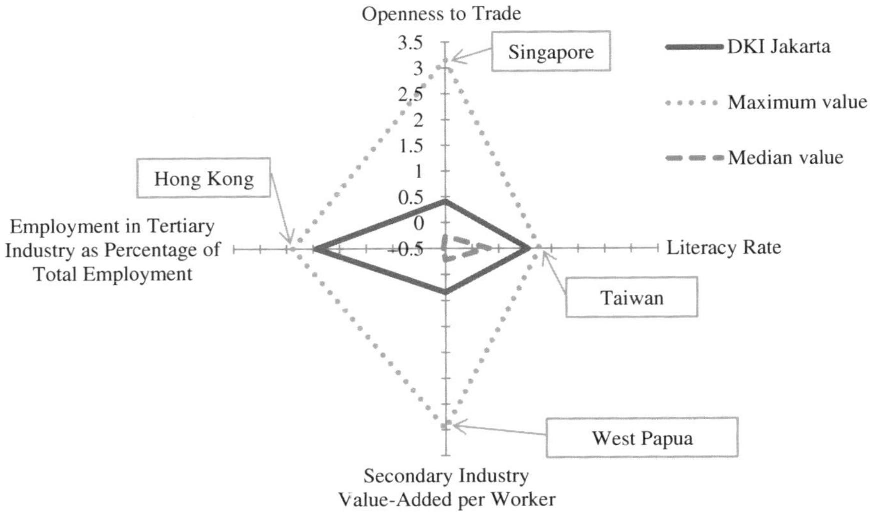

Source: Asia Competitiveness Institute.

determinants which are associated with growth slowdown in this combined group of upper-middle-income and high-income economies, namely Openness To Trade, Literacy Rate, Secondary Industry Value Added per Worker, and Employment in Tertiary Industry as Percentage of Total Employment. The solid line shows the standardised score for DKI Jakarta. The dashed line represents the median score for all economies in the combined group of upper-middle-income and high-income economies across ASEAN, Greater China, India, and Indonesia, while the dotted line denotes the maximum score for those economies.

DKI Jakarta performed better than the median scores of the combined group of upper-middle-income and high-income economies in all determinants considered. In particular, its standardised scores for Literacy Rate and Employment in Tertiary Industry as Percentage of Total Employment were relatively high and close to the maximum scores attained by Taiwan and Hong Kong respectively. In order to mitigate the risk of experiencing economic growth slowdown, DKI Jakarta could draw on its high Literacy Rate to further enhance its Secondary Industry Value Added per Worker.

East Java, Indonesia

Lower-middle-income economy

Figure 4.16 shows the relative strengths and weaknesses of East Java, which was a lower-middle-income economy in 2012 according to the income classification we adopt. As discussed in Section 4.6.1, we found four determinants which are associated with growth slowdown in this particular income group, namely Old Dependency Ratio, Literacy Rate, Foreign Direct Investment Inflows as Percentage of GRDP, and Employment in Tertiary Industry as Percentage

Figure 4.16: East Java's Strengths and Weaknesses

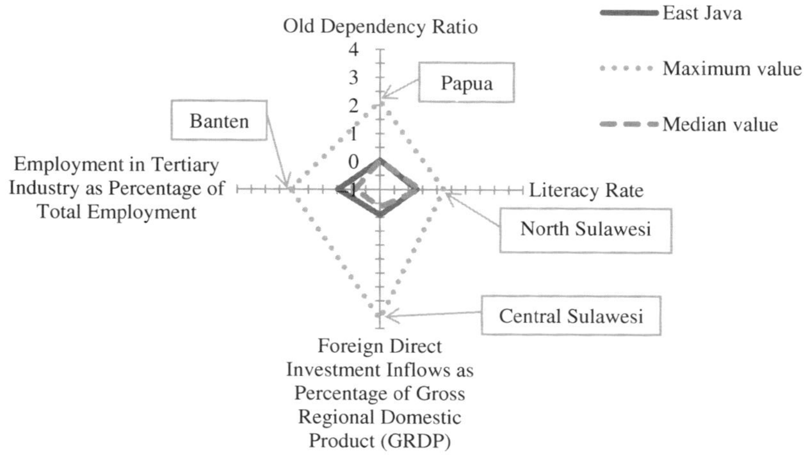

Source: Asia Competitiveness Institute.

of Total Employment. The solid line shows the standardised score for East Java. The dashed line represents the median score for all economies in the lower-middle-income group across ASEAN, Greater China, India, and Indonesia, while the dotted line denotes the maximum score for those economies.

In general, East Java's standardised scores for the various determinants considered were rather close to the median scores of the lower-middle-income group. The two determinants in which East Java performed slightly better than the median were Foreign Direct Investment Inflows as Percentage of GRDP and Employment in Tertiary Industry as Percentage of Total Employment, even though, there is still much room for further improvement. With the standardised score for Literacy Rate at 0.2851 which was lower than the median score of 0.4026, East Java should consider widening access to basic education, thereby unleashing its human capital potential to contribute in higher value-added activities within the service sector.

East Kalimantan, Indonesia

High-income economy

Figure 4.17 shows the relative strengths and weaknesses of East Kalimantan, which was a high-income economy in 2012 according to the income classification we adopt. As mentioned in Section 4.4.2, due to data constraint, we have combined the analysis of high-income economies with that of the upper-middle-income economies. As discussed in Section 4.6.1, we found four determinants which are associated with growth slowdown in this combined group of upper-middle-income and high-income economies, namely Openness To Trade, Literacy Rate, Secondary Industry Value Added per Worker, and Employment in Tertiary Industry as Percentage of Total Employment. The solid line shows the standardised score for East Kalimantan. The dashed line represents the median score for all economies in the combined group of

Figure 4.17: East Kalimantan's Strengths and Weaknesses

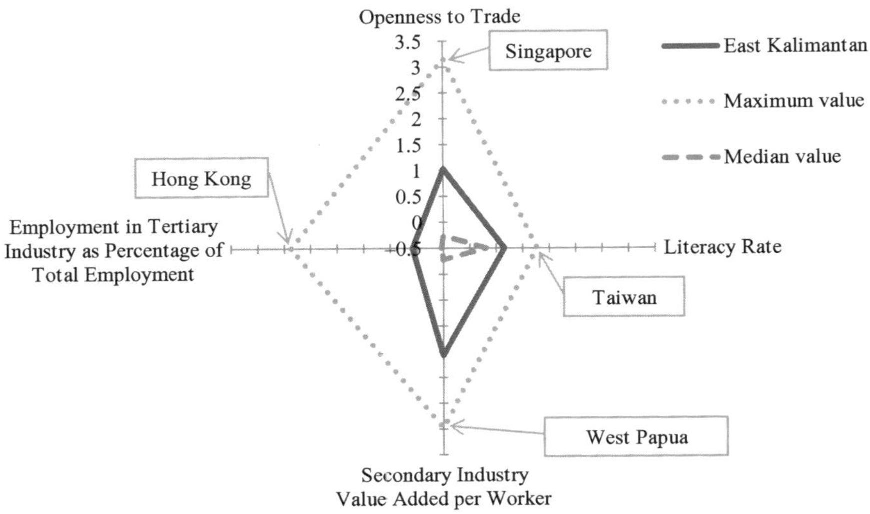

Source: Asia Competitiveness Institute.

upper-middle-income and high-income economies across ASEAN, Greater China, India, and Indonesia, while the dotted line denotes the maximum score for those economies.

East Kalimantan performed better than the median scores of the combined group of upper-middle-income and high-income economies in all determinants. However, as shown in Figure 4.17, there is still much room for improvement for all determinants as their standardised scores were far from the respective maximum scores. In order to mitigate the risk of experiencing economic growth slowdown, East Kalimantan could draw on its relatively better performing Literacy Rate to further improve its Employment in Tertiary Industry as Percentage of Total Employment.

East Nusa Tenggara, Indonesia

Low-income economy

Figure 4.18 shows the relative strengths and weaknesses of East Nusa Tenggara, which was a low-income economy in 2012 according to the income classification we adopt. As discussed in Section 4.6.1, we found three determinants which are associated with growth slowdown in this particular income group, namely Length of Road per capita, Literacy Rate, and Foreign Direct Investment Inflows as Percentage of GRDP. The solid line shows the standardised score for East Nusa Tenggara. The dashed line represents the median score for all economies in the low-income group across ASEAN, Greater China, India, and Indonesia, while the dotted line denotes the maximum score for those economies.

In general, East Nusa Tenggara's standardised scores for the various determinants considered were rather close to the median scores of the low-income group, with noticeable gap between

Figure 4.18: East Nusa Tenggara's Strengths and Weaknesses

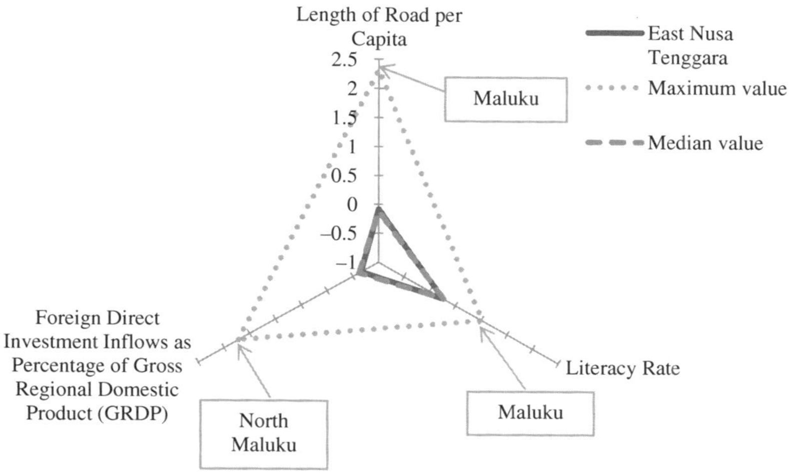

Source: Asia Competitiveness Institute.

East Nusa Tenggara's standardised scores and the maximum scores. In order to attract the much needed foreign direct investment, East Nusa Tenggara should first provide more reliable and better quality infrastructure as it performed poorly in Length of Road per capita. With standardised score for Literacy Rate at 0.2636 (lower than the median score of 0.2663), East Nusa Tenggara should also consider widening access to basic education, thereby unleashing its human capital potential to contribute in higher value-added activities.

Gorontalo, Indonesia

Low-income economy

Figure 4.19 shows the relative strengths and weaknesses of Gorontalo, which is a low-income economy according to the income classification we adopt. As discussed in Section 4.6.1, we found three determinants which are associated with growth slowdown in this particular income group, namely Length of Road per Capita, Literacy Rate, and Foreign Direct Investment Inflows as Percentage of GRDP. The solid line shows the standardised score for Gorontalo. The dashed line represents the median score for all economies in the low-income group across ASEAN, Greater China, India, and Indonesia, while the dotted line denotes the maximum score for those economies.

In general, Gorontalo performed better than the median scores of the low-income group in all determinants considered. However, Gorontalo could consider attracting more foreign direct investment to its economy, bringing in the much needed capital, managerial expertise and technology for continued economic growth, as its standardised score for the Foreign Direct Investment Inflows as Percentage of GRDP was still far from the maximum score. Relatively high Literacy Rate is Gorontalo's strength, with a standardised score of 0.8500

Figure 4.19: Gorontalo's Strengths and Weaknesses

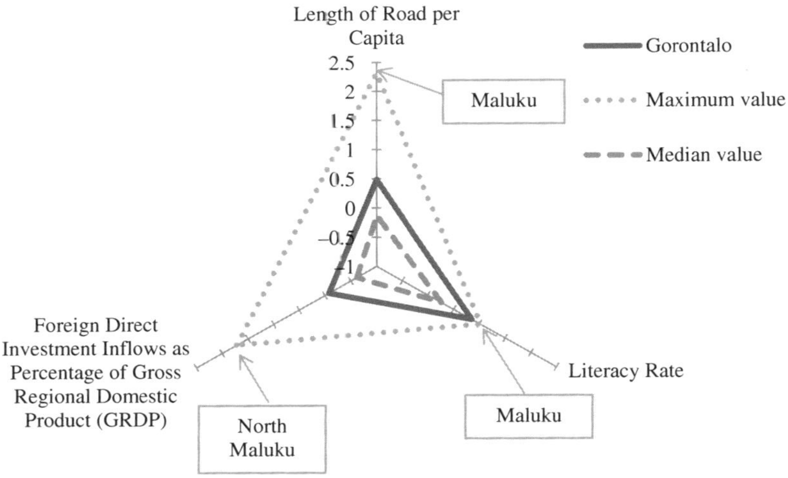

Source: Asia Competitiveness Institute.

which was rather close to the maximum score of 1.0180 by Maluku. However, tapping solely on Gorontalo's forte in high literacy rate to increase its attractiveness as destination for foreign direct investment is insufficient; it must work on improving its infrastructure provision as well. As shown in the Figure 4.19, although Gontaralo's score for Length of Road per Capita was above the median, it was still way below the maximum score, signifying room for improvement.

Jambi, Indonesia

Lower-middle-income economy

Figure 4.20 shows the relative strengths and weaknesses of Jambi, which was a lower-middle-income economy in 2012 according to the income classification we adopt. As discussed in Section 4.6.1, we found four determinants which are associated with growth slowdown in this particular income group, namely Old Dependency Ratio, Literacy Rate, Foreign Direct Investment Inflows as Percentage of GRDP, and Employment in Tertiary Industry as Percentage of Total Employment. The solid line shows the standardised score for Jambi. The dashed line represents the median score for all economies in the lower-middle-income group across ASEAN, Greater China, India, and Indonesia, while the dotted line denotes the maximum score for those economies.

In general, Jambi performed better than the median scores of the lower-middle-income group in all the determinants considered. Favourable demographic landscape along with majority of the population being equipped with basic education, as demonstrated in the relatively high standardised scores of Jambi in Old Dependency Ratio and Literacy Rate, are Jambi's strengths. However, Jambi has much to work on in terms of Foreign Direct Investment Inflows as Percentage of

Figure 4.20: Jambi's Strengths and Weaknesses

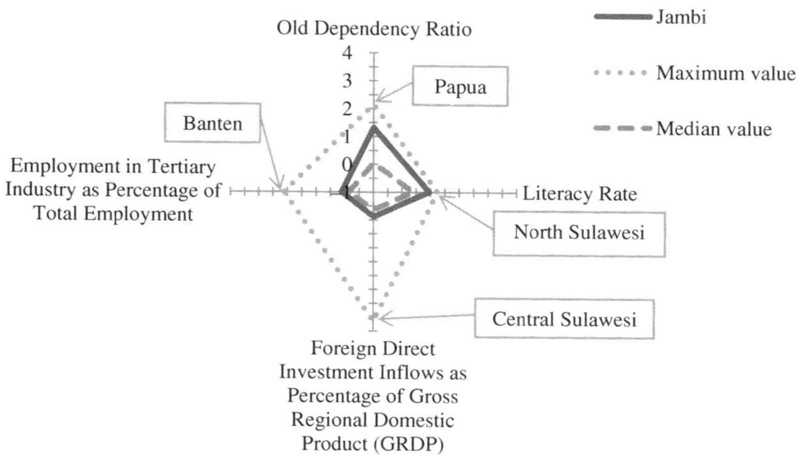

Source: Asia Competitiveness Institute.

GRDP and Employment in Tertiary Industry as Percentage of Total Employment. Jambi could consider attracting more foreign direct investment into its economy, bringing in the much needed capital, managerial expertise and technology for continued economic growth.

Lampung, Indonesia

Lower-middle-income economy

Figure 4.21 shows the relative strengths and weaknesses of Lampung, which was a lower-middle-income economy according to the income classification we adopt. As discussed in Section 4.6.1, we found four determinants which are associated with growth slowdown in this particular income group, namely Old Dependency Ratio, Literacy Rate, Foreign Direct Investment Inflows as Percentage of GRDP, and Employment in Tertiary Industry as Percentage of Total Employment. The solid line shows the standardised score for Lampung. The dashed line represents the median score for all economies in the lower-middle-income group across ASEAN, Greater China, India, and Indonesia, while the dotted line denotes the maximum score for those economies.

In general, Lampung performed better than the median scores of the lower-middle-income group in all determinants considered except for Foreign Direct Investment Inflows as Percentage of GRDP. Lampung's standardised score for Foreign Direct Investment Inflows as Percentage of GRDP was a tad lower than the median score, signalling a possible area for improvement by attracting more foreign direct investment to its economy, bringing in the needed capital, managerial expertise and technology for continued economic growth. Relatively high Literacy Rate is Lampung's strength, with a standardised score of 0.8725 which was rather close to the maximum value of 1.2460 in North Sulawesi.

Figure 4.21: Lampung's Strengths and Weaknesses

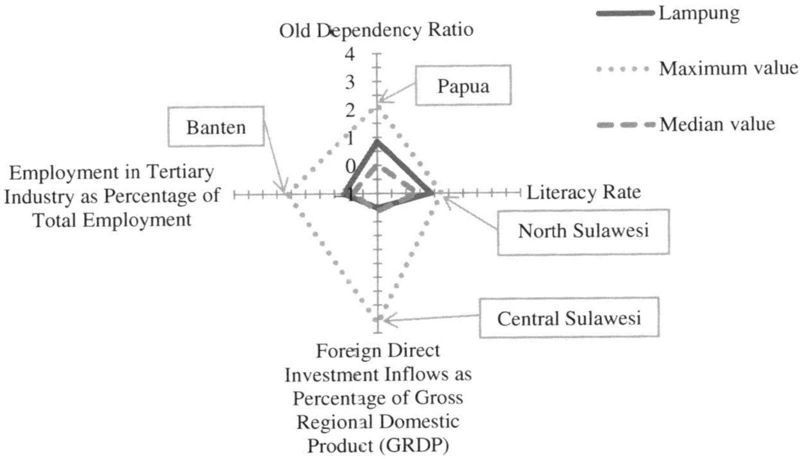

Source: Asia Competitiveness Institute.

Maluku, Indonesia

Low-income economy

Figure 4.22 shows the relative strengths and weaknesses of Maluku, which was a low-income economy in 2012 according to the income classification we adopt. As discussed in Section 4.6.1, we found three determinants which are associated with growth slowdown in this particular

Figure 4.22: Maluku's Strengths and Weaknesses

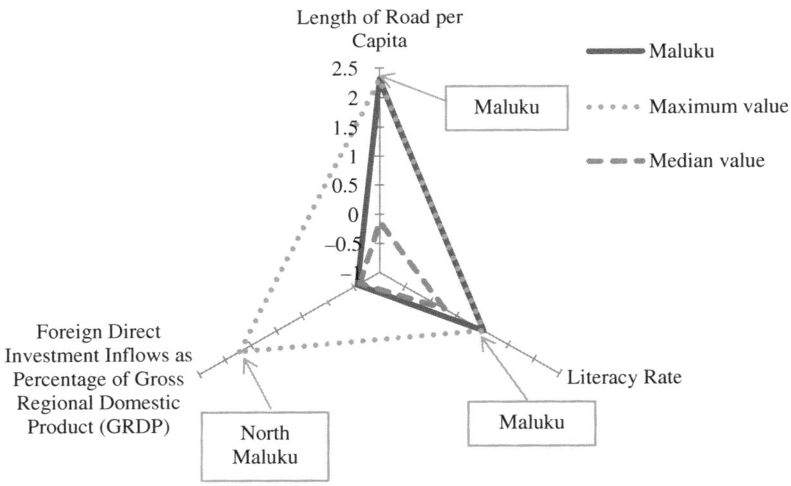

Source: Asia Competitiveness Institute.

income group, namely Length of Road per Capita, Literacy Rate, and Foreign Direct Investment Inflows as Percentage of GRDP. The solid line shows the standardised score for Maluku. The dashed line represents the median score for all economies in the low-income group across ASEAN, Greater China, India, and Indonesia, while the dotted line denotes the maximum score for those economies.

Maluku has done well in most of the determinants considered. Its scores of Length of Road per Capita and Literacy Rate were the maximum scores in the low-income group. However, Maluku could consider attracting more foreign direct investment to its economy, bringing in the much needed capital, managerial expertise and technology for continued economic growth, as its standardised score for the Foreign Direct Investment Inflows as Percentage of GRDP was still far from the maximum score. By tapping on Maluku's forte in high literacy rate and adequate infrastructure, it can work towards becoming an attractive destination for foreign direct investment.

North Maluku, Indonesia

Low-income economy

Figure 4.23 shows the relative strengths and weaknesses of North Maluku, which was a low-income economy in 2012 according to the income classification we adopt. As discussed in Section 4.6.1, we found three determinants which are associated with growth slowdown in this particular income group, namely Length of Road per Capita, Literacy Rate, and Foreign Direct Investment Inflows as Percentage of GRDP. The solid line shows the standardised score for North Maluku. The dashed line represents the median score for all economies in the low-income

Figure 4.23: North Maluku's Strengths and Weaknesses

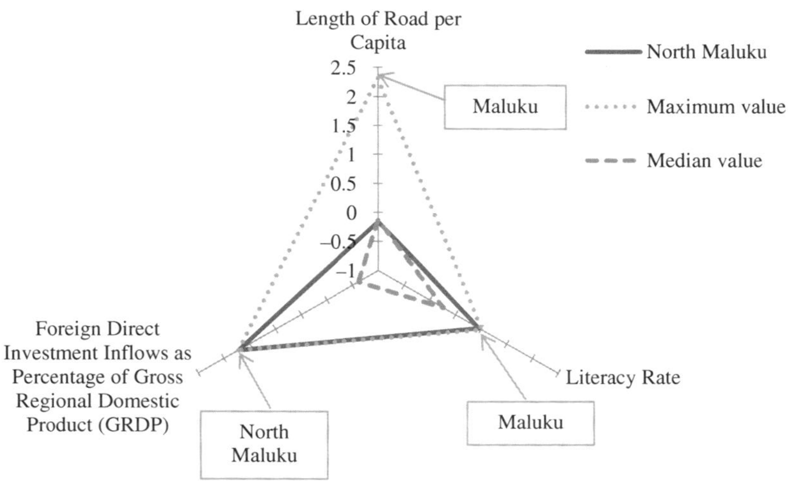

Source: Asia Competitiveness Institute.

group across ASEAN, Greater China, India, and Indonesia, while the dotted line denotes the maximum score for those economies.

North Maluku has demonstrated outstanding achievement in most of the determinants considered, with their standardised scores that are close to the maximum scores of the low-income group. Moreover, its standardised score for Foreign Direct Investment Inflows as Percentage of GRDP at 1.7218 was the maximum score. In order to further minimise North Maluku's risk of experiencing growth slowdown, North Maluku could consider improving its Length of Road per Capita, as its score was still slightly below the median score. Basic infrastructure development is vital for low-income economies like North Maluku to realise its potential for greater economic returns as it allows for better provision of services and enabling businesses to grow and expand.

North Sulawesi, Indonesia

Lower-middle-income economy

Figure 4.24 shows the relative strengths and weaknesses of North Sulawesi, which was a lower-middle-income economy in 2012 according to the income classification we adopt. As discussed in Section 4.6.1, we found four determinants which are associated with growth slowdown in this particular income group, namely Old Dependency Ratio, Literacy Rate, Foreign Direct Investment Inflows as Percentage of GRDP, and Employment in Tertiary Industry as Percentage of Total Employment. The solid line shows the standardised score for North Sulawesi. The dashed line represents the median score for all economies in the lower-middle-income group across ASEAN, Greater China, India, and Indonesia, while the dotted line denotes the maximum score for those economies.

Figure 4.24: North Sulawesi's Strengths and Weaknesses

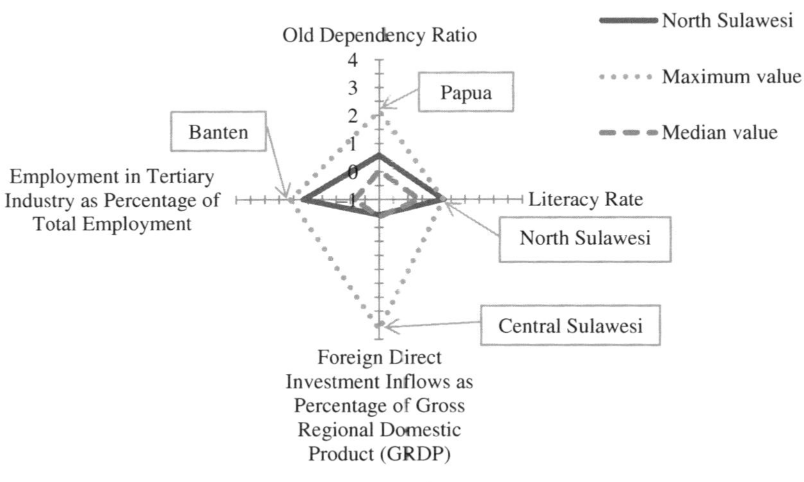

Source: Asia Competitiveness Institute.

In general, North Sulawesi performed better than the median scores of the lower-middle-income group in most of the determinants considered. The standardised score for North Sulawesi's Literacy Rate at 1.2460 was also the maximum score for the lower-middle-income group. Favourable demographic landscape along with majority of the population being equipped with basic education, as demonstrated by the relatively high standardised scores of Old Dependency Ratio and Literacy Rate respectively, are North Sulawesi's strengths. However, North Sulawesi could consider attracting more foreign direct investment to its economy, bringing in the needed capital, managerial expertise and technology for continued economic growth, as its standardised score for the Foreign Direct Investment Inflows as Percentage of GRDP was slightly below the median score.

North Sumatra, Indonesia

Lower-middle-income economy

Figure 4.25 shows the relative strengths and weaknesses of North Sumatra, which was a lower-middle-income economy in 2012 according to the income classification we adopt. As discussed in Section 4.6.1, we found four determinants which are associated with growth slowdown in this particular income group, namely Old Dependency Ratio, Literacy Rate, Foreign Direct Investment Inflows as Percentage of GRDP, and Employment in Tertiary Industry as Percentage of Total Employment. The solid line shows the standardised score for North Sumatra. The dashed line represents the median score for all economies in the lower-middle-income group across ASEAN, Greater China, India, and Indonesia, while the dotted line denotes the maximum score for those economies.

In general, North Sumatra performed better than the median scores of the lower-middle-income group in all the determinants considered. Favourable demographic landscape along with

Figure 4.25: North Sumatra's Strengths and Weaknesses

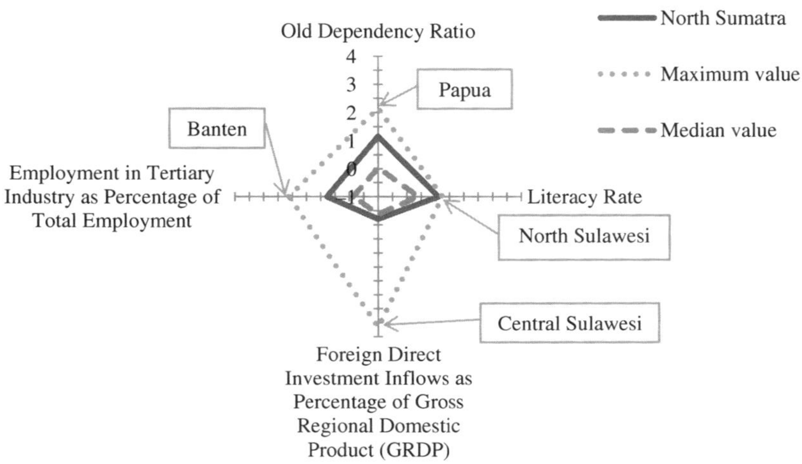

Source: Asia Competitiveness Institute.

the majority of the population being equipped with basic education, as demonstrated by the relatively high standardised scores in Old Dependency Ratio and Literacy Rate, are North Sumatra's strength. However, North Sumatra has much to work on in terms of Foreign Direct Investment Inflows as Percentage of GRDP. North Sumatra could consider attracting more foreign direct investment to its economy, bringing in the much needed capital, managerial expertise and technology for continued economic growth.

Papua, Indonesia

Lower-middle-income economy

Figure 4.26 shows the relative strengths and weaknesses of Papua, which was a lower-middle-income economy in 2012 according to the income classification we adopt. As discussed in Section 4.6.1, we found four determinants which are associated with growth slowdown in this particular income group, namely Old Dependency Ratio, Literacy Rate, Foreign Direct Investment Inflows as Percentage of GRDP, and Employment in Tertiary Industry as Percentage of Total Employment. The solid line shows the standardised score for Papua. The dashed line represents the median score for all economies in the lower-middle-income group across ASEAN, Greater China, India, and Indonesia, while the dotted line denotes the maximum score for those economies.

The performances of Papua in the various determinants were rather mixed. The standardised scores for Papua's Old Dependency Ratio and Foreign Direct Investment Inflows as Percentage of GRDP were close to the maximum scores of the lower-middle-income group. In fact, Papua attained the maximum score for Old Dependency Ratio. On the other hand, the fact that the

Figure 4.26: Papua's Strengths and Weaknesses

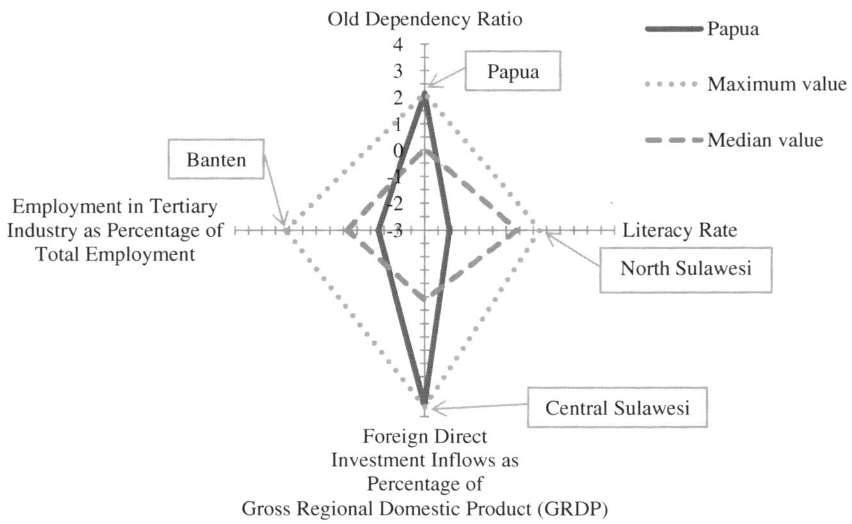

Source: Asia Competitiveness Institute.

standardised scores of Papua in Literacy Rate and Employment in Tertiary Industry as Percentage of Total Employment were much lower than the respective median scores signal the pressing need for improvement in these aspects. Though Papua enjoys a favourable demographic landscape, the majority of its population are not well equipped with basic education. Papua could consider improving its Literacy Rate, thereby unleashing its human capital potential to contribute in higher value-added activities within the service sector.

Riau, Indonesia

High-income economy

Figure 4.27 shows the relative strengths and weaknesses of Riau, which was a high-income economy in 2012 according to the income classification we adopt. As mentioned in Section 4.4.2, due to data constraint, we have combined the analysis of high-income economies with that of the upper-middle-income economies. As discussed in Section 4.6.1, we found four determinants which are associated with growth slowdown in this combined group of upper-middle-income and high-income economies, namely Openness To Trade, Literacy Rate, Secondary Industry Value Added per Worker, and Employment in Tertiary Industry as Percentage of Total Employment. The solid line shows the standardised score for Riau. The dashed line represents the median score for all economies in the combined group of upper-middle-income and high-income economies across ASEAN, Greater China, India, and Indonesia, while the dotted line denotes the maximum score for those economies.

Riau performed better than the median scores of the combined group of upper-middle-income and high-income economies in all determinants considered. In particular, its standardised scores

Figure 4.27: Riau's Strengths and Weaknesses

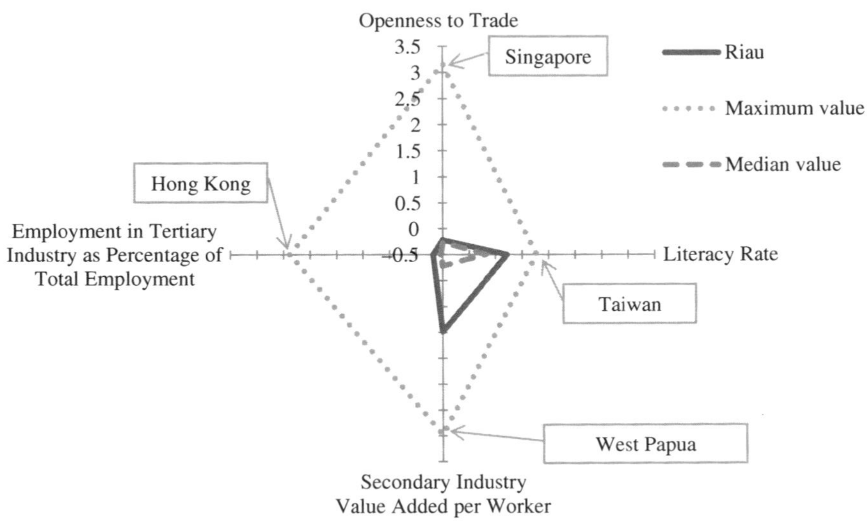

Source: Asia Competitiveness Institute.

for Literacy Rate and Secondary Industry Value Added per Worker were relatively high, though gaps still existed between Riau's standardised scores and the maximum scores attained by Taiwan and West Papua respectively. In order to mitigate the risk of experiencing economic growth slowdown, Riau could draw on its high Literacy Rate to further enhance its Employment in Tertiary Industry as Percentage of Total Employment.

Riau Islands, Indonesia

Upper-middle-income economy

Figure 4.28 shows the relative strengths and weaknesses of Riau Islands, which was an upper-middle-income economy in 2012 according to the income classification we adopt. As mentioned in Section 4.4.2, due to data constraint, we have combined the analysis of upper-middle-income economies with that of the high-income economies. As discussed in Section 4.6.1, we found four determinants which are associated with growth slowdown in this combined group of upper-middle-income and high-income economies, namely Openness To Trade, Literacy Rate, Secondary Industry Value Added per Worker, and Employment in Tertiary Industry as Percentage of Total Employment. The solid line shows the standardised score for Riau Islands. The dashed line represents the median score for all economies in the combined group of upper-middle-income and high-income economies across ASEAN, Greater China, India, and Indonesia, while the dotted line denotes the maximum score for those economies.

In general, Riau Islands performed better than the median scores of the combined group of upper-middle-income and high-income economies in all determinants considered, except for

Figure 4.28: Riau Islands' Strengths and Weaknesses

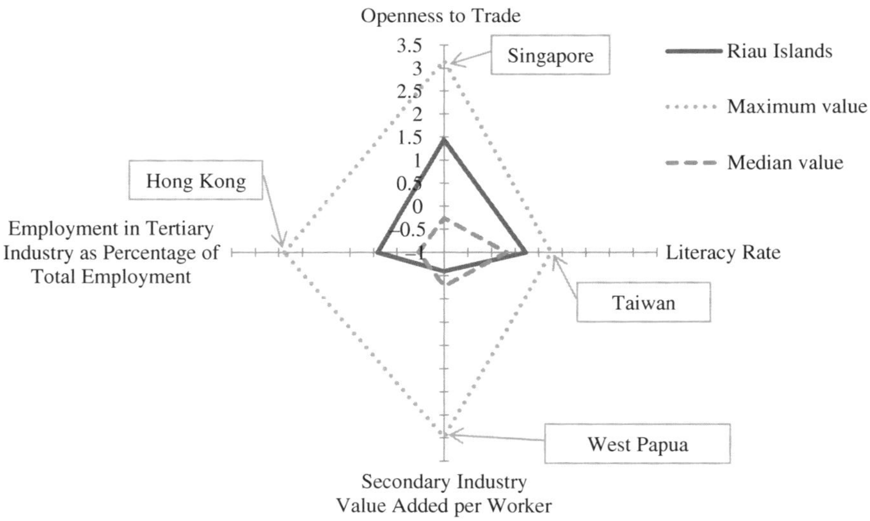

Source: Asia Competitiveness Institute.

Secondary Industry Value Added per Worker. Openness to Trade was Riau Islands' strength, with a standardised score of 1.4426, roughly half of that of Singapore. In order to mitigate the risk of experiencing economic growth slowdown, Riau Islands could draw on its high Literacy Rate to further enhance its Secondary Industry Value Added per Worker.

South Kalimantan, Indonesia

Lower-middle-income economy

Figure 4.29 shows the relative strengths and weaknesses of South Kalimantan, which was a lower-middle-income economy in 2012 according to the income classification we adopt. As discussed in Section 4.6.1, we found four determinants which are associated with growth slowdown in this particular income group, namely Old Dependency Ratio, Literacy Rate, Foreign Direct Investment Inflows as Percentage of GRDP, and Employment in Tertiary Industry as Percentage of Total Employment. The solid line shows the standardised score for South Kalimantan. The dashed line represents the median score for all economies in the lower-middle-income group across ASEAN, Greater China, India, and Indonesia, while the dotted line denotes the maximum score for those economies.

In general, South Kalimantan performed better than the median scores of the lower-middle-income group in all determinants considered. However, it could consider attracting more foreign direct investment to its economy, bringing in the needed capital, managerial expertise and technology for continued economic growth, as its standardised score for Foreign Direct Investment Inflows as Percentage of GRDP was still far from the maximum score. Relatively high Literacy

Figure 4.29: South Kalimantan's Strengths and Weaknesses

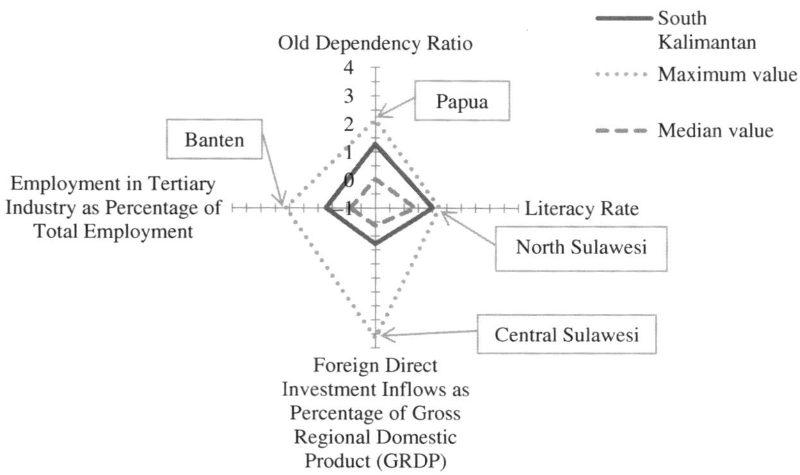

Source: Asia Competitiveness Institute.

Rate was South Kalimantan's strength with a standardised scores of 1.003 which was rather close to the maximum value of 1.2460 in North Sulawesi.

South Sulawesi, Indonesia

Lower-middle-income economy

Figure 4.30 shows the relative strengths and weaknesses of South Sulawesi, which was a lower-middle-income economy in 2012 according to the income classification we adopt. As discussed in Section 4.6.1, we found four determinants which are associated with growth slowdown in this particular income group, namely Old Dependency Ratio, Literacy Rate, Foreign Direct Investment Inflows as Percentage of GRDP, and Employment in Tertiary Industry as Percentage of Total Employment. The solid line shows the standardised score for South Sulawesi. The dashed line represents the median score for all economies in the lower-middle-income group across ASEAN, Greater China, India, and Indonesia, while the dotted line denotes the maximum score for those economies.

In general, South Sulawesi performed better than the median scores of the lower-middle-income group in all determinants considered, except for Literacy Rate. Its standardised score for Literacy Rate was a tad lower than the median score, signalling a possible area for improvement by widening access to basic education. Relatively high Employment in Tertiary Industry as Percentage of Total Employment was South Sulawesi's strength, with a standardised score of 0.8974, almost half of that of the maximum score in Banten. South Sulawesi could consider improving its Literacy Rate, thereby unleashing its human capital potential to contribute in higher value-added activities within the service sector.

Figure 4.30: South Sulawesi's Strengths and Weaknesses

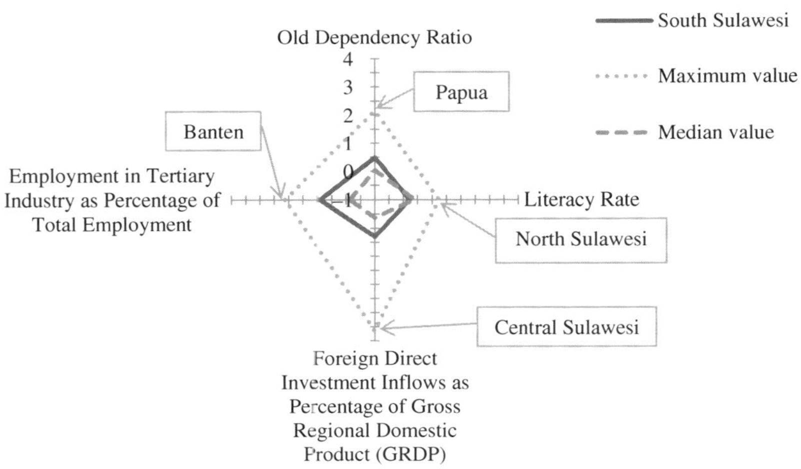

Source: Asia Competitiveness Institute.

South Sumatra, Indonesia

Lower-middle-income economy

Figure 4.31 shows the relative strengths and weaknesses of South Sumatra, which was a lower-middle-income economy in 2012 according to the income classification we adopt. As discussed in Section 4.6.1, we found four determinants which are associated with growth slowdown in this particular income group, namely Old Dependency Ratio, Literacy Rate, Foreign Direct Investment Inflows as Percentage of GRDP, and Employment in Tertiary Industry as Percentage of Total Employment. The solid line shows the standardised score for South Sumatra. The dashed line represents the median score for all economies in the lower-middle-income group across ASEAN, Greater China, India, and Indonesia, while the dotted line denotes the maximum score for those economies.

In general, South Sumatra performed better than the median scores of the lower-middle-income group in all determinants considered, except for Employment in Tertiary Industry as Percentage of Total Employment. Relatively high Literacy Rate was South Sumatra's strength, with a standardised score of 1.0502 which was rather close to the maximum value of 1.2460 in North Sulawesi. South Sumatra could tap on its high literacy rate to increase its Employment in Tertiary Industry as Percentage of Total Employment.

Figure 4.31: South Sumatra's Strengths and Weaknesses

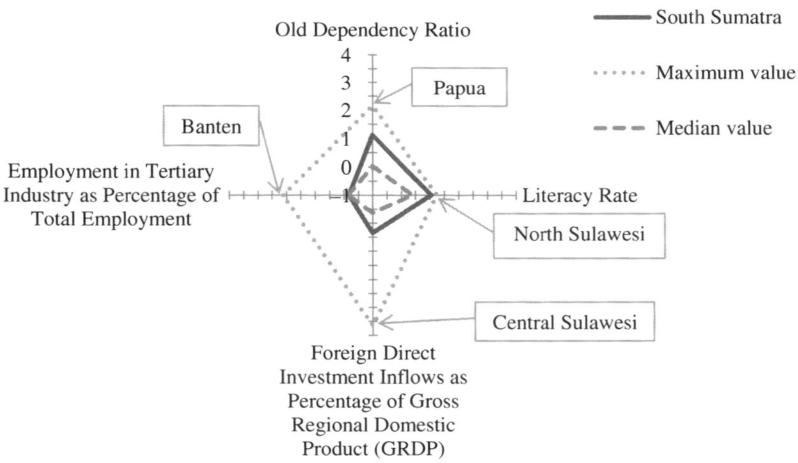

Source: Asia Competitiveness Institute.

Southeast Sulawesi, Indonesia

Lower-middle-income economy

Figure 4.32 shows the relative strengths and weaknesses of Southeast Sulawesi, which was a lower-middle-income economy in 2012 according to the income classification we adopt.

Figure 4.32: Southeast Sulawesi's Strengths and Weaknesses

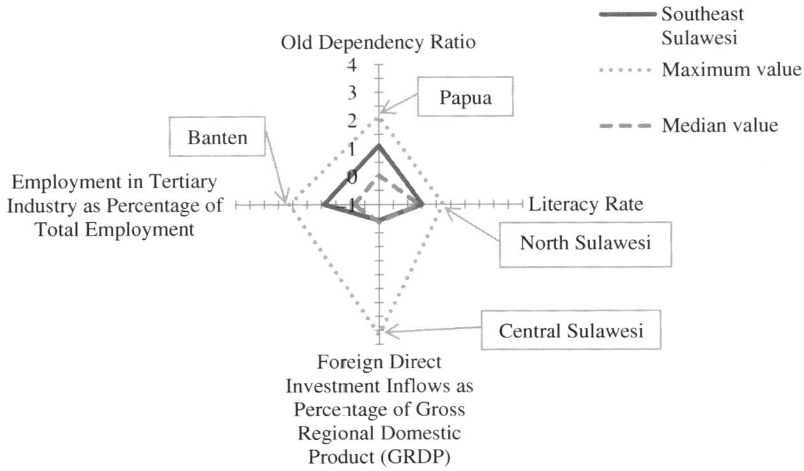

Source: Asia Competitiveness Institute.

As discussed in Section 4.6.1, we found four determinants which are associated with growth slowdown in this particular income group, namely Old Dependency Ratio, Literacy Rate, Foreign Direct Investment Inflows as Percentage of GRDP, and Employment in Tertiary Industry as Percentage of Total Employment. The solid line shows the standardised score for Southeast Sulawesi. The dashed line represents the median score for all economies in the lower-middle-income group across ASEAN, Greater China, India, and Indonesia, while the dotted line denotes the maximum score for those economies.

The performances of Southeast Sulawesi in the various determinants were rather mixed. The standardised scores for Southeast Sulawesi's Literacy Rate and Foreign Direct Investment Inflows as Percentage of GRDP were close to the median scores of the lower-middle-income group, suggesting much room for improvement in these aspects. On the other hand, Southeast Sulawesi had a relatively high score for Employment in Tertiary Industry as Percentage of Total Employment and a relatively low score for Old Dependency Ratio. Though Southeast Sulawesi enjoyed a favourable demographic landscape, the majority of its population were not well equipped with basic education. Southeast Sulawesi could consider improving its Literacy Rate, thereby unleashing its human capital potential to contribute in higher value-added activities within the service sector.

West Java, Indonesia

Lower-middle-income economy

Figure 4.33 shows the relative strengths and weaknesses of West Java, which was a lower-middle-income economy in 2012 according to the income classification we adopt. As discussed in Section 4.6.1, we found four determinants which are associated with growth slowdown in this

Figure 4.33: West Java's Strengths and Weaknesses

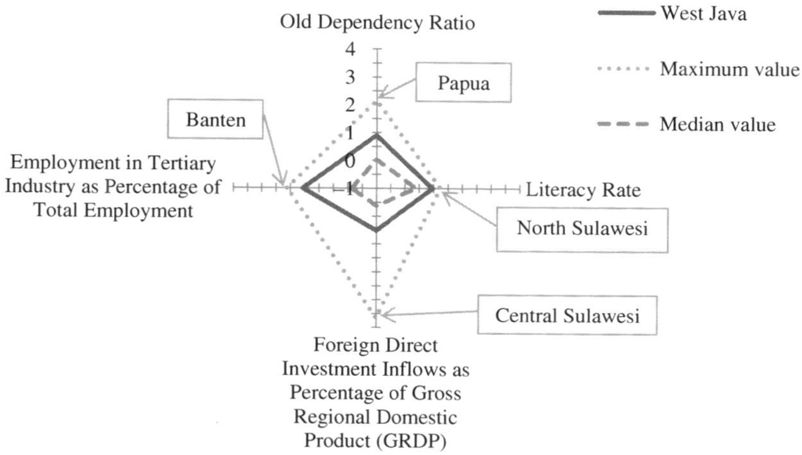

Source: Asia Competitiveness Institute.

particular income group, namely Old Dependency Ratio, Literacy Rate, Foreign Direct Investment Inflows as Percentage of GRDP, and Employment in Tertiary Industry as Percentage of Total Employment. The solid line shows the standardised score for West Java. The dashed line represents the median score for all economies in the lower-middle-income group across ASEAN, Greater China, India, and Indonesia, while the dotted line denotes the maximum score for those economies.

In general, West Java performed better than the median scores of the lower-middle-income group in all determinants considered. However, West Java could consider attracting more foreign direct investment to its economy, bringing in the needed capital, managerial expertise and technology for continued economic growth, as its standardised score for the Foreign Direct Investment Inflows as Percentage of GRDP was still far from the maximum score. Relatively high Literacy Rate and Employment in Tertiary Industry as Percentage of Total Employment were West Java's strengths, with standardised scores of 0.9779 and 1.5618 respectively. The scores were rather close to the maximum scores that were achieved by North Sulawesi and Banten, respectively.

West Kalimantan, Indonesia

Lower-middle-income economy

Figure 4.34 shows the relative strengths and weaknesses of West Kalimantan, which is a lower-middle-income economy according to the income classification we adopt. As discussed in Section 4.6.1, we found four determinants which are associated with growth slowdown in this particular income group, namely Old Dependency Ratio, Literacy Rate, Foreign Direct Investment Inflows as Percentage of GRDP, and Employment in Tertiary Industry as Percentage

Figure 4.34: West Kalimantan's Strengths and Weaknesses

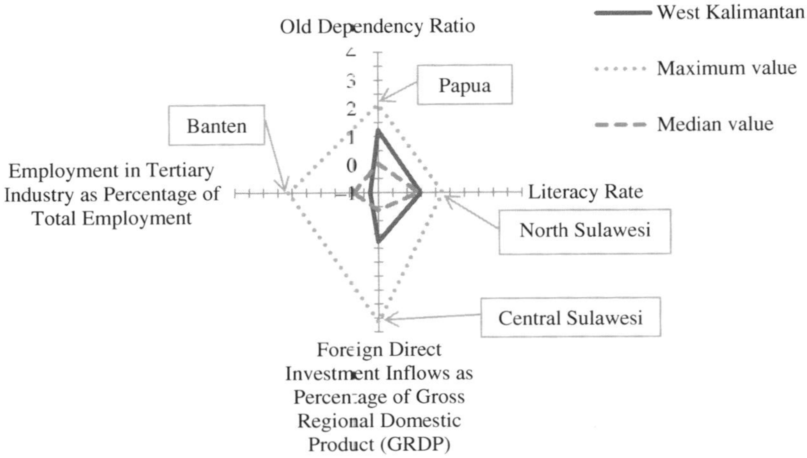

Source: Asia Competitiveness Institute.

of Total Employment. The solid line shows the standardised score for West Kalimantan. The dashed line represents the median score for all economies in the lower-middle-income group across ASEAN, Greater China, India, and Indonesia, while the dotted line denotes the maximum score for those economies.

The performance of West Kalimantan in the various determinants was rather mixed. West Kalimantan's standardised scores for Old Dependency Ratio and Foreign Direct Investment Inflows as Percentage of GRDP were noticeably higher than the median scores, while its score for Literacy Rate was close to the median score. On the other hand, the score for Employment in Tertiary Industry as Percentage of Total Employment was relatively low for West Kalimantan. There is much room for improvement if West Kalimantan wants to minimise its risk of undergoing growth slowdown in the lower-middle-income group.

West Nusa Tenggara, Indonesia

Low-income economy

Figure 4.35 shows the relative strengths and weaknesses of West Nusa Tenggara, which was a low-income economy in 2012 according to the income classification we adopt. As discussed in Section 4.6.1, we found three determinants which are associated with growth slowdown in this particular income group, namely Length of Road per Capita, Literacy Rate, and Foreign Direct Investment Inflows as Percentage of GRDP. The solid line shows the standardised score for West Nusa Tenggara. The dashed line represents the median score for all economies in the low-income group across ASEAN, Greater China, India, and Indonesia, while the dotted line denotes the maximum score for those economies.

Out of the three determinants considered, West Nusa Tenggara's standardised scores for two determinants were below the respective median scores by a large margin, including the Length

Figure 4.35: West Nusa Tenggara's Strengths and Weaknesses

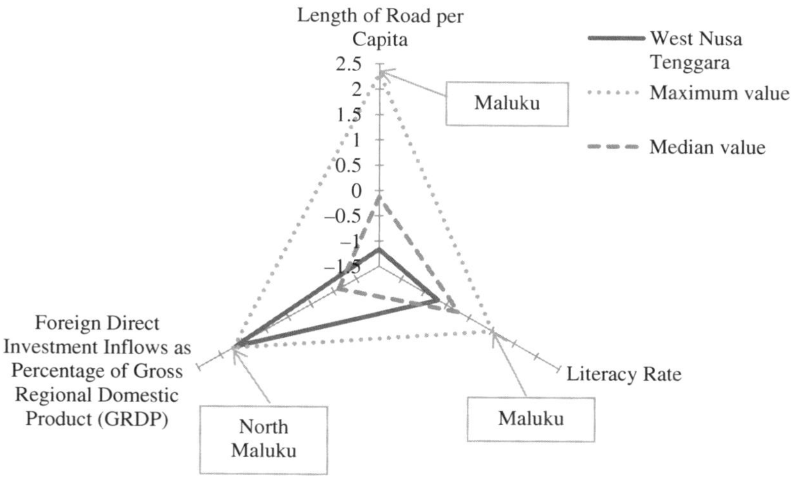

Source: Asia Competitiveness Institute.

of Road per Capita and Literacy Rate. However, Foreign Direct Investment Inflows as Percentage of GRDP was West Nusa Tenggara's strength, with a standardised score of 1.6756 which was rather close to the maximum score of 1.7218 achieved by North Maluku. In order to avoid economic growth slowdown, West Nusa Tenggara could consider drawing upon its strength in attracting foreign direct investment to provide more reliable and better quality infrastructure and people's access to basic education.

West Papua, Indonesia

Upper-middle-income economy

Figure 4.36 shows the relative strengths and weaknesses of West Papua, which was an upper-middle-income economy in 2012 according to the income classification we adopt. As mentioned in Section 4.4.2, due to data constraint, we have combined the analysis of upper-middle-income economies with that of the high-income economies. As discussed in Section 4.6.1, we found four determinants which are associated with growth slowdown in this combined group of upper-middle-income and high-income economies, namely Openness To Trade, Literacy Rate, Secondary Industry Value Added per Worker, and Employment in Tertiary Industry as Percentage of Total Employment. The solid line shows the standardised score for West Papua. The dashed line represents the median score for all economies in the combined group of upper-middle-income and high-income economies across ASEAN, Greater China, India, and Indonesia, while the dotted line denotes the maximum score for those economies.

The performances of West Papua in the various determinants were rather mixed. West Papua's standardised score for Employment in Tertiary Industry as Percentage of Total Employment was close to the median scores of the combined group of upper-middle-income and high-income

Figure 4.36: West Papua's Strengths and Weaknesses

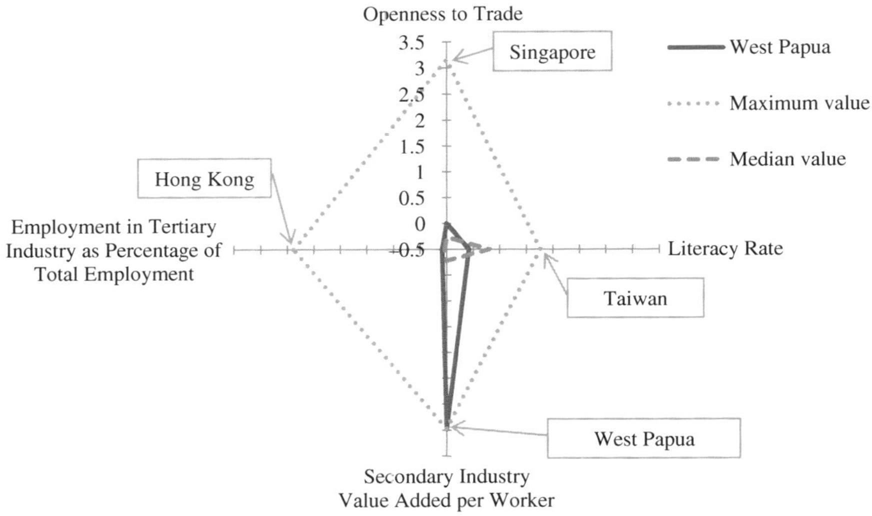

Source: Asia Competitiveness Institute.

economies, suggesting that there is much room for improvement in this aspect. On the other hand, relatively high Openness To Trade and Secondary Industry Value Added per Worker were West Papua's strengths. Moreover, West Papua has achieved the maximum score for Secondary Industry Value Added per Worker with a standardised score of 2.9808. However, its standardised score for Literacy Rate was a noticeably lower than the median score, signalling a possible area for improvement by widening access to basic education.

West Sulawesi, Indonesia

Low-income economy

Figure 4.37 shows the relative strengths and weaknesses of West Sulawesi, which was a low-income economy in 2012 according to the income classification we adopt. As discussed in Section 4.6.1, we found three determinants which are associated with growth slowdown in this particular income group, namely Length of Road per Capita, Literacy Rate, and Foreign Direct Investment Inflows as Percentage of GRDP. The solid line shows the standardised score for West Sulawesi. The dashed line represents the median score for all economies in the low-income group across ASEAN, Greater China, India, and Indonesia, while the dotted line denotes the maximum score for those economies.

The standardised scores for West Sulawesi's Length of Road per Capita and Foreign Direct Investment Inflows as Percentage of GRDP were a tad lower than the respective median scores, signalling possible areas of improvement. As for Literacy Rate, West Sulawesi's standardised score was only slightly higher than the median score of 0.2663 at 0.2690. Basic infrastructure development is vital for low-income economies like West Sulawesi to realise its potential for

Figure 4.37: West Sulawesi's Strengths and Weaknesses

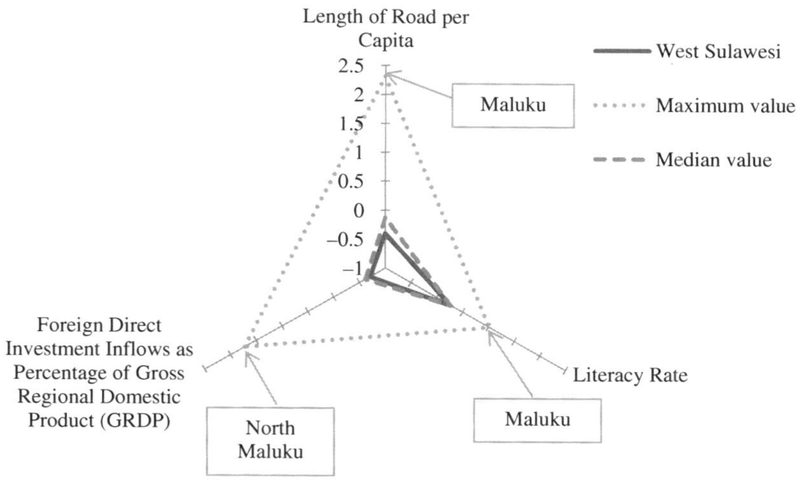

Source: Asia Competitiveness Institute.

greater economic returns by providing better services and enabling businesses to grow and expand. At the same time, it is crucial for West Sulawesi to improve its Literacy Rate which can unleash its human capital potential to contribute in higher value-added activities.

West Sumatra, Indonesia

Lower-middle-income economy

Figure 4.38 shows the relative strengths and weaknesses of West Sumatra, which was a lower-middle-income economy in 2012 according to the income classification we adopt. As discussed in Section 4.6.1, we found four determinants which are associated with growth slowdown in this particular income group, namely Old Dependency Ratio, Literacy Rate, Foreign Direct Investment Inflows as Percentage of GRDP, and Employment in Tertiary Industry as Percentage of Total Employment. The solid line shows the standardised score for West Sumatra. The dashed line represents the median score for all economies in the lower-middle-income group across ASEAN, Greater China, India, and Indonesia, while the dotted line denotes the maximum score for those economies.

In general, West Sumatra performed better than the median scores of the lower-middle-income group in most of the determinants considered. However, West Sumatra could consider attracting more foreign direct investment to its economy, bringing in the needed capital, managerial expertise and technology for continued economic growth, as its standardised score for Foreign Direct Investment Inflows as Percentage of GRDP was slightly below the median score. Relatively high Literacy Rate is West Sumatra's strength, with a standardised score of 1.0271 which was rather close to the maximum value of 1.2460 achieved by North Sulawesi. West Sumatra

Figure 4.38: West Sumatra's Strengths and Weaknesses

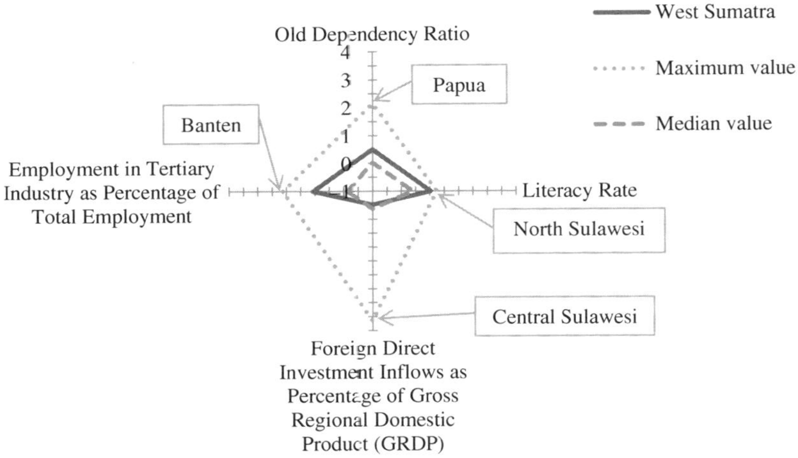

Source: Asia Competitiveness Institute.

could tap on its high literacy rate to increase its Employment in Tertiary Industry as Percentage of Total Employment.

4.8 Policy Implications and Concluding Notes

The Indonesian government has focused on improving the quality of economic growth to be green, more inclusive and sustainable. The emphases of the National Medium Term Development Plan 2015–2019 (RPJMN 2015–2019) include "inclusive and sustainable growth, increasing value added of natural resources with the sustainable approach, increasing quality of the environment, disaster mitigation and tackling climate change" (London School of Economics and Political Science, 2015).

In this context, our research differs from the existing literature on middle-income trap and growth slowdowns in Indonesia by studying this issue at the sub-national rather than at the macro level. Despite a general increase in level of GRDP per capita for the sub-national economies of Indonesia since we started to track them in 1990, disparity still exists across economies. According to the income thresholds classification we adopted, there were only three economies in the high-income group at 2013 which included DKI Jakarta, East Kalimantan, and Riau, while two economies attained the upper-middle-income status, namely Riau Islands and West Papua. Conversely, six economies were still stuck in the low-income group, specifically Gorontalo, Maluku, North Maluku, West Nusa Tenggara, East Nusa Tenggara, and West Sulawesi. The rest of the 22 economies were in the lower-middle-income group as of 2013.

By conducting both logistics and probit estimations as well as employing the Bayesian Model Averaging (BMA) techniques, we found that growth slowdowns in various income groups tend to be associated with different sets of determinants. Growth slowdown in the low-income group is mainly associated with high level of GRDP per Capita, low Literacy Rate, low Foreign Direct

Investment Inflows as Percentage of GRDP and short Length of Road per Capita. On the other hand, lower-middle-income economies are more likely to experience growth slowdown when they have higher level of GRDP per Capita, lower Foreign Direct Investment Inflows as Percentage of GRDP, higher Old Dependency Ratio, lower Employment in Tertiary Industry as Percentage of Total Employment, and lower Literacy Rate. As for the combined group of upper-middle-income and high-income economies, growth slowdown for economies in this group is associated with high GRDP per Capita, low Openness To Trade, low Literacy Rate, low Employment in Tertiary Industry as Percentage of Total Employment, and low Secondary Industry Value added per Worker.

Having identified the underlying drivers of growth slowdown in each income group, we assessed whether each sub-national economy of Indonesia is prone to experience growth deceleration. Overall, we discovered that sub-national economies in Indonesia have a positive outlook with an average of a 10% chance of experiencing growth slowdown in the 2012–2017 period. Among all economies in our sample, sub-national economies in Indonesia have the lowest average predictive probability of slowdown.[38] Riau is the most likely to slow down among all Indonesia sub-national economies and yet its probability of slowdown is still smaller than 0.5. Nevertheless, the caveat to this finding is that a low probability number may reflect growth stagnation, in which initial growth rates were so slow that the definition of growth slowdown does not apply.

In general, the chief policy implication of our study lies in the variables that had been identified as significant by our income group-specific models. Peer-learning is important in formulating policies to combat growth slowdown. The sub-national economies in Indonesia can benchmark their performances in the relevant policy dimensions against other Asian developing economies to identify their relative strengths and weaknesses and promote the necessary reforms to mitigate the risk of growth slowdown.

References

Abbas, S. Ali, Nazim Belhocine, Asmaa ElGanainy, and Mark Horton. 2010. "A Historical Public Debt Database." IMF Working Paper No. 10/425, International Monetary Fund (IMF), Washington D.C.

Agenor, Pierre-Richard. 2015. "Caught in the Middle? The Economics of Middle-Income Trap", FERDI Working Paper No. 142. *Fondation pour les études et recherches sur le développement international* (FERDI), Clermont-Ferrand.

Aiyar, Shekhar, Romain Duval, Damien Puy, Yiqun Wu, and Longmei Zhang. 2013. "Growth Slowdows and the Middle-Income Trap." IMF Working Paper No. 13/71, International Monetary Fund (IMF), Washington D.C.

Azariadis, Costas, and John Stachurski. 2005. "Poverty Traps." in *Handbook of Economic Growth*, edited by Philippe Aghion and Steven N. Durlauf, 1A:295–384. Amsterdam: Elsevier.

Barro, Robert J., and Jong Wha Lee. 2013. "A New Data Set of Educational Attainment in the World, 1950–2010." *Journal of Development Economics* 104 (C): 184–198.

[38]The average predictive probabilities of Greater China and India are 0.56872 and 0.43071, respectively.

Benkovskis, K., B. Bluhm, E. Bobeica, C. Osbat, and S. Zeugner. 2015. "An Empirical Analysis of Competitiveness Drivers Using Bayesian Model Averaging."

Bloom, David E., David Canning, and Jaypee Sevilla. 2003. "Geography and Poverty Traps." *Journal of Economic Growth* 8(4): 355–378.

Bluedorn, John, Rupa Duttagupta, Jaime Guajardo, and Petia Topalova. 2013. "Capital Flows Are Fickle: Anytime, Anywhere." IMF Working Paper No. 13/183, International Monetary Fund (IMF), Washington D.C.

Brock, W. A. 2001. "What Have We Learned from a Decade of Empirical Research on Growth? Growth Empirics and Reality." *The World Bank Economic Review* 15(2): 229–272.

Bulman, David, Maya Eden, and Ha Nguyen. 2014. "Transitioning from Low-Income Growth to High-Income Growth: Is There a Middle Income Trap?" 7104. The World Bank Policy Research Working Paper No. 7104, The World Bank, Washington D.C.

Cooper, Andrew, and Jongryn Mo. 2013. "Middle Power Leadership and the Evolution of the G20." *Global Summitry Journal* 1: 1–14.

Dehn, Jan. 2014. "The High Income Trap." *The Emerging View*. Available at: https://www.ashmoregroup.com/sites/default/files/article-docs/June 14 High Income trap.pdf.

Eichengreen, Barry, Donghyun Park, and Kwanho Shin. 2012. "When Fast-Growing Economies Slow Down: International Evidence and Implications for China." *Asian Economic Papers* 11: 42–87.

Eichengreen, Barry, Donghyun Park, and Kwanho Shin. 2013. "Growth Slowdowns Redux: New Evidence on the Middle-Income Trap." NBER Economic Research Paper Series No. 18673, National Bureau of Economic Research (NBER), Massachusetts.

Felipe, Jesus. 2012a. "Tracking the Middle-Income Trap: What Is It, Who Is in It, and Why? Part 1." ADB Working Paper No. 306, Asian Development Bank (ADB), Manila.

Felipe, Jesus. 2012b. "Tracking the Middle-Income Trap: What Is It, Who Is in It, and Why? Part 2." ADB Working Paper No. 307, Asian Development Bank (ADB), Manila.

Flaaen, Aaron, Ejaz Ghani, and Saurabh Mishra. 2013. "How to Avoid Middle Income Traps? Evidence from Malaysia." The World Bank Policy Research Working Papers No. 6427, The World Bank, Washington D.C.

Gill, Indermit Singh, and Homi Kharas. 2007. *An East Asian Renaissance: Ideas for Economic Growth*. The World Bank, Washington D.C.

Gill, Indermit Singh, and Homi Kharas. 2015. "The Middle-Income Trap Turns Ten", The World Bank Policy Research Working Paper No. 7403, The World Bank, Washington D.C.

González-Aguado, Carlos, and Enrique Moral-Benito. 2013. "Determinants of Corporate Default: A BMA Approach." *Applied Economics Letters* 20(6): 511–514.

Hausmann, Ricardo, Lant Pritchett, and Dani Rodrik. 2005. "Growth Accelerations. Journal of Economic Growth." *Journal of Economic Growth* 10(4): 303–329.

Hausmann, Ricardo, Jason Hwang, and Dani Rodrik. 2005. "What you export matters". NBER Economic Research Paper Series No. 11905, National Bureau of Economic Research (NBER), Massachusetts.

Hausmann, Ricardo, Francisco Rodríguez, and Rodrigo Wagner. 2006. "Growth Collapses." 136. CID Working Paper No. 146, Center for International Development (CID), Harvard University, Massachusetts.

Im, Fernando Gabriel, and David Rosenblatt. 2013. "Middle-Income Traps: A Conceptual and Empirical Survey." The World Bank Policy Research Working Paper No. 6594, The World Bank, Washington D.C.

International Monetary Fund. 2015. "World Economic Outlook: Adjusting to Lower Commodity Prices." Available at: http://www.imf.org/external/pubs/ft/weo/2015/02/pdf/text.pdf (accessed on February 25, 2016).

Jalan, Jyotsna, and Martin Ravallion. 2002. "Geographic Poverty Traps? A Micro Model of Consumption Growth in Rural China." *Journal of Applied Econometrics* 17(4): 329–346.

Jerzmanowski, Michal. 2006. "Empirics of Hills, Plateaus, Mountains and Plains: A Markov-Switching Approach to Growth." *Journal of Development Economics* 81(2): 357–385.

Kasenda, Daniel. 2015. "Can Asian Developing Countries Stuck In A "Middle-Income Trap" Learn From South Korea's Economic Development Experience?", GDN Working Paper No.86. Global Development Network (GDN), Washington D.C.

Kyozuka, Tamaki. 2016. "ASEAN Bloc's Exports Drop for First Time in 6 Years." *Nikkei Asian Review*, February 24. Available at: http://asia.nikkei.com/Politics-Economy/Economy/ASEAN-bloc-s-exports-drop-for-first-time-in-6-years (accessed on February 25, 2016).

London School of Economics and Political Science. 2015. "National Medium Term Development Plan 2015-2019 (RPJMN 2015–2019)." Available at: http://www.lse.ac.uk/GranthamInstitute/law/national-medium-term-development-plan-2015-2019-rpjmn-2015-2019/ (accessed on February 25, 2016).

Maddison, James. 2010. "Statistics on World Population, GDP and Per Capita GDP, 1-2008AD." Available at: http://www.ggdc.net/maddison/oriindex.htm (accessed on August 11, 2015).

Neumann, Frederic. 2015. "Time to Talk about the High Income Trap." *Nikkei Asian Review*, May 24. Available at: http://asia.nikkei.com/Viewpoints/Economeister/Time-to-talk-about-the-high-income-trap (accessed on February 23, 2016).

Pritchett, Lant. 2000. "Understanding Patterns of Economic Growth: Searching for Hills among Plateaus, Mountains, and Plains." *The World Bank Economic Review* 14(2): 221–250.

Quah, Danny T. 1993. "Empirical Cross-Section Dynamics in Economic Growth." *European Economic Review* 37(2–3): 426–434.

Reddy, Sanjay, and Camelia Minoiu. 2008. "Real Income Stagnation of Countries 1960–2001." *The Journal of Development Studies* 45(1): 1–23.

Rhee, Changyong. 2012. "Indonesia Risks Falling Into the Middle-Income Trap." Asian Development Bank Op-Ed/Opinion. Available at: http://www.adb.org/news/op-ed/indonesia-risks-falling-middle-income-trap-changyong-rhee (accessed on February 25, 2016).

Sambijantoro, Satria. 2013. "RI at Middle-Income Crossroad." *The Jakarta Post*, December 13. Available at: http://www.thejakartapost.com/news/2013/12/13/ri-middle-income-crossroad.html (accessed on February 23, 2016).

Tan, Khee Giap, Lian Xiao and Xie Teleixi. 2016. "Growth Slowdown Analysis for Greater China Economies" *Journal of Economics and Development Studies*, 4(2): 129–144, June 2016 [US].

Tan, Khee Giap, Trieu Duong Luu Nguyen and Lian Xiao. 2017 "Empirical Analysis of Growth Slowdown in ASEAN." *The Journal of Developing Areas* [Forthcoming].

Tan, Khee Giap, Trieu Duong Luu Nguyen, and Sangiita Yoong Wei Cher. 2016. "An Empirical Investigation of Growth Slowdown Analysis for India's Sub-National Economies."*ACI Technical*

Working Paper #06-2016, Asia Competitiveness Institute, Lee Kuan Yew School of Public Policy, National University of Singapore, June.

Tan, Khee Giap, Le Phuong Anh Nguyen, Sasidaran Gopalan and Trieu Duong Luu Nguyen. 2017. *2015 Annual Competitiveness Analysis, Agricultural Productivity and Development Vision for ASEAN-10.* Singapore: World Scientific.

Tan, Khee Giap, Sangiita Yoong Wei Cher, Sasidaran Gopalan and Le Phuong Anh Nguyen. 2016. *2014 Annual Competitiveness Ranking and Simulation Study for ASEAN-10 and Development Strategies to Enhance Asia Economic Connectivity*. Singapore: World Scientific.

The Conference Board. 2015. "Output, Labor and Labor Productivity, 1950-2015, Total Economy Database, May 2015 Version." Available at: https://www.conference-board.org/data/economydatabase/index.cfm?id=27762 (accessed on August 11, 2015).

The World Bank. 2014. *Indonesia Development Policy Review 2014 - Indonesia: Avoiding the Trap*. The World Bank, Jakarta.

Wei, Shang Jin. 2015. "PRC's Slowdown for Asia's Growth – Key Takeaways." Asian Development Blog, July 25. Available at: http://blogs.adb.org/blog/prc-s-slowdown-asia-s-growth-key-takeaways (accessed on February 23, 2016).

Woo, Wing Thye. 2012. "China Meets the Middle-Income Trap: The Large Potholes in the Road to Catching-Up." *Journal of Chinese Economic and Business Studies* 10(4): 313–336.

Ye, Longfeng and Peter Robertson. 2016. "Identifying prisoners of the middle-income trap", Available at: http://www.voxeu.org/article/identifying-prisoners-middle-income-trap (accessed on April 29, 2016).

Yusuf, Shahid, and Kaoru Nabeshima. 2009. "Can Malaysia Escape the Middle-Income Trap? A Strategy for Penang." The World Bank Policy Research Working Paper No. 4971, The World Bank, Washington D.C.

Zhang, Derong. 2014. "The Mechanism of the Middle Income Trap and the Potential Factors Influencing China's Economic Growth" *Frontiers of Economics in China* 9(3): 499–528.

Zhang, Longmei, and Damien Puy. 2015. "Growth Slowdown: Are Frontier and Developing Asian Economies Different?" in *Frontier and Developing Asia: The Next Generation of Emerging Markets*, edited by Alfred Schipke. International Monetary Fund, Washington D.C.

Discussant Note 4.1[1]

Growth Slowdown Analysis by Income Thresholds for Indonesia's Sub-national Economies

Dr Kirida Bhaopichitr

Research Director
Thailand Development Research Institute (TDRI), Thailand

Good afternoon everyone, I would like to thank the ACI, especially Professor Tan for inviting me here today. If you remember we had a similar conference last November, and I was also here. I can see the progress that has been made since then. I would like to congratulate the team for doing such comprehensive research, especially the young researchers from the ACI who have been putting in a lot of hard work. They have been crunching all these data for us to have a very comprehensive explanation of the slowdown that different countries in ASEAN and also the sub-national units in Indonesia as well as in China and India have been experiencing.

With the good work that the team has already done, I probably have more observations and questions than answers to offer to them. Let me start with some observations that I have on the results that they have presented.

The observations that I have are on the main page which shows the results. The paper claims that there are these important determinants, as you can say, of growth slowdown in each income group for the economies. The different explanations that the paper offers make up a 95-page PowerPoint of slides. For some of them, there may be more in-depth explanations than others. For those that I still have not understood, please allow me to ask some questions. I would like to focus on two of the main determinants: openness to trade and the old dependency ratio.

The paper claims that if upper- and middle-income countries had high openness to trade, then the probability of that country slowing down would be less. This conclusion was based on the negative sign in front of the coefficient for the openness to trade variable in the regression tables. In this new normal world where growth is slowing down around the world and world trade is

[1]The contents of this discussion note were delivered during the Asia Competitiveness Institute (ACI)-World Bank ASEAN Economic Forum, on 9 September 2016, in Singapore

also slowing down, I am not sure if this still holds. The chart on screen shows the latest data from the World Bank. The next one is the IMF world forecast. As evident from these charts, in this new normal world, one of the main characteristics is that world growth will slow down. This is because of volatility or what they now call VUCA which stands for Volatility, Uncertainty, Complexity and Ambiguity. There are a lot of uncertainties and one of the things that have also happened is trade consolidation. For instance, the US may have been using inputs from Asia to produce goods but they are consolidating the supply chain, meaning that they are producing more in Mexico or in Latin America. Even China is doing the same thing. They are trying to produce closer to home to reduce the costs of production and logistics.

Let us now look at how world growth data compares to world trade data. We observe that before the Lehman Brother Crisis in the US, when the world economy grew by 1%, world trade would roughly increase by 2%, so the relation is one to two. After the Crisis we see that that relationship has softened. Now, when world growth expands by percent, instead of world trade growing by 2%, it only grows by 1%. This has really affected countries that are open to trade, especially countries that are export-oriented like Thailand and Malaysia. To make a long story short, world growth is growing slower than before, and in addition to that, world trade is slowing even more. As such, countries that are open to trade may actually have higher probability of slowing down instead of having a lower probability of slowing down as the paper suggested. This is something that happens because the world changes so quickly. It is not that there is something wrong with the model, but it is just that with the new data coming out in recent years, we can see that the structure of world trade has changed. As a result, its impact on countries that are very open can be different.

In addition, I would like show you the example of Thailand. The Thailand Development Research Institute has conducted a constant share analysis to decompose the different determinants of export growth. There are four main components: (i) export growth depends on growth in world trade, (ii) export growth depends on conditions in the country that we export to, (iii) export growth depends on the commodity that we actually export, and (iv) export growth depends on competitiveness. As you can see, in the case of Thailand, the world trade effect is pretty significant. Hence, if world trade slows down, it will very much affect Thailand's exports. We also extend the analysis for other countries; and if the ACI is interested, we can partner on this research, not only at the country level but also the sub-national level.

Next, I would also like to make an observation about old age dependency ratio. The paper says when old age dependency in a country rises, the probability of a country slowing down would increase. That makes sense because if you have more old people and fewer working-age people, it reduces your economy's growth potential. However, the paper suggests that the effect is only significant for lower-middle-income countries. Is that because many of the middle-income countries are still very protective of their labor market? Singapore is aging but is already a high-income country, and it welcomes talents from overseas to supplement their workforce. In contrast, middle-income and lower income countries, like Thailand, do not welcome foreign talents. Clearly, the relationship between old age dependency ratio and the probability of growth slowdown may change if the underlying policies change. Being more open to immigrants, especially skilled workers, may help middle-income countries.

I also have a few questions. I like the paper because the model has yielded a lot of results. However, I would like the team to explain the reasons behind some of these results. One of the charts shows that upper-middle income and high-income economies in ASEAN have a higher probability of getting into a slowdown. I am wondering why this is the case. One possible explanation might be that these ASEAN countries are more open to trade, so now that trade is slowing down, the probability of economic growth slowdown has risen. However, this is probably not the reason because the data used in this paper is only until 2013. Hence, I am not sure why that is the case.

The second question is that when the research team takes into account all the economies and not just ASEAN, they found that the probability of lower-middle income economies slowing down is actually quite high. The graph is in a concave fashion which means that when we are at this level, the probability of you slowing down is higher than when you are in a high-income area. I'm not sure why that is the case. But if that is really the case, we can argue for the middle-income trap. If you are in the middle-income group, your chances of slowing down are much higher, so you can try to become high-income before you are trapped in there. This is a powerful result if it is going to prove the existence of a middle-income trap.

The last question concerns the chart that shows a comparison of Singapore with other countries in different dimensions. Now that we know that there are different reasons for why Singapore may grow at a slower rate, I'm also interested to know which determinants we should focus on if we want to reduce the probability of Singapore slowing down. Which bottleneck is the most problematic that we need to address first? I think such analysis is something useful which could be added into the paper. The authors may then suggest which policy should be implemented in order to reduce the probability of growth slowdown.

Discussant Note 4.2[1]

Growth Slowdown Analysis by Income Thresholds for Indonesia's Sub-national Economies

Dr Darwin Marcelo

Infrastructure Economist
The World Bank Group

I have two sets of comments, one on the methods and models, and the other one on the results.

First, this is a very interesting research, addresses a very relevant question and includes a huge effort to prepare the data, especially because the numbers are at the sub-regional level. Last year, The World Bank worked together with NUS and ACI to obtain similar information at the national level. This process was very complicated, so what you have achieved here is remarkable.

On the methods and models, the search for slowdown episodes started with a window of five years. The selection of that window is rather arbitrary. A question I would ask to the researchers is what would have happened if you had a longer or shorter window. This is relevant because the number of episodes may change if the window is narrower or wider. When trying to explain the probability of occurrence of a slowdown episode, the window selection may affect the results. This window also has a direct effect on the time series presented. The study used a twenty-year dataset, but with a five-year window, 10 years of data are lost. The analysis detected a slowdown only for a period of 10 years, from 1998 to 2008. One may think that most slowdowns happened after 2008 and before 1998. Therefore, the selection of this window is very important, because it has two repercussions on the results of the model.

On the results, it would be useful if you can include the classification statistics, given that the whole point of the exercise is to make a prediction and assess the probability of a slowdown episode. Two indicators should have been presented; sensitivity and specificity. Sensitivity means the fraction of events that are correctly classified and specificity means fraction of non-events that are correctly classified. This will give the reader an idea of how powerful the model

[1]The contents of this discussion note were delivered during the Asia Competitiveness Institute (ACI)-World Bank ASEAN Economic Forum, on 9 September 2016, in Singapore

is. Furthermore, given that the suggested probabilistic model is trying to predict the probability of occurrence of a slowdown event, it should also be contrasted against the observed results to give the reader an idea of how powerful the model is.

I also think that it is highly possible that observations are clustered at the country level because the units of observation are at the sub-regional level. This might lead to standard error bias, but more importantly, coefficient bias, which could lead to a wrong conclusion. Therefore, I suggest to perform a test to be completely sure that this kind of phenomenon (clustering at the country level) is not present. The intuition is that a country is exposed to the same macroeconomic environment. Observations may not be independent because they correspond to sub-regions within a country. All the sub-regions are exposed to the same macroeconomic factors and so they may be clustered.

The results are striking. For a country like Singapore, there is a very high probability of experiencing a slowdown event. And then, when we look at the sub-regional level there are many economies that have about 40% probability for facing a slowdown event.

Results suggest that the richer the sub-national region is, the higher the probability of a slowdown episode is. Again, what happens when you have clustering? You may have a region within a country that is getting richer and that has a high probability of facing a slowdown. But it may happen that all the regions inside a country growth at the same time because they are clustered at the country level. I would not consider the sub-regional levels as micro nations, I would consider the sub-region as a cluster inside a country. Again, regions are similar in terms of legislation, language, trade relations, national government, etc.

Finally, regarding the implications of the model, I have the following question: what is the space that governments have or what are the instruments that governments have to reduce the probability of a slowdown, especially when the country is a middle-income or high-income one? According to the model, one of the determinants of growth slowdown is the literacy rate. Well, increasing the literacy rate is very complicated when the nation is already well educated, as in the case of Singapore.

Chapter 5

2016 Inaugural Ease of Doing Business Index on Attractiveness to Investors, Business Friendliness and Competitive Policies (EDB Index ABC) for Indonesian Provinces

5.1 Introductory Notes

Non-market considerations such as transaction costs matter for economic growth. The less burdensome it is for firms to conduct its business, the more likely it is for business activities to flourish, and the more likely it is for the economy to grow. One of the most notable initiatives that measures a firm's formal transaction costs in a given location is the annual 'Doing Business' (DB) index calculated by the World Bank. Since the DB index was first launched in 2003, it has become the gold standard in measuring the quality of business regulations. Several countries and sub-national entities have even adopted the DB ranking as a formal key performance indicator.

Despite the popularity of this index, empirical support remains ambiguous. When *de facto* experiences from the World Bank Enterprise Surveys are matched with *de jure* results as reported in DB reports, there are weak associations between the two (Hallward-Driemeier and Pritchett, 2015), suggesting that formal regulations may only play a partial role in shaping firms' perceptions towards the ease of doing business. Also, others point out that explanatory weaknesses of the DB index stem from sampling issues, especially due to the fact that an entire country's score is calculated based on surveys conducted in one or two cities only. In short, while the DB index may help to understand the extent of formal non-market challenges facing firms in a certain location, it fails to explain in a convincing manner the actual investment and economic growth therein.

To better understand economic competitiveness and to paint a more complete picture of ease of doing business, it is imperative that formal regulatory aspects (such as Responsiveness to Businesses as measured by the DB index) are taken into account together with economic factors. These include macro-level variables, such as market potential and infrastructure resilience, as well as micro-level variables such as profitability, cost-effectiveness, and the facilitating of business operations. Additionally, the role of government at multiple levels, especially their policies in managing competition, is similarly paramount and should also be taken into consideration.

It is with this intention that we at the Asia Competitiveness Institute (ACI), Lee Kuan Yew School of Public Policy, National University of Singapore, propose a new, and more holistic approach to measure Ease of Doing Business (EDB), which aims to allow for a better approximation of investment and competitiveness. The framework takes into account three major aspects or 'environments' of doing business: (1) Attractiveness to Investors, (2) Business Friendliness, and (3) Competitive Policies (hence ABC), which we call "EDB Index ABC". Acknowledging the importance of aspects measured by the World Bank's DB index, these indicators are included as part of the second environment (Business Friendliness), but the key remains that they only form a part of the EDB Index ABC.

To operationalise this tool and to respond to calls for a bottom-up approach in understanding the ease of doing business, we apply the EDB Index ABC to 33 Indonesian provinces. This choice reflects our view of the importance and potentials of the Indonesian economy. The country achieved a decade of robust economic growth during the 2000s, until it was slowed down by the global slump in commodity prices. Indonesia is now intent on reviving such growth largely through investment promotion. With a total population of over 250 million, and the fact that the country has achieved much stride in its decentralisation measures during the past 15 years, each of the Indonesian provinces merits to be treated as a unit of analysis. We have also been tracking over 100 variables related to the competitiveness of 33 Indonesian provinces since 2012 (Tan *et al.*, 2013, 2015; Tan and Amri, 2013), and so we would have interesting data on competitiveness to compare against that on ease of doing business.

The remainder of the chapter is presented as follow: first, we present a background on the Indonesian economy and investment inflows into the country and its provinces, followed by a literature review on doing business and how it has been measured, especially by the World Bank's DB index (Section 5.2). Second, we present ACI's EDB Index ABC, including the framework covering the three environments (Attractiveness to Investors, Business Friendliness, and Competitive Policies), the indicators used, data sources, and how the overall index is calculated (Section 5.3). Afterwards, we present the empirical findings (ranking, standardised scores, geographical spread, etc.) of the EDB Index ABC on 33 Indonesian provinces. Such findings are presented for the Overall EDB Index ABC as well as for each of the environments therein. We also present the findings from a policy simulation that gauges the extent to which each province could improve their EDB Index ABC, given hypothetical progress in their weakest indicators (Section 5.4.). Finally, we present some notable conclusions from the research, and highlight some policy implications (Section 5.5.).

5.2 Literature Review

5.2.1 Investment Trends in Indonesia

Indonesia achieved a period of political stability and respectable GDP growth, which averaged at 5.7% annually between 2004 and 2013. Reports forecasted that if Indonesia were able to keep an annual GDP growth rate of 7.0%, the world's fourth most populous country would become the seventh largest economy in the world by 2030 (Oberman *et al.*, 2012).

A substantial portion of Indonesia's growth in the 2000s was driven by a rising price of raw commodities, fuelled by fast growth in other parts of the world, most notably China. Like many countries that experienced 'Dutch disease,' Indonesia did not do enough to diversify its economic base, and to some extent underwent 'deindustrialisation' (Yulisman, 2015). The country is currently experiencing its lowest level of industrialisation since the Asian Financial Crisis: manufacturing industries' contribution to national gross domestic product (GDP) has steadily declined from 29% in 2001 to 23% in 2014, according to data from the Central Statistics Agency (BPS). As global demand slowed and commodity prices fell, Indonesia was left with a meagre 4.7% growth rate in 2015 — much lower than the 5.7% initially targeted by the state budget (Rusmana, 2016), and well below those achieved by Myanmar (8.3%), Vietnam (6.5%) and the Philippines (6.0%).

To realise its aspirations to become the seventh largest economy in the world by 2030, the Indonesian government is targeting a return to a 7.0% GDP growth rate before the end of President Joko Widodo (Jokowi)'s first term in 2019, where private sector investment will generate the bulk of such growth (Parlina, 2014). To support the initiative, the Indonesia Investment Coordinating Board (BKPM) has targeted an average annual increase of Foreign Direct Investment (FDI) by 15.1% between 2015 and 2019 (The Wall Street Journal, 2015). Recognising the challenges faced by investors, among the President's priorities to attract investment is to curtail red tape, simplify investment licencing and improve business certainty. For instance, at the Asian edition of the *World Economic Forum* in April 2015, the Indonesian President Jokowi famously remarked, "Please come and invest in Indonesia — if you have any problem, call me" (The Straits Times, April 20, 2015).

Indonesia's drive to increase FDI seems to have yielded some results: Indonesia's FDI net inflow has increased steadily from about US$5 billion in 2009 to US$28.5 billion in 2014, according to BKPM data on realised gross investment inflows. Indonesia has slowly been reaping more proportion of the world's FDI inflow, from a low of 0.4% in 2009 (just after the global financial crisis) to a high of 1.8% in 2014. Also, as a proportion of GDP, FDI has risen from 2.0% to 3.4% within the same period (see Figure 5.1). Despite the improvement, however, Indonesia still has much catching up to do: comparable ASEAN countries have reported higher FDI net inflow as percentage of GDP in 2013. These include Vietnam (5.2%), Malaysia (3.7%), and Thailand (3.7%).

At the sub-national level, Indonesia is seeing some interesting trends related to the distribution of FDI inflows of late. Of the country's six major regions, Java, the pulse of the Indonesia's economy where 60% of the population resides, has traditionally attracted the bulk of FDI for multiple decades. Since 2008, however, interest in other regions has grown in line with the national aspiration towards broad-based development across the country. The share of FDI to Java almost halved from 91% in 2009 to 53% in 2015. Meanwhile, Kalimantan and Sumatra regions are the biggest beneficiaries of this change in inflows (see Figure 5.2).

The top five out of 33 provinces — DKI Jakarta, West Java, Banten, East Java, and East Kalimantan — together collect 68% of the total FDI that goes into Indonesia between 2007 and 2015. It needs to be noted that the first four are located in Java. But as mentioned, investors are diversifying into other provinces. Data from BKPM show that the proportion of FDI that goes

Figure 5.1: Share of FDI into Indonesia (%), 2001–2014

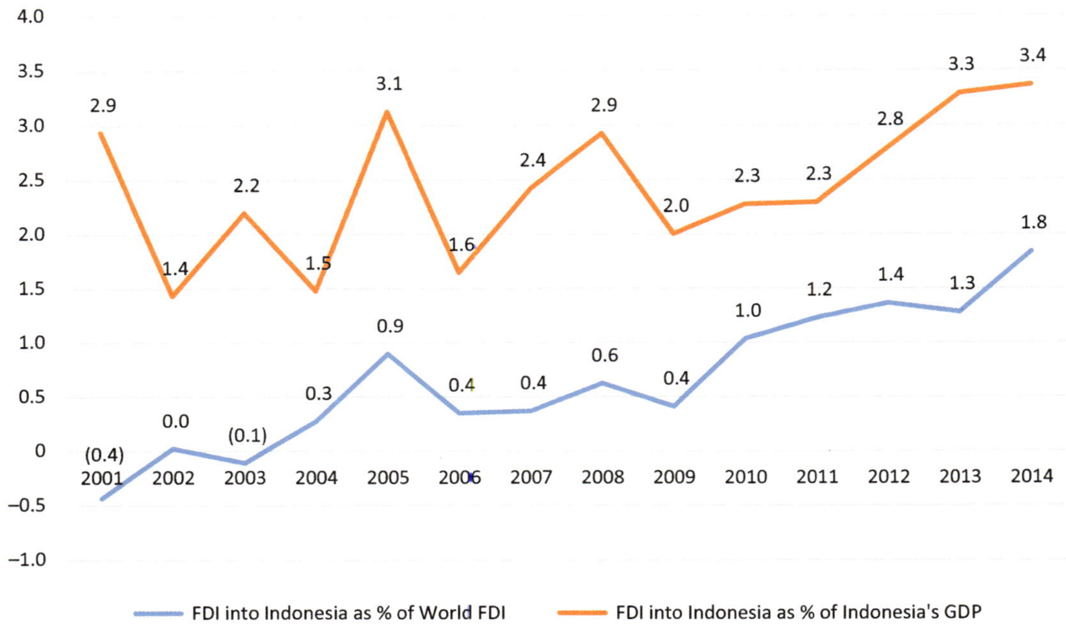

Source: Asia Competitiveness Institute, based on UNCTAD data.

Figure 5.2: Share of FDI into Indonesian Regions (as % of Total FDI Inflows), 2001–2015

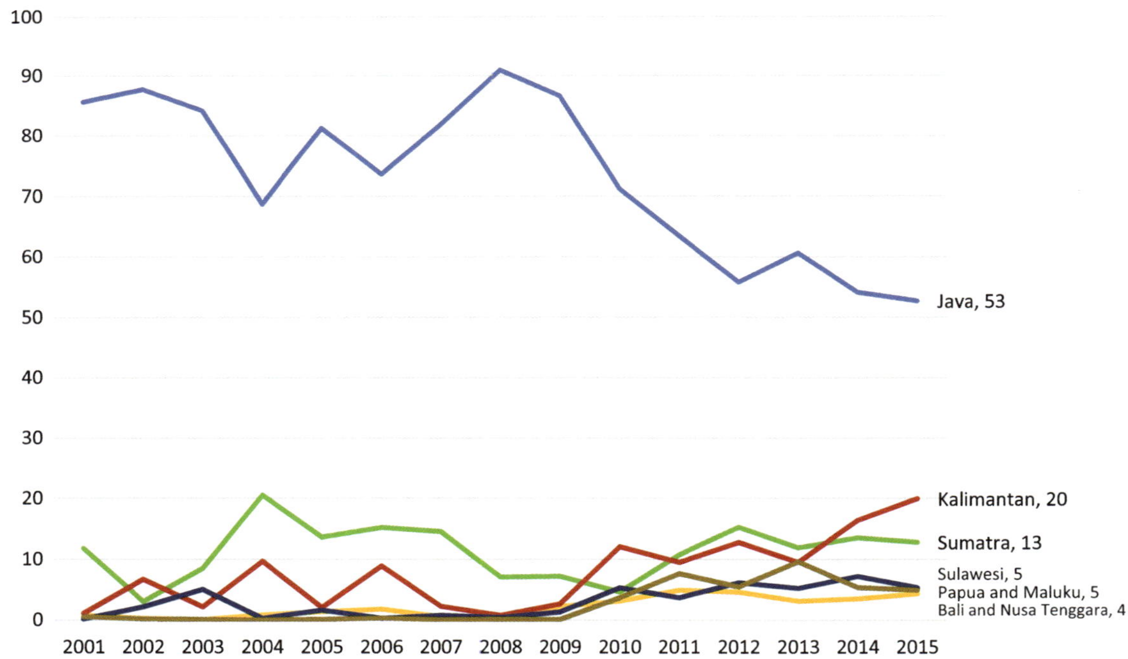

Source: Asia Competitiveness Institute, based on BKPM data.

outside of the top-five provinces has increased from 23.1% (slightly less than a quarter) during the 1998–2006 period to 32% (almost a third) during the 2007–2015 period.

The regional and provincial changes in FDI trends merit further investigations and at ACI, we believe that a holistic bottom-up evaluation of business friendliness and economic competitiveness provides more useful insights and guide future policy directions.

5.2.2 Measuring the Ease of Doing Business: An Overview

Since the World Bank's Doing Business (DB) index was launched in 2003 (World Bank, 2003), there has been a growing wealth of literature that uses the index to measure the influence of the ease of doing business on economic growth, foreign direct investment, and entrepreneurship among others. Many countries desire improvements in DB rankings to the extent that it is used as a key performance indicator in some governments. For example, Indonesia's 'Roadmap for Bureaucracy Reform' for 2010–2014 targets an improvement in Indonesia's international DB ranking, from 122nd place in 2009 to 75th place in 2014.[1] The DB exercise argues that the pro-business role of the government in formulating and implementing competitive policies is paramount without which very often market forces are either slow or too weak to act.

The purpose of the DB index is simple: to reflect the ease of doing business in a country. Countries are ranked based on the time and costs to complete procedures that are considered relevant to small- and medium-sized domestic firms. In the latest 2017 edition, these are *Starting a Business, Dealing with Construction Permits, Getting Electricity, Registering Property, Getting Credit, Protecting Minority Investors, Paying Taxes, Trading Across Borders, Enforcing Contracts, and Resolving Insolvency* (World Bank, 2016). The rankings of countries are determined by sorting the aggregate distance to frontier scores on these aspects. The distance to frontier score captures the gap between an economy and the best performing one. While the intuitive appeal of the DB index is apparent to policymakers, there are likewise obvious design and conceptual weaknesses.

As popular as this index is, the empirical support for DB is controversial. Using DB components as proxy to business regulations, improvements in regulatory quality have been found to have a positive effect on GDP per capita growth, and similarly positive interaction with FDI and FDI inflows (Djankov, McLiesh, and Ramalho, 2006; Busse and Groizard, 2008; Jayasuriya, 2011). A single rank improvement in DB and trade-related indicators specifically is associated with a significant increase of FDI by 0.5% and 0.7%, respectively (Corcoran and Gillanders, 2015).

However, the usefulness of this index is not without detractors; the framework, reliability, and accompanying recommendations in the annual reporting of the DB index have been questioned throughout the years as well. For example, when countries improve in rankings, the cost or the trade-offs that have been made and the interaction effects on other factors become unclear (Arruñada, 2007; Berg and Cazes, 2008; Ravallion, 2012). The 'Employing Workers' indicator is particularly troublesome: the DB index ranking system favours deregulation of the labour

[1]Minister for State Apparatus and Bureaucracy Reform Regulation No. 20/2010 on Road Map of Bureaucracy Reform: 2010–2014.

market on the premise that formality and employment would improve. Policies such as minimum wages, working hours, employment protection, fixed-term contracts and social security generate positive externalities that Berg and Cazes (2008) argue cannot be encouraged across all countries. As the Independent Evaluation Group (2008) puts it, the indicator captures the letter but not the spirit of the International Labour Organization's conventions.

The desired effect of ranking improvements is not equally experienced by all countries. There is a marginal return to countries that have enjoyed improvements in the past. Developing countries may not see an increase in FDI inflows from DB improvements, possibly due to *de jure* and *de facto* divergences while on the other end of the spectrum, relatively poor and well-governed countries see a positive effect in investments and economic growth (Eifert, 2009; Jayasuriya, 2011). Lower cost of procedures may be influenced by scale more than efficiency, thus favouring developed countries (Arruñada, 2007).

Furthermore, DB is based on the principle that lowering time and cost of procedures of starting a business will increase entrepreneurship. A study across 39 countries between 2000 and 2005 which disaggregated entrepreneurs by their status — whether actual or prospective, out of need or interest — showed that the impact of entry regulations is not significant across the board (Stel, Storey, and Thurik, 2007). Those who started businesses out of need were affected by minimum capital and labour market regulations and chose informality to avoid start-up procedures. However, when entrepreneurship is measured more generally, the number of procedures will significantly and negatively affect the number of businesses registered and the governance will significantly influence entry rates as shown by Klapper *et al.* (2007).

From a methodological perspective, DB also comes under criticism. DB surveys a select group of experts in one or two cities in each country as representative cases for Ease of Doing Business in the whole country. In the context of Indonesia, the cities of Jakarta and Surabaya were chosen (World Bank, 2016). Sub-national reports are produced in 2010 and 2012 for up to 14 cities on selected indicators (World Bank, 2010; 2012). While the team behind DB argues that there is no need for a large sample size given the nature of the study, critics — even within the World Bank — argue that having few respondents is a source for concern. For example, there may be respondents who do not have the requisite extensive knowledge of local laws and regulations or exposure in an alternative regime which pose risks to the veracity of the data collected (Davis and Kruse, 2007; Independent Evaluation Group, 2008).

When it comes to indicators, there are issues in reliability, accuracy, and explanatory powers (Independent Evaluation Group, 2008). Employing factor analysis and Cronbach's alpha models, it was argued that most indicators had low explanatory powers: 18 out of 41 variables are considered to be dispensable and only four out of 10 indicators are reliable (Pinheiro-Alves and Zambujal-Oliveira, 2012). Contribution of variables to explain the variance in DB is low. The scales used within the indicators are also heterogeneous. Moreover, the construction of the indicators is undermined by the opaque process through which variables are selected, selection bias and the simplistic coding of responses (Davis and Kruse, 2007; Berg and Cazes, 2008). The DB also measures regulations in isolation, not considering the regulatory history of a given country, stage of development, complexity of a regulatory regime, path dependencies in procedures and country-level nuances (Arruñada, 2007; Davis and Kruse, 2007; Independent Evaluation Group, 2008).

One of the major issues in interpreting the results of the DB report is the assumption that firms comply fully with the prevailing business regulations. When *de facto* experiences in the World Bank Enterprise Surveys are matched with *de jure* results reported in DB reports, there are weak associations between the two, particularly when regulations are more burdensome, leading some to conclude that there is "water in the regulations" (Hallward-Driemeier and Pritchett, 2015). Furthermore, firms that report faster turnaround times experience this favourable treatment across the board; there are marked differences in experience between firms in the same country than a firm in different countries. In some countries, a fall in time needed for a procedure may be reported in the DB index when in fact the time required rose due to enforcement of or compliance to the regulatory change. Furthermore, entrepreneurs also face additional time and costs not captured by DB such as intermediaries and non-mandatory procedures; in countries with low-quality regulations, there are additional costs of hiring advisors and legal services that add up to total transaction costs (Arruñada, 2007).

Nevertheless, Indonesia has achieved steady improvement in the overall DB ranking from being in the 129th position in the 2012 report, to the 91st position out of 189 countries in the 2017 report (World Bank, 2016) (see Figure 5.3). The most notable improvements are in *Getting Electricity* (up from 161st to 49th between 2012 and 2017), and *Getting Credit* (up from 126th to 62nd during the same period). However, there were deteriorations in *Protecting Minority Investors* (down from 46th to 70th), *Trading Across Borders* (down from 39th to 108th), and *Dealing with Construction Permits* (down from 71st to 116th). Regardless of the improvements and deteriorations, Indonesia has consistently fared poorly in *Starting a Business* (fluctuating from a low of 175th to a high of

Figure 5.3: Indonesia's Position in the World Bank's Ease of Doing Business Rankings, Relative to Selected Countries (2012–2017)

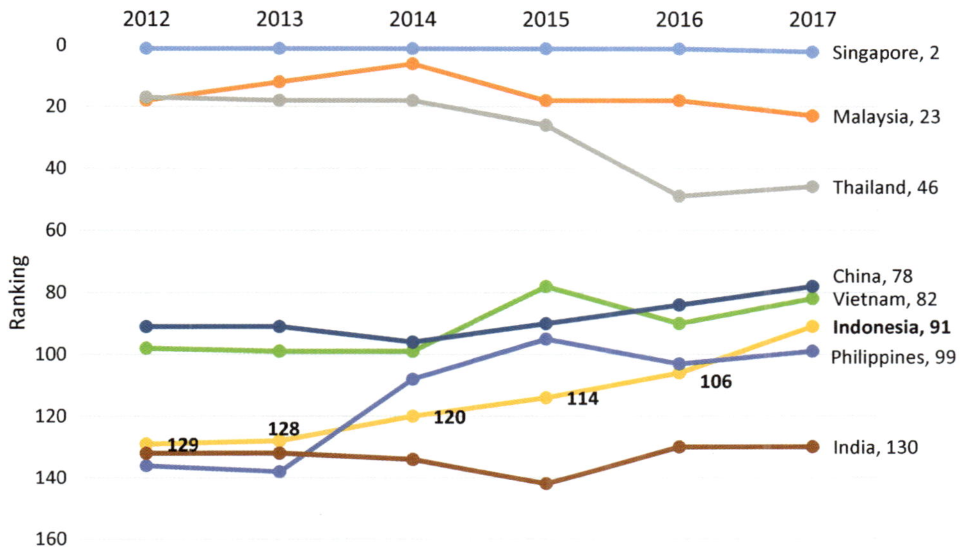

Source: World Bank data, compiled by Asia Competitiveness Institute.

151st), and *Enforcing Contracts* (fluctuating from a low of 172nd to a high of 144th). Lack of infrastructure and legal clarity remains a major obstacle for businesses.

As mentioned earlier, one of the criticisms in adopting these figures for the whole of Indonesia is that it is based on data that come from two cities only: Jakarta and Surabaya which are the country's largest and second largest cities. Considering the depth of decentralisation measures that the country has adopted, Indonesia's sub-national peculiarities cannot be fully appreciated and addressed by targeting national policy and procedural impediments. While the central government can drive certain national policies,[2] governments at the provincial, city (*kota*), and regency (*kabupaten*) levels have relative independence in formulating policies related to economic sectors and public services, and vary in implementation capacities. Indonesia's decentralisation policies remain dynamic, with more attention being placed at the city- and district-level governments during the onset of adopting the policy (2001–2008), and increasing role of provincial governments as coordinator of local governments (2008 onwards).

Acknowledging the need for sub-national analysis, the World Bank has applied the DB index to 14 cities in 2010 (World Bank, 2010) and 20 cities in 2012 (World Bank, 2012). Only three aspects of DB were measured: Starting a Business, Dealing with Construction Permits, and Registering Property. We see some consistency in terms of which cities were doing well for each of these aspects. For example, Yogyakarta City (in DI Yogyakarta province) was first in terms of Starting a Business both in 2010 and 2012. Bandung City (in West Java province) and Jakarta both did well in Registering Property, jointly ranked first in 2012 while holding first and second places respectively in 2010. Meanwhile, Balikpapan City (in East Kalimantan province) did rather well for Dealing with Construction Permits, improving from eighth place in 2010 to first place in 2012.

While the sub-national DB analysis is indeed useful, the World Bank has not conducted an update for Indonesian cities beyond 2012. This may reflect the challenges of conducting such analysis at the sub-provincial level, as Indonesia has 498 districts (93 cities and 405 regencies) altogether. Conducting a DB analysis at the provincial level (Indonesia has 34 provinces as of 2016) may be more manageable and in line with efforts by the central government to strengthen the role of provinces as the coordinator of relatively autonomous local governments. However, the city-level and provincial-level analysis of DB would not be expressly comparable as they involve different governing institutions.

As discussed in the prior section, the explanatory power and policy recommendations that accompany the DB country report are relatively thin. While there is merit to regulatory reforms underpinned by the DB index, the knock-on effect of attracting foreign direct investments is not well-established.

To consider a more specific, provincial-level and more holistic analysis which includes Attractiveness to Investors, Business Friendliness, and Competitive Policies, we turn to ACI's EDB Index ABC, the framework and methodology of which will be explained in the following section.

---

[2]E.g. defence, police, military, monetary, justice, foreign affairs, and religious affairs.

5.3 Research Methodology

5.3.1 ACI's Ease of Doing Business Index ABC Framework

ACI's EDB Index ABC is proposed as a more holistic analytical tool on ease of doing business at the sub-national level, applicable to both domestic as well as foreign firms. It is a bottom-up approach that considers business perspectives and local government practices at the micro level through survey data combined with publicly available macroeconomic data through formal statistical publications.

With the intention of covering the different stages of business investment in a particular location, the EDB Index ABC captures three different aspects or 'environments' of doing business, namely Attractiveness to Investors (A), Business Friendliness (B) and Competitive Policies (C) which are further broken down into five 'sub-environments' and ultimately detailed down into 74 indicators (see Figure 5.4 for the framework, and Appendix 6 for the full list of indicators).

First, Attractiveness to Investors (A) measures the comparative advantage of a location that comes into consideration when firms are considering where to invest. These are the factors that a firm would compare and contrast as *ex-ante* factors, before it decides or makes a commitment to invest in said location. This environment, consisting of two sub-environments and 28 indicators, captures basic factors that make a province attractive as an investment destination. From investors' point of view, the sub-environment *Infrastructure Resilience and Market Potential*, which includes 21 indicators, stands out as the key considerations when making decisions on where to invest. The other sub-environment is *Profitability and Cost Effectiveness*, which includes cost of labour, ease of obtaining land and property, as well as taxation matters. This sub-environment is composed of seven indicators.

Figure 5.4: ACI's EDB Index ABC Framework

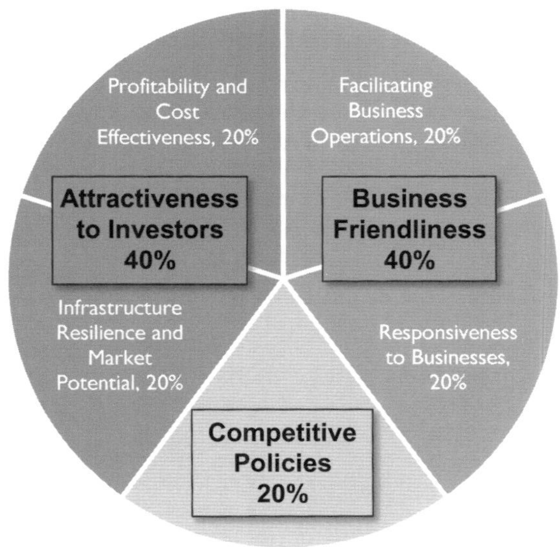

Source: Asia Competitiveness Institute.

Second, Business Friendliness (B) measures the ease of functioning that comes into consideration when firms are already committed to an investment, but still may pull out despite some costs. These are the factors that a firm would scrutinise as *ex-post* factors, after it made the commitment to invest. This environment, which consists of two sub-environments and 24 indicators, covers extensive factors that create a friendly ecosystem for businesses. The first sub-environment, *Facilitating Business Operations*, is composed of 14 indicators and includes ease of getting favourable labour supply, accessing financial services and obtaining reliable local suppliers. Additionally, investors value security where businesses are isolated from disruptions triggered by crime, violence, and political instability. The second sub-environment, *Responsiveness to Businesses*, entails factors related to firms' assessment on the regulatory procedures and bureaucracy imposed by the government. This includes 10 indicators which are most similar to the aspects measured in the World Bank's DB index, such as ease of starting a business and ease of paying corporate taxes.

The third environment, Competitive Policies (C), evaluates the existence of policies and practices that facilitate ease of doing business at the provincial level, making the province more competitive compared to its peers from a regulatory point of view. Environment C is not broken down into any further sub-environments. Instead, it is composed of 22 indicators which capture whether related business procedures are in place rather than dwelling into its actual implementation. Most of the indicators examine ideal procedures in provincial one-stop-service agency (PTSP) and how extensive the deployment of e-governance as a tool is to disseminate information to potential investors and ease the process of acquiring business licenses.

5.3.2 Indicators and Data Sources

The data used to construct the index is based on 74 indicators at the provincial level, in which (a) 20 indicators are secondary data for the year 2013, collected from the Indonesian government's formal statistical publications in 2015, and (b) 54 indicators are primary data collected by ACI from each of the 33 Indonesian provinces between May and October of 2015. Out of the 54 indicators derived from primary data, 32 were based on ACI's EDB Index ABC surveys to business operators in each province, 11 were based on ACI surveys to one-stop-service agencies in each province, and another 11 were generated by ACI team's assessment of the one-stop-service's e-government practices, conducted from September to October 2015.

For the 32 perception indicators under the EDB Index ABC survey, ACI collected the data in collaboration with The Employers' Association of Indonesia (APINDO). The surveys were largely perception-based, and responses were recorded through an electronic response system and coded using a Likert scale. ACI also visited each provincial government's one-stop-service units or *Pelayanan Terpadu Satu Pintu* (PTSP) and recorded the availability of related services with a yes (1) or no (0) measurement which contributes towards 11 indicators. For the remaining 11 primary indicators, e-government practice among PTSP units is accessed based on availability of relevant features in their respective websites and, again, recorded with a yes (1) or no (0) measurement. Secondary data are gathered from secondary sources such as the Central Statistical

Agency (BPS), World Bank Indonesia Database for Policy and Economic Research (INDO-DAPOER), Bank Indonesia and other statistical data providers such as CEIC.

5.3.3 The Standardised Score

The index is calculated by using a nested approach, where indicator scores are aggregated into their respective sub-environment scores, sub-environment scores aggregated into their respective environment scores, and finally the environment scores aggregated into the overall index (similar to the methodology used in the calculation of ACI's Competitiveness Index, explained earlier in Chapter 2). Each indicator carries equal weight into its respective sub-environment. Similarly, each of the sub-environments carries equal weight into its respective environment.

However, in aggregating the three environments into the Overall EDB Index ABC, we have opted to provide 40% weight for each of environments A (Attractiveness to Investors) and B (Business Friendliness), while the remaining 20% weight is provided for environment C (Competitive Policies). The justification for a smaller weight for environment C is based on empirical literature which has shown that while *de jure* factors matter, it may not be the most important consideration for business activities to take place.

Given the different units of each indicator, a standardised score is calculated to harmonise the indicators as a relative comparison to see the performance of a certain province in comparison to the average province. The standardised score method has been utilised and developed in our publications (e.g., see Tan *et al.*, 2013; 2015). See Appendix 2 for a technical explanation on computing the rankings.

5.3.4 *What-if* Simulation Analysis

In an effort to provide more than just ranking tables, we also explore ways for the provinces to improve their EDB Index ABC standings. Through data analysis, we obtain not only rankings but also each province's relative strengths and weaknesses from the distribution of stronger and weaker indicators. The '*What-if*' simulation crafted by ACI is basically a recalculation of the index where a province improves its top 20% weakest indicators to the average level of all provinces involved in the study, assuming all other provinces' scores remain constant. The simulation would allow us to see various levels of improvements that a province could potentially achieve.

Again, the method to conduct the *What-if* analysis for EDB Index ABC is similar to that used in conducting the *What-if* competitiveness analysis (see Chapter 2 for more details).

5.4 Ease of Doing Business Index ABC Results

5.4.1 Ranking and Scores for Overall EDB Index ABC

The Overall EDB Index ABC ranking for 33 Indonesian provinces, as shown in Table 5.1, is computed based on the methodology outlined earlier. The EDB Index ABC measures a province's performance relative to the average performance of all 33 provinces covered in the study.

Table 5.1: Rankings and Scores of Overall Ease of Doing Business Index ABC, 2016

				Environment Std. Scores		
Rank	Province	Region	Overall EDB Index ABC Std. Score	Attractiveness to Investors	Business Friendliness	Competitive Policies
1	South Sulawesi	Sulawesi	1.8570	1.7003	2.3700	−1.0063
2	DKI Jakarta	Java	1.6182	1.7497	1.9000	−1.0825
3	East Java	Java	1.5415	0.7906	0.8231	2.6951
4	Central Java	Java	1.4857	0.9086	1.8280	0.2349
5	West Java	Java	1.2494	1.1545	0.5511	1.3889
6	Bali	Bali–Nusa Tenggara	1.0885	0.3820	1.2047	1.0086
7	North Sulawesi	Sulawesi	0.9274	0.9880	1.0374	−0.4876
8	Central Sulawesi	Sulawesi	0.9128	1.3637	0.5246	−0.2696
9	DI Yogyakarta	Java	0.8654	0.3667	0.7846	1.0222
10	South Kalimantan	Kalimantan	0.4203	0.3844	0.6074	−0.3687
11	Aceh	Sumatra	0.2346	0.7858	−0.4303	0.1902
12	Banten	Java	0.2331	1.2448	−0.7624	−0.0695
13	Gorontalo	Sulawesi	0.2140	0.5062	−0.3512	0.5121
14	West Nusa Tenggara	Bali–Nusa Tenggara	0.1678	0.5054	0.0708	−0.5080
15	East Kalimantan	Kalimantan	0.1505	−0.0413	−0.4475	1.5557
16	Central Kalimantan	Kalimantan	0.0971	0.1601	0.3318	−0.6109
17	Bangka Belitung Islands	Sumatra	0.0646	0.3502	−0.4915	0.5306
18	Southeast Sulawesi	Sulawesi	−0.0042	−0.4849	0.3440	0.2655
19	West Kalimantan	Kalimantan	−0.0348	−0.3733	−0.2307	1.0744
20	Lampung	Sumatra	−0.1108	0.8021	0.3312	−2.6922
21	Maluku	Maluku–Papua	−0.1387	−1.1896	0.6529	0.5403
22	East Nusa Tenggara	Bali–Nusa Tenggara	−0.1933	−0.3998	−0.1786	0.4141
23	Riau	Sumatra	−0.3516	−0.1214	−0.8279	0.5479
24	North Maluku	Maluku–Papua	−0.7069	−0.6247	−0.3502	−0.7661
25	Papua	Maluku–Papua	−0.7978	−0.7355	−0.2349	−1.1243
26	Bengkulu	Sumatra	−0.8323	−0.8220	−0.4874	−0.5789
27	West Sulawesi	Sulawesi	−1.0218	−1.1624	−0.5243	−0.5520
28	North Sumatra	Sumatra	−1.2099	−1.1444	−1.2889	0.2184
29	South Sumatra	Sumatra	−1.2252	−1.6937	−0.8647	0.4094
30	Riau Islands	Sumatra	−1.3921	−0.5102	−1.6399	−1.0485
31	West Papua	Maluku–Papua	−1.4492	−1.4913	−0.6204	−1.3445
32	West Sumatra	Sumatra	−1.8133	−1.2637	−1.9282	−0.5829
33	Jambi	Sumatra	−1.8458	−2.0848	−1.7030	0.4840

Source: Asia Competitiveness Institute.

Figure 5.5: Geographical Spread for Overall EDB Index ABC

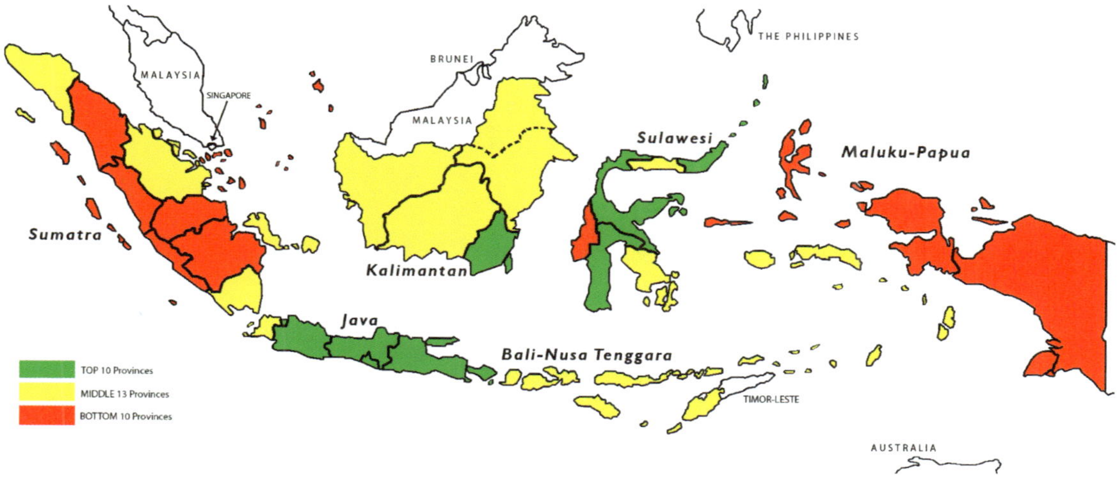

Source: Asia Competitiveness Institute.

Figure 5.6: Top-five and Bottom-five Provinces for Overall EDB Index ABC

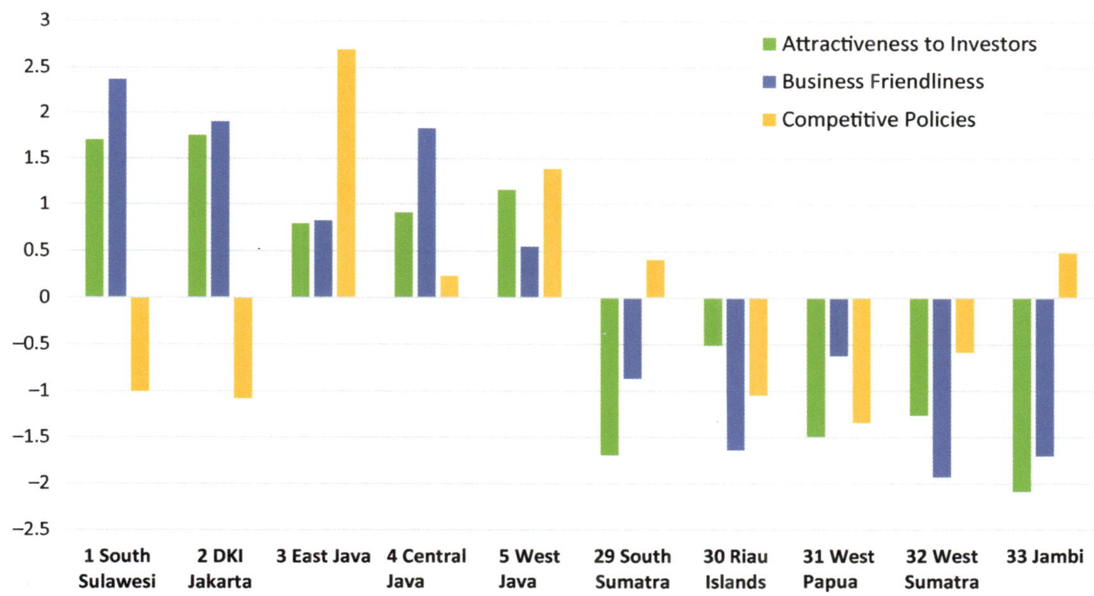

Source: Asia Competitiveness Institute.

A score of zero indicates that the province is an average performer while a positive score indicates that the performance of the province is better than the average of all cities in this study. Vice versa, a negative score indicates lower than average performance.

Table 5.1 shows that South Sulawesi is ranked the highest, followed by DKI Jakarta, East Java, Central Java, and West Java. When the scores are mapped as shown in Figure 5.5, provinces in the Java, Sulawesi, and Kalimantan regions generally fare better than those in the Sumatra, Bali–Nusa Tenggara, and Maluku–Papua regions. To highlight, five out of six Java provinces, as well as three out of six Sulawesi provinces are within the top-10. At the other end of the spectrum, provinces in the Maluku–Papua and Sumatra regions occupy the bottom positions. Three out of four Maluku–Papua provinces, as well as six out of 10 Sumatra provinces are within the bottom-10 of the table. Despite receiving a growth in FDI inflows especially in the mining sector, operating in Sumatran provinces is challenging for businesses.

Diving deeper into factors that provide advantages to the top-five provinces, the diversity of provincial characteristics and local regulations becomes clear (Figure 5.6). South Sulawesi and DKI Jakarta (ranked first and second, respectively) are strong on *Attractiveness to Investors*, *Business Friendliness* but weak on *Competitive Policies*. East Java, Central Java, and West Java (ranked third, fourth, and fifth, respectively) are more well-rounded in that they achieve positive scores in all three environments. However, each of them excels in different aspects. East Java fares extremely well in *Competitive Policies*, but less so in *Attractiveness to Investors* and *Business Friendliness*. Central Java, on the other hand, has a very favourable score for *Business Friendliness* that is comparable to DKI Jakarta's, but fares just slightly better than average on *Competitive Policies*. West Java is the most balanced among the top-five provinces with better than average scores across all three environments.

When the bottom-five provinces are examined, we generally see weak scores across all three environments (A, B, and C), except for South Sumatra and Jambi. Interestingly, these two provinces benefit from marginally better-than-average scores for *Competitive Policies*. However, a common trait across all bottom-five provinces is that they suffer from poor *Attractiveness to Investors* and *Business Friendliness*.

5.4.2 Ranking and Scores by Three Environments

Attractiveness to Investors

Zooming in to the first environment, in terms of Attractiveness to Investors, DKI Jakarta leads the rankings, followed by South Sulawesi, Central Sulawesi, Banten and West Java (see Table 5.2). When the scores are mapped as shown in Figure 5.7, we find that provinces in the Java and Sulawesi regions tend to perform better than those in the remaining four regions. Similar to the geographic spread for Overall EDB Index ABC, five out of six Java provinces, as well as three out of six Sulawesi provinces are included within the top-10. Among the bottom-ranked, all four provinces in the Maluku–Papua region occupy the bottom-10 portion of the table. The Sumatra region also deserves attention as five out of 10 provinces therein are also included within the bottom-10.

Among the top-five provinces for environment A (see Figure 5.8), it is interesting to note that DKI Jakarta and South Sulawesi again surface as the best two provinces (albeit in different sequences). DKI Jakarta is an obvious frontrunner with the indicators in this environment

Table 5.2: Rankings and Scores for Attractiveness to Investors, 2016

Rank	Province	Region	Environment Std. Score for Attractiveness to Investors	Sub-environment Std. Scores: Infrastructure Resilience & Market Potential	Sub-environment Std. Scores: Profitability & Cost Effectiveness
1	DKI Jakarta	Java	1.7497	1.9002	0.7242
2	South Sulawesi	Sulawesi	1.7003	1.5906	0.9597
3	Central Sulawesi	Sulawesi	1.3637	0.1843	1.8611
4	Banten	Java	1.2448	1.3011	0.5661
5	West Java	Java	1.1545	1.3028	0.4289
6	North Sulawesi	Sulawesi	0.9880	0.5546	0.9273
7	Central Java	Java	0.9086	0.6662	0.6966
8	Lampung	Sumatra	0.8021	−0.1701	1.3732
9	East Java	Java	0.7906	1.9396	−0.7538
10	Aceh	Sumatra	0.7858	−0.2361	1.4147
11	Gorontalo	Sulawesi	0.5062	−0.7128	1.4720
12	West Nusa Tenggara	Bali–Nusa Tenggara	0.5054	−0.1838	0.9419
13	South Kalimantan	Kalimantan	0.3844	1.2063	−0.6298
14	Bali	Bali–Nusa Tenggara	0.3820	0.9793	−0.4062
15	DI Yogyakarta	Java	0.3667	0.9351	−0.3851
16	Bangka Belitung Islands	Sumatra	0.3502	−0.5320	1.0574
17	Central Kalimantan	Kalimantan	0.1601	−0.1637	0.4039
18	East Kalimantan	Kalimantan	−0.0413	1.1913	−1.2532
19	Riau	Sumatra	−0.1214	−0.0866	−0.0955
20	West Kalimantan	Kalimantan	−0.3733	−0.5537	−0.0063
21	East Nusa Tenggara	Bali–Nusa Tenggara	−0.3998	−0.7498	0.1501
22	Southeast Sulawesi	Sulawesi	−0.4849	−0.8276	0.1003
23	Riau Islands	Sumatra	−0.5102	0.0824	−0.8476
24	North Maluku	Maluku–Papua	−0.6247	−1.2280	0.2910
25	Papua	Maluku–Papua	−0.7355	−1.3133	0.2101
26	Bengkulu	Sumatra	−0.8220	−0.5450	−0.6879
27	North Sumatra	Sumatra	−1.1444	−0.5285	−1.1881
28	West Sulawesi	Sulawesi	−1.1624	−1.6547	−0.0889
29	Maluku	Maluku–Papua	−1.1896	−0.7957	−0.9886
30	West Sumatra	Sumatra	−1.2637	−0.8577	−1.0378
31	West Papua	Maluku–Papua	−1.4913	−1.2431	−0.9938
32	South Sumatra	Sumatra	−1.6937	0.0470	−2.5874
33	Jambi	Sumatra	−2.0848	−1.4987	−1.6284

Source: Asia Competitiveness Institute.

Figure 5.7: Geographical Spread for Attractiveness to Investors, 2016

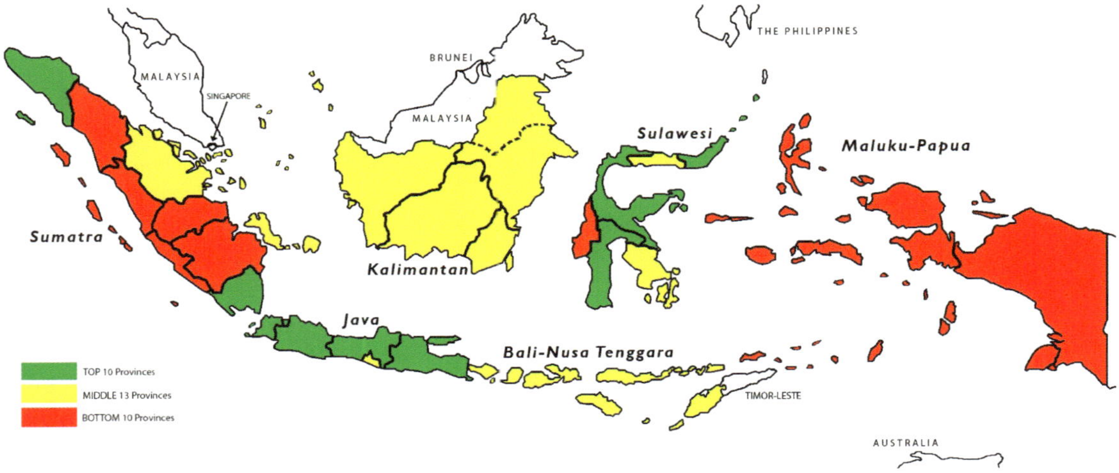

Source: Asia Competitiveness Institute.

Figure 5.8: Top-five and Bottom-five Provinces for Attractiveness to Investors, 2016

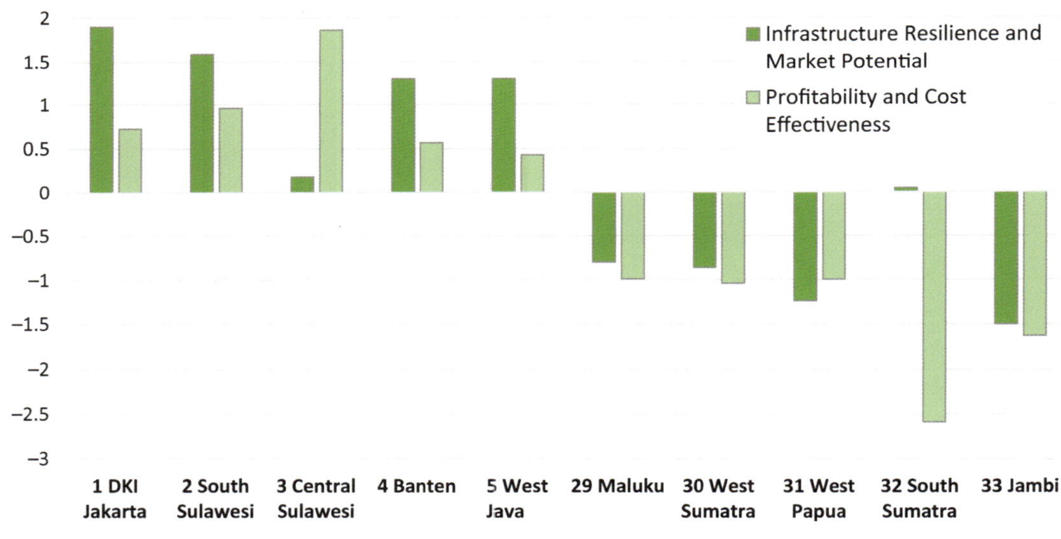

Source: Asia Competitiveness Institute.

capturing its claim to the share of infrastructure (roads, power, telecommunications), human capital and consumers compared to the rest of Indonesia although the operating costs of businesses are pushed upwards due to higher labour costs and tax. South Sulawesi stands out for its conflict and dispute resolution mechanism and regulatory control. Banten and West Java enjoy geographical advantages with large foreign and domestic markets with more favourable labour costs compared to DKI Jakarta, as well as attractive tax incentives and subsidy structures. It is interesting to note that four out of the top-five provinces obtained substantially higher scores for the Infrastructure Resilience and Market Potential sub-environment compared to the scores for the Profitability and Cost Effectiveness sub-environment. Central Sulawesi is the odd one out as it has substantially higher score for Profitability and Cost Effectiveness, while performing just above average for Infrastructure Resilience and Market Potential. The province is particularly attractive in this sense due to favourable local taxes and fees.

The bottom-five provinces are all unfavourable on both sub-environments but again, there is one odd province, which is South Sumatra. Interestingly, South Sumatra fares substantially below average for Profitability and Cost Effectiveness, but achieves just above-average score for Infrastructure Resilience and Market Potential. Upon further scrutiny, we find that fees for registering property in South Sumatra is among the highest in Indonesia. Maluku, West Papua, West Sumatra, and Jambi have poor Information, Communications, and Technology (ICT)/internet infrastructure. The high rental costs for office and land spaces in Jambi and West Papua add significantly to the cost of doing business in those provinces.

Business Friendliness

For the environment of Business Friendliness, South Sulawesi is ranked first, ahead of DKI Jakarta, Central Java, Bali, and North Sulawesi (see Table 5.3). Again, similar to results from the overall index and the first environment, both South Sulawesi and DKI Jakarta emerge in the top positions. South Sulawesi's strength is in its governance, with relatively lower crime and corruption that disrupt businesses. Both North Sulawesi and South Sulawesi demonstrate high procedural effectiveness, meaning that permits and clearances are relatively easier to get and investor protection regulations are above average. South Sulawesi also has strong intellectual property (IP) protection and dispute and conflict resolution mechanisms. Businesses located in DKI Jakarta benefit from strong credit availability and market of middle management talent. Meanwhile, skilled production workers are more readily available in Central Java and Bali. At the bottom-end of the table, Sumatra deserves dire attention as seven out of its 10 provinces are ranked among the bottom-10.

All top-five provinces in this environment show positive scores for both sub-environments, with both Sulawesi provinces (South Sulawesi and North Sulawesi) faring much better in terms of Responsiveness to Businesses, while the Java–Bali provinces (DKI Jakarta, Central Java, and Bali) demonstrate better scores for Facilitating Business Operations (see Figures 5.9 and 5.10).

Meanwhile, all the bottom-five provinces are located in Sumatra, plagued by high levels of crime, corruption and security issues. In Riau Islands, tension between labour unions and management is substantially above average, and security is also a major issue. Jambi's effectiveness in approving and clearing procedures for new businesses, land and property as well as construction permits and protecting investor rights are notably problematic. All bottom-five provinces scored below average for both sub-environments of Facilitating Business Operations as well as Responsiveness to Businesses.

Table 5.3: Rankings and Scores for Business Friendliness, 2016

Rank	Province	Region	Environment Std. Score for Business Friendliness	Sub-environment Std. Scores	
				Facilitating Business Operations	Responsiveness to Businesses
1	South Sulawesi	Sulawesi	2.3700	1.1505	2.8165
2	DKI Jakarta	Java	1.9000	2.4726	0.7077
3	Central Java	Java	1.8280	2.1784	0.8813
4	Bali	Bali–Nusa Tenggara	1.2047	1.8016	0.2149
5	North Sulawesi	Sulawesi	1.0374	0.0933	1.6431
6	East Java	Java	0.8231	1.6722	–0.2944
7	DI Yogyakarta	Java	0.7846	0.9822	0.3310
8	Maluku	Maluku–Papua	0.6529	0.0735	1.0193
9	South Kalimantan	Kalimantan	0.6074	0.4631	0.5535
10	West Java	Java	0.5511	0.7076	0.2149
11	Central Sulawesi	Sulawesi	0.5246	–0.9829	1.8611
12	Southeast Sulawesi	Sulawesi	0.3440	–0.4781	1.0539
13	Central Kalimantan	Kalimantan	0.3318	0.3462	0.2092
14	Lampung	Sumatra	0.3312	0.3922	0.1621
15	West Nusa Tenggara	Bali–Nusa Tenggara	0.0708	0.2955	–0.1770
16	East Nusa Tenggara	Bali–Nusa Tenggara	–0.1786	–1.0871	0.7882
17	West Kalimantan	Kalimantan	–0.2307	0.2563	–0.6424
18	Papua	Maluku–Papua	–0.2349	–0.1474	–0.2458
19	North Maluku	Maluku–Papua	–0.3502	–0.1550	–0.4312
20	Gorontalo	Sulawesi	–0.3512	–0.0312	–0.5567
21	Aceh	Sumatra	–0.4303	–1.3937	0.6735
22	East Kalimantan	Kalimantan	–0.4475	–0.3948	–0.3543
23	Bengkulu	Sumatra	–0.4874	–0.3876	–0.4282
24	Bangka Belitung Islands	Sumatra	–0.4915	–0.3207	–0.5019
25	West Sulawesi	Sulawesi	–0.5243	–0.3556	–0.5221
26	West Papua	Maluku–Papua	–0.6204	–0.4019	–0.6365
27	Banten	Java	–0.7624	–0.5526	–0.7235
28	Riau	Sumatra	–0.8279	–0.5139	–0.8718
29	South Sumatra	Sumatra	–0.8647	–0.9061	–0.5413
30	North Sumatra	Sumatra	–1.2889	–0.8858	–1.2715
31	Riau Islands	Sumatra	–1.6399	–1.3339	–1.4110
32	Jambi	Sumatra	–1.7030	–0.8494	–2.0011
33	West Sumatra	Sumatra	–1.9282	–1.7077	–1.5197

Source: Asia Competitiveness Institute.

Figure 5.9: Geographical Spread for Business Friendliness, 2016

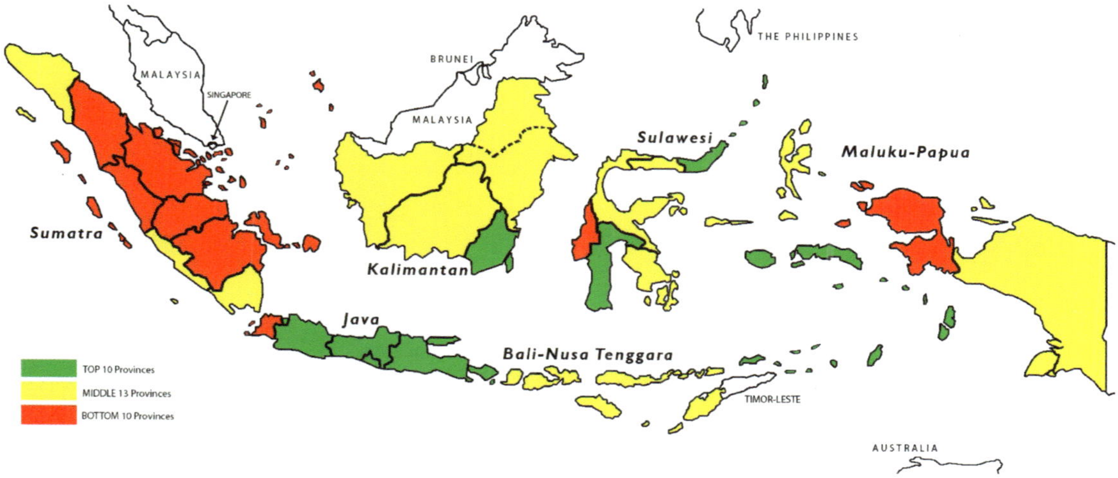

Source: Asia Competitiveness Institute.

Figure 5.10: Top-five and Bottom-five Provinces for Business Friendliness, 2016

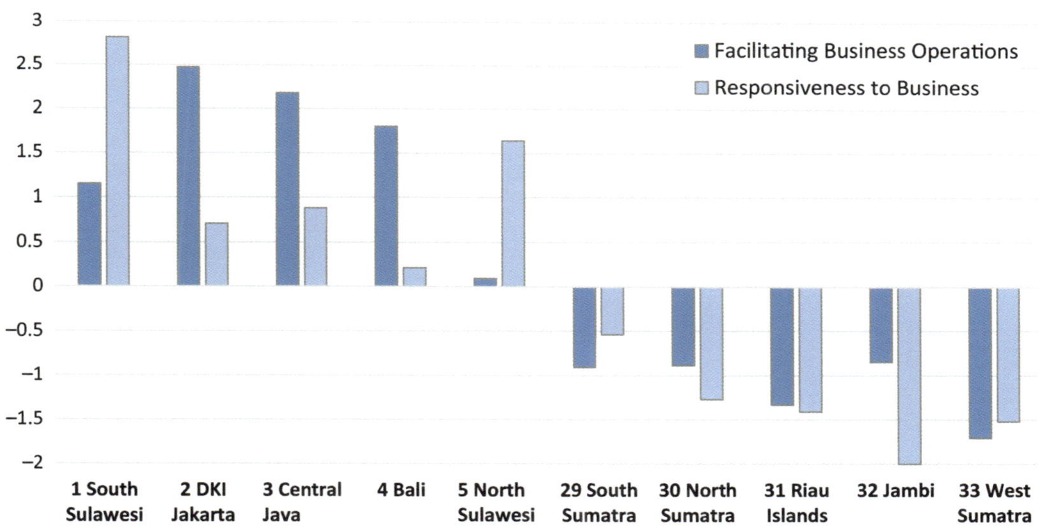

Source: Asia Competitiveness Institute.

Competitive Policies

For the third environment Competitive Policies, we see a more varied distribution of performance, both in terms of scores (see Table 5.1), as well as geographical spread (see Figure 5.11). Each of Indonesia's regions has at least one province which achieved a top-10 position.

Figure 5.11: Geographical Spread for Competitive Policies, 2016

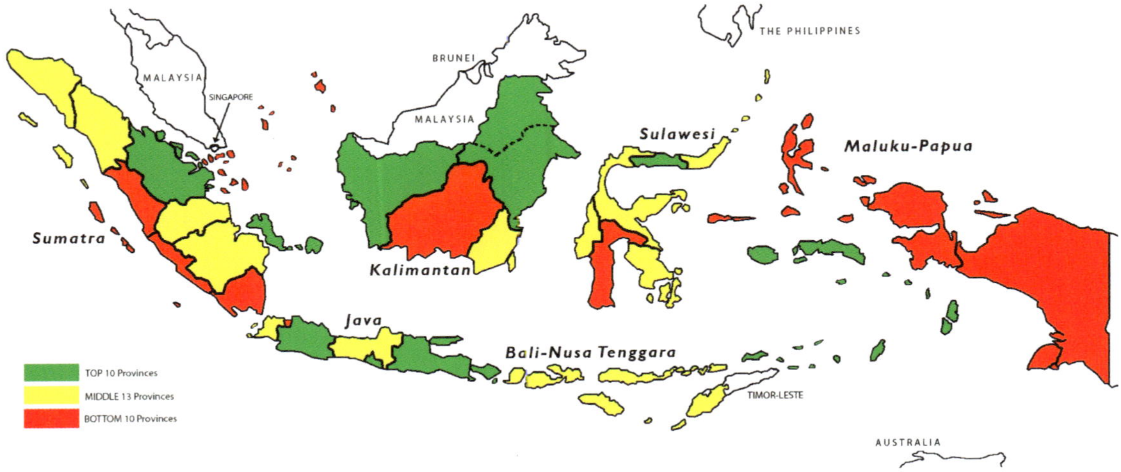

Source: Asia Competitiveness Institute.

Figure 5.12: Top-five and Bottom-five Provinces for Competitive Policies, 2016

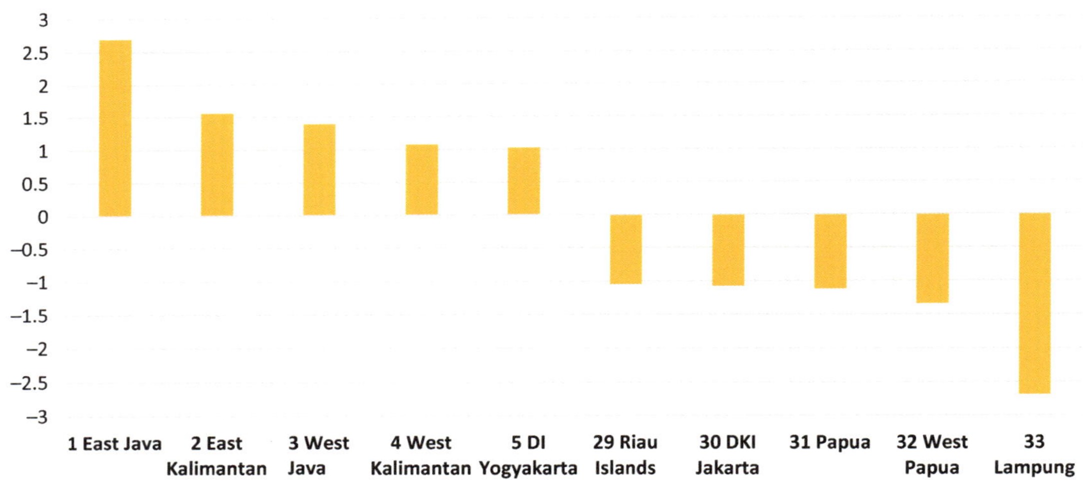

Source: Asia Competitiveness Institute.

Among the top-five, in terms of scores, East Java pulls far ahead of the other provinces with its user-friendly one-stop-service website providing essential information and services for businesses. Next in line, East Kalimantan, West Java, West Kalimantan and DI Yogyakarta are above average in this area but variously lacking in information on certain procedures, as well as on application submission and tracking services (see Figure 5.12).

Similar to the best-performing provinces, the bottom-10 provinces are also scattered across various regions. In terms of scores, most of the bottom-five provinces obtained scores which are clustered closely except for Lampung which notably scored the least, particularly because its one-stop-service had the least number of user features. Interestingly, South Sulawesi and DKI Jakarta, which consistently obtained the best scores for environments A and B, are among the bottom-five performers for environment C.

5.4.3 *What-if* Simulation Analysis on Overall EDB Index ABC

Each province's ranking and score before and after the simulation are presented in Table 5.4. Post-simulation, provinces which see the greatest jump by improving their respective weakest indicators are East Nusa Tenggara (up 16 places, from 22nd to sixth), Papua (up 14 places, from 25th to 11th), and West Papua (up 13 places, from 31st to 18th). In the case of East Nusa Tenggara, most of its weakest indicators are related to procedural inefficiencies and weaknesses in the one-stop-service, internal factors that can be independently addressed by the local government. For Papua and West Papua, on top of procedural constraints, infrastructure growth is needed to bring the province on par with the rest. The central government's plans to invest in infrastructure in eastern Indonesia could ameliorate this constraint in the long term.

That is not to say that top-ranked provinces do not have more to do: the scores of South Sulawesi's, DKI Jakarta's and East Java's weakest indicators are as much below average as the bottom-ranked provinces for certain indicators, meaning that provincial performance is uneven across the environments. Improvements in a one-stop-service's user-friendliness and functionalities and a review of local taxation structure could cement South Sulawesi and DKI Jakarta's top positions. For East Java, the weakest indicators span across several areas, such as banking penetration, rental costs of land/office space, and ease of obtaining approvals and permits and legal recourse. Thus, the involvement and coordination of different agencies is necessary towards lifting the province's performance.

5.4.4 *What-if* Simulation Analysis on Three Environments

What-if simulations are also conducted for each of the three environments (A, B, and C) to see the extent to which a province could improve its environments. For Attractiveness to Investors (see Table 5.5), three provinces, in particular, show that they could jump substantially: West Papua (up 18 places, from 31st to 13th), East Kalimantan (up 15 places, from 18th to third), and Papua (up 13 places, from 25th to 12th). West Papua's top-20% weakest indicators are dominated by those related to Attractiveness to Investors, such as (1) Cost of Renting Land/Office Space, (2) Ease of Obtaining New Sewerage Connection, and (3) Quality of Mobile Phone Coverage, such that an improvement in these would substantially raise the environment's score. Similarly, for the case of East Kalimantan, indicators related to Attractiveness to Investors also make up the province's weakest areas, such as (1) Minimum

Table 5.4: *What-if* Simulation for Overall EDB Index ABC, 2016

	Rank		Score	
Economy	**Before**	**After**	**Before**	**After**
Aceh	11	7	0.2346	1.0294
Bali	6	2	1.0885	1.5844
Bangka Belitung Islands	17	10	0.0646	0.8191
Banten	12	7	0.2331	0.9845
Bengkulu	26	18	−0.8323	0.0086
Central Java	4	1	1.4857	2.0518
Central Kalimantan	16	10	0.0971	0.7265
Central Sulawesi	8	2	0.9128	1.5600
DI Yogyakarta	9	3	0.8654	1.5231
DKI Jakarta	2	1	1.6182	2.5108
East Java	3	1	1.5415	2.0993
East Kalimantan	15	5	0.1505	1.2304
East Nusa Tenggara	22	6	−0.1933	1.0876
Gorontalo	13	7	0.2140	0.9264
Jambi	33	24	−1.8458	−0.6922
Lampung	20	10	−0.1108	0.6870
Maluku	21	10	−0.1387	0.8152
North Maluku	24	17	−0.7069	0.0501
North Sulawesi	7	4	0.9274	1.4867
North Sumatra	28	22	−1.2099	−0.2125
Papua	25	11	−0.7978	0.2925
Riau	23	11	−0.3516	0.2832
Riau Islands	30	23	−1.3921	−0.2696
South Kalimantan	10	7	0.4203	0.9648
South Sulawesi	1	1	1.8570	2.6445
South Sumatra	29	18	−1.2252	−0.0569
Southeast Sulawesi	18	10	−0.0042	0.6699
West Java	5	2	1.2494	1.7220
West Kalimantan	19	10	−0.0348	0.5716
West Nusa Tenggara	14	10	0.1678	0.6442
West Papua	31	18	−1.4492	−0.0022
West Sulawesi	27	20	−1.0218	−0.0858
West Sumatra	32	26	−1.8133	−0.8566

Source: Asia Competitiveness Institute.

Table 5.5: *What-if* Simulation for Attractiveness to Investors, 2016

Economy	Rank		Score	
	Before	After	Before	After
Aceh	10	6	0.7858	1.0208
Bali	14	5	0.3820	1.1364
Bangka Belitung Islands	16	11	0.3502	0.7369
Banten	4	3	1.2448	1.5714
Bengkulu	26	19	−0.8220	−0.1245
Central Java	7	2	0.9086	1.6642
Central Kalimantan	17	11	0.1601	0.6941
Central Sulawesi	3	3	1.3637	1.6180
DI Yogyakarta	15	4	0.3667	1.2926
DKI Jakarta	1	1	1.7497	2.6481
East Java	9	1	0.7906	1.6661
East Kalimantan	18	3	−0.0413	1.5091
East Nusa Tenggara	21	11	−0.3998	0.6266
Gorontalo	11	6	0.5062	1.0739
Jambi	33	27	−2.0848	−1.0089
Lampung	8	7	0.8021	0.9239
Maluku	29	18	−1.1896	0.0531
North Maluku	24	20	−0.6247	−0.1765
North Sulawesi	6	3	0.9880	1.4844
North Sumatra	27	26	−1.1444	−0.7629
Papua	25	12	−0.7355	0.4470
Riau	19	18	−0.1214	0.1180
Riau Islands	23	17	−0.5102	0.1658
South Kalimantan	13	11	0.3844	0.7598
South Sulawesi	2	1	1.7003	2.3645
South Sumatra	32	20	−1.6937	−0.2898
Southeast Sulawesi	22	18	−0.4849	0.0810
West Java	5	3	1.1545	1.6163
West Kalimantan	20	17	−0.3733	0.2764
West Nusa Tenggara	12	8	0.5054	0.8079
West Papua	31	13	−1.4913	0.3275
West Sulawesi	28	19	−1.1624	−0.0879
West Sumatra	30	25	−1.2637	−0.7439

Source: Asia Competitiveness Institute.

Wage per Month, (2) Ease of Obtaining Reliable Power Supply, and (3) High Tax as Major Obstacle for Operating a Business.

For Business Friendliness (see Table 5.6), the biggest improvements are potentially reaped by North Sumatra (up 14 places, from 30th to 16th), Riau (from 28th to 16th), Banten (from 27th to 15th), and Bangka Belitung Islands (from 24th to 12th). For North Sumatra, eight out of 15 weakest indicators are related to Business Friendliness, including (1) Tension between Labour Unions and Management, (2) Lack of Corruption, (3) Ease of Obtaining Approval and Clearance for Starting a New Business. Similarly for Riau and Banten, labour relations, corruption, and business registration issues form hurdles that stunt their Business Friendliness. For Bangka Belitung Islands, many of the issues in this environment are related to the availability and quality of manpower and value chain. These include: (1) Ease of Recruiting Skilled Production Workers, (2) Ease of Recruiting Professionals and Management Staff, and (3) Relationship with Local Suppliers.

For Competitive Policies (see Table 5.7), there are possibilities for big jumps, as shown by DKI Jakarta (up 23 places, from 30th to seventh), Central Kalimantan (up 19 places, from 26th to seventh), and Bengkulu (up 17 places, from 24th to seventh). All the indicators in this environment are related to the performance of the provincial PTSP's website.

5.4.5 Median and Maximum Web Analysis

To better understand the characteristics of the top- and bottom-ranked provinces against the median province, sub-environment scores for South Sulawesi (ranked first) and Jambi (ranked 33rd) are compared to the median and maximum scores within each sub-environment (see Figures 5.13 and 5.14). Although South Sulawesi ranked first for Overall EDB Index ABC and obtained very high scores for four out of five sub-environments, it does not fare well in Competitive Policies. Its score in this sub-environment is even substantially lower than that of the median score. Meanwhile, Jambi's position is quite interesting because its sub-environment scores are mostly below those of the median, but it had favourable score for Competitive Policies. Looking at its worst-performing sub-environments, Jambi as the bottom-ranked province is dragged down by high cost structure and long regulatory procedures.

Comparing the scores of South Sulawesi and Jambi to the maximum scores for said sub-environments, we see that South Sulawesi obtained the highest score for Responsiveness to Businesses and scored close to maximum scores for the other sub-environments, except for Competitive Policies, in which it fared below average. Jambi's scores, on the other hand, still show a long distance away from the maximum scores, except for Competitive Policies. Interestingly, it can be argued that the top-performing province in terms of EDB Index ABC is lacking one aspect wherein the bottom-performing province excels.

Table 5.6: *What-if* Simulation for Business Friendliness, 2016

Economy	Rank		Score	
	Before	After	Before	After
Aceh	21	12	–0.4303	0.3434
Bali	4	4	1.2047	1.3008
Bangka Belitung Islands	24	12	–0.4915	0.3772
Banten	27	15	–0.7624	0.1005
Bengkulu	23	16	–0.4874	–0.1449
Central Java	3	3	1.8280	1.8280
Central Kalimantan	13	12	0.3318	0.3975
Central Sulawesi	11	5	0.5246	1.1115
DI Yogyakarta	7	6	0.7846	0.9657
DKI Jakarta	2	2	1.9000	2.0151
East Java	6	5	0.8231	1.0669
East Kalimantan	22	16	–0.4475	0.0175
East Nusa Tenggara	16	5	–0.1786	1.0055
Gorontalo	20	15	–0.3512	0.2826
Jambi	32	26	–1.7030	–0.6620
Lampung	14	10	0.3312	0.5561
Maluku	8	5	0.6529	1.1468
North Maluku	19	15	–0.3502	0.1853
North Sulawesi	5	4	1.0374	1.2285
North Sumatra	30	16	–1.2889	–0.1658
Papua	18	15	–0.2349	0.2062
Riau	28	16	–0.8279	–0.0137
Riau Islands	31	25	–1.6399	–0.5678
South Kalimantan	9	6	0.6074	0.8234
South Sulawesi	1	1	2.3700	2.4550
South Sumatra	29	18	–0.8647	–0.2541
Southeast Sulawesi	12	6	0.3440	0.8728
West Java	10	6	0.5511	0.9005
West Kalimantan	17	15	–0.2307	0.1598
West Nusa Tenggara	15	15	0.0708	0.1548
West Papua	26	16	–0.6204	–0.0446
West Sulawesi	25	16	–0.5243	–0.1250
West Sumatra	33	28	–1.9282	–0.8875

Source: Asia Competitiveness Institute.

Table 5.7: *What-if* Simulation for Competitive Policies, 2016

	Rank		Score	
Economy	**Before**	**After**	**Before**	**After**
Aceh	17	4	0.1902	1.2736
Bali	6	4	1.0086	1.2786
Bangka Belitung Islands	9	7	0.5306	0.9458
Banten	18	11	–0.0695	0.4837
Bengkulu	24	7	–0.5789	0.5719
Central Java	15	4	0.2349	1.0453
Central Kalimantan	26	7	–0.6109	0.6213
Central Sulawesi	19	7	–0.2696	0.6150
DI Yogyakarta	5	3	1.0222	1.3982
DKI Jakarta	30	7	–1.0825	0.6773
East Java	1	1	2.6951	2.7181
East Kalimantan	2	2	1.5557	1.7059
East Nusa Tenggara	12	7	0.4141	0.9614
Gorontalo	10	7	0.5121	0.8711
Jambi	11	7	0.4840	0.6875
Lampung	33	19	–2.6922	–0.3019
Maluku	8	7	0.5403	0.7668
North Maluku	27	17	–0.7661	0.1744
North Sulawesi	21	14	–0.4876	0.3448
North Sumatra	16	4	0.2184	1.0492
Papua	31	19	–1.1243	–0.1874
Riau	7	7	0.5479	0.8833
Riau Islands	29	19	–1.0485	–0.2234
South Kalimantan	20	7	–0.3687	0.5617
South Sulawesi	28	7	–1.0063	0.9430
South Sumatra	13	7	0.4094	0.8703
Southeast Sulawesi	14	7	0.2655	0.6757
West Java	3	2	1.3889	1.6402
West Kalimantan	4	4	1.0744	1.3355
West Nusa Tenggara	22	7	–0.5080	0.5589
West Papua	32	23	–1.3445	–0.5740
West Sulawesi	23	18	–0.5520	0.0967
West Sumatra	25	18	–0.5829	0.0050

Source: Asia Competitiveness Institute.

Figure 5.13: Median Competitiveness Web for Top- and Bottom-ranked Provinces, 2016

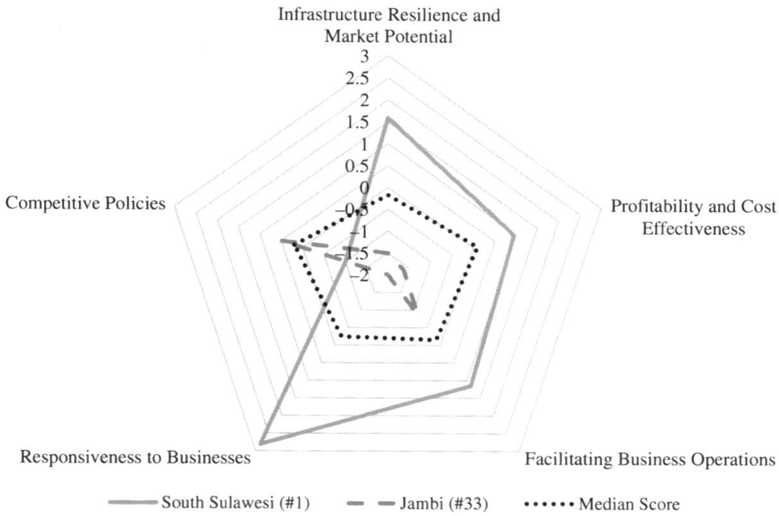

Source: Asia Competitiveness Institute.

Figure 5.14: Maximum Competitiveness Web for Top- and Bottom-ranked Provinces, 2016

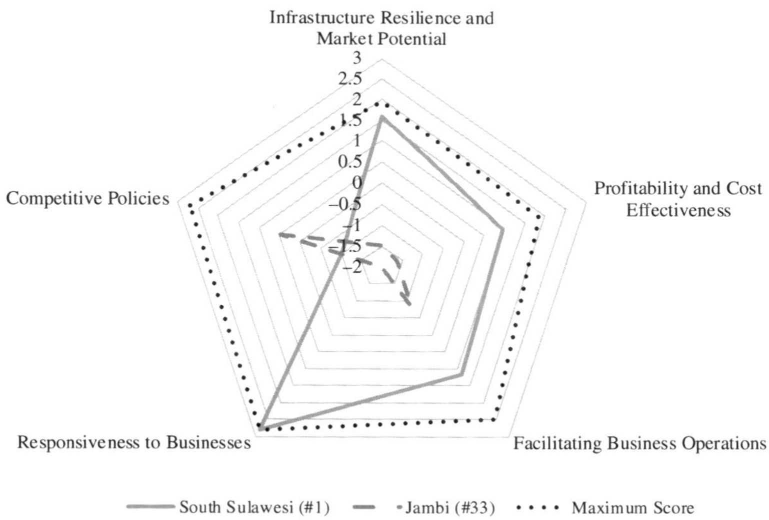

Source: Asia Competitiveness Institute.

5.5 Policy Implications and Concluding Notes

The EDB Index ABC offers a more holistic way in looking at how the non-market transaction costs of doing business interact with market aspects such as profitability and cost effectiveness, as well as regulatory factors such as competitive policies, in influencing sub-national competitiveness. In response to criticisms of the World Bank's DB index, we adopt the aspects measured in the DB index and place them in a wider framework of Ease of Doing Business which include Attractiveness to Investors, Business Friendliness, and Competitive Policies.

In terms of the explanatory powers of the three different environments (A, B, and C), it seems that A and B have a stronger and a more consistent role. All the top-five provinces in Overall EDB Index ABC show positive scores for A and B. Correspondingly, all bottom-five provinces obtain negative scores for A and B (again, see Figure 5.6).

While the role of A and B seem undisputable, the role of C is more ambiguous. The first- and second-ranked provinces (South Sulawesi and DKI Jakarta) have negative scores for C. One possibility is that these provinces did not take C very seriously, considering they were already very strong in A and B. At the same time, two of the bottom-five provinces still managed to achieve positive scores for C. The geographical spread for Competitive Policies (see Figure 5.11) highlights that regional advantages are less obvious in this environment as the management of one-stop-services and technology deployment capacity of each province are relatively independent, unlike other factors that require critical mass such as infrastructure networks and labour.

Figure 5.15 shows that five provinces demonstrate above-average results in all three sub-environments: East Java (ranked third), Central Java (fourth), West Java (fifth), Bali (sixth) and DI Yogyakarta (ninth). All five belong within the top-10. On the other hand, Figure 5.16 highlights that although South Sulawesi (first) and DKI Jakarta (second) have the highest scores for the Overall EDB Index ABC, the Competitive Policies scores of these provinces are below average. The same condition applies for North Sulawesi (seventh), Central Sulawesi (eighth), and South Kalimantan (10th). Interestingly, it can be argued that the top-10 are made up of provinces which fare well in either all three environments (A, B, and C), or simply two environments (A and B, but not C). The case of Lampung (ranked 20th) shows that if it had obtained better scores for the Competitive Policies environment, it might have been ranked among the top-10, taking over South Kalimantan's place.

Figure 5.15: Five Provinces with Positive Scores across All Three Environments (ABC)

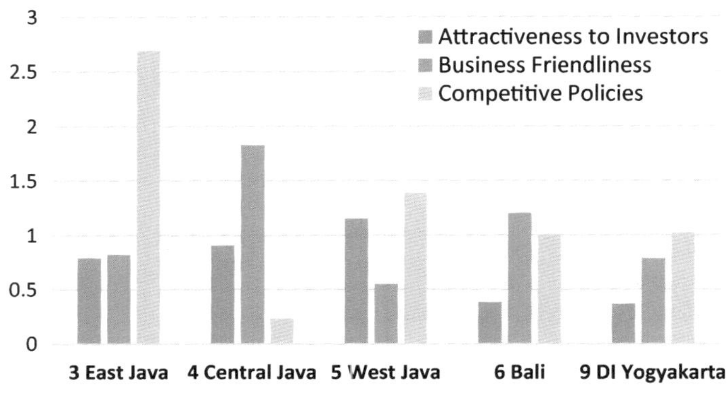

Source: Asia Competitiveness Institute.

Figure 5.16: Eight Provinces with Positive Scores for Attractiveness to Investors and Business Friendliness

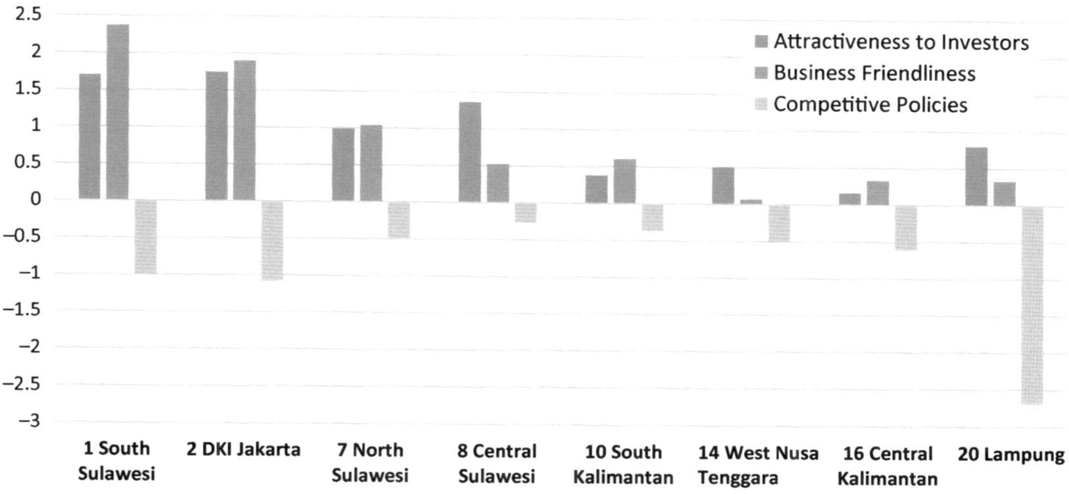

Source: Asia Competitiveness Institute.

Figure 5.17: Scatterplot of ACI's 2016 Competitiveness Scores and 2016 EDB Index ABC Scores for 33 Indonesian Provinces

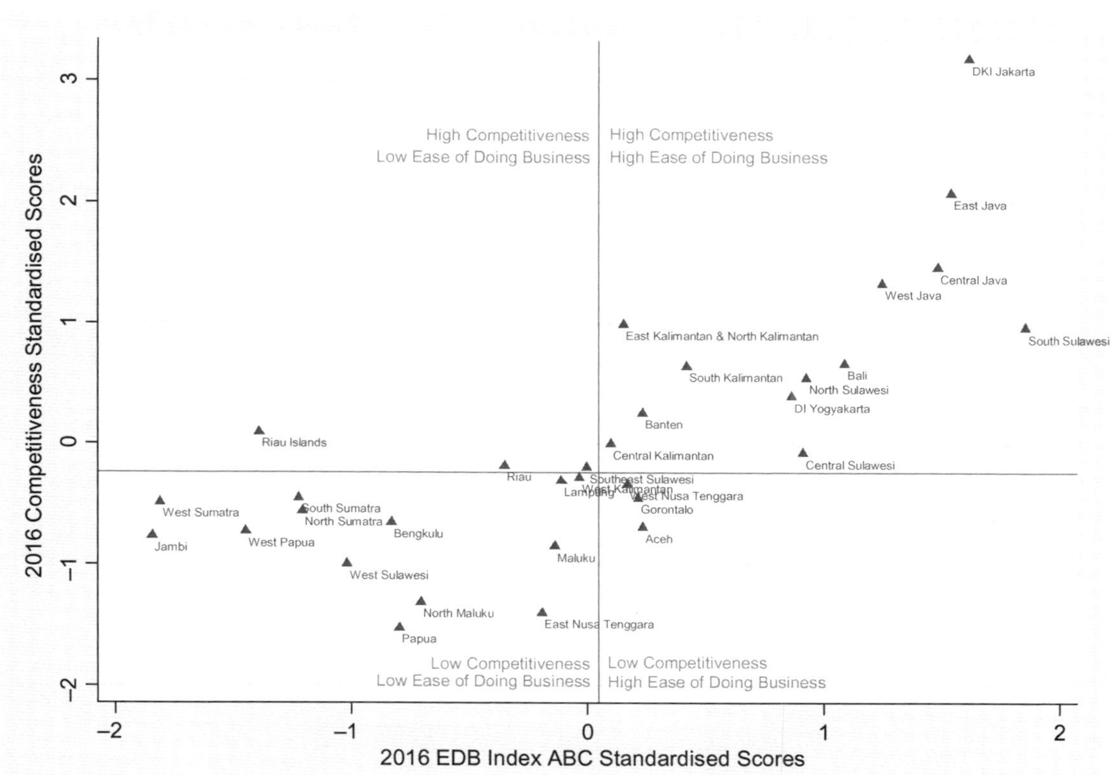

Source: Asia Competitiveness Institute.

5.5.1 Comparing ACI's EDB Index ABC Scores and ACI's Competitiveness Index Scores

So far, there seems to be a positive association between ACI's EDB Index ABC and ACI's Competitiveness Index for 33 Indonesian provinces. The scatterplot between the two indices shows that provinces with high level of competitiveness also tend to show high levels of Ease of Doing Business (see Figure 5.17). This seems to suggest that a holistic approach to ease of doing business may be able to provide a better approximation of an economy's competitiveness level, although the direction of causality (if any) remains to be further explored.

5.5.2 Comparing ACI's EDB Index ABC Scores and Foreign Direct Investment

We also see some association between the EDB Index ABC and average FDI inflow for the past three years for 33 Indonesian provinces (see Figure 5.18), although the level of correlation may be less obvious. Out of six provinces which occupy the top-left quadrant (high FDI but low EDB), four are rich in natural resources, meaning more than 30% of its GRDP is generated from

Figure 5.18: Scatterplot of ACI's 2016 EDB Index ABC Scores and FDI Inflows for 33 Indonesian Provinces

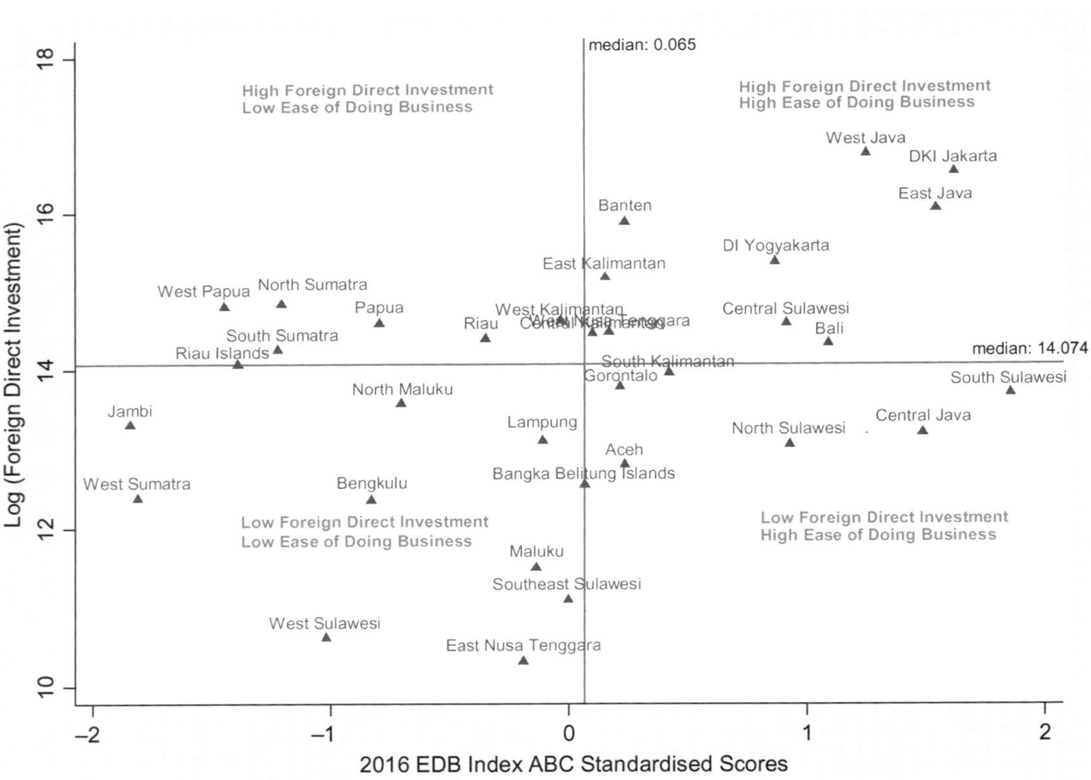

Source: Asia Competitiveness Institute.

oil, gas, and other mining-related activities. These four provinces are: Riau, Papua, West Papua, and South Sumatra. This highlights the complexity of the issue.

5.5.3 Concluding Notes

For provinces in eastern Indonesia, such as Papua and West Papua, on top of procedural constraints, infrastructure growth is needed to bring the provinces on par with the rest. The central government's plans to invest in infrastructure in eastern Indonesia could ameliorate this constraint in the long term.

That is not to say that top-ranked provinces do not have more to do: the scores of South Sulawesi, DKI Jakarta and East Java's weakest indicators are as much below average as the bottom-ranked provinces for certain indicators, meaning that provincial performance is uneven across the environments. Improvements in PTSP's user-friendliness and functionalities and a review of local taxation structure could cement South Sulawesi and DKI Jakarta's top positions. For East Java, the weakest indicators span across several areas, such as banking penetration, rental costs of land/office space, and ease of obtaining approvals and permits and legal recourse. Thus, the involvement and coordination of different agencies is necessary towards lifting a province's performance.

Under the current government's sixth economic package, eight special economic zones are to be established across the country. Their locations are in Banten (ranked 12th), West Nusa Tenggara (14th), East Kalimantan (15th), North Maluku (24th), North Sumatra (28th) and South Sumatra (29th). Notably, these provinces are middling at best in ACI's EDB Index ABC, indicating more room for future policy improvements to complement existing measures such as tax holidays and discounts to facilitate strong investor interest.

Despite its methodological simplicity, if the EDB Index ABC were able to gauge the level of competitiveness and economic potential of an area to a satisfactory level, it would not be impossible to utilise it as a guide for investment policies and regulations.

References

Arruñada, Benito. 2007. "Pitfalls to Avoid When Measuring Institutions: Is Doing Business Damaging Business?" *Journal of Comparative Economics* 35 (4): 729–47. doi:10.1016/j.jce.2007.08.003.

Berg, Janine, and Sandrine Cazes. 2008. "Policymaking Gone Awry: The Labor Market Regulations of the Doing Business Indicators." *Comparative Labor Law & Policy Journal* 29 (4): 349.

Bhagyashree, Garekar. 2015. "Indonesia President Widodo to Investors: Call Me If You Have Any Problems." *The Straits Times*, April 20. Available at http://www.straitstimes.com/asia/se-asia/indonesia-president-widodo-to-investors-call-me-if-you-have-any-problems.

Busse, Matthias, and José Luis Groizard. 2008. "Foreign Direct Investment, Regulations and Growth." *World Economy* 31 (7): 861–86. doi:10.1111/j.1467-9701.2008.01106.x.

Corcoran, Adrian, and Robert Gillanders. 2015. "Foreign Direct Investment and the Ease of Doing Business." *Review of World Economics* 151 (1): 103–26. doi:10.1007/s10290-014-0194-5.

Davis, Kevin E., and Michael B. Kruse. 2007. "Taking the Measure of Law: The Case of the Doing Business Project: Taking the Measure of Law." *Law & Social Inquiry* 32 (4): 1095–1119. doi:10.1111/j.1747-4469.2007.00088.x.

Djankov, Simeon, Caralee McLiesh, and Rita Maria Ramalho. 2006. "Regulation and Growth." *Economics Letters* 92 (3): 395–401. doi:10.1016/j.econlet.2006.03.021.

Eifert, Benjamin P. 2009. "Do Regulatory Reforms Stimulate Investment and Growth? Evidence from the Doing Business Data, 2003-07." Available at http://www.cgdev.org/publication/do-regulatory-reforms-stimulate-investment-and-growth-evidence-doing-business-data-2003.

Hallward-Driemeier, M., and L. Pritchett. 2015. "How Business Is Done in the Developing World: Deals versus Rules." *Journal of Economic Perspectives* 29 (3): 121–40. doi:10.1257/jep.29.3.121.

Independent Evaluation Group. 2008. "Doing Business: An Independent Evaluation — Taking the Measure of the World Bank-IFC Doing Business Indicators." IEG Independent Evaluations & Annual Reviews. Washington, DC: The World Bank. Available at https://openknowledge.worldbank.org/handle/10986/6467.

Jayasuriya, Dinuk. 2011. "Improvements in the World Bank's Ease of Doing Business Rankings: Do They Translate into Greater Foreign Direct Investment Inflows?: Policy Research Working Papers." The World Bank. Available at http://elibrary.worldbank.org/doi/abs/10.1596/1813-9450-5787.

Klapper, Leora, Raphael Amit, Mauro F. Guillen, and Quesada, Juan Manuel. 2007. "Entrepreneurship And Firm Formation Across Countries." Policy Research Working Papers. The World Bank. Available at http://elibrary.worldbank.org/doi/abs/10.1596/1813-9450-4313.

Oberman, Raoul, Richard Dobbs, Arief Budiman, Fraser Thompson, and Morten Rosse. 2012. "The Archipelago Economy: Unleashing Indonesia's Potential." McKinsey Global Institute. Available at http://www.mckinsey.com/global-themes/asia-pacific/the-archipelago-economy.

Parlina, Ina. 2014. "Jokowi Aims for 7 Percent Annual Growth." *The Jakarta Post*, December 24. Available at http://www.thejakartapost.com/news/2014/12/24/jokowi-aims-7-percent-annual-growth.html.

Pinheiro-Alves, Ricardo, and João Zambujal-Oliveira. 2012. "The Ease of Doing Business Index as a Tool for Investment Location Decisions." *Economics Letters* 117 (1): 66–70. doi:10.1016/j.econlet.2012.04.026.

Ravallion, Martin. 2012. "Mashup Indices of Development." *The World Bank Research Observer* 27 (1): 1–32. doi:10.1093/wbro/lkr009.

Rusmana, Yoga. 2016. "Indonesian GDP Growth Misses Target in 2015, Ministry Reports." *Bloomberg.com*, January 3. Available at https://www.bloomberg.com/news/articles/2016-01-03/indonesian-gdp-growth-misses-target-in-2015-ministry-reports.

Stel, André van, David J. Storey, and A. Roy Thurik. 2007. "The Effect of Business Regulations on Nascent and Young Business Entrepreneurship." *Small Business Economics* 28 (2/3): 171–86. doi:10.1007/s11187-006-9014-1.

Tan, Khee Giap, and Mulya Amri. 2013. "Subnational Competitiveness and National Performance: Analysis and Simulation for Indonesia." *Journal of CENTRUM Cathedra: The Business and Economics Research Journal* 6 (2): 173–192.

Tan, Khee Giap, Mulya Amri, Linda Low, and Kong Yam Tan. 2013. *Competitiveness Analysis and Development Strategies for 33 Indonesian Provinces*. Singapore: World Scientific.

Tan, Khee Giap, Nurina Merdikawati, Mulya Amri, and Blake Harley Berger. 2015. *2014 Annual Competitiveness Analysis and Development Strategies for Indonesian Provinces*. Singapore: World Scientific.

The Wall Street Journal. 2015. "Indonesia's Investment Aims — The Numbers." *The Wall Street Journal*, June 15. http://blogs.wsj.com/briefly/2015/06/15/indonesias-investment-aims-the-numbers/.

World Bank. 2003. "Doing Business 2004 — Understanding Regulations." http://www.doingbusiness.org/reports/global-reports/doing-business-2004.

World Bank. 2010. "Doing Business in Indonesia 2010." Doing Business — Subnational Series. Washington, D.C.

World Bank. 2012. "Doing Business in Indonesia 2012." Doing Business — Subnational Series. Washington, D.C.

World Bank. 2016. "Doing Business 2017 — Equal Opportunity for All." World Bank. Available at http://www.doingbusiness.org/reports/global-reports/doing-business-2017.

Yulisman, Linda. 2015. "Kadin Proposes Special Funding Body to Support Industry." *The Jakarta Post*, May 8. Available at http://www.thejakartapost.com/news/2015/05/08/kadin-proposes-special-funding-body-support-industry.html.

Discussant Note 5.1[1]

2016 Inaugural Ease of Doing Business Index on Attractiveness to Investors, Business Friendliness and Competitive Policies (EDB Index ABC) of Indonesian Provinces

Ms Paramita Dasgupta

Practice Manager, Asia, Trade & Competitiveness
The World Bank Group

The Ease of Doing Business Index ABC presentation by Asia Competitiveness Institute (ACI) is organized in two broad heads, and I only limit my comments to address those two. The first is a brief overview and some responses to The World Bank Group's approach of Doing Business and the importance of subnational benchmarking surveys. The second is a set of issues and comments that I would like to share about ACI's EDB Index ABC.

First, on the importance of benchmarking surveys in the World Bank. Under the Investment Climate pillar of the World Bank Group's Trade and Competitiveness Global Practice, ease of doing business and streamlining business environment and regulatory issues are at the heart of the work we do.

One, Doing Business is one of the World Bank's global benchmarking tool that makes comparisons across 189 countries and selected cities at the subnational and regional level. The report which has been in operation since 2002 focuses on domestic small and medium-sized enterprises (SMEs). While country coverage, survey scope and number of indicators have increased over the years, the basic objective of why we initiated this whole exercise has not changed. The World Bank's Doing Business aims to provide an objective measure of regulations and their enforcement on SMEs, which remain as predominant source of employment in each country.

[1] The contents of this discussion note were delivered during the Asia Competitiveness Institute (ACI)-World Bank ASEAN Economic Forum, on 9 September 2016, in Singapore.

Second, as this exercise is conducted in 189 countries, it is difficult to expand the number of cities we cover. However, the World Bank deals with this limitation by focusing on the other commercial cities, in countries with population of more than 100 million. Thus, in countries like Indonesia, India, Mexico, and the United States, we have introduced a second commercial city. The paper does indicate differences in data and heterogeneity of data, which is precisely the reason why the World Bank started the sub-national data series about ten years ago.

The sub-national data exercise is extremely powerful and has a huge potential to initiate reform dialogue and reform action. In large federations like India, it has had a huge peer-to-peer impact in terms of facilitating dialogue, and sharing of the good practices. Building on the comment that was made in the Indonesian study, there was a relation running in India, that if only Indian States compared and shared their best practices, they would improve from the ranking of 140 to anywhere close to 50. So, the good practices actually lie in the country but the main implementation and practice vary.

We also agree fully with the comment that World Bank's Doing Business is certainly not a comprehensive indicator. In fact, the Frequently Asked Questions (FAQs) section on Doing Business website shows that the number one misconception is that Doing Business is supposed to be a comprehensive indicator of business environment in the country, which is absolutely untrue. The World Bank Group use itself, and encourage others to use multiple data sets for coming up with the baseline assessments of situations in any country. In fact, we ourselves refer to FDI data, citizen engagement and rule-making surveys, doing business and the law, and a number of other global benchmarks that the World Bank itself conduct. There are also others that have been conducted by other agencies, including the ACI.

In fact, Doing Business does not measure a number of important aspects of business environment. For example, it does not measure current macroeconomic stability, security, corruption, labor skills, and underlying quality of institutions and infrastructure, all of which are absolute fundamental process of the basic competitiveness of any location. While the limitations are fully noted and very well understood, we do see Doing Business as a dialogue-starter, and as a good reflection of investor sentiment in any country. Normally, within any country dialogue, the first four or five years go into data dispute and data debate. There is an optimistic and positive trend wherein the world is now moving to more data dialogue and dialogue around reform and action, which is the way to go.

Let me move to the ACI EDB Index ABC and as I've mentioned in the start, we are actually delighted that such a comprehensive report or study have been undertaken as part of the Memorandum of Understanding (MOU) signed earlier this morning, between the World Bank Group and National University of Singapore (NUS). We are hoping that there will be more opportunity to do work together, especially on sub-national benchmarking exercise, and we really look forward to that.

The World Bank have had more comprehensive sub-national benchmarking exercises like ACI EDB Index ABC in some countries like Kenya, Nigeria, Spain, Mexico. We found each of these exercises to be a very powerful tool for reform dialogue. So, we are hoping that the Indonesian authority will be considering some of the findings of the study into its policy priority.

I think the EDB Index ABC methodology takes into account all three data sources that we normally consider for surveys. It refers to outcome data like 'kilometers of roads' and 'number of firms registered'. It also looks at output data, perception and experience-based data. Output-based data is interesting because it is actionable. However, the World Bank do not rely only on '*de jure* factors' but we also look at the '*de facto*' of doing business because it is not only about the regulation, cost fees or the strategic timelines on paper. The Doing Business also looks at '*de facto*' experience of the private sector, in terms of actual time-taken, actual fees paid including informal fees, as well as how the one-stop shop functions in practice (whether it is truly an effective one-stop shop, or "one-more stop shop"), which is often the case in most of the markets that we work on.

So, we have several comments about the ACI EDB Index ABC study. First, whether there has been a prioritization or some kind of the research on the relevance of each of the indicators that have been considered. In order to be comprehensive, the study has about 74 indicators, making the exercise fairly complex. However, there might be room for some consolidation, which could perhaps happen through some kind of more internal desk review of the relevance of each indicator. So, we would base it on private sector feedback, or whichever that strongly pinpoints, such as signs or larger weights assigned to certain indicators in particular.

Second, it could also be good for us to understand who the respondents from the firm perception data are. A large multinational firm may have a different experience from a small-sized domestic firm, and hence there should be a clarification on that. There are couple of dimensions that are relevant for investors which do not seem to be included (in the study) and yet are very important for the certainty of the business environment. These include how frequent the business regulations are changing in the country, and how intense the consultative changes are, such as whether the businesses in private sector are involved in those decisions made to change the regulatory environment. We do not get an indication or sense that these factors are being considered in the indicators listed.

Given the periodicity and comparability, which makes benchmarking very powerful, we are wondering whether ACI are planning to undertake this exercise on a more regular basis. If so, it would be good to get a sense of what the plans are, and how ACI and the World Bank could perhaps collaborate on strengthening our approach and approaching this together.

It is interesting that while there are differences in data used; World Bank's sub-national Doing Business data for Indonesia in 2012 and ACI EDB Index ABC data in 2015–16, and differences in the approach of methodology, the results are comparable. For instance, East Kalimantan (which is represented by Balikpapan) in the Doing Business study came up number one in construction permits, and even in EDB Index ABC study, East Kalimantan ranks number two in the environment of Competitive Policies.

On the other hand, in the World Bank's sub-national Doing Business data for Indonesia, South Sulawesi (which is represented by Makassar) ranks number 17 in 'starting business.' However, based on the EDB Index ABC study, South Sulawesi ranks number one in the overall index. This is reflective of the impressive policy reforms that have been undertaken in the province, and the data is now confirming this. There is a powerful message in that, there is basically consistency in the results irrespective of the approaches we have.

As the government of Indonesia is very committed to doing business reform agenda, cutting across provinces beyond Jakarta, the World Bank are working very closely with Jakarta authority, particularly in ease of doing business, and sharing work with University of Indonesia to share the good practices from Jakarta and other leading provinces. It will be great to see how we (ACI and the World Bank) can explore further collaboration together.

Discussant Note 5.2[1]

2016 Inaugural Ease of Doing Business Index on Attractiveness to Investors, Business Friendliness and Competitive Policies (EDB Index ABC) of Indonesian Provinces

Ms Kristy Tsun-Tzu Hsu

Director, Taiwan ASEAN Studies Center
Chung-Hua Institution for Economic Research, Taiwan

My institute does not follow ease of doing business benchmarking or other studies, but we do follow or watch closely Taiwanese industries in this region. So the points I will be making may complement those made by the other discussant because I can share with you investors' potential point of view. The methodologies used in Asia Competiveness Institute (ACI) Ease of Doing Business Index ABC (EDB Index ABC) is a combination of secondary and survey data collected from field trips to Indonesia, which are organized in collaboration with the Employers' Association of Indonesia (APINDO). APINDO is a very important organization in Indonesia. Their involvement makes the assessment more business relevant.

Taiwan has been investing in Southeast Asia since the 1980s. To date, accumulated foreign direct investments (FDI) from Taiwan into this region amount to around USD 100 to 150 billion. As Taiwan has been investing heavily in this region, businesses would want to know more about such benchmarking and assessment data, which could help them make business decisions.

From the perspective of Taiwanese investors, most of the indicators listed in the study's 'Attractiveness to Investors' environment are very important. Stable and sufficient supply of labor force including semi-skilled and skilled workers, ease of obtaining electricity, and availability of large-sized land are also among investors' considerations. In particular, investors

[1]The contents of this discussion note were delivered during the Asia Competitiveness Institute (ACI)-World Bank ASEAN Economic Forum, on 9 September 2016, in Singapore.

consider labor-intensive and clustering of manufacturing industries, such as textile, garments, and footwear, and automobile and spare parts.

Based on experiences, Yangon and Phnom Penh are very difficult places for Taiwanese investors. In the past two years, there have been visits from hundreds of delegations to these places. However, it has been difficult to access Yangon and Phnom Penh and buy large-scale land there due to high cost. So far, there have not been large-scale investment activities by Taiwanese companies in these two regions. This implies that large-scale land for developing industry-based clusters is very important for large-scale investors.

For export-oriented investors, whether the host country has Free Trade Agreement (FTA) networks is very important. As Taiwan has existing networks in the region, Taiwanese investors would always look for places with more FTA networks, so that products exported from the host economy can be subjected to low or zero tariffs to export destinations. To illustrate, in the past few years after Vietnam announced their participation in the Trans-Pacific Partnership (TPP) negotiations, FDI inflows flooded into Vietnam as investors leveraged on Vietnam's TPP membership and exported to US marketplace. Such was also observed in Cambodia after Cambodia became eligible for the Generalized System of Preferences (GSP) treatment by the European Union (EU). We see a lot of investment going into Cambodia, as investors take advantage of Cambodia's GSP treatment when they export products to European countries. So, Taiwanese companies are now waiting for the news on whether Myanmar is going to be granted GSP treatment by the United States. If this happens, there would be many Taiwanese companies who would consider to invest in Myanmar in the next few years.

As for the study's 'Business Friendliness' environment, having stable supply chains is most important for Taiwanese and Korean investors, particularly those who are heavily participating in Global Value Chains (GVCs). This means that investors always consider whether they can have clustering of supporting industries in the host economies, and local suppliers in the host countries who can help secure access to raw and semi materials and parts for their operations. Furthermore, an important phenomenon observed is the increasing tension between labor and firms in some countries. Increasing strikes in Cambodia and Vietnam, amounting to hundreds of strikes in a year have already deterred some Taiwanese investors. For example a large footwear manufacturer, which employed 160,000 workers in Vietnam, suffered many strikes and had to look at neighboring countries to diversify its operations.

With regards to 'security' which is another indicator in the study's 'Business Friendliness' environment, Taiwanese investors experience different political situation in Taiwan, wherein they do not observe diplomatic relations with all of the countries where they heavily invest in. As such, Taiwanese investors are more concerned about investment protection, particularly for large-scaled investment. For this reason, companies always consider investment protection when they look for opportunities in countries like Indonesia.

The study's 'Competitive Policies' environment is also very important and several indicators from this environment may be more relevant in regards to less developed countries. For instance, under the sub-national or provincial level assessments, the local government and administrative procedures are very important considerations for investors. Hence, while the World Bank Doing Business ranking demonstrates improvements in government performance or reforms, it provides less information for business decision-making. Large companies would thus pay and engage companies like KPMG or McKinsey, because their materials and assessment help them more. So, compared to the World Bank assessment of Doing Business, ACI EDB Index ABC have new indicators which may reflect more business perspective. This can perhaps help more potential investors who are searching for locations for investment.

As this study uses sub-national level data or indicators, it may be useful to differentiate roles of central and provincial government in affecting or improving the general and specific issues demonstrated by certain indicators. For example, minimum wage issues, and implementation and enforcement of national law such as protection of intellectual property rights may be under the purview of national government. In such cases, what would be the role of state or provincial government? There is also a need to consider different situations in different provinces, such as situations in landlocked provinces or provinces with different level of industrialization.

Finally, a very important case to share is the case of Foxconn or Hon Hai Technology Group, which is the world's largest ICT product manufacturer and supplier. Four years ago, Foxconn went to Indonesia to seriously investigate locations where they can build their operation base. However, one and half years ago, they decided to go to India. Foxconn already had a lot of manufacturing orders from Oppo, Xiaomi, Huawei, HTC and some other Taiwan smartphones, and the most recent developments indicate that the iPhone manufacturer decides to outsource iPhone manufacturing to Foxconn's operations in India.

Foxconn's decision to move from Indonesia to India has nothing to do with ease of doing business because these two countries may perform similarly in ease of doing business indicators. Instead, Foxconn's decision reflects two major considerations or motives adopted by large companies like theirs.

First is about the worthiness or intention of their clients which are the large brand owners — Huawei, Xiaomi, HTC and iPhone. Since their client asks them to invest in India, they have to follow through with their client's request and go. Second consideration is ironic, because openness to trade which typically can attract more FDI, can sometimes become the opposite. Foxconn's decision to go to India is due to India's local content policy two years ago, which raised a lot of cost for imported cellphones. This forces the brand owners as well as manufacturers like Foxconn to consider manufacturing inside India, so they could reduce the cost. So, the openness to trade sometimes may lead to increase in FDI, but sometimes it may be the opposite as is the case for Foxconn.

Also, when Foxconn decide to invest in India, the company brings a lot of clusters of suppliers with them, and many Taiwanese and Korean companies follow in their footsteps. As a result, India begin to build the supply chain of smartphones. This scenario may have interesting and significant implications, which we could consider when we do ease of doing business assessment in this project.

Chapter 6
Conclusion

6.1 Summary of Key Findings

The Asia Competitiveness Institute (ACI) is committed to evaluate competitiveness and related issues in the economies of Southeast Asia (i.e. ASEAN-10 countries)[1] in the context of a rising China[2] and India.[3] Annual analyses at the sub-national level has been ACI's forte, an approach that is relevant given the vast and diverse characteristics of large countries such as Indonesia, China, and India. This book presents the results of our latest research, reflecting a deep interest to track provincial and regional competitiveness in Indonesia, and to put forward an empirical approach based on our rich sub-national database.

As an overview and introduction to the book, Chapter 1 starts by providing a brief account of Indonesia's most recent macroeconomic development and ends by presenting the breakdown of the overall structure of this book. As the country strives to revive its economic growth, hampered by low commodity prices and weak external demand, Indonesia is pushing for public spending in infrastructure development. To enable a high level of public investment, the country is boosting receipts from tax collection and tourism, as well as attracting more investment by adopting wide-ranging reforms to improving the ease of doing business. The success of such strategies depends on efforts conducted at both the national and sub-national levels.

Chapter 2 provides the results of ACI's 2016 annual analysis on Indonesia's provincial-level competitiveness. Provinces from the Java region remain among the most competitive while those from the Maluku–Papua region tend to stay lagging. There are only minor changes observed among the top-10 provinces and bottom-five compared to the previous years' research results. Meanwhile, we see more dynamic changes in the standardised scores of mid-range provinces.

---

[1] See ACI's publications of competitiveness analysis for ASEAN countries (Tan *et al.*, 2016, 2017a). More specifically, ACI also published competitiveness studies of Indonesia at the provincial and regional levels (Tan *et al.*, 2013, 2015a, 2015b, 2017b, 2017c).

[2] See ACI's publications of competitiveness analysis for China (Tan, Yuan, and Xie, 2017; Tan, Yuan, and Yoong, 2015; Tan *et al.*, 2014a).

[3] See ACI's publications of competitiveness analysis for India (Tan, Gopalan, and Tandon, 2017; Tan *et al.* 2014b, 2015c).

There remains a challenge in identifying the characteristics of provinces with high and low competitiveness. Having a strong manufacturing sector has been argued to be correlated with competitiveness, but West Papua, Bangka Belitung Islands, North Sumatra (among the most industrialised provinces where 54.2%, 28.2%, and 27.8% of the GRDP in 2013 were generated from the secondary industries, respectively) were ranked 27th, 20th, and 24th in our latest competitiveness ranking. Also, in our conversation with many Indonesian stakeholders, having abundant natural resources was often proposed as explanation to the performance of provinces such as East Kalimantan (ranked fifth). However, this again was proven untrue when comparing against the performance of Riau and West Papua (where oil and gas accounted for 45% and 49% of the GRDP in 2013, respectively), which were ranked 15th and 27th. Similarly, having an archipelagic character was often offered as explanation to lagging performance of certain provinces. Many archipelagic provinces do exhibit challenges, as shown by the low ranking obtained by East Nusa Tenggara (ranked 32nd), North Maluku (31st) and Maluku (29th). However, again, we see exceptions such as North Sulawesi and Riau Islands which did quite well, being ranked ninth and 12th, respectively.

Chapter 3 provides the results of ACI's 2016 annual analysis on Indonesia's regional-level competitiveness. The findings are generally intuitive to many policymakers' understanding of regional disparity in the country, but the weak performance of Sumatra region does provide new insight. The Sumatra region for many years has been considered as the more developed part of the country, being located next to the Malacca Strait, but ACI's regional competitiveness ranking for the past three years ranks the region fourth, below Java, Kalimantan, and Sulawesi. In terms of regional disparity, the most notable gap appears to take place between Java and all other regions.

The growth slowdown analysis of Indonesia's provinces presented in Chapter 4 shows that without having certain characteristics, economic growth in the provinces faces risks of major slowdown. Such characteristics differ across the various provinces based on their income groups, but Literacy Rate persists as the indicator that applies to all groups. For low-income and lower middle-income provinces, FDI Inflows matter, while for high-income and upper-middle income provinces, Openness to Trade plays an important role. The analysis also calls for a better management of higher growth rates recently experienced by Riau and East Kalimantan, and preparation in anticipation of growth slowdown.

Chapter 5 presents ACI's inaugural analysis on Ease of Doing Business based on the exploration of three environments: Attractiveness to Investors, Business Friendliness, and Competitive Policies. This research finds some correlation between the standardised scores for the EDB Index ABC and those for the Overall Competitiveness Index. Dividing the results into four quadrants, Indonesian provinces which have high EDB Index ABC scores tend to also have high Overall Competitiveness scores, and vice versa (see the scatterplot diagram in Figure 5.17). Only three provinces belong to the quadrant that shows relatively high EDB Index ABC, but rather low Overall Competitiveness: West Nusa Tenggara, Gorontalo, and Aceh. Also, only three provinces belong to the quadrant that shows relatively low EDB Index ABC, but rather high Overall Competitiveness: Riau, Riau Islands, and Southeast Sulawesi. Keep in mind, though, that many of these six provinces are mapped around the middle of the scatterplot diagram.

6.2 Concluding Remarks: Indonesia as a Rising Middle Power

Indonesia's overall competitiveness is tied to its leaders' ability to corral support at the central and local governments to see the bureaucratic reforms through and ensure that growth is broad-based across regions. With the end of the commodity supercycle, Indonesia can no longer afford to tolerate the structural weaknesses in its economy.

For economic growth to be sustainable, allowing Indonesia to take on its role as a rising middle power, each province in Indonesia has a role to play in improving its own competitiveness from macroeconomic management, governance, financial, business and labour conditions to infrastructure development.

6.2.1 Dealing with Bureaucracy

With Indonesia's decentralised structure, the momentum for reform is contingent on local bureaucratic capacity to implement central government policies and to initiate regional and provincial-specific reforms. At the national level, President Jokowi has a freer hand in selecting his team and setting policies that steers Indonesia in the direction of reforms. But the quality and policy leanings of local government leaders are determined by local politics.

The dynamics between governors, regents and city mayors also need to be considered to understand why some provinces are ahead of the game. Technocratic governors have gained popularity and innovation in public services, such as digitising permit and license applications, a measure of competitiveness, is taking place in some provinces. However, it may take more cajoling before such reforms happen sufficiently fast and become widespread.

The environment of Government and Institutional Setting within ACI's competitiveness framework, particularly the Institutions, Governance, and Leadership sub-environment, help us to see the variation of these factors among provinces (see Chapter 2, particularly Table 2.3). Provinces in Sulawesi tend to show marked progress in these matters and it is timely for other provinces to learn how they achieved such progress.

6.2.2 Improving Human Capital

Human capital constraints in less economically vibrant provinces must be recognised. Except for Aceh, unemployment rates have trended down across the board, but significant wage differentials and better opportunities in formal employment in larger cities and neighbouring countries such as the Philippines and Malaysia drain much-needed talent. Seasonal, informal employment among youth is also high, and there is a shortage of higher skilled workers in the private sector. Productivity gains is hard to achieve given the structural issues in the labour market.

ACI's competitiveness framework, especially the environment of Quality of Life and Infrastructure Development, and more specifically, the Standard of Living, Education, and Social Stability sub-environment allows us to identify the range of standardised scores among provinces in this aspect (see Chapter 2, particularly Table 2.5). The improvement of human capital depends on both the quantity and quality of spending on education and healthcare.

In this regard, we find discrepancy between the quantity of local government spending on education and the quality of education that is provided. Some provinces (such as Jambi, Central Kalimantan, and West Sulawesi) obtain relatively high scores on hard indicators related to education, such as Student–Teacher Ratio, but low scores on the related soft indicators, including Perceived Quality of Education based on ACI's surveys.

While improvements in hard indicators are an important indication of quantity of spending, the discrepancy between performance in hard indicators and perceived performance in soft indicators highlights the need to improve the quality of public spending. This issue has been raised a number of times (Negara, 2016; World Bank, 2017) and ACI's research provides added value in the form of empirical findings to justify such argument.

6.2.3 Developing Infrastructure

Ageing infrastructure and lack of connectivity have been among the most important concerns raised about Indonesia. While former president Susilo Bambang Yudhoyono (SBY) stewarded Indonesia's economy into shape, it has been at the expense of infrastructure development in the last decade. Under President Jokowi, more than 200 National Strategic Projects have been announced via Presidential Regulation 3/2016 and 102/2016 encompassing the development of roads, railways, ports, airports, dams, water, electricity, special economic zones, affordable housing and oil and gas, agriculture and maritime infrastructure across all provinces. All projects are expected to be completed by 2019. Some of these projects are familiar to Indonesians: the Jakarta Mass Rapid Transit (MRT) project has more than two decades of history.

As of December 2016, 16 projects have been completed on the back of Rp 25.9 trillion investments, the biggest among them are the Kalibaru port (Rp 12 trillion — an expansion of the Tanjung Priok port) and Terminal 3 of Jakarta's Soekarno–Hatta International Airport (Rp 4.7 trillion), which adds significantly to the airport's capacity to match regional rivals in Malaysia and Singapore (Ariyanti, 2016).

The sheer number of projects demonstrate the desperate need for infrastructure development in the country. Weighed down by bureaucratic constraints, President Jokowi has taken a gamble with this ambitious plan instead of focusing on several keystone projects for quick wins. But his top-down push does inspire popular support especially bringing the much-needed connectivity to the Eastern provinces such as Papua and Sulawesi.

For some of these projects, details on investment terms, availability of government guarantees and timeline are not readily available, making it potentially challenging for foreign investors to navigate. Unsurprisingly, delays in land acquisition, alleged corruption and cronyism in the procurement process and cost revisions and overruns among others have surfaced. To accelerate the implementation of these national projects, President Jokowi issued a decree effective from 6 December 2016, enabling private firms to undertake land acquisitions if the project is not budgeted or ministries or government agencies have insufficient budget (Tobing, 2016). His target of achieving 35,000 MW power-generating capacity by 2019 is certainly behind schedule and is currently being reconsidered, while the estimated cost of the trans-Java railway linking Jakarta and Surabaya has quadrupled (Alifandi, 2016).

6.2.4 Spreading Growth Engines

ACI's research on competitiveness and ease of doing business shows that the performance of Indonesia's economy is still based on the performance of a few growth centres. The country's growth centres are still largely found in the Java region, and to a smaller extent, in the provinces of South Sulawesi, Riau Islands, and North Sumatra. East Kalimantan and Riau are among the natural resource-rich provinces with substantial public revenue and are developing fast. However, their growth has been largely based on prices of commodities, and they are currently being impacted by the commodity price bust.

This, again, highlights the need for Indonesia to develop a robust manufacturing sector that is not based on natural resources. West Papua has a large manufacturing sector that contributes to 54% of the provincial GRDP in 2013. However, most of the manufacturing activities taking place there is related to the processing of oil and gas. Aside from those dealing with commodities, Indonesia's manufacturing centres are mostly found along the northern coast of Java (namely, in DKI Jakarta, Banten, West Java, Central Java, and East Java), where manufacturing activities therein collectively contribute to 69% of Indonesia's total manufacturing output in 2013. Aside from that taking place in Java, manufacturing mostly takes place in Riau Islands (more specifically, Batam) and North Sumatra.

Indonesia's efforts to develop and spread manufacturing capacity to other parts of the country should be welcomed. The master plan for national industry development identifies 14 industrial estates outside of Java that are to be developed between 2015 and 2019. These include two estates in Maluku–Papua region, five in Sulawesi region, four in Kalimantan region, and three in Sumatra region (see Table 6.1). Many of these estates are to be developed into processing centres of the regions' nearby natural resources, therefore their performance would still be prone to commodity price fluctuations. But nevertheless, this is an improvement down the value chain, compared to the current tendency to export raw, unprocessed materials. It is also consistent with the Indonesian Ministry of Industry's strategy to develop the Java-based industrial estates into high technology-based industries and those geared to produce consumer goods, while the non-Java estates will be prioritised to develop natural resource-based industries.

As part of the effort to increase investment and support economic growth, Indonesia is developing Special Economic Zones (SEZs). Based on the most recent 2009 law on the matter, firms operating in the SEZs would get fiscal incentives in the form of reduced tax rates and import duties, as well as non-fiscal incentives such as those related to one-stop services, property ownership, and immigration. As of January 2017, there have been 10 approved SEZs, while the list of SEZ applications under review is also growing.

While the policy to support SEZs is welcomed, the readiness of the regency or province where the zone is being proposed should also be considered. For example, only two of the earmarked SEZs are currently in development while six others are hampered by bureaucratic issues at the ministerial and regional levels (Jakarta Post, 2016). ACI's research on both provincial competitiveness (Chapter 2) and ease of doing business (Chapter 5) shows that some of the provinces where SEZs are designated are among the middle and worst performers (see Table 6.2). Tourism potential played a substantial role in the approval of some SEZs. For example, Tanjung Lesung (Banten), Morotai (North Maluku), Mandalika (West Nusa Tenggara), and Tanjung

Table 6.1: Industrial Estates to be Developed Outside Java, 2015–2019

No.	Location of Industrial Estate	Province	Core-Industry	Anchor Company
1	Teluk Bintuni	West Papua	Fertilizers and petrochemicals	PT. Pupuk Indonesia
2	Buli, East Halmahera	North Maluku	Ferronickel	PT. Feni Haltim
3	Bitung	North Sulawesi	Agro-based and logistics	PT. Pelindo
4	Konawe	Southeast Sulawesi	Ferronickel	Jiangsu Delong Nickel Industry Co. Ltd
5	Morowali	Central Sulawesi	Ferronickel	PT. Sulawesi Mining Investment
6	Palu	Central Sulawesi	Rattan, agro-based, others	PT. Bangun Palu Sulteng
7	Bantaeng	South Sulawesi	Ferronickel	Pt. Hwadi and Bantaeng Sigma Energi
8	Ketapang	West Kalimantan	Alumina	Pt. Well Harvest Winning Alumina Refinery
9	Mandor, Landak	West Kalimantan	Rubber-based	N.A.
10	Batulicin, Tanah Bumbu	South Kalimantan	Steel iron	PT. Meratus Jaya Iron and Steel
11	Jorong, Tanah Laut	South Kalimantan	Steel iron and agro-based	PT. Semeru Surya, PT. Delta Prima Iron Steel
12	Tanggamus	Lampung	Maritime	PT. Repindo Jagat Raya
13	Kuala Tanjung	North Sumatra	Alumina	PT. Inalum
14	Sei Mangkei	North Sumatra	Oleochemicals	PT. Unilever Oleochemical Indonesia

Source: Ministry of Industry, Indonesia (Facts & Figures 2016), compiled by Asia Competitiveness Institute.

Table 6.2: Special Economic Zones in Indonesia

No.	Location/Name of SEZ	Province	Year of Approval	Province's Ranking in ACI's 2016 …	
				Overall Competitiveness	EDB Index ABC
1	Sei Mangkei	North Sumatra	2012	24	28
2	Tanjung Lesung	Banten	2012	11	12
3	Palu	Central Sulawesi	2014	14	8
4	Bitung	North Sulawesi	2014	9	7
5	Morotai	North Maluku	2014	31	24
6	Tanjung Api-api	South Sumatra	2014	22	29
7	Mandalika	West Nusa Tenggara	2014	19	14
8	Maloy Batuta Trans Kalimantan (MBTK)	East Kalimantan	2014	5	15
9	Tanjung Kelayang	Bangka Belitung Islands	2016	20	17
10	Sorong	West Papua	2016	27	31

Source: Indonesia National Board of SEZs (http://kek.go.id/), compiled by Asia Competitiveness Institute.

Kelayang (Bangka Belitung Islands), and to a large extent, also Sorong (West Papua) were given SEZ status to capitalise on the scenic location potential. However, without addressing deeper structural challenges, tax breaks and incentives may have limited appeal to investors.

6.3 Future Research Agenda: Nexus between Exchange Rates and FDI Inflows

The world economy appears to enter into turbulent times once again. Nearly eight years have passed since the global financial crisis of 2007–2009, but global economic growth is yet to be back on its rails. The most recent global growth numbers from the International Monetary Fund (IMF)'s World Economic Outlook (WEO) offer no reason for optimism, with growth projections downbeat and downgraded relative to previous years. Specifically, the October 2016 IMF WEO forecasts global growth to be 3.1% in 2016, lower not only relative to 2015 but also a far cry from the average global growth rate of 4.5% between 2000 and 2007 before the global financial crisis began.

Much of this underwhelming performance in terms of economic growth comes from the continued growth stagnation of the Advanced Economies that have experienced a notable slowdown in their average growth rate of about 2.7% pre-global financial crisis. Fears of 'secular stagnation' in the advanced economies aside, the growth projections of emerging market and developing economies in 2016 was around 4.2% which is not impressive either, especially when viewed in historical context where they posted an average growth of about 6.6% from the turn of the millennium till the global financial crisis.

Emerging market economies in Asia more generally and countries like Indonesia particularly are still better off than their counterparts in the rest of the world and still manage to contribute to the growth of the region on the whole. However, there have been legitimate concerns about the process of 'deglobalisation' of trade and financial flows which could not only potentially reverse the economic gains brought about by global economic interconnectedness so far but also wield a negative influence on the sustainability of growth in Asian economies such as Indonesia, moving forward. Indeed, recent data appear to suggest notably sharp and sustained declines in global trade as well as cross-border capital flows (particularly banking flows) in recent years, which are being viewed as the beginning of the process of deglobalisation.

It must be reiterated that the gradual normalisation of the United States (US) monetary policy has begun and consequently have generated fears that there will be a repeat of the 'taper tantrum' that battered countries like Indonesia in 2013. Changes in the US monetary policies have always exerted significant spillover effects on countries like Indonesia, especially pronounced during the period following the global financial crisis. While ultra-loose monetary policies in the form of quantitative easing resulted in currency appreciations due to massive capital inflows, the tapering of the same through interest rate hikes generated massive capital outflows and consequent currency depreciations. The severity of the impact was more on fragile emerging economies like Indonesia with relatively weak macroeconomic fundamentals. Thus, the ebbs and flows of international capital flows sensitive to US monetary policy changes have in general given rise to a variety of policy challenges concerning monetary and exchange rate management in countries like Indonesia, which in turn has a significant bearing on its overall macroeconomic and financial stability.

More generally, currency swings in Indonesia matter because of the potential macroeconomic implications they can have on its trade and foreign investments. Viewed particularly in the context of the importance of trade and foreign investments to Indonesia, one of the most significant challenges for the policymakers is to understand the potential implications of exchange rate volatility on trade flows as well as foreign investments.

There is particularly a large extant academic literature that has well documented the importance of foreign direct investment (FDI) inflows to emerging markets as a source of supplementing domestic capital, technology and skills that in turn help accelerate economic growth. Policymakers also tend to have a preference to attract FDI compared to other types of capital flows (such as portfolio flows), as FDI is considered relatively more stable than the rest.

As noted in Chapter 5, one must not forget the heavily skewed nature of FDI inflows into Indonesia's sub-national economies. For instance, on average, between 2000 and 2009, 82.3% of the FDI inflows have been directed to provinces in Java, with DKI Jakarta, West Java, Banten, and East Java consistently being the largest recipients of FDI inflows, although more peripheral provinces such as East Kalimantan, Riau, and Papua are catching up.

Past research suggests that a variety of 'pull' factors ranging from skill endowments to robust institutions to locational advantages (to just name a few) determine the extent of FDI that flows into a country. From this list, an important but underexamined factor relates to the behaviour of exchange rates and how it affects FDI inflows. Thus, one of the many determinants on FDI concerns the movements of exchange rates both in terms of their levels and volatility.

How do we expect exchange rate movements to affect FDI inflows? Let us take the example of the rupiah depreciation. In theory, we can expect three different effects through which a weakening of Indonesian rupiah will affect FDI inflows into the country. First, through wealth effects, a depreciation of the rupiah will make its assets cheap and can encourage FDI inflows.

Second, through the demand effects, a cheaper rupiah makes it less attractive for firms to repatriate profits back to home country which will in turn lead to higher reinvestment of retained earnings in Indonesia.

Third, through cost-competitiveness effects, when FDI is export-promoting in nature, firms using Indonesia as an export platform tend to experience lowering of export costs when the rupiah depreciates which will lead to a greater inflow of FDI. If FDI is more domestic market-oriented, then again a depreciation induces FDI because of wealth effects.

While this seemingly looks straightforward, there are three caveats to bear in mind. If the country is part of a supply chain and has lowvalue-add, then changes in exchange rates (levels) might not have a significant effect. Similarly, if there are strong expectations of sustained and further depreciation of the rupiah, it may actually impede further FDI from flowing into Indonesia. Finally, expectations of rupiah depreciation can also reduce repatriation of retained earnings.

Despite the lack of consensus, theory gives us a broad idea as to what to expect about the relationship between exchange rates and FDI inflows. However, is empirical evidence consistent with theory? Most studies on this issue have focused on advanced economies primarily, with very little empirical work dedicated to understand the dynamics in major emerging markets like Indonesia. The broader point that cost competitiveness remains one of the crucial determining variables affecting FDI inflows cannot be ignored and in fact sustaining cost competitiveness has become a prerequisite for countries like Indonesia to continue being an attractive destination for global FDI inflows.

Given this context, our future research will attempt to understand the determinants of FDI inflows at the sub-national level in Indonesia, with a specific focus on real effective exchange rates (REER) and REER volatility. Given the sparse work that exists to date on one of the important policy issues as to whether exchange rates matter or not in attracting FDI inflows, we investigate how movements in REER (both in levels and volatility) affect FDI inflows to its sub-national economies. Further, given that the world has seen a proliferation of global value chains in the way international trade transactions take place and that Indonesia is plugged into this network quite densely, it naturally becomes important to understand what role exchange rate movements both in terms of levels and volatility play on the country's trade flows, which will also be part of our future research agenda.

References

Alifandi, A. 2016. "Slow progress on Indonesia's power plant construction programme indicates continuing operational issues despite government political commitment." *IHS Global Insight Daily Analysis*. May 2013.

Ariyanti, F. 2016. "Daftar 16 Proyek Strategis Nasional yang Sudah Terbangun." *Liputan6*. Dec 8, 2016. Available at http://bisnis.liputan6.com/read/2673561/daftar-16-proyek-strategis-nasional-yang-sudah-terbangun.

Negara, Siwage Dharma. 2016. "Indonesia's 2016 Budget: Optimism Amidst Global Uncertainties." 3. ISEAS Perspective. Singapore: ISEAS - Yusof Ishak Institute.

Tan, Khee Giap, Mulya Amri, Linda Low, and Kong Yam Tan. 2013. *Competitiveness Analysis and Development Strategies for 33 Indonesian Provinces*. Singapore: World Scientific.

Tan, Khee Giap, Mulya Amri, Nurina Merdikawati, and Nursyahida Ahmad. 2017b. *2015 Annual Competitiveness Analysis and Development Strategies for Indonesian Provinces*. Asia Competitiveness Institute — World Scientific Series. Singapore: World Scientific. Available at http://www.worldscientific.com/worldscibooks/10.1142/10246.

Tan, Khee Giap, Sasidaran Gopalan, and Anuja Tandon. 2017. *2015 Agricultural Total Factor Productivity and Competitiveness Analysis for States and Federal Territories and Five Regions of India*. Singapore: World Scientific. Available at http://www.worldscientific.com/worldscibooks/10.1142/10231.

Tan, Khee Giap, Linda Low, Kartik Rao, and Kong Yam Tan. 2015c. *2014 Regional Competitiveness Analysis and a Master Plan on Regional Development Strategies for India: Annual Competitiveness Update and Evidence on Economic Development Model for Selected States of India*. Book, Whole. Singapore: World Scientific.

Tan, Khee Giap, Linda Low, Kong Yam Tan, and Kartik Rao. 2014b. *Annual Analysis of Competitiveness, Simulation Studies and Development Perspective for 35 States and Federal Territories of India: 2000–2010*. Book, Whole. Singapore: World Scientific.

Tan, Khee Giap, Nurina Merdikawati, Mulya Amri, and Blake Harley Berger. 2015b. *2014 Annual Competitiveness Analysis and Development Strategies for Indonesian Provinces*. Singapore: World Scientific.

Tan, Khee Giap, Nurina Merdikawati, Mulya Amri, and Kong Yam Tan. 2015a. *2014 Provincial and Inaugural Regional Competitiveness Analysis: Safeguarding Indonesia's Growth Momentum.* Singapore: World Scientific.

Tan, Khee Giap, Nurina Merdikawati, Mulya Amri, and Kong Yam Tan. 2017c. *2015 Agricultural Productivity, Decentralisation, and Competitiveness Analysis for Provinces and Regions of Indonesia.* Asia Competitiveness Institute — World Scientific Series. Singapore: World Scientific. Available at http://www.worldscientific.com/worldscibooks/10.1142/10245.

Tan, Khee Giap, Le Phuong Anh Nguyen, Sasidaran Gopalan, and Nguyen Trieu Duong Luu. 2017a. *2015 Annual Competitiveness Analysis, Agricultural Productivity and Development Vision for ASEAN-10.* Singapore: World Scientific. Available at http://www.worldscientific.com/worldscibooks/10.1142/10219.

Tan, Khee Giap, Sangiita Wei Cher Yoong, Sasidaran Gopalan, and Le Phuong Anh Nguyen. 2016. *2014 Annual Competitiveness Ranking and Simulation Study for ASEAN-10 and Development Strategies to Enhance Asia Economic Connectivity*. Singapore: World Scientific. Available at http://www.worldscientific.com/worldscibooks/10.1142/10004.

Tan, Khee Giap, Randong Yuan, and Teleixi Xie. 2017. *2015 Estimation of Agricultural Productivity and Annual Update of Competitiveness Analysis for Greater China*. Singapore: World Scientific. Available at http://www.worldscientific.com/worldscibooks/10.1142/10244.

Tan, Khee Giap, Randong Yuan, and Sangiita Wei Cher Yoong. 2015. *2014 Annual Provincial and Regional Competitiveness Analysis for Greater China Economies: Development Strategies under the New Normal*. Book, Whole. Singapore: World Scientific.

Tan, Khee Giap, Randong Yuan, Sangiita Wei Cher Yoong, and Yang Mu. 2014a. *Annual Analysis of Competitiveness, Simulation Studies and Development Perspective for 34 Greater China Economies: 2000–2010*. Book, Whole. Singapore: World Scientific Publishing Co. Pte. Ltd.

World Bank. 2017. "Indonesia Economic Quarterly, January 2017: Sustaining Reform Momentum." Text/HTML. World Bank. Available at http://www.worldbank.org/en/country/indonesia/publication/indonesia-economic-quarterly-january-2017.

Appendices

Appendix 1

List of Indicators for the 2016 Competitiveness Index and Ranking for Indonesian Provinces and Regions

No.	Indicator	Unit	Source
1	**MACROECONOMIC STABILITY**		
1.1	**Regional Economic Vibrancy**		
1.1.01	Gross Regional Domestic Product (GRDP)	Rupiah (Million), 2000 Constant Prices	BPS, Statistics Indonesia
1.1.02	Gross Regional Domestic Product (GRDP), Non-oil & gas	Rupiah (Million), 2000 Constant Prices	(indicator 1.1.01) & BPS, Statistics Indonesia
1.1.03	GRDP Growth	Percentage Change per Annum, 2000 Constant Prices	BPS, Statistics Indonesia
1.1.04	GRDP per Capita	Rupiah (Million), 2000 Constant Prices	BPS, Statistics Indonesia, GRDP of Provinces in Indonesia by Industrial Origin
1.1.05	GRDP per Capita, Non-oil & gas	Rupiah (Million), 2000 Constant Prices	BPS, Statistics Indonesia, GRDP of Provinces in Indonesia by Industrial Origin
1.1.06	GRDP of Primary Industry	Rupiah (Million), 2000 Constant Prices	INDO-DAPOER, World Bank Group
1.1.07	GRDP of Secondary Industry	Rupiah (Million), 2000 Constant Prices	INDO-DAPOER, World Bank Group
1.1.08	GRDP of Tertiary Industry	Rupiah (Million), 2000 Constant Prices	INDO-DAPOER, World Bank Group

(Continued)

(Continued)

No.	Indicator	Unit	Source
1.1.09	Gross Domestic Fixed Capital Formation	Rupiah (Million), 2000 Constant Prices	BPS, Statistics Indonesia, GRDP of Provinces in Indonesia by Expenditure
1.1.10	Inflation (R)	Percentage Change per Annum	BPS, Statistics Indonesia, Statistical Yearbook of Indonesia
1.2	**Openness to Trade and Services**		
1.2.01	Exports	Rupiah (Million), 2000 Constant Prices	PUSDATIN, Ministry of Trade
1.2.02	Exports, Non-oil & gas	Rupiah (Million), 2000 Constant Prices	PUSDATIN, Ministry of Trade
1.2.03	Imports	Rupiah (Million), 2000 Constant Prices	PUSDATIN, Ministry of Trade
1.2.04	Imports, Non-oil & gas	Rupiah (Million), 2000 Constant Prices	PUSDATIN, Ministry of Trade
1.2.05	Openness to Trade	Ratio	(indicators 1.1.01, 1.2.01, 1.2.03)
1.3	**Attractiveness to Foreign Investors**		
1.3.01	Foreign Direct Investment, Last 3 Year Average	US Dollars (Million), Current Market Prices	BPS, Statistics Indonesia, Statistical Yearbook of Indonesia
1.3.02	Domestic Direct Investment, Last 3 Year Average	Rupiah (Billion)	BPS, Statistics Indonesia, Statistical Yearbook of Indonesia
1.3.03	Investment Promotion and Management	Index	ACI Survey (2015)
	Based on responses by business owners, academics, and government officials in each province, to the following survey questions: 1. The Provincial Government has a clear strategy to attract investors; 2. The Provincial Government has done well to market the province to investors; 3. The Provincial Government channels money for appropriate development purposes/ projects.		
2	**GOVERNMENT AND INSTITUTIONAL SETTING**		
2.1	**Government Policies and Fiscal Sustainability**		
2.1.01	Government Revenue	Rupiah (Thousand), 2000 Constant Prices	BPS, Statistics Indonesia, *Financial Statistics of Province Government*
2.1.02	Tax Revenue	Rupiah (Thousand), 2000 Constant Prices	BPS, Statistics Indonesia, *Financial Statistics of Province Government*
2.1.03	Tax Revenue per Government Revenue	Ratio	(indicators 2.1.01, 2.1.02)
2.1.04	Government Expenditure	Rupiah (Thousand), 2000 Constant Prices	BPS, Statistics Indonesia, *Financial Statistics of Province Government*

(Continued)

(Continued)

No.	Indicator	Unit	Source
2.1.05	Fiscal Balance	Rupiah (Thousand), 2000 Constant Prices	(indicators 2.1.01, 2.1.04)
2.2	**Institutions, Governance, and Leadership**		
2.2.01	Lack of Corruption	Index	ACI Survey (2015)
	Based on responses by business owners and academics in each province, to the following survey questions: 1. Corruption is not a severe problem; 2. Corruption is not a common practice among firms in the province; 3. Public contracts are awarded based on meritocracy (not favouritism or kickbacks).		
2.2.02	Crime Rate (R)	Rate per 100,000 population	BPS, Statistics Indonesia, Statistical Yearbook of Indonesia
2.2.03	Security	Index	ACI Survey (2015)
	Based on responses by business owners and academics in each province, to the following survey questions: 1. The political condition (including ethnic and religious relations) in the province is stable; 2. Control of crimes and violence in the province is effective; 3. Businesses and citizens don't have to worry about their property rights.		
2.2.04	Government Inclusiveness and Accountability	Index	ACI Survey (2015)
	Based on responses by business owners, academics, and government officials in each province, to the following survey questions: 1. In this province, the government makes significant efforts to communicate policies and regulations to businesses and citizens; 2. In this province, the government carefully considers the voice of businesses and citizens in making their policy decisions; 3. In this province, government officials have high sense of accountability.		
2.2.05	Government Progress & Expectation	Index	ACI Survey (2015)
	Based on responses by business owners and academics in each province, to the following survey questions: 1. The current government is committed to improve its performance; 2. The government in this province has improved its performance in the past three years; 3. The government in this province will improve its performance in the next three years.		
2.2.06	Government Efficiency	Index	ACI Survey (2015)
	Based on responses by business owners and academics in each province, to the following survey questions: 1. Cost of dealing with permits and other public documents or matters is not burdensome; 2. Time to deal with permits and other public documents or matters is not burdensome; 3. Administrative requirement to deal with permits and other public documents or matters is not burdensome.		

(Continued)

(*Continued*)

No.	Indicator	Unit	Source
2.2.07	Coordination of Local Governments	Index	ACI Survey (2015)
	Based on responses by business owners, academics, and government officials in each province, to the following survey questions: 1. Laws and regulations across different local governments in the province are harmonized; 2. There is good collaboration and coordination among local governments within the province.		
2.2.08	Provincial Governing Capacity	Index	ACI Survey (2015)
	Based on responses by business owners, academics, and government officials in each province, to the following survey question: 1. There is good coordination among government agencies at the provincial level.		
2.3	**Competition, Regulatory Standards, and Rule of Law**		
2.3.01	Regulatory Governance	Index	ACI Survey (2015)
	Based on responses by business owners, academics, and government officials in each province, to the following survey questions: 1. In this province, the government has made regulations pertaining to my business clearer (more transparent); 2. In this province, the government has made regulations pertaining to my businesses less burdensome; 3. My business receives fair treatment from regulators in this province.		
2.3.02	Rule of Law	Index	ACI Survey (2015)
	Based on responses by business owners and academics in each province, to the following survey questions: 1. In the province, contracts are respected and enforced; 2. In the province, judiciary bodies are independent and fair; 3. In the province, judiciary services are readily accessible; 4. In this province, the government regulators follow closely the laws and regulations in their enforcement.		
2.3.03	Vibrancy of Competition and Collaboration	Index	ACI Survey (2015)
	Based on responses by business owners and academics in each province, to the following survey questions: 1. Competition among firms is fair; 2. My firm has close relationship with local suppliers; 3. Demand by customers in the province is strong and sophisticated; 4. Firms in the province has good platforms and incentives for collaboration.		
3	**FINANCIAL, BUSINESSES, AND MANPOWER CONDITIONS**		
3.1	**Financial Deepening and Business Efficiency**		
3.1.01	Bank Deposits	Rupiah (Million), 2000 Constant Prices	Bank of Indonesia, Indonesia Banking Statistics
3.1.02	Bank Loans	Rupiah (Million), 2000 Constant Prices	Bank of Indonesia, Indonesia Banking Statistics
3.1.03	Non-Performing Loans (R)	Rupiah (Million), 2000 Constant Prices	Bank of Indonesia, Indonesia Banking Statistics

(*Continued*)

(Continued)

No.	Indicator	Unit	Source
3.1.04	Non-Performing Loans per Total Bank Loans (R)	Ratio	(indicators 3.1.02, 3.1.03)
3.1.05	Number of Bank Branches or Offices	Number	Bank of Indonesia, Indonesia Banking Statistics
3.1.06	Population per Number of Bank Branches or Offices (R)	Ratio	(indicators 3.1.05, 4.1.01)
3.1.07	Ease of Dealing With Banks	Index	ACI Survey (2015)
	Based on responses by business owners in each province, to the following survey questions: 1. Administrative requirement to borrow money from banks is not burdensome; 2. Interest rate for borrowing money from banks is not burdensome; 3. Banks are generally responsive to your firm's needs.		
3.1.08	Firms' Performance	Index	ACI Survey (2015)
	Based on responses by business owners in each province, to the following survey questions: 1. This year 2015 your firm's revenue is estimated to ....; 2. Next year 2016 your firm's revenue is expected to ....; 3. This year 2015 your firm's employment figure is estimated to ...; 4. Next year 2016 your firm's employment figure is expected to		
3.1.09	Firms' Strategy	Index	ACI Survey (2015)
	Based on responses by business owners in each province, to the following survey question: 1. In order to enhance your company's performance, how likely is your company to engage in each of the strategy options listed below in the next few years? 1. Cut costs, streamline business? 2. Spend more on promotion/ ads? 3. Improve skills and motivation of employees? 4. Upgrade production process? 5. Introduce new products.		
3.1.10	Firms' Human Resource Capacity	Index	ACI Survey (2015)
	Based on responses by business owners, academics and government officials in each province, to the following survey questions: 1. The skills of your employees are adequate for their job requirements; 2. Your firm has invested substantially in employee training programs the past 3 years; 3. Your firm will invest substantially in employee training programs the next 3 years.		
3.1.11	Firms' Equipment Capacity	Index	ACI Survey (2015)
	Based on responses by business owners in each province, to the following survey questions: 1. The technology and equipment used for your firm's main production process is up-to-date; 2. Your firm is using the technology and equipment to its optimal capacity; 3. Your firm will invest in upgrading its equipment over the next five years.		
3.1.12	Firms' Application of IT	Index	ACI Survey (2015)
	Based on responses by business owners in each province, to the following questions: 1. Your firm has invested substantially in IT in the past three years; 2. Your firm will invest significantly in IT over the next three years; 3. The status of your company's internet connection; 4. The status of your company's website.		

(Continued)

(Continued)

No.	Indicator	Unit	Source
3.1.13	Firms' Innovation	Index	ACI Survey (2015)
	Based on responses by business owners, academics and government officials in each province, to the following survey questions: 1. Your firm has introduced many new products or product features over the past three years; 2. Your firm has applied many innovative methods in production process over the past three years; 3. Your firm spends substantially on Research and Development.		
3.2	**Labour Market Flexibility**		
3.2.01	Labour Force	Number	BPS, Statistics Indonesia, Statistical Yearbook of Indonesia
3.2.02	Labour Force Participation Rate	Ratio	(indicators 3.2.01, 4.1.01)
3.2.03	Employment	Number	BPS, Statistics Indonesia, Statistical Yearbook of Indonesia
3.2.04	Employment in Primary Industry	Number	BPS, Statistics Indonesia, Statistical Yearbook of Indonesia
3.2.05	Employment in Secondary industry	Number	BPS, Statistics Indonesia, Statistical Yearbook of Indonesia
3.2.06	Employment in Tertiary Industry	Number	BPS, Statistics Indonesia, Statistical Yearbook of Indonesia
3.2.07	Unemployment Rate (R)	Percentage	(indicator 3.2.01) & BPS, Statistics Indonesia, Statistical Yearbook of Indonesia
3.2.08	Minimum Wage per Month (R)	Rupiah, Current Market Prices	BPS, Statistics Indonesia, Statistical Yearbook of Indonesia
3.2.09	Labour Relations	Survey Data	ACI Survey (2015)
	Based on responses by business owners, academics and government officials in each province, to the following survey questions: 1. It is not difficult to recruit skilled production workers; 2. It is not difficult to recruit skilled professionals and management staff; 3. Workers generally have good discipline and motivated to work; 4. There is no tension between labour unions and management.		
3.3	**Productivity Performance**		
3.3.01	Overall Labour Productivity	Rupiah (Million) per person-year, 2000 Constant Prices	(indicators 1.1.01, 3.2.03)
3.3.02	Overall Labour Productivity, Non-oil & gas	Rupiah (Million) per person-year, 2000 Constant Prices	(indicators 1.1.02, 3.2.03)
3.3.03	Primary Industry Productivity	Rupiah (Million) per person-year, 2000 Constant Prices	(indicators 1.1.06, 3.2.04)

(Continued)

(*Continued*)

No.	Indicator	Unit	Source
3.3.04	Secondary Industry Productivity	Rupiah (Million) per person-year, 2000 Constant Prices	(indicators 1.1.07, 3.2.05)
3.3.05	Tertiary Industry Productivity	Rupiah (Million) per person-year, 2000 Constant Prices	(indicators 1.1.08, 3.2.06)
4	**QUALITY OF LIFE AND INFRASTRUCTURE DEVELOPMENT**		
4.1	**Physical Infrastructure**		
4.1.01	Population	Persons, Year-end	INDO-DAPOER, World Bank Group
4.1.02	Population Growth	Percentage Change per Annum	INDO-DAPOER, World Bank Group
4.1.03	Urban Population	Percentage of Total Population	ACI's estimates based on data by INDO-DAPOER, World Bank Group
4.1.04	Length of Paved Roads	Kilometres	BPS, Statistics Indonesia, *Transportation Statistics*
4.1.05	Registered Motor Vehicles	Number	BPS, Statistics Indonesia, *Transportation Statistics*
4.1.06	Registered Motor Vehicles per KM of paved road (R)	Ratio	(indicators 4.1.05, 4.1.04)
4.1.07	Cargo at Inter-island Seaport	Tons	BPS, Statistics Indonesia, Statistical Yearbook of Indonesia
4.1.08	Cargo at International Seaport	Tons	BPS, Statistics Indonesia, Statistical Yearbook of Indonesia
4.1.09	Passengers of Domestic Air Traffic	Number	BPS, Statistics Indonesia, *Transportation Statistics*
4.1.10	Passengers of International Air Traffic	Number	BPS, Statistics Indonesia, *Transportation Statistics*
4.1.11	Households with Pipe Water Services	Percentage of households	BPS, Statistics Indonesia, Statistical Yearbook of Indonesia
4.1.12	Households with State Electricity Services	Percentage of households	BPS, Statistics Indonesia, Statistical Yearbook of Indonesia
4.1.13	Ease of Acquiring Property	Index	ACI Survey (2015)
	Based on responses by business owners, academics and government officials in each province, to the following survey questions: 1. It is not difficult to acquire land for opening or expanding business in the province; 2. The cost of renting land/ office space in the province is not burdensome.		

(*Continued*)

(*Continued*)

No.	Indicator	Unit	Source
4.1.14	Quality of Physical Infrastructure	Index	ACI Survey (2015)
	Based on responses by business owners and academics in each province, to the following survey questions: 1. Quality of Power supply …; 2. Quality of Water supply …; 3. Quality of Roads …; 4. Quality of sea port ….; 5. Quality of airports ….; 6. Quality of public transportation….		
4.2	**Technological Infrastructure**		
4.2.01	Telephone Ownership	Percentage of households	BPS, Statistics Indonesia, *Trends of Selected Socio-Economic Indicators of Indonesia*
4.2.02	Handphone Ownership	Percentage of households	BPS, Statistics Indonesia, *Trends of Selected Socio-Economic Indicators of Indonesia*
4.2.03	Desktop Computer Ownership	Percentage of households	BPS, Statistics Indonesia, *Trends of Selected Socio-Economic Indicators of Indonesia*
4.2.04	Laptop Computer Ownership	Percentage of households	BPS, Statistics Indonesia, *Trends of Selected Socio-Economic Indicators of Indonesia*
4.2.05	Internet Access at Home	Percentage of households	BPS, Statistics Indonesia, *Welfare Statistics*
4.2.06	Internet Access at Office	Percentage of households	BPS, Statistics Indonesia, *Welfare Statistics*
4.2.07	Internet Access at School	Percentage of households	BPS, Statistics Indonesia, *Welfare Statistics*
4.2.08	Internet Access in Handphone	Percentage of households	BPS, Statistics Indonesia, *Welfare Statistics*
4.2.09	Quality of Technological Infrastructure	Index	ACI Survey (2015)
	Based on responses by business owners and academics in each province, to the following survey questions: 1. Quality of mobile phone coverage …; 2. Access/coverage of internet …; 3. Speed of internet access ….		
4.3	**Standard of Living, Education, and Social Stability**		
4.3.01	Adult Illiteracy Rate (R)	Percentage of Adults	INDO-DAPOER, World Bank Group
4.3.02	Mean Years of Schooling	Years	BPS, Statistics Indonesia, *Trends of Selected Socio-Economic Indicators of Indonesia*

(*Continued*)

(Continued)

No.	Indicator	Unit	Source
4.3.03	School Enrolment Rate (Primary)	Percentage	INDO-DAPOER, World Bank Group
4.3.04	School Enrolment Rate (Junior High)	Percentage	INDO-DAPOER, World Bank Group
4.3.05	School Enrolment Rate (Senior High)	Percentage	INDO-DAPOER, World Bank Group
4.3.06	Student–Teacher Ratio (Primary) (R)	Ratio	BPS, Statistics Indonesia, Statistical Yearbook of Indonesia
4.3.07	Student–Teacher Ratio (Junior High) (R)	Ratio	BPS, Statistics Indonesia, Statistical Yearbook of Indonesia
4.3.08	Student–Teacher Ratio (Senior High) (R)	Ratio	BPS, Statistics Indonesia, Statistical Yearbook of Indonesia
4.3.09	Human Development Index	Index	INDO-DAPOER, World Bank Group
4.3.10	Life Expectancy at Birth	Years	Ministry of Health, *Indonesia Health Profile*
4.3.11	Gini Ratio (R)	Ratio	BPS, Statistics Indonesia
4.3.12	Urban Population Growth	Percentage Per Annum	(indicator 4.1.03)
4.3.13	Population per Health Facility (R)	Ratio	Ministry of Health
4.3.14	Population per Medical Worker (R)	Ratio	Ministry of Health
4.3.15	Environmental Quality Index	Index	Ministry of Environment
4.3.16	Fatalities due to Natural Disaster (R)	Number	BPS, Statistics Indonesia, Statistical Yearbook of Indonesia
4.1.17	Quality of Education Based on responses by business owners, academics and government officials in each province, to the following survey questions: 1. Quality of secondary/vocational education in this province is very good compared to other provinces; 2. Quality of higher education/university in the province is very good compared to other provinces.	Index	ACI Survey (2015)
4.3.18	Quality of Healthcare Based on responses by business owners, academics and government officials in each province, to the following survey questions: 1. Quality of basic health services in this province is very good compared to other provinces; 2. Quality of general health services in this province is very good compared to other provinces; 3. Quality of advanced health services (specialists, etc.) in this province is very good compared to other provinces.	Index	ACI Survey (2015)
4.3.19	Affordability and Accessibility of Goods Based on responses by business owners, academics and government officials in each province, to the following survey questions: 1. The price of staple goods in this province is quite affordable for most people; 2. In this province, secondary/luxury goods is quite easy to find, for those who can afford them.	Index	ACI Survey (2015)

Appendix 2

Algorithm for Computing the Provincial and Regional Competitiveness Index and Ranking

A step-by-step description of the ranking process is described below for N regions (or provinces, respectively), M indicators and C environments, with each environment comprising S sub-environments.

Algorithm: Ranking Methodology

(1) Compute the mean value of indicator j $(j = 1, \ldots, M)$,

$$\overline{X}_j = \frac{1}{N}\sum_{i=1}^{N} X_{ij}$$

where X_{ij} represents the value that region i $(i = 1, \ldots, N)$ takes for indicator j.

(2) For each indicator j $(j = 1, \ldots, M)$, calculate its standard deviation (SD),

$$SD_j = \sqrt{\frac{1}{N}\sum_{i=1}^{N}(X_{ij} - \overline{X}_j)^2}$$

(3) Compute the standardised value of indicator (SVI) that each region i $(i = 1, \ldots, N)$ takes under each of the indicators j $(j = 1, \ldots, M)$,

$$SVI_{ij} = \frac{X_{ij} - \overline{X}_j}{SD_j}$$

(4) Compute the 'ranked' standardised value of indicator (RSVI) that each region i $(i = 1, \ldots, N)$ takes under each of the indicators j $(j = 1, \ldots, M)$:

$$RSVI_{ij} = \begin{cases} SVI_{ij}, & \textit{if a higher value is better} \\ -SVI_{ij}, & \textit{if a lower value is better} \end{cases}$$

(5) For each indicator, j (j = 1, …, M), a ranking can be obtained for regions: regions with a higher value of RSVI for indicator j are ranked ahead of those with a lower value.

(6) For each region i (i = 1, …, N), calculate the RSVI for each sub-environment k (k = 1, …, S) belonging to environment l (l = 1, …, C),

$$Raw\_RSVI_{i,lk} = \frac{1}{y_{lk}}\sum_{p=1}^{y_{lk}} RSVI_{i,j_{lk,p}}$$

$$Mean\_RSVI_{lk} = \frac{1}{N}\sum_{i=1}^{N} Raw\_RSVI_{i,lk}$$

$$SD\_RSVI_{lk} = \sqrt{\frac{1}{N}\sum_{i=1}^{N}(Raw\_RSVI_{i,lk} - Mean\_RSVI_{lk})^2}$$

$$RSVI_{i,lk} = \frac{Raw\_RSVI_{i,lk} - Mean\_RSVI_{lk}}{SD\_RSVI_{lk}}$$

where y_{lk} is the total number of indicators under sub-environment k of environment l and ($RSVI_{i,jlk,1}$, …, $RSVI_{i,jlk,ylk}$) are the RSVIs for region i that make up sub-environment k of environment l.

(7) For each region i (i = 1, …, N), calculate the RSVI for each environment l (l = 1, …, C),

$$Raw\_RSVI_{i,l} = \frac{1}{S_l}\sum_{k=1}^{S_l} RSVI_{i,lk}$$

$$Mean\_RSVI_{l} = \frac{1}{N}\sum_{i=1}^{N} Raw\_RSVI_{i,l}$$

$$SD\_RSVI_{l} = \sqrt{\frac{1}{N}\sum_{i=1}^{N}(Raw\_RSVI_{i,l} - Mean\_RSVI_{l})^2}$$

$$RSVI_{i,l} = \frac{Raw\_RSVI_{i,l} - Mean\_RSVI_{l}}{SD\_RSVI_{l}}$$

where ($RSVI_{i,l1}$, …, $RSVI_{i,lS}$) are the RSVIs for the S sub-environments under each environment l.

(8) Overall rank score of region i (i = 1, …, N),

$$Raw\_R_i = \frac{1}{C}\sum_{l=1}^{C} RSVI_{i,l}$$

$$Mean\_R = \frac{1}{N}\sum_{i=1}^{N} Raw\_R_i$$

$$SD\_R = \sqrt{\frac{1}{N}\sum_{i=1}^{N}(Raw\_R_i - Mean\_R)^2}$$

$$R_i = \frac{Raw\_R_i - Mean\_R}{SD\_R}$$

Regions with a higher *Ri* are ranked ahead of those with lower value of *Ri*, and the region with the highest *Ri* is the most competitive region.

Step (5) provides the ranking of each region for each individual indicator. To achieve this ranking, Step (4) adjusts the value of the SVIs so that a higher value will lead to a better ranking in terms of 'competitiveness'. Depending on the nature of the indicator in question, a higher or lower value may reflect a more 'competitive' region. Take, for instance, the sub-indicators 'Gross Regional Domestic Product (GRDP)' and 'Unemployment Rate'. A higher GRDP but a lower 'unemployment rate' suggests better economic performance, which makes a region more 'competitive'. In most cases where a higher value is better (e.g. GRDP), the SVIs of regions are considered, and those with a higher SVI value will have a better ranking. However, for indicators where the inverse is true (e.g. Unemployment Rate), the 'negative SVI' values are compared between regions and a lower SVI value will lead to a better ranking. Step (4) thus seeks to make all standardised values of all indicators consistent for ranking purposes.

Step (6) determines the sub-environment rankings of each region. The average RSVI of all the indicators in the sub-environment is calculated, restandardised across all the regions and compared to other regions. Regions with a higher average RSVI rank better in the sub-environment. Although the number of indicators varies for each sub-environment, there are three sub-environments for each of the four environments. The aggregate score for each sub-environment is given an equivalent weighting: 33.33% of their respective environment's score.

To arrive at the ranking for each environment, the RSVIs of the sub-environments are averaged and restandardised across all the regions as detailed by Step (7). Finally, Step (8) requires the RSVI values of each environment to be averaged and restandardised across all the regions to determine the overall ranking of the region. Regions with a higher RSVI are ranked ahead of those with a lower RSVI.

Identical weights are assigned to each environment as they represent equivalent significance to the computation of Overall Competitiveness Index. This method is repeated and applied consistently across all the regions to ensure precision of the rankings. Mathematically, this can be illustrated as follows:

Overall Competitiveness Index: = 25% × (Macroeconomic Stability)
+ 25% × (Government and Institutional Setting)
+ 25% × (Financial, Businesses, and Manpower Conditions)
+ 25% × (Quality of Life and Infrastructure Development)

Appendix 3

Notes on Data Aggregation of Competitiveness Indicators from Provincial to Regional Level

No.	Indicator	Unit	Reversed Indicator	Calculated as in
1	MACROECONOMIC STABILITY			
1.1	**Regional Economic Vibrancy**			
1.1.01	Gross Regional Domestic Product (GRDP)	Rupiah (Million), 2000 Constant Prices		Approach 1
1.1.02	Gross Regional Domestic Product (GRDP), Non-oil & gas	Rupiah (Million), 2000 Constant Prices		Approach 1
1.1.03	GRDP Growth	Percentage Change per Annum, 2000 Constant Prices		Approach 2
1.1.04	GRDP per Capita	Rupiah (Million), 2000 Constant Prices		Approach 2
1.1.05	GRDP per Capita, Non-oil & gas	Rupiah (Million), 2000 Constant Prices		Approach 2
1.1.06	GRDP of Primary Industry	Rupiah (Million), 2000 Constant Prices		Approach 1
1.1.07	GRDP of Secondary Industry	Rupiah (Million), 2000 Constant Prices		Approach 1
1.1.08	GRDP of Tertiary Industry	Rupiah (Million), 2000 Constant Prices		Approach 1
1.1.09	Gross Domestic Fixed Capital Formation	Rupiah (Million), 2000 Constant Prices		Approach 1
1.1.10	Inflation	Percentage Change per Annum	R	Approach 3

(Continued)

(Continued)

No.	Indicator	Unit	Reversed Indicator	Calculated as in
1.2	**Openness To Trade and Services**			
1.2.01	Exports	Rupiah (Million), 2000 Constant Prices		Approach 1
1.2.02	Exports, Non-oil & gas	Rupiah (Million), 2000 Constant Prices		Approach 1
1.2.03	Imports	Rupiah (Million), 2000 Constant Prices		Approach 1
1.2.04	Imports, Non-oil & gas	Rupiah (Million), 2000 Constant Prices		Approach 1
1.2.05	Openness To Trade	Ratio		Approach 2
1.3	**Attractiveness To Foreign Investors**			
1.3.01	Foreign Direct Investment, Last 3 Year Average	US Dollars (Million), Current Market Prices		Approach 1
1.3.02	Domestic Direct Investment, Last 3 Year Average	Rupiah (Billion)		Approach 1
1.3.03	Investment Promotion and Management	Index (Survey Data)		Approach 3
2	**GOVERNMENT AND INSTITUTIONAL SETTING**			
2.1	**Government Policies and Fiscal Sustainability**			
2.1.01	Government Revenue	Rupiah (Thousand), 2000 Constant Prices		Approach 1
2.1.02	Tax Revenue	Rupiah (Thousand), 2000 Constant Prices		Approach 1
2.1.03	Tax Revenue/Government Revenue	Ratio		Approach 2
2.1.04	Government Expenditure	Rupiah (Thousand), 2000 Constant Prices		Approach 1
2.1.05	Fiscal Balance	Rupiah (Thousand), 2000 Constant Prices		Approach 1
2.2	**Institutions, Governance and Leadership**			
2.2.01	Lack of Corruption	Index (Survey Data)		Approach 3
2.2.02	Crime Rate	Rate Per 100,000 population	R	Approach 3
2.2.03	Security	Index (Survey Data)		Approach 3
2.2.04	Government Inclusiveness and Accountability	Index (Survey Data)		Approach 3
2.2.05	Government Progress & Expectation	Index (Survey Data)		Approach 3

(Continued)

(Continued)

No.	Indicator	Unit	Reversed Indicator	Calculated as in
2.2.06	Government Efficiency	Index (Survey Data)		Approach 3
2.2.07	Coordination of Local Governments	Index (Survey Data)		Approach 3
2.2.08	Provincial Governing Capacity	Index (Survey Data)		Approach 3
2.3	**Competition, Regulatory Standards and Rule of Law**			
2.3.01	Regulatory Governance	Index (Survey Data)		Approach 3
2.3.02	Rule of Law	Index (Survey Data)		Approach 3
2.3.03	Vibrancy of Competition and Collaboration	Index (Survey Data)		Approach 3
3	**FINANCIAL, BUSINESSES AND MANPOWER CONDITIONS**			
3.1	**Financial Deepening and Business Efficiency**			
3.1.01	Bank Deposits	Rupiah (Million), 2000 Constant Prices		Approach 1
3.1.02	Bank Loans	Rupiah (Million), 2000 Constant Prices		Approach 1
3.1.03	Non-Performing Loans	Rupiah (Million), 2000 Constant Prices	R	Approach 1
3.1.04	Non-Performing Loans per Total Bank Loans	Ratio	R	Approach 2
3.1.05	Number of Bank Branches or Offices	Number		Approach 1
3.1.06	Population per Number of Bank Branches or Offices	Ratio	R	Approach 2
3.1.07	Ease of Dealing With Banks	Index (Survey Data)		Approach 3
3.1.08	Firms' Performance	Index (Survey Data)		Approach 3
3.1.09	Firms' Strategy	Index (Survey Data)		Approach 3
3.1.10	Firms' Human Resource Capacity	Index (Survey Data)		Approach 3
3.1.11	Firms' Equipment Capacity	Index (Survey Data)		Approach 3
3.1.12	Firms' Application of IT	Index (Survey Data)		Approach 3
3.1.13	Firms' Innovation	Index (Survey Data)		Approach 3
3.2	**Labour Market Flexibility**			
3.2.01	Labour Force	Number		Approach 1
3.2.02	Labour Force Participation Rate	Ratio		Approach 2

(Continued)

(Continued)

No.	Indicator	Unit	Reversed Indicator	Calculated as in
3.2.03	Employment	Number		Approach 1
3.2.04	Employment in Primary Industry	Number		Approach 1
3.2.05	Employment in Secondary Industry	Number		Approach 1
3.2.06	Employment in Tertiary Industry	Number		Approach 1
3.2.07	Unemployment Rate	Percentage	R	Approach 2
3.2.08	Minimum Wage per Month	Rupiah, Current Market Prices	R	Approach 3
3.2.09	Labour Relations	Index (Survey Data)		Approach 3
3.3	**Productivity Performance**			
3.3.01	Overall Labour Productivity	Rupiah (Million) per person-year, 2000 Constant Prices		Approach 2
3.3.02	Overall Labour Productivity, Non-oil & gas	Rupiah (Million) per person-year, 2000 Constant Prices		Approach 2
3.3.03	Primary Industry Productivity	Rupiah (Million) per person-year, 2000 Constant Prices		Approach 2
3.3.04	Secondary Industry Productivity	Rupiah (Million) per person-year, 2000 Constant Prices		Approach 2
3.3.05	Tertiary Industry Productivity	Rupiah (Million) per person-year, 2000 Constant Prices		Approach 2
4	**QUALITY OF LIFE AND INFRASTRUCTURE DEVELOPMENT**			
4.1	**Physical Infrastructure**			
4.1.01	Population	Persons, Year-end		Approach 1
4.1.02	Population Growth	Percentage Change per Annum		Approach 3
4.1.03	Urban Population	Percentage of Total Population		Approach 3
4.1.04	Length of Paved Roads	Kilometres		Approach 1
4.1.05	Registered Motor Vehicles	Number		Approach 1
4.1.06	Registered Motor Vehicles per KM of paved road	Ratio	R	Approach 2
4.1.07	Cargo at Inter-island Seaport	Tons		Approach 1
4.1.08	Cargo at International Seaport	Tons		Approach 1

(Continued)

(*Continued*)

No.	Indicator	Unit	Reversed Indicator	Calculated as in
4.1.09	Passengers of Domestic Air Traffic	Number		Approach 1
4.1.10	Passengers of International Air Traffic	Number		Approach 1
4.1.11	Households with pipe water services	Percentage of households		Approach 3
4.1.12	Households with state electricity services	Percentage of households		Approach 3
4.1.13	Ease of Acquiring Property	Index (Survey Data)		Approach 3
4.1.14	Quality of Physical Infrastructure	Index (Survey Data)		Approach 3
4.2	**Technological Infrastructure**			
4.2.01	Telephone Ownership	Percentage of households		Approach 3
4.2.02	Handphone Ownership	Percentage of households		Approach 3
4.2.03	Desktop Computer Ownership	Percentage of households		Approach 3
4.2.04	Laptop Computer Ownership	Percentage of households		Approach 3
4.2.05	Internet Access at Home	Percentage of households		Approach 3
4.2.06	Internet Access at Office	Percentage of households		Approach 3
4.2.07	Internet Access at School	Percentage of households		Approach 3
4.2.08	Internet Access in Handphone	Percentage of households		Approach 3
4.2.09	Quality of Technological Infrastructure	Index (Survey Data)		Approach 3
4.3	**Standard of Living, Education and Social Stability**			
4.3.01	Adult Illiteracy Rate	Percentage of Adults	R	Approach 3
4.3.02	Mean Years of Schooling	Years		Approach 3
4.3.03	School Enrolment Rate (Primary)	Percentage		Approach 3
4.3.04	School Enrolment Rate (Junior High)	Percentage		Approach 3
4.3.05	School Enrolment Rate (Senior High)	Percentage		Approach 3
4.3.06	Student-Teacher Ratio (Primary)	Ratio	R	Approach 3
4.3.07	Student-Teacher Ratio (Junior High)	Ratio	R	Approach 3

(*Continued*)

(*Continued*)

No.	Indicator	Unit	Reversed Indicator	Calculated as in
4.3.08	Student-Teacher Ratio (Senior High)	Ratio	R	Approach 3
4.3.09	Human Development Index	Index		Approach 3
4.3.10	Life Expectancy at Birth	Years		Approach 3
4.3.11	Gini Ratio	Ratio	R	Approach 3
4.3.12	Urban Population Growth	Percentage Per Annum		Approach 3
4.3.13	Population per Health Facility	Ratio	R	Approach 3
4.3.14	Population per Medical Worker	Ratio	R	Approach 3
4.3.15	Environmental Quality Index	Index		Approach 3
4.3.16	Fatalities due to Natural Disaster	Number	R	Approach 3
4.1.17	Quality of Education	Index (Survey Data)		Approach 3
4.3.18	Quality of Healthcare	Index (Survey Data)		Approach 3
4.3.19	Affordability and Accessibility of Goods	Index (Survey Data)		Approach 3

Source: Asia Competitiveness Institute.

Appendix 4

Determinants of Growth Slowdown for the Low-income Group, Lower-middle-income Group and Combined Group of Upper-middle-income and High-income Economies, Probit Specification

	Growth Slowdown Models		
Income Groups	**Low-Income**	**Lower-Middle-Income**	**Combined Group of Upper-Middle-Income and High-Income Economies**
GRDP per Capita	0.0007** (0.0003)	0.0003*** (0.0001)	0.0002*** (0.00004)
Literacy Rate	–0.0171** (0.0069)	–0.0124* (0.0065)	–0.0937*** (0.0364)
Foreign Direct Investment Inflows as Percentage of GRDP	–0.2135** (0.1010)	–0.0997*** (0.0266)	
Length of Road per Capita	–0.0068* (0.0039)		
Employment in Tertiary Industry as Percentage of Total Employment		–0.0165** (0.0065)	–0.0263** (0.0103)
Old Dependency Ratio		0.0378** (0.0164)	
Openness to Trade			–0.0057*** (0.0018)
Secondary Industry Value-added per Worker			–0.00001** ($4.72e^{-6}$)
Constant	–0.5704 (0.5692)	–0.4116 (0.6006)	9.1347*** (3.3867)
No. of Observations	358	667	147
Pseudo R^2	0.0660	0.0857	0.1234

Note: Numbers in the parentheses are standard errors. *, **, and *** denote the coefficient is significant at 10% level, 5% level, and 1% level, respectively.

Source: Asia Competitiveness Institute.

Appendix 5

Predictive Probabilities of Growth Slowdown for Indonesia Sub-national Economies for the Period 2012–2017 (Based on Probit Specification of the Income-group Specific Growth Slowdown Models)

Economy	Income Group Which Economy Belongs to in 2012	Probability of Experiencing Growth Slowdown during 2012–2017
Aceh	Lower-Middle-Income	0.09189
Bali	Lower-Middle-Income	0.05119
Bangka Belitung Islands	Lower-Middle-Income	0.16289
Banten	Lower-Middle-Income	0.00362
Bengkulu	Lower-Middle-Income	0.06520
Central Java	Lower-Middle-Income	0.14248
Central Kalimantan	Lower-Middle-Income	0.03764
Central Sulawesi	Lower-Middle-Income	0.00483
DI Yogyakarta	Lower-Middle-Income	0.09772
DKI Jakarta	High-Income	0.20246
East Java	Lower-Middle-Income	0.20866
East Kalimantan	High-Income	0.31568
East Nusa Tenggara	Low-Income	0.05991
Gorontalo	Low-Income	0.01802
Jambi	Lower-Middle-Income	0.11931
Lampung	Lower-Middle-Income	0.12299
Maluku	Low-Income	0.05427

(*Continued*)

(*Continued*)

Economy	**Income Group Which Economy Belongs to in 2012**	**Probability of Experiencing Growth Slowdown during 2012–2017**
North Maluku	Low-Income	0.00000
North Sulawesi	Lower-Middle-Income	0.08985
North Sumatra	Lower-Middle-Income	0.13878
Papua	Lower-Middle-Income	0.03564
Riau	High-Income	0.39184
Riau Islands	Upper-Middle-Income	0.03734
South Kalimantan	Lower-Middle-Income	0.06452
South Sulawesi	Lower-Middle-Income	0.08565
South Sumatra	Lower-Middle-Income	0.13865
Southeast Sulawesi	Lower-Middle-Income	0.07886
West Java	Lower-Middle-Income	0.05319
West Kalimantan	Lower-Middle-Income	0.06150
West Nusa Tenggara	Low-Income	0.00017
West Papua	Upper-Middle-Income	0.12318
West Sulawesi	Low-Income	0.15128
West Sumatra	Lower-Middle-Income	0.13527
Average		**0.10135**

Note: Average reported is simple average.

Source: Asia Competitiveness Institute.

Appendix 6

List of Indicators for the 2016 Ease of Doing Business Index: Attractiveness to Investors, Business Friendliness, Competitive Policies for Indonesian Provinces

No.	Environments, Sub-environments, Indicators	Measurement	Source
	Environment 1. Attractiveness to Investors		
	Sub-environment 1.1. Infrastructure Resilience & Market Potential		
1	Roads in good condition	Percentage	Indo Dapoer Database, calculated by ACI
2	Cargo at inter-island seaport	Tons	Statistics Indonesia (2014)
3	Cargo at international seaport	Tons	Statistics Indonesia (2014)
4	Ease of exporting and importing standardised cargo by sea	Likert Scale	ACI Business Survey (2015)
5	Passengers of domestic air traffic	Number	Transportation Statistics (2014)
6	Passengers of international air traffic	Number	Transportation Statistics (2014)
7	Quality of airport	Likert Scale	ACI Business Survey (2015)
8	Availability and efficiency of transport and logistic infrastructure	Likert Scale	ACI Business Survey (2015)
9	Ease of obtaining power supply	Likert Scale	ACI Business Survey (2015)
10	Ease of obtaining water supply	Likert Scale	ACI Business Survey (2015)
11	Ease of obtaining sewerage connection	Likert Scale	ACI Business Survey (2015)
12	Ease of obtaining ICT infrastructure	Likert Scale	ACI Business Survey (2015)
13	Households with internet access	Percentage	Welfare Statistics (2014), calculated by ACI
14	Speed of internet access	Likert Scale	ACI Business Survey (2015)

(Continued)

(*Continued*)

No.	Environments, Sub-environments, Indicators	Measurement	Source
15	Households with mobile phone ownership	Percentage	Welfare Statistics (2014), calculated by ACI
16	Quality of mobile phone coverage	Likert Scale	ACI Business Survey (2015)
17	Population	Number	Statistics Indonesia (2014)
18	Domestic market size index	Index	Indo Dapoer Database, calculated by ACI
19	Foreign market size index	Index	Indo Dapoer Database, calculated by ACI
20	Foreign direct investment	Rupiah	Statistics Indonesia (2014)
21	Domestic direct investment	Rupiah	Statistics Indonesia (2014)
	Sub-environment 1.2. Profitability & Cost Effectiveness		
1	Minimum wage per month	Rupiah	Statistics Indonesia (2014)
2	Overall labour productivity	Rupiah	Statistics Indonesia (2014)
3	Flexibility of labour laws	Likert Scale	ACI Business Survey (2015)
4	Local taxes & fees as obstacle to operating a business	Likert Scale	ACI Business Survey (2015)
5	Ease of availing tax incentives and subsidies	Likert Scale	ACI Business Survey (2015)
6	Cost of renting land/office space as not burdensome	Likert Scale	ACI Business Survey (2015)
7	Registration of property as obstacle to operating a business	Likert Scale	ACI Business Survey (2015)
	Environment 2. Business Friendliness		
	Sub-environment 2.1. Facilitating Business Operations		
1	Labour force	Number	Statistics Indonesia (2014)
2	Labour force participation rate	Percentage	Statistics Indonesia (2014), calculated by ACI
3	Unemployment rate	Percentage	Statistics Indonesia (2014)
4	Ease of recruiting production workers	Likert Scale	ACI Business Survey (2015)
5	Ease of recruiting professionals	Likert Scale	ACI Business Survey (2015)
6	Capable and motivated workers	Likert Scale	ACI Business Survey (2015)
7	Tension between labour and firms	Likert Scale	ACI Business Survey (2015)
8	Ratio of bank deposits to GRDP	Percentage	Bank Indonesia
9	Ratio of bank loans to GRDP	Percentage	Bank Indonesia
10	Ease of dealing with banks	Likert Scale	ACI Business Survey (2015)
11	Relationship with local suppliers	Likert Scale	ACI Business Survey (2015)
12	Crime rate per 100,000 population	Number	Statistics Indonesia (2014)
13	Security	Likert Scale	ACI Business Survey (2015)

(*Continued*)

(*Continued*)

No.	Environments, Sub-environments, Indicators	Measurement	Source
14	Lack of corruption	Likert Scale	ACI Business Survey (2015)
	Sub-environment 2.2. Responsiveness to Business		
1	Ease of paying corporate taxes	Likert Scale	ACI Business Survey (2015)
2	Ease of starting a business	Likert Scale	ACI Business Survey (2015)
3	Ease of obtaining land and property title	Likert Scale	ACI Business Survey (2015)
4	Ease of obtaining construction permit	Likert Scale	ACI Business Survey (2015)
5	Ease of obtaining environmental clearance	Likert Scale	ACI Business Survey (2015)
6	Ease of filing industrial disputes	Likert Scale	ACI Business Survey (2015)
7	Conflict resolution through courts	Likert Scale	ACI Business Survey (2015)
8	Investor protection regulation	Likert Scale	ACI Business Survey (2015)
9	Implementation and enforcement of intellectual property rights	Likert Scale	ACI Business Survey (2015)
10	Ease of obtaining support from local investment board	Likert Scale	ACI Business Survey (2015)
	Environment 3. Competitive Policies		
1	One-Stop-Service (PTSP) receives local permit applications?	Yes/No	ACI PTSP Survey (2015)
2	Reduction/elimination of fees for local permit applications?	Yes/No	ACI PTSP Survey (2015)
3	Statutory time limit for processing applications?	Yes/No	ACI PTSP Survey (2015)
4	Sanction if time limit not met?	Yes/No	ACI PTSP Survey (2015)
5	Authority to issue local permits? (acts on behalf of respective agencies)	Yes/No	ACI PTSP Survey (2015)
6	Fixed timeline for seeking clarification for rejected applications?	Yes/No	ACI PTSP Survey (2015)
7	Provides clearance and approval of incentives?	Yes/No	ACI PTSP Survey (2015)
8	Integrated information system to transfer & share data among government agencies?	Yes/No	ACI PTSP Survey (2015)
9	Concise guidebook covering business registration, including procedures?	Yes/No	ACI PTSP Survey (2015)
10	Computerised tracking system for internal monitoring of permit applications?	Yes/No	ACI PTSP Survey (2015)
11	Computerised permit application tracking system accessible to customers?	Yes/No	ACI PTSP Survey (2015)
12	Website provides information on types of permits that can be processed?	Yes/No	ACI Assessment (2015)
13	Website provides information on time needed to process permits?	Yes/No	ACI Assessment (2015)
14	Website provides information on cost of applying permits?	Yes/No	ACI Assessment (2015)
15	Website provides information on required documents to apply for permits?	Yes/No	ACI Assessment (2015)

(*Continued*)

(*Continued*)

No.	Environments, Sub-environments, Indicators	Measurement	Source
16	Website allows users to download permit application?	Yes/No	ACI Assessment (2015)
17	Website allows users to submit permit application?	Yes/No	ACI Assessment (2015)
18	Website allows users to file complaint?	Yes/No	ACI Assessment (2015)
19	Website allows users to track their application?	Yes/No	ACI Assessment (2015)
20	Website provides province-specific information on doing business regulations?	Yes/No	ACI Assessment (2015)
21	Website provides 'Frequently Asked Questions'?	Yes/No	ACI Assessment (2015)
22	Website provides contact information?	Yes/No	ACI Assessment (2015)

Source: Asia Competitiveness Institute.

Appendix 7

Algorithm for Computing the EDB Index ABC and Ranking

A step-by-step description of the ranking process is described below for N regions (or provinces respectively), M indicators and C environments, with each environment comprising S sub-environments.

Algorithm: Ranking Methodology

(1) Compute the mean value of practical indicator j ($j = 1, \ldots, M$),

$$\overline{X}_j = \frac{1}{N}\sum_{i=1}^{N} X_{ij}$$

where X_{ij} represents the value that province i ($i = 1, \ldots, N$) takes for practical indicator j.

(2) For each practical indicator j ($j = 1, \ldots, M$), calculate its standard deviation (SD),

$$SD_j = \sqrt{\frac{1}{N}\sum_{i=1}^{N}(X_{ij} - \overline{X}_j)^2}$$

(3) Compute the standardised value of indicator (SVI) that each province i ($i = 1, \ldots, N$) takes under each of the practical indicators j ($j = 1, \ldots, M$),

$$SVI_{ij} = \frac{X_{ij} - \overline{X}_j}{SD_j}$$

(4) Compute the ranked standardised value of indicator (RSVI) that each province i ($i = 1, \ldots, N$) takes under each of the practical indicators j ($j = 1, \ldots, M$):

$$RSVI_{ij} = \begin{cases} SVI_{ij}, & \text{if a higher value is better} \\ -SVI_{ij}, & \text{if a lower value is better} \end{cases}$$

(5) For each of the practical indicators j ($j = 1, \ldots, M$), a ranking can be obtained for provinces. Provinces with a higher value of RSVI for indicator j are ranked ahead of those with a lower value.

(6) For each province i ($i = 1, \ldots, N$), calculate the RSVI for each sub-environment k ($k = 1, \ldots, S$) belonging to environment l ($l = 1, \ldots, C$),

$$Raw\_RSVI_{i,lk} = \frac{1}{y_{lk}} \sum_{p=1}^{y_{lk}} RSVI_{i,j_{lk,p}}$$

$$Mean\_RSVI_{lk} = \frac{1}{N} \sum_{i=1}^{N} Raw\_RSVI_{i,lk}$$

$$SD\_RSVI_{lk} = \sqrt{\frac{1}{N} \sum_{i=1}^{N} (Raw\_RSVI_{i,lk} - Mean\_RSVI_{lk})^2}$$

$$RSVI_{i,lk} = \frac{Raw\_RSVI_{i,lk} - Mean\_RSVI_{lk}}{SD\_RSVI_{lk}}$$

where y_{lk} is the total number of practical indicators under sub-environment k of environment l and (*RSVIi,jlk,*1 , …, *RSVIi,jlk,ylk*) are the RSVIs for province i that make up sub-environment k of environment l.

(7) For each province i ($i = 1, \ldots, N$), calculate the RSVI for each environment l ($l = 1, \ldots, C$),

$$Raw\_RSVI_{i,l} = \frac{1}{S_l} \sum_{k=1}^{S_l} RSVI_{i,lk}$$

$$Mean\_RSVI_{l} = \frac{1}{N} \sum_{i=1}^{N} Raw\_RSVI_{i,l}$$

$$SD\_RSVI_{l} = \sqrt{\frac{1}{N} \sum_{i=1}^{N} (Raw\_RSVI_{i,l} - Mean\_RSVI_{l})^2}$$

$$RSVI_{i,l} = \frac{Raw\_RSVI_{i,l} - Mean\_RSVI_{l}}{SD\_RSVI_{l}}$$

Where (*RSVIi,l*1, …, *RSVIi,lS*) are the RSVIs for the S sub-environments under each environment l.

(8) Overall rank score of province i ($i = 1, \ldots, N$),

$$Raw\_R_i = \frac{1}{C} \sum_{l=1}^{C} RSVI_{i,l}$$

$$Mean\_R = \frac{1}{N}\sum_{i=1}^{N} Raw\_R_i$$

$$SD\_R = \sqrt{\frac{1}{N}\sum_{i=1}^{N}(Raw\_R_i - Mean\_R)^2}$$

$$R_i = \frac{Raw\_R_i - Mean\_R}{SD\_R}$$

The provinces with a higher R_i are ranked ahead of those with a lower value of R_i, and the province with the highest R_i is the most liveable province.

Step 5 of the algorithm provides the ranking of each province for each individual practical indicator. To achieve this ranking, Step 4 of the algorithm adjusts the value of the SVIs so that a greater ease of doing business is represented by a higher RSVI value of the indicators. Depending on the nature of the indicator in question, a higher or lower value may reflect a higher level of ease of doing business in the said province. Step 4 of the algorithm thus seeks to make the standardised values of all practical indicators consistent for the purpose of ranking.

Step 6 of the algorithm determines the sub-environment rankings of each province. The average RSVIs of all the indicators in the sub-environment are calculated and compared across provinces. Those with a higher average RSVI rank better in the sub-environments. To arrive at the province ranking for each environment, the RSVIs of the sub-environment are aggregated as stipulated in Step 7 of the algorithm.

Finally, Step 8 of the ranking algorithm requires the RSVI values of each environment to be summed up to determine the overall ranking of the province. Provinces with a higher RSVI are ranked ahead of those with a lower RSVI.

The aggregate score for each three environment (A, B, and C) is given different weights within the EDB Index ABC. This method is repeated and applied consistently across all the provinces. Mathematically, this can be illustrated as follows:

EDB Index ABC = 40% × (Attractiveness to Investors)
+ 40% × (Business Friendliness)
+ 20% × (Competitive Policies)

Asia Competitiveness Institute - World Scientific Series

(Continued from page vi)

2015 Estimation of Agricultural Productivity and Annual Update of Competitiveness Analysis for Greater China: Optimising Agricultural Productivity and Promoting Innovation Driven Growth
by Tan Khee Giap, Yuan Randong & Xie Teleixi (Lee Kuan Yew School of Public Policy, NUS, Singapore)

2015 Agricultural Total Factor Productivity and Competitiveness Analysis for States and Federal Territories and Five Regions of India: Annual Competitiveness Update and Evidence on the Agricultural Development Models for Selected Indian States
by Tan Khee Giap, Sasidaran Gopalan & Anuja Tandon (Lee Kuan Yew School of Public Policy, NUS, Singapore)

2015 Agricultural Productivity, Decentralisation, and Competitiveness Analysis for Provinces and Regions of Indonesia
by Tan Khee Giap, Nurina Merdikawati, Mulya Amri & Tan Kong Yam (Lee Kuan Yew School of Public Policy, NUS, Singapore)

2015 Annual Competitiveness Analysis and Development Strategies for Indonesian Provinces
by Tan Khee Giap, Mulya Amri, Nurina Merdikawati & Nursyahida Ahmad (Lee Kuan Yew School of Public Policy, NUS, Singapore)

2014

2014 Annual Competitiveness Ranking and Simulation Study for ASEAN-10 and Development Strategies to Enhance Asia Economic Connectivity
by Tan Khee Giap, Sangiita Yoong Wei Cher, Sasidaran Gopalan & Nguyen Le Phuong Anh (Lee Kuan Yew School of Public Policy, NUS, Singapore)

2014 Annual Provincial and Regional Competitiveness Analysis for Greater China Economies: Development Strategies under the New Normal
by Tan Khee Giap, Yuan Randong & Sangiita Yoong Wei Cher (Lee Kuan Yew School of Public Policy, NUS, Singapore)

2014 Regional Competitiveness Analysis and a Master Plan on Regional Development Strategies for India: Annual Competitiveness Update and Evidence on Economic Development Model for Selected States of India
by Tan Khee Giap, Linda Low, Kartik Rao & Tan Kong Yam (Lee Kuan Yew School of Public Policy, NUS, Singapore)

2014 Provincial and Inaugural Regional Competitiveness Analysis: Safeguarding Indonesia's Growth Momentum
by Tan Khee Giap, Nurina Merdikawati, Mulya Amri & Tan Kong Yam (Lee Kuan Yew School of Public Policy, NUS, Singapore)

2014 Annual Competitiveness Analysis and Development Strategies for Indonesian Provinces
by Tan Khee Giap, Nurina Merdikawati, Mulya Amri & Blake Harley Berger (Lee Kuan Yew School of Public Policy, NUS, Singapore)

2013

Annual Analysis of Competitiveness, Simulation Studies and Development Perspective for 34 Greater China Economies: 2000–2010
by Tan Khee Giap, Yuan Randong, Sangiita Yoong Wei Cher & Yang Mu (Lee Kuan Yew School of Public Policy, NUS, Singapore)

Annual Analysis of Competitiveness, Simulation Studies and Development Perspective for 35 States and Federal Territories of India: 2000–2010
by Tan Khee Giap, Linda Low, Tan Kong Yam & Kartik Rao (Lee Kuan Yew School of Public Policy, NUS, Singapore)

Competitiveness Analysis and Development Strategies for 33 Indonesian Provinces
by Tan Khee Giap, Mulya Amri, Linda Low & Tan Kong Yam (Lee Kuan Yew School of Public Policy, NUS, Singapore)